Un-Roman Sex

Gender, Sexuality, and
Lovemaking in the Roman
Provinces and Frontiers

Edited by Tatiana Ivleva and Rob Collins

Routledge
Taylor & Francis Group

LONDON AND NEW YORK

First published 2020
by Routledge
2 Park Square, Milton Park, Abingdon, Oxon OX14 4RN

and by Routledge
52 Vanderbilt Avenue, New York, NY 10017

Routledge is an imprint of the Taylor & Francis Group, an informa business

British Library Cataloguing-in-Publication Data
A catalogue record for this book is available from the British Library

Library of Congress Cataloging-in-Publication Data
Names: Ivleva, Tatiana, editor. | Collins, Rob, editor.
Title: Un-Roman sex : gender, sexuality, and lovemaking in the Roman provinces and frontiers / edited by Tatiana Ivleva and Rob Collins.
Identifiers: LCCN 2019056031 (print) | LCCN 2019056032 (ebook) |
ISBN 9781138284029 (hardback) | ISBN 9781315269894 (ebook)
Subjects: LCSH: Sex customs–Rome–History. | Gender identity–Rome. |
Rome–Customs and manners.
Classification: LCC HQ13 .U6 2020 (print) | LCC HQ13 (ebook) |
DDC 392.60937–dc23
LC record available at https://lccn.loc.gov/2019056031
LC ebook record available at https://lccn.loc.gov/2019056032

ISBN: 978-1-138-28402-9 (hbk)
ISBN: 978-1-315-26989-4 (ebk)

Typeset in Times New Roman
by Swales & Willis, Exeter, Devon, UK

Contents

Illustrations

Figures

Tables

Plates

Contributors

Rob Collins is a specialist of Roman frontier studies and small finds, with a particular focus on late antiquity, and his research explores themes of identity, place, and regionality. His monograph, *Hadrian's Wall and the End of Empire* (2012), was the first comprehensive study of a late Roman frontier. Other publications include *Hadrian's Wall 2009–2019* (2019), *Roman Military Architecture on the Frontiers* (2015), and *Finds from the Frontier* (2010). Rob is a Lecturer at Newcastle University, UK.

Robyn Crook is a PhD candidate and Social Sciences and Humanities Research Council of Canada Scholar in the Department of Anthropology and Archaeology at the University of Calgary. Her PhD focuses on gender and identity in northern Britain, with special attention paid to women's lives. Robyn has worked in the UK, southern Italy, and in Canada doing Roman, Precontact, and Historical Archaeology for over ten years.

Matthew G. Fittock is the Finds Liaison Officer for Bedfordshire and Hertfordshire. Prior to this he studied at the University of Reading where his Masters and PhD theses focussed on ceramic "pipeclay" figurines in Roman Britain. His research interests include object fragmentation and the expression of cultural and social identities through Roman material culture. As a Committee Member of the Roman Finds Group he has been the editor of their bi-annual newsletter, *Lucerna*, since 2015.

Stefanie Hoss is a post-excavation small finds specialist of Roman and Byzantine metal, glass, and worked bone at Small Finds Archaeology in the Netherlands, and a Lecturer at the University of Cologne. Her research interests revolve around the question as to what material remains can reveal about the social habits of the Roman and post-Roman world. Her publications include monographs on the Roman and Byzantine culture of bathing and the bathhouses in Palestine, on the Roman military belt from the first to the third centuries, as well as (co-)edited volumes on Roman toilets, Roman militaria, and Roman small finds.

Tatiana Ivleva has a special interest in the study of provincial corporeal culture in its various embodiments, ranging from personal dress adornments made of copper alloy and glass to the epigraphic visibility of sexual and other relationships. As a material culture specialist of the Roman frontier and provincial regions, her research showcases the power of everyday objects in disentangling the past activities of the inhabitants at the edges of the Roman world. Her publications include *Embracing the Provinces: Society and Material Culture of the Roman Frontier Regions* (2018) and papers on migration and mobility, family formations in the Roman army, and experimental archaeology. Tatiana is Visiting Research Fellow at Newcastle University, UK.

Sarah Levin-Richardson is an Assistant Professor of Classics at the University of Washington, Seattle. A specialist in Roman sexuality, graffiti, and Pompeii, her publications include *The Brothel of Pompeii: Sex, Class, and Gender on the Margins of Roman Society* (Cambridge 2019), "*fututa sum hic*: Female Subjectivity and Agency in Pompeian Sexual Graffiti", and "Revisiting Roman Sexuality: Agency and the Conceptualization of Penetrated Males", co-authored with Deborah Kamen. In 2017, she won the Barbara McManus Award for Best Published Paper from the Women's Classical Caucus for "Lusty Ladies in the Roman Imaginary" (co-written with Kamen).

Adam Parker is the Assistant Curator of Archaeology at the Yorkshire Museum and a PhD student in Classical Studies at the Open University, researching the archaeology of magic in Roman Britain. He has published widely on the materiality and ephemerality of magic in the Roman world and recently co-edited (with Stuart McKie) the volume *Material Approaches to Roman Magic: Occult Objects and Supernatural Substances* (TRAC Themes in Roman Archaeology 2, Oxbow, 2018).

John Pearce is a Senior Lecturer in Archaeology at King's College London. His research interests lie in Roman archaeology, especially the provinces of north-west Europe and Italy. In particular his focus lies on Roman funerary rituals and commemoration, on documents and writing in the Roman provinces, and on "small finds", that is artefacts such as items of adornment and utensils, as a source for understanding Roman society. A current emphasis in his research lies on the figural decoration of these objects as an understudied aspect of Roman visual culture.

Kaja Stemberger was awarded her PhD in Classics for a thesis on Roman mortuary archaeology at King's College London in 2018. She currently lives and works in her native country of Slovenia in commercial archaeology. Roman archaeology has been her lifelong passion, and besides mortuary archaeology she has a keen interest in identity studies and experimental archaeology.

Alissa M. Whitmore is a Roman archaeologist with research interests in small finds, gender, public space, and ancient magic. She has published on phallic pendants and bathhouses, and currently advises undergraduate Anthropology and Classical Studies students at Iowa State University.

Preface and acknowledgements

The genesis of *Un-Roman Sex* started with an informal discussion between the editors at the 2014 Reading RAC/TRAC conference. This stimulated the organisation of two sessions by the editors, first, *Sex in the Frontiers*, at the 23rd Limes Congress/International Congress of Roman Frontier Studies in Ingolstadt in 2015, and, second, *Make Love, Not War! Sex, Gender, and Family in the Roman Provinces*, at the Roman Archaeology Conference held in Rome in 2016. We would like to thank the organisers of both conferences for providing a platform for discussion of matters of sexuality in the Roman provinces. Interest in the sessions stimulated us to consider a volume of its own. Some of the contributors who presented in the two sessions have published in the proceedings of the 23rd Limes Congress; others have been earmarked to appear elsewhere. New contributors have been commissioned and we are very grateful to all presenting and contributing authors in helping us to make the topic of sex and sexuality more pronounced within Roman provincial scholarship. We offer special thanks to all our authors for their time and effort in writing, but above all for their patience during the revision stages and final preparation of the manuscript.

The editors would like to extend their thanks to Elizabeth Risch (née Thomasson), Ella Halstead, and Amy Davis-Poynter at Routledge for their assistance and patience while this volume was in process. We thank Mark Locicero for his work in improving the English of some of the chapters and our colleagues who offered help with peer reviewing. Their insights and suggestions on individual chapters helped this volume achieve the form that we envisaged. Many colleagues and friends were supportive throughout the process of pulling it together, inspiring us through discussion, occasional gentle teasing, and in some cases outright discomfort. Tatiana wishes to express her personal thanks to her husband Joep van Rijn who assisted with images and a few maps, and provided steadfast support at different stages of the manuscript production.

We would like to thank MATCH and the Research Committee of HCA, both at Newcastle University, for supporting indexing and colour printing costs for this volume.

Abbreviations

AE	*L'Année Épigraphique*
Artefacts	*Online Collaborative Encyclopedia of Archaeological Small Finds* http://artefacts.mom.fr/
Beazley Archive	*University of Oxford Classical Art Research Center* www.beazley.ox.ac.uk/index.htm
CIL	*Corpus Inscriptionum Latinarum*
CLE	Bücheler, E. and Lommatzsch, E. (1930). *Carmina Latina Epigraphica*. Leipzig: [n.s.].
CSIR I.1	Phillips, E. (1977). *Corpus Signorum Imperii Romani, vol. 1 fasc. 1: Great Britain, Corbridge, Hadrian's Wall East of the North Tyne*. Oxford: Oxford University Press.
CSIR I.6	Coulston, J. and Phillips, E. (1988). *Corpus Signorum Imperii Romani, vol. 1 fasc. 6: Great Britain, Hadrian's Wall West of the North Tyne and Carlisle*. Oxford: Oxford University Press.
CSIR Deutschland II, 06	Boppert, W. (1992). *Corpus Signorum Imperii Romani. Deutschland II.6: Zivile Grabsteine aus Mainz und Umgebung*. Mainz: Verlag des römisch-germanischen Zentralmuseums in Kommission bei Dr. Rudolf Habelt.
EDCS	*Epigraphik-Datenbank Clauss/Slaby*, www.manfredclauss.de/
Esperandieu V	Espérandieu, E. (1913). *Recueil Général des Bas-Reliefs de la Gaule Romaine. Tome 5. Belgique; première partie*. Paris: Imprimerie National.
Esperandieu XI	Espérandieu, E. (1928). *Recueil Général des Bas-Reliefs, Statues et Bustes de la Gaule Romaine. Tome XI, Supplement*. Paris: Imprimerie National.
Illpron	Hainzmann, M. and Schubert, P. (1986). *Inscriptionum Lapidarium Latinarum Provinciae Norici usque ad annum MCMLXXXIV repertarum indices*. Berlin: [n.s.].

LIMC	*Lexicon Iconographicum Mythologiae Classicae, 1981–2009*. Zürich and Munich: Artemis Verlag.
lupa.at	*Ubi erat lupa* catalogue of Roman sculpture: http://lupa.at/
MANN	Museo Archeologico Nazionale di Napoli: www.museoarcheologiconapoli.it/en/collections/
PAN	Portable Antiquities of the Netherlands: www.portable-antiquities.nl/pan/#/public
PAS	Portable Antiquities Scheme: https://finds.org.uk/
RIB	Collingwood, R.G. and Wright, R.P. (1965–). *Roman Inscriptions of Britain*. Oxford: Clarendon.
Tab. Vindol. II	Bowman, A.K., Thomas, J.D. and Adams, J.N. (1994). *The Vindolanda Writing-Tablets: (Tabulae Vindolandenses II)*. London: British Museum.
Tab. Vindol. III	Bowman, A.K. and Thomas, J.D. (2003). *The Vindolanda Writing Tablets: Tabulae Vindolandenses*, vol. III. London: British Museum.
Wellcome Collection	https://wellcomecollection.org/works

1 Venus' mirror

Reflections of gender and sexuality in the Roman Empire

Tatiana Ivleva and Rob Collins

Introduction: gender and sex on display

Un-Roman Sex is intended to contest the current state of scholarship on Roman gender and sexuality, as well as to promote an agenda that increases the visibility and impact of evidence from the Roman provinces and frontiers by utilising material culture beyond its current role of illustrating textual analyses.

The first goal of the volume is to introduce gender and sexuality as appropriate variables of historical and archaeological analysis of the Roman provinces and frontiers through a number of case studies that map the complexity of gender and sexual identities within the Roman Empire. Long-standing interest in these subjects by Classicists (see below) has largely bypassed Roman archaeologists of the provinces and frontiers. Whenever references are made within Classical scholarship to the data outside the Mediterranean basin, they are either incomplete, superficial, or even misguided. For example, Skinner (2014: 269) observes that in Roman culture "sex was [...] unashamedly on display", but primarily refers to Mediterranean evidence. Thus, *Un-Roman Sex* is a response to John Clarke's (2003) *Roman Sex: 100 B.C. to A.D. 250*, where he explores the range of sexual representations and texts alluding to the sexual activities, using the examples limited to the Mediterranean region. Sexual imagery also pervaded the provinces, as evidenced by the numerous archaeological discoveries of objects bearing depictions of phalluses or sexual scenes. Provincials, too, were surrounded by sex and sexual imagery, but there is no comprehensive informed volume that tackles this issue. There is a remarkable silence on the topic, and it is time to make some noise.

The second goal of the volume is to chart the perceptions of sexualities in provincial and peripheral settings through application of wide-ranging methodologies, some of which are imported or imposed models and paradigms established through the Classics, others are introduced for the first time. In this regard, *Un-Roman Sex* is a starting point for archaeologists of the Roman imperial period, especially those working outside of the Mediterranean basin, to engage with Roman sexuality via the material culture of the era. While not denying the significant contributions made through Classical scholarship, the volume acknowledges that the strengths, benefits, and limitations of archaeological evidence are different from those of texts and "fine" art. Given the sheer quantity of archaeological material from the Roman imperial period, found inside and outside the Roman Empire, there are thousands of objects that have great potential to contribute to our understanding of sexuality in this period. Furthermore, paradigms and models built on texts or fine art will always be biased toward the elite, those Mediterranean-based classes of the 1st centuries B.C. and A.D. that are not broadly representative of the population of the wider empire across space or time, though there are some notable exceptions (Kamen and Levin-Richardson 2015a, 2015b). Therefore, any desire to formulate any model(s) of Roman sexuality that has a basis in evidence outside of 1st-century A.D. Italy *must* engage with archaeological data.

The third goal of the volume is to explore how genders and sexualities in the provinces and frontiers may or may not have differed from that of the Mediterranean basin. The Roman Empire consisted of more lands and peoples than those of the Italian peninsula, and each new conquest brought new societies into the imperial fold. Roman culture, due in large part to the gross dominance of imperial politics and economics, was often advantaged in new territories incorporated into the empire, a process generally encapsulated by the term "Romanisation". Romanisation, however, was not unilateral or universal; reception of various aspects of Roman culture was discrepant for individuals in provincial and barbarian societies (Webster 2001; Mattingly 2004, 2006, 2011; Revell 2009, 2015, 2016; Eckardt 2014). If we are to understand the constructions of gender and sex identities outside Roman Italy, the limitations of Latin authors proselytising an elite androcentric view on sexuality must be acknowledged, especially when sex identity may be deeply enshrined in cultural context and upbringing, which meant "non-elite" and "non-Mediterranean" for a vast proportion of the population of the Roman Empire. How were Roman norms and expectations of sexuality met in these societies, and how did local custom contest, mitigate, or give way to the metropolitan-Mediterranean elite culture of the ruling classes of the early Roman Empire?

This volume, therefore, examines the subject of human sexuality and gender variability at the edge of the Roman world, presenting a divergence or alternative to the dominant Romano-Hellenistic model of sex and erotic experience. By developing approaches to the study of ancient gender and sexuality in the provincial setting, it provides whenever possible a view that is grounded in a perspective of the cultures comprising the Roman Empire. Additionally, *Un-Roman Sex* is an important-yet-neglected topic in elucidating the processes contributing to the political and cultural incorporation of the provinces in the Roman Empire. The juxtaposition of multiple cultural views on sex impacts on the formation of social relations and gender dynamics. Our desire is also to introduce a new set of evidence comprising epigraphic and material culture sources and with their help point to future directions of research that will ultimately lead to enhancing our view of provincial sexuality and gender dynamics. Before introducing our contributors, however, it is necessary to provide a broad-brush review of the topics' development in both Classical and Roman provincial scholarship. For decades, Classical studies conducted intensive discussions and dissections of sexuality and gender, but these subjects have barely surfaced as methodological or theoretical concerns in Roman archaeology. The following section aims to explore the reasons why.

"We may have lost the battle, but not the war": sexuality and identity wars in classical and Roman provincial scholarship

Starting in the 1970s, the Classics has experienced the "sexuality wars", and in the closing decades of the 20th century and early decades of this century, Roman archaeology has experienced its own revolution fighting through "Romanisation and identity wars".

Classicists' interest in the topic can be dated to 1978 when Kenneth Dover's volume, *Greek Homosexuality*, was published, providing the first step in a new direction of scholarship of ancient sexual activities and desires. Directly building upon Dover's work, Foucault's original French-language text and its immediate English translation of *History of Sexuality* provided a new paradigm for the topic in two volumes (1985[1984], 1986[1984]), resetting the foundation of ancient sexuality in the 1980s. The volumes clearly stated that sexuality as a category is very much a product of modernity invented over the course of the 19th century. Significantly, this meant that the concept itself, and other categories deriving from it, such as the binary division of homosexuality and heterosexuality, were not applicable to Greek and Roman cultures, as those societies thought with their own categories (Holmes 2012: 80). It is the teasing out of these categories that gave rise to the study of gender and sexuality among Classicists. Yet, the emergence of strong, even vehement disagreements has been referred to as the "sexuality wars" with debates circling around historicising Greek and Roman sexual taxonomies. At the heart of the debate is whether these ancient taxonomies are limited to specific historical formations, or if they have any utility for understanding modern categories of sexuality, providing analogies for non-conformative (marginalised, non-heterosexual) individuals (Skinner 1997; Flemming 2010: 799; Holmes 2012: 82, 93, 109; Chapter 11). Having reached the second decade of the 21st century, "the ancient sexuality wars are [...] over" for Classical scholarship (Ormand and Blondell 2015: 3), with a consensus on "making resonant, effective connections between the past and the present" with contextualised historical analysis (Holmes 2012: 110; Masterson et al. 2015a: 7). This holistic approach to exploring both emic and etic categories of past and present sex and gender systems allows us to transcend the rhetoric inherited from modern binary divisions, making the scholarship value-free, inclusive, and impartial (Ormand and Blondell 2015: 15).

In contrast, for Roman provincial and frontier scholarship, the wars were fought over the Romanisation and identity paradigms. The prominence of both themes, which were developed in parallel to each other, can be connected with the growing dissatisfaction of the unilateral imperialism of the traditional Romanisation paradigm that dominated Roman archaeology through the course of the 20th century. In this paradigm the inhabitants of various provinces were seen as adhering and emulating (elite and civilised) Roman cultural norms and practices, to the best of their abilities. Emerging in the post-colonial thought of the later 1990s, the debate on the redefinition or abandonment of the term "Romanisation" has been sustained into recent years (on the debate see Webster 2001; Mattingly 2004, 2011; Hingley 2005; Schörner 2005; Gardner 2013), but a theoretical and conceptual vacuum was created within which "identity" took centre-stage. This concept provided enough space for the development of different perspectives on the interaction between Roman and indigenous societies, "liberating Roman archaeology from the Roman-native dichotomy, encouraging research into regional, sub-ethnic, gender, and class identities" (Pitts 2007: 693). Yet, the growing interest in this research theme rather quickly backfired as identity started to be regarded as a substitute and synonym for the "R-word", which led to it being studied for its own sake with research mainly focusing on cataloguing various types of identities and the way they can be determined from the archaeological record (on the debate see, among others, Brubaker and Cooper 2000; Insoll 2007; Pitts 2007; Revell 2009; Versluys 2014). The term became overused in Roman archaeology, and a quest to move beyond it is well underway, with the term "globalisation" now acquiring a prominent spot in Roman provincial studies but not in Roman frontier ones (Hingley 2005; Mattingly 2011; Gardner 2013; Naerebout 2014; Pitts and Versluys 2015; but see Eckardt 2014). This paradigm provides an all-inclusive, non-binary understanding for any sort of developments occurring in the provincial milieu, ranging from direct inter-provincial relationships to more complex networks concurrently working at multiple scales such as intra-provincial, inter-provincial, core-periphery, and diffused centralities.

In short, the Classicists' sexuality wars have rarely surfaced within Roman provincial disciplines. Yet, while it seems that provincial archaeologists have not participated in this sexuality and gender discourse, they have not remained completely silent on the subject.

The last three decades of scholarship fought hard for the inclusion of gender matters into mainstream Roman provincial discourse. These developments can be attributed to the pioneering and groundbreaking work of female scholars Eleanor Scott, Lindsay Allason-Jones, and Carol van Driel-Murray for gender, and Catherine Johns for sexual imagery. The appearance of the gender question in Roman provincial scholarship is tied up with the arrival of a new conference platform in the 1990s: the Theoretical Roman Archaeology Conference (TRAC), initiated by Eleanor Scott. This was the place where controversial topics and ideas could be raised, promoted, and openly discussed without the danger that the researchers would be stigmatised or ridiculed (Scott 1993; Revell 2010; van Driel-Murray and Allason-Jones, personal communication). The work of these female scholars has generated a wide-ranging literature on topics such as the presence of women and children in Roman military camps and soldiers' marriage and/or cohabitation rights and practices (Allason-Jones 1995, 1999, 2004, 2005; van Driel-Murray 1995, 1997, 1998; James 2006). At first glance, it seems that these developments in Roman provincial archaeology chronologically coincided with a rise in publications on gender and sexuality in Classics, but also with the growth of post-processual thought in Roman archaeology in general (Revell 2010: 2). However, these developments were not direct outcomes of these processes. According to Carol van Driel-Murray and Lindsay Allason-Jones (personal communication), they were never consciously seeking to engage with gender studies or post-processual theoretical archaeology. They were driven down the path of looking for women in the archaeological record for a number of simple reasons. First, there was the emerging professionalisation of artefact studies and specialists beyond the utilitarian application of small finds for dating archaeological contexts (Lindsay Allason-Jones, personal communication). Second, numerous assemblages of female-associated finds on Roman-period sites led them to realise that women needed to be put back into the picture—and exploration of exactly what women were doing on a particular site logically followed identification of their presence (Carol van Driel-Murray and Lindsay Allason-Jones, personal communication). Third, the androcentric biases and presumptions in reading the small finds also contributed to the urgency to tackle the issue of the gendered meaning behind specific artefacts or assemblages, making Lindsay Allason-Jones enquire as to what constitutes a typical military assemblage (Allason-Jones 1995, 1999). In short, scholars of the traditional frontier narrative required that the presence of women and children had to be proven rather than assumed, and now most scholars at least acknowledge their presence within the confines of military communities even if there are still debates about *where* women and children resided (Hodgson 2014; Le Bohec 2017).

Yet, those studies that placed women firmly within the annals of frontier and provincial histories have primarily focused on the methods of identifying women in the archaeological record (Allison 2006, 2007, 2009, 2013; Tomas 2011) and the investigation of women's roles in various provincial societies, especially in the Roman military (Stoll 2006; Brandl 2008; van Driel-Murray 2008; Greene 2011, 2012, 2013, 2015a, 2015b, 2016, 2017; Foubert 2013; Hemelrijk and Woolf 2013; Tomas 2015; Klein 2017; van Enckevort 2017; Vanhoutte and Verbrugge 2017; Juntunen 2018; Ivleva Forthcoming). Though informative and important, these studies have only constituted the data and phenomena to be documented and discussed, inhibited by the persistent and constant barrier that the presence of women had to be proven. This has constrained opportunities to engage with wider theoretical frameworks on gender and broaden the perspectives for exploring various gender categories, sexuality, and embodiment distinct to the provinces (Revell 2010). The current problems for the study of gender in Roman provincial circles can be summarised as an "add women and stir" approach (borrowing from Knapp 1998: 368).

Sex and sexuality are also found in mainstream Roman scholarship of imperial expansion, but explored through the themes of colonialism, subjugation, and power. Whittaker (2004: 115–43) and Mattingly (2011: 94–121) highlight how the terminology and imagery of sex is employed to speak about imperialism and domination, such that sexuality and sexual exploitation are formative for the construction of power relations and the subjugation of the native population. Indeed, for the Romans, sex was yet another weapon in the armoury of imperial conquest and expansion. Roman authors wrote about sexual violence in the provinces and the rape of the captives to underscore the power of Roman soldiers, and thus the imperial armies (Phang 2001: 256, n. 127; Williams 2010: 112–16, 139; Leitao 2014: 240). We have accounts of the use of Batavian captives "for sexual exploitation" (Tacitus, *Histories* 4.14), which may have been one of the causes for Civilis' rebellion in A.D. 70; the rape of Boudicca's daughters is also sometimes considered as one of the major causes of the A.D. 60 revolt in Britannia (Whittaker 2004: 120–1; Mattingly 2011: 112). Phang (2001: 267–8) cautions that this is a topos, and we must be careful how common we perceive rape and sex as weapons of empire (but see the rape scenes on the Columns of Trajan and Marcus Aurelius, or the imperial reliefs from the Sebasteion at Aphrodisias; Whittaker 2004: 117, 121–2; Mattingly 2011: 117–19). The Latin language has a lexicon that can be applied to discussions of power and domination in both societal and sexual contexts. Words describing the masculinity of Roman soldiers, *imperium* ("dominion") and *fortitudo* ("strength"), are clear examples of the intersection of sex and power. However, many aspects of life were perceived through the lens of power, and sex and sexuality were not as preclusively linked to imperial language as Whittaker or Mattingly would lead us to believe. Graffiti, albeit from an Italian urban environment, provides examples of sexual language that is not employed for imperialist messaging (see examples in Kamen and Levin-Richardson 2015a, 2015b), and this highlights the underlying ethnocentric and androcentric expectations of the historical and political genres of elite Roman writers and audiences. It is important to explicitly acknowledge this point, as it is these very same sources that are most likely to provide accounts of people and events in the provinces and frontiers (see Chapter 6).

When the idea for this volume was born at the joint RAC and TRAC meeting in Reading in 2014, there followed a series of sessions, first at the International Congress of Roman Frontier Studies in Ingolstadt in 2015 (Collins and Ivleva 2018) and, second, at the Roman Archaeology Conference held in Rome in 2016. During these sessions, we witnessed first-hand that sex and gender stereotypes still affect the biases and assumptions within provincial scholarship. Sex appears "as a 'present absence'" in provincial archaeology (borrowing from Weston 2011[1998]: 11). There were and still are obstructions in the handling and interpretation of material pertaining to gender and sexuality; one can still perceive the ghettoisation of research on these themes. Sex-based research of any historical period is met with "embarrassment, titillation, and a hefty dose of 'oooh Matron' due to contemporary cultural ambivalence toward sexuality" (Lister 2019). Furthermore, the "sex act is the most private of all acts in most societies, and sexuality is a field where boundaries are sharply drawn" (Lyons and Lyons 2011a: 3). Thus, the research was and is still perceived as filthy or inappropriate, embarrassing, distasteful, or vulgar, a subject that does not deserve a serious investigation (Weston (2011[1998]: 19). As session coordinators we have encountered similar attitudes, with some members of the audience projecting their own values onto the topic, commenting that the subject is "too hot and too sexy" to be truly scholarly.

The fight for inclusion and equity therefore continues, and we can confidently call them our Roman provincial archaeology sexuality wars. More *theoretically informed* research into gender and sexuality in Roman provincial and frontier scholarship is required, and these themes should have a central position in the analysis of Roman-era human relations (Baker 2003 and Revell 2010 have previously made similar calls). Engaging with these subjects will help us to comprehend the social constructions of particular human roles and relationships to explore why specific decisions or choices were made by the provincial inhabitants rather than a progressive revision of top-down historical narratives. But we also need to and can take it further. For instance, we can engage more openly with the globalisation paradigm. Principal debates revolving around the application of globalisation, or glocalisation, to the study of the Roman Empire have by-passed the study of gender and sexuality. As noted above, the Roman provinces were not homogeneous entities and cannot be studied or understood using a one-size-fits-all mentality. The challenge lies in revealing aspects of local diversity, communal and individual choice, and the coexistence of various local responses towards new concepts of gender and sex in the pre-existing and developing environments of a provincial and/or frontier setting. In this volume we aim to illuminate this multiplicity and multivocality of provincial reflections on their own gender and sexual realities. Alongside it, we explore various approaches and methodologies in order to move beyond structural and theoretical binaries of Classical and Roman provincial scholarship and build bridges between the two disciplines.

The provinces laid bare: toward an archaeological approach to the study of gender and sexuality in Roman provincial studies

The chapters in this volume are united in a shared commitment to tease out the shape and function of provincial sexuality through textual and material culture evidence, primarily dating to the period of the first three centuries A.D. Contributors bring their own voices, experiences, and perspectives to the topic, and in some cases our editorial views and opinions do not necessarily coincide with the ideas or interpretations expressed by our contributors. The important point is that they position themselves within an analytical and theoretical framework to give form to the data itself. While this has been achieved in most cases, it is notable that there is a recurrence of cataloguing the variety of sexual practices, gender spectra, and distribution of erotic images. This is telling, and the necessity to catalogue data is strongly indicative of how little evidence from outside Italy has been presented in a consistent and regular fashion. Indeed, many of the chapters in this volume offer the first presentation of a cohesive, thematic dataset.

There are some points to consider before introducing our contributors and major themes. Roman archaeology in general does not attach itself to any of the contemporary schools or theories in gender or sexuality studies, such as queer theory or intersectionality. Nor does it actively engage in the discussion of the sex/gender distinction compared to other archaeologies of other periods (e.g. Voss and Schmidt 2000). It is to be hoped that this volume will provoke a serious debate necessitating the reconceptualisation of these analytical categories within the field of provincial studies. Our first step in that direction is to provide a brief review of the concepts used in this volume, mainly to provide insight into the contemporary meaning of the terms.

The volume deals with the topics of sex, gender, and sexuality. All three are difficult to define, even more so in how they relate to each other, as each discipline, be it anthropology, sociology, or archaeology, has its own dominant ideas. Compare, for instance, one Classicist's perception where "sex is not the same as gender and sexuality but is refined and expanded on in those terms" (Masterson et al. 2015a: 1), with the archaeological viewpoint advanced by Voss and Schmidt (2000: 2) where "sexuality is related to both biological sex and gender, and simultaneously is quite distinct from them". Interdependency of sex, gender, and sexuality makes it difficult to advance the primacy of a specific term, as some scholars put the spotlight on sexuality as the defining element in human matters (Halperin et al. 1990: 3–4; Skinner 1997) or on sex as a reflection of gender and sexuality (Masterson et al. 2015a: 1 and 7).

Sexuality comes as a "signifier with numerous, sometimes contradictory, referents" (Lyons and Lyons 2011a: 2), usually used to describe specific forms of human behaviours (sexual drive or (un)conscious impulses) and refer to all kinds of sexual relations (Voss and Schmidt 2000: 2). Sexuality is, however, seen as a modern phenomenon, following upon Foucault's perception that

> sexuality *per se* did not exist [...] in *any* society, *anywhere*, much before the nineteenth century because sexuality is the result of the modern deployment of a particular set of discourses that came into being relatively late in the history of the West.
>
> (quote from Ormand and Blondell 2015: 8 analysing
> Foucault 1978; italics in original)

Taken to its extreme, one *could* argue that ancient sexuality did not exist. However, as all existing definitions of any terms should be situated within the social contexts of past societies, many scholars employ the notion of "sexuality" as long as it is understood on its own terms without drawing parallels to our own culturally specific perceptions of what constitutes sexuality (Skinner 1997; Halperin 1998: 109; Voss and Schmidt 2000: 3; Ormand and Blondell 2015: 13).

Gender acts as an analytical category, the result of environmental and cultural conditioning in early childhood, and differentiates itself from biological sex with which one is born. In other words, to be a woman or a man is not a biological condition but rather something imposed on a child, or, as French writer Simone de Beauvoir wrote in 1952, "one is not born, but rather becomes, a woman" (de Beauvoir 1953[1952]). Such neat differentiations of "gender is culture, and biological sex is nature", are naturally problematic as they reinforce categorisation where sex is fixed and gender can go any way (Rubin 1975; Voss and Schmidt 2000: 15; Pilcher and Whelehan 2017: 59). For a different perspective one can refer to the works of Judith Butler (1990), who obliterates the idea that sexual difference is rooted in the body. In her works, there is no distinction between socially constructed gender or biological sex, because sex is already gender (Butler 1990: 6). Concepts such as male and female or man and woman are not absolute: they are performed on a daily basis. When an individual dresses, walks, acts, talks, or moves according to the social expectations of the said individual's gender/sex, they sustain the regulatory ideal of what is expected for that gender/sex and also consolidate/make the norm of being that gender/sex. For example, the stereotype of the femme fatale depicted in film noire captures the behaviours (facial expression, posture, and language) and accessories (makeup, clothing, and jewellery) of a specific womanly identity; while this is taken from a popular mass genre, it provides a hyperbolic example of the recursive perception and performance of gender/sex. The example further illustrates how gender can be enmeshed with sexuality.

This volume is structured along the lines of sex, femininity, and masculinity, and we are mindful that such divisions reinforce the binary views on gender as social and sex as physical, and the oversimplified polarisation of masculinity versus femininity. The choice is conscious, however, as we wanted to depart from our own discipline where "gender" equals women and sexually tinted imagery is considered iconographically pornographic. We believe that such a threefold division will allow us to show the intersections and the relationships between sex, gender, and sexuality at its fullest. Following Skinner (1997: 13), this made our complex dataset elastic and adaptable by accommodating different readings of evidence. Gazing at an image of what is clearly sexual intercourse, by modern and ancient standards, raised the question of the social significance of the intercourse: decontextualisation of such an act makes it meaningless in the same way as decontextualising figurines of the goddess of Love or images of male and female genitals, and seeing them as eroticising and sexually arousing (Part I). Similarly, how do images of vulvas and naked female bodies comply with ancient discourse on femininity (Part II)? In our view, discussion of the material fingerprint of masculinities (the phallus is one such example) tallies with the masculinities enacted in daily life; the sexual practices of those practising/performing hegemonic masculinities prompts consideration of where sex ends and discourse on sexuality begins (Part III). It is precisely these intersections that we are interested in unravelling, as a key part in our investigative processes of provincial modes of sex, gender, and sexuality.

Apart from struggling with multiple terminologies, we and our contributors had to confront yet another obstacle. Our primary focus is on the provinces and frontiers, and our aim is to untangle emic views in gender and sexuality matters, but the Mediterranean (Roman) perspective could not be completely removed from any of the case studies. In part, so much has been written within the Classical discipline that we cannot avoid including comparanda and ideas. Indeed, the length of time Classicists have been studying these topics and the sheer amount of volumes available offer us a rather rewarding vista (e.g. most recently Hubbard 2014; Skinner 2014; Blondell and Ormand 2015; Masterson et al. 2015b). This imbalance underscored the editorial decision not to prescribe the "ultimate" methodology for the study of the topic, but rather to allow the contributors to probe various methodologies, openly borrowing some from anthropologies, Classics, and archaeologies of sexuality of other periods. Each contribution has its own strategies and each stands in its own right, which has provided the opportunity to showcase multivocalities and multiplicities of provincial sexualities and genders without resolving to homogeneous, over-generalised perspectives. This multivocality is enhanced moreover through the international and educational backgrounds of the contributors.

Part I: Seeing (beyond) sex explores the archaeology of sex, revealing how it was interwoven into the social fabric through the use of material culture. There is an abundance of evidence for the omnipresence of sexual imagery in the provinces: couplings of men with women adorning public architecture, "daily" household utensils, and dress. John Pearce, Matthew Fittock and Adam Parker explore these material manifestations of sexual imagery and the layered meanings of the iconography as portrayed in a specific type of object, one in which the portability of these objects generates further complexity, or context, to interpretation. Their contributions show how sex is truly "a present absent", but not from the historical narrative but rather from the function of the objects themselves. While Pearce analyses objects depicting explicit sexual acts and Parker focuses on explicit (to a modern audience) artefacts depicting male and female genitals, Fittock has selected a group of artefacts exhibiting more implicit and arbitrary imagery depicting the naked female body.

Pearce explores a sexual scene involving three individuals on a knife handle from Roman Britain. As with every archaeological artefact, multi-dimensional readings of this scene can be proposed and images on it do more than portray a sex act (Morgan 2018: 44). As "images [in general] move us when they offer something we want or need: to be entertained, intrigued, frightened, encouraged, scolded, inspired" (Morgan 2018: 56), so this sexual scene becomes more than just being about the sex. The viewers' and users' age, status, social background, upbringing, origin, and so on could have made them "read" the scene beyond the obvious representation of an acrobatic sexual intercourse. It could have been read as a citation joke (that is now lost on us) and thus entertain the viewer and the user. It could have acted as a protective image aimed at safeguarding an individual during shaving, albeit note the double-layered meaning behind an object being possibly a shaving knife and a protective symbolic meaning of a scene. Close physical encounters involving such objects with sexual scenes is another matter: sensory experience may have added another layer of meaning onto an already complex scene. Therefore, Pearce's exploration of what the image of sexual intercourse does, how it does it, and the role of cultural conditioning when such an image is observed or a knife is handled emphasises that experiencing and seeing sex in a provincial context is never a fixed or static perspective. For the volume as a whole, Pearce's opening chapter foregrounds that any image we associate with sex (e.g. genitals) or sexual activity (e.g. same-sex couples involved in a sexual relationship) enables a range of interpretative possibilities not necessarily in agreement with each other or with modern expectations and perceptions. While this is not a novel statement, it does come up as a common thread throughout the volume, and even when it does not explicitly feature, it should be taken into the equation.

Matthew Fittock is the first contribution that takes a materialist approach by exploring exactly these contextual, material, and spatio-temporal entanglements foregrounded by Pearce through the analyses of pipeclay Venus figurines found throughout Roman Britain. Fittock emphasises the inherited ambiguity of the whole "pipeclay Venus figurine package": the figurine itself, the material it is made of, and the types, practices of use and deposition all contributed to various nuances in how an object with an image of Venus was perceived. In these instances, Venus is no longer the goddess of love and sex, but more about protection and fertility. Figurines tell us the fascinating yet mundane stories of immigrants from Gaul to Britain, of family losses and dangers of childbearing in antiquity, and of daily religious practices in household shrines. There is nothing sexual about them. Understanding ancient sexuality also means being able to desexualise objects and perspectives, be they ancient or modern.

Adam Parker's chapter continues with themes of sexual images acting as protective mechanisms, of their inherited ambiguity, and of their multiple apotropaic functionalities, adding a magical twist to the interpretation and discussion. While not completely divesting the images of sexuality, his analysis highlights the different perceptions of phallic and vulvate presence in the Roman world, in which the sexuality of a phallus and vulva may be secondary or even tertiary to its symbolic function. Being an unmissable part in the apotropaic toolkit in a province of Britannia, images of phalluses and vulvas feature on a wide-range of objects of human and animal adornment made in a variety of materials. This indicates that provincials may have mixed and matched materials, images, and functions for the purpose of individualised protection. This knowledge adds yet another layer to the understanding and perceiving of contextually informed, protective-not-sexual phalluses and vulvas in the past, though this time it adds another dimension—a realm of (personalised) magic.

Part II: Representations and performance of the feminine (or is it?) addresses facets of ancient femininity in three distinct contributions. Excessive, somewhat obsessive, emphasis on putting women back into the picture in Roman provincial research, as described above, has created a false equation between gender studies and women (Revell 2010). Therefore, in this section, while chapters continue to explore the ever elusive and "present absence" of women, and their lady parts, combined they do act as a springboard for redefining the focus of gender as a topic in the provincial setting by going beyond the "add women and stir" approach and beyond the de facto assumption of the presence of women and children in military forts.

Stefanie Hoss's opening contribution takes us on yet another materialist journey, this time zooming-in on the presentation of female genitals in art and the material culture of Mediterranean and north-western provincial societies.

Physiological accuracy, while achievable by artisans in antiquity, was eschewed in favour of more ambiguous and symbolic representations. Exploring the causes for such a development, she shows how in every society depictions of vulvas come in different shapes, sizes, and materials, suggesting the existence of divergent societal views and perspectives on how this female organ should be executed. Yet, in spite of the differences, a similar thread emerged in Hoss's analysis: every society's urge not to depict female genitals in their full and accurate physiological glory was, actually, foregrounded in a taboo. From the material non-presentation of female genitals, the part moves onto material representations of femininity and representations of ideal provincial female gender in words and images. Robyn Crook's summative essay warns us to pay greater attention to the nexus of class and gender in Roman Britain, as portrayed in accounts of elite and non-elite women in textual sources. A glimpse of a society more equal than previously suggested comes forward in her conclusion, where women enjoyed a set of privileges and relative freedom on a day-to-day basis. Looking at the data through the perspective of group identity, Crook, however, emphasises that much of the evidence may in fact be idealised representation of a female gender embedded in group ideals of a perfect woman. This complex interplay between peer and individual perception, or shall we say, hegemonic and non-hegemonic femininity, is yet another reminder in this part of the complexity involved in untangling emic and etic perspectives on genders in a provincial setting. Kaja Stemberger moves the discussion further by focusing on gender differences in relation to or in juxtaposition with social status, culture, and ethnicity. Her case study foregrounds the subject of agency through assessment of the burial record of two Roman colonies in the territory of modern Slovenia. Stemberger critiques historicising accounts of how attire was interpreted in the past, which supported ethno-nationalist readings of the evidence. In fact, the difference between the two cemeteries and treatments of the dead provide a firm rebuttal of many of the underlying assumptions of the concept of Romanisation. All in all, this section focuses on how provincial femininity operated through a system of hegemonic ideal—where the vulva and its image simply did not fit into an archetype—and how the impeccable intersected with an individual agency in the formation of a non-ideal, non-hegemonic view.

Part III: The stuff of "man" presents three case studies that explicitly address masculinity and its physical embodiment: the phallus, be it flaccid or erect. Opening the part is Tatiana Ivleva's chapter, which engages with same-sex sexual relationships and issues of manliness in the Roman army stationed at the edges of the Roman world. Scrutinising the epigraphic sources for the evidence of same-sex sexual relations between soldiers and their male slaves, as well as between soldiers, she asks whether there were links with Roman masculine and sexual protocols operating in the centre of the empire. Her chapter is yet another prime example of how Classical and Roman archaeology scholarship deviate. The former was filled with discussions on male same-sex sexual relations and explorations of masculine categories in Latin texts and imagery to the point where the term "sexuality" became somewhat synonymous with same-sex sexual relations (Masterson et al. 2015a: 5). The latter evolved within a "default heterosexual matrix" stating that men of the provinces were heterosexually masculine without embracing the variety of masculinities or allowing for alternative readings of sexual relations (Masterson et al. 2015a: 5).

The following two chapters deal with the, by default, "manliest", but not necessarily masculine, matter—the phallus—through a discrete analysis of material representations of male genitals in resting and excited states. Rob Collins takes a very materialist perspective on the erect phallus, cataloguing the presence and diversity of stone-carved examples from the World Heritage Site of Hadrian's Wall. The large assemblage of phalluses from the Wall enables a consideration of the use of the phallus as an apotropaic symbol relative to a monumental "place" and more discrete "places", as well as through time. In this regard, the archaeology challenges notions of limited episodic use of the phallus and demonstrates a preference for specific placement, extending the notion of a frontier barrier beyond the merely physical into the metaphysical. Alissa Whitmore focuses on pendants of flaccid phalli, highlighting Rome's cultural interactions with the East. The apotropaic concept remains, though the manner of presentation of the phallus alongside other amulets and its archaeological context is at some variance with the ithyphallic pendants known from Western provinces. Charting the physical and contextual flaccid phallic amulets' journeys from the West to the East, Whitmore's contribution adds another "power" level to the depicted penis. Alongside apotropaic function, the role of flaccid, as opposed to the erect, exemplars in the protection of children's future virility is yet to be explored fully (on the protective power of erect phalli for the children's benefit, see Parker 2015). Taken together, and in contrast to Hoss's conclusion on non-representation of the vulva, both chapters highlight the phallic omnipresence. It was socially acceptable to depict phalluses in various materials and display on diverse media, but it could also be observed, worn, and curated by people of various status, genders, sexes, and ages, including animals. Furthermore, the diversity in the phallic depictions, with Collins developing a typology of ithyphallic stone-carvings via the corpus of Hadrian's Wall, is intriguing. An experiment detailed in Appendix 5.1 of Hoss's contribution suggests the penis is usually drawn in two uniform ways, flaccid or erect, with the vulva depicted in numerous, most often unrecognisable, manners. While we aim not to draw boundaries between female and male matters, it does become clear that when it comes to genitals, societal boundaries, norms, acceptances, and taboos remain firm.

Naturally, there is a certain degree of overlap in the contributions between the three parts in terms of subject matter, and the papers could be ordered differently to highlight other shared themes. Crook, Stemberger, and Ivleva, for example, highlight gender constructs in different media, produced for and consumed by different audiences. Parker's and Whitmore's chapters can be comfortably read alongside those of Pearce, Fittock, and Hoss in terms of the role of (pseudo)-sexualised imagery in portable objects, while Whitmore, Parker, and Hoss more specifically consider the role of adornment and visibility of such objects. Similar theoretical viewpoints on masculinity, femininity, and gender are shared in the chapters by Ivleva and Crook.

A theme that emerged in Stemberger's and Collins's chapters is the issue of language (also Voss and Schmidt 2000: 2). Collins makes use of English slang and humour to develop his phallus typology, which may be jarring for some scholars and seen as inappropriate. But is it so? Some aspects of sexuality, primarily anatomical, have clearly defined clinical and medical terminology, though strict employment of clinical terminology is not always appropriate, for example in the translation of poetry. Other aspects, such as sexual positions, have variable terminologies that not only depend on language, but also frame cultural perceptions and prejudices, and have a further layer of baggage by way of appropriate scholarly use. This is further emphasised in Stemberger's chapter where she confronts the problem that Slovenian language does not distinguish between sex and gender. The ability to frame discourse with a useful terminology relies on the presence of a viable lexicon, in which concepts can be meaningfully separated, in Stemberger's case with an interpretative necessity to distinguish gender (as a social construct) from (biological) sex. The extent to which one feels bound to contemporary scholarly language is therefore a significant factor, and one that is further mitigated by the socio-economic position of the scholarly author, not least class, gender, and nationality, as well as the perceived expectations of her/his audiences.

For most authors in this volume, familiar historic societies have been seen in a new light through integrating sexuality and gender perspectives into the analysis of those societies (Weston 2011[1998]: 8). Collins's intriguing conclusion on the "phallic force field" protecting the barrack blocks provided new knowledge on the processes going on within a military fort, showcasing how space was literally embodied. Magical aspects of sexuality resurface in Parker's chapter. New questions were brought to light. How did children perceive the abundance of the genital images? How did audiences react to someone wearing a flaccid or erect phallic pendant, or a vulva used to decorate horse harnesses, especially when such objects were located to draw the eye of the viewer (Whitmore, Parker, and Hoss)? This surely contrasts with scenes of people participating in sexual acts, which were not always linked to their representational value (Pearce, see also Clarke 2001). Looking at masculinity and same-sex sexual relations made Ivleva reconsider the most romanticised story from Roman Britain, that of Regina, the native Catuvellaunian (British) girl married to Barates of Palmyra. Is it a true love story, a story of sexual abuse, or even one of fatalistic compromise (see also Baird 2015)? Situated as we are within the Romanisation and imperialism paradigms, and their deconstruction, to what extent are we receptive to the plausibility of more egalitarian provincial societies, at least in terms of gender and sexual behaviour (Crook and Ivleva)?

More images of phalluses, vulvas, and sexual intercourses may have existed in the past, but they were deliberately destroyed by 19th- and 20th-century archaeologists and/or curators due to their perception of pornographic imagery, a theme that emerges in a number of contributions (Pearce, Parker, Hoss, Ivleva, and Collins). The *gabinetto segreto* is known from Italy, but not in the European north-west, as far as the editors are aware. Yet, similar tendencies, to keep the sexual images under lock and key, or even to destroy them completely, have been recorded in 18th- and 19th-century academic circles, albeit seemingly not on the same massive scale as for the Mediterranean. Images perceived as erotic or pornographic were observed and noted, but there was a reluctance to discuss them with scholars before moving on without further commenting on the imagery. Commentary was often brief, oblique, or allusive, and we are fortunate when destruction is noted, such as the penis "so offensive to chaste Eyes" found at Maryport in northern England (Gordon 1726: 100). Another issue highlighted in Whitmore's chapter is the deliberate mixing of sexualised and mundane artefacts found on different sites and in different contexts to increase their sale value—a practice recorded in 19th-century Sardinia, but surely these might have been more common than we actually realise. One cannot know what has been thrown away or combined together, leaving us with the misguided information on context, date, and associated assemblage. Therefore, while the data presented in this volume showcases its density in Roman provinces and beyond, one may ponder whether we are dealing with a fraction of what has survived and how trustworthy our contextual data is. In this regard, a comparison with other provinces, such as those of the Upper and Lower Danube or in the Middle East, may be a fruitful endeavour, as it will allow scholars to contrast and compare the results deriving from the studies presented here. Are the numbers in some way similar? Are different academic (and religious) backgrounds responsible for the level of survival and tolerance toward the ancient sexual imagery? Or does it all boil down to archaeological recovery biases, with objects made in inorganic, durable materials prone to greater survival (Parker)?

What is missing from the volume is a "Part IV: Fluidity of gender(s) and sex". Ideally, such a section would complete the volume by discussing evidence for non-conformative and alt-genders, sexual practices that deviated from the protocols operating at the Empire's centre, or material embodiments of sexuality that do not include images of or allusions to genitals or sexual scenes. At the time of this volume's production, such research was non-existent. Considering how conscious contemporary scholarship on ancient sexuality is regarding the existence of "third genders" (Matić 2012; Moral 2016), as editors we did not want to fall into the perpetual loop of dividing and numbering genders. Therefore, we avoided inviting contributions on the "usual suspects", like the *gallus* from Catterick (Cool 2002: 29–30), simultaneously curating the hope that the volume will inspire "out-of-the-box" thinking when a desire to label an "unusual" burial excavated in the provinces arises (for inspiration, see Surtees and Dyer 2020). Neither did we wish to project our "fantasies" and search for sex in places where no sex was intended, especially since the erotically charged images of genitals and sexual intercourse were not necessarily perceived in antiquity as alluding to sex (as they would in the eyes of a modern audience) as our contributions in Parts I–III indicate (see also Johns 1982).

We leave this search to our successors knowing well that we have raised the bar high. Therefore, instead of "Part IV", to draw the whole volume together we have asked Sarah Levin-Richardson, scholar of ancient sexuality in the discipline of Classics, to consider the contributions to the volume relative to the topic in her home discipline. Such closure should be seen as an attempt to build bridges between the disciplines of Classics and Roman (provincial) archaeology in matters of sexuality. Our hope in this regard is to make it a norm that at least two to three contributions dealing with the (archaeological) evidence from the wider empire of the first four centuries A.D. will feature in subsequent volumes on sex in antiquity. Provincial sex and genders should not become a "present absence" in Classics; neither should they spark an interest and enthusiasm, and then "fade away" (paraphrasing the title of Halperin 2015).

Conclusion

In this volume, we add texture to the provincial discourse on sexuality and gender, and show how sex and gender issues were woven into the very fibre of daily life in the provinces and frontiers. Sexual imagery decorated household structures and public buildings, but also the necks of the inhabitants. We can envision the use of sexual language in everyday (humorous) talk, in magic spells or votive dedications, yet we still struggle to vocalise our evidence (when we have any). Assessing the production, role, and impact of everyday gender fluidities provides another means of understanding the realities of multicultural provinces and frontiers. In all, our adventure exploring different gender and sexual discourses and dynamics has shown us the diversity of data, highlighting the volume of evidence to be found outside of peninsular Italy, as well as a greater spread of chronologies. The collected evidence indicates a highly varied picture of people living under diverse sexual regimes, holding different views on masculinity and femininity, and following unique dynamics in sexual matters. To some, such interpretations of sexual and gender variability may seem frustratingly speculative; however, teasing out the subtleties without recourse to analogies with the present was a rewarding analytical strategy. In addition, the evidence has proven suitable for asking questions along different trajectories, integrating notions of gender, family, and sexuality with contextualised readings of space and ideology.

As a whole, the volume emphasises the urgency in approaching the topics as a lived experience in the provinces, rather than from the perspective of a "present absence" narrative. We hope this volume will demonstrate that provincial constructions of sex must constitute a discrete research area, not only within the general field of provincial studies but also within the field of ancient sexuality as a whole. This is why we wish not only to stay rigidly within the provincial discourse, but to position sexuality and gender in Roman provinces and frontiers within a broader and deeper context of the ancient world. Thus, there is work to be done, not least in overcoming the challenges specific to our discipline. But this divergence between the traditional datasets and approaches of Classicists and archaeologists indicates exciting avenues for further scholarship and opens up a fertile and vast area of study positioned at the intersection of both disciplines. We hope the essays in this volume establish a foundation for Roman archaeologists to engage with these exciting topics and act as a forum for the generation of scholars who will expand the field without the fear of ghettoisation. While as editors we feel that this is a pleasure delayed, the knowledge that this book may spark many other projects is rewarding.

Bibliography

Allason-Jones, L. (1995). "'Sexing' Small Finds", in P. Rush (ed.), *Theoretical Roman Archaeology: Second Conference Proceedings*. Avebury: Aldershot, 22–32.

Allason-Jones, L. (1999). "Women and the Roman Army in Britain", in A. Goldsworthy and I.P. Haynes (eds), *The Roman Army as a Community, Including Papers of a Conference held at Birkbeck College, University of London on 11–12 January, 1997*. Journal of Roman Archaeology Supplementary Series no 34. Portsmouth, RI: Journal of Roman Archaeology, 41–51.

Allason-Jones, L. (2004). "The Family in Roman Britain", in M. Todd (ed.), *A Companion to Roman Britain*. Oxford: Wiley, 273–88.

Allason-Jones, L. (2005). *Women in Roman Britain*. London: British Museum Press.

Allison, P.M. (2006). "Mapping for Gender. Interpreting Artefact Distribution Inside 1st- and 2nd-century AD Forts in Roman Germany", *Archaeological Dialogues*, 13(1): 1–20.

Allison, P.M. (2007). "Artefact Distribution within the Auxiliary Fort at Ellingen: Evidence for Building Use and for the Presence of Women and Children", *Bericht der römische-germanischen Kommission*, 87: 387–452.

Allison, P.M. (2009). "The Women in the Early Forts: GIS and Artefact Distribution Analyses in 1st and 2nd Century Germany", in A. Morillo, N. Hanel and E. Martin (eds), *Limes XX: Estudios Sobre la Frontera Romana*, Anejos de *Gladius* 13. vol. 3, Madrid: C.S.I.C., 1193–201.

Allison, P.M. (2013). *People and Spaces in Roman Military Bases*. Cambridge: Cambridge University Press.

Baird, J.A. (2015). "On Reading the Material Culture of Ancient Sexual Labor", *Helios*, 42(1): 163–75.

Baker, P. (2003). "A Brief Comment on the TRAC Session Dedicated to the Interdisciplinary Approaches to the Study of Roman Women", in G. Carr, E. Swift and J. Weekes (eds), *TRAC 2002: Proceedings of the Twelfth Annual Theoretical Roman Archaeology Conference, Canterbury 2002*. Oxford: Oxbow Books, 140–46.

Blondell, R. and Ormand, K. eds, (2015). *Ancient Sex. New Essays*. Columbus, OH: The Ohio State University Press.

Brandl, U. ed, (2008). *Frauen und römisches Militär. Beiträge eines runden Tisches in Xanten vom 7. Bis 9. Juli 2005*. British Archaeological Reports International Series 1759. Oxford: Archaeopress.

Brubaker, R. and Cooper, F. (2000). "Beyond 'Identity'", *Theory and Society*, 29: 1–47.

Butler, J. (1990). *Gender Trouble: Feminism and the Subversion of Identity*. London: Routledge.

Clarke, J. (2001). *Looking at Lovemaking. Constructions of Sexuality in Roman Art, BC 100 – AD 250*. Berkeley: University of California Press.

Clarke, J. (2003). *Roman Sex 100 BC – 250 AD*. New York: Harry N. Abrams.

Collins, R. and Ivleva, T. (2018). "Introduction: Sex on the Frontiers. Textual and Material Representations of Human Sexuality at the Edge of Empire", in Sommer and Matešić (2018), 1035–38.

Cool, H.E.M. (2002). "An Overview of the Small Finds from Catterick", in P.R. Wilson (ed.), *Cataractonium: Roman Catterick and Its Hinterland. Excavations and Research, 1958–1997. Vol 2*. York: Council for British Archaeology, 24–43.

de Beauvoir, S. (1953[1952]). *The Second Sex*. Trans. By H.M. Parsley. New York: Knopf.

Dover, K. (1978). *Greek Homosexuality*. Harvard, MA: Harvard University Press.

Eckardt, H. (2014). *Objects and Identities: Roman Britain and the North-Western Provinces*. Oxford: Oxford University Press.

Flemming, R. (2010). "Sexuality", in A. Barchiesi and W. Scheidel (eds), *The Oxford Handbook of Roman Studies*. Oxford: Oxford University Press, 797–815.

Foubert, L. (2013). "Female Travellers in Roman Britain: Vibia Pacata and Julia Lucilla", in Hemelrijk and Woolf (2013), 391–403.

Foucault, M. (1978[1976]). *The History of Sexuality. Vol. 1. An Introduction*. Trans. By R. Hurley. New York: Penguin Books.

Foucault, M. (1985[1984]). *The History of Sexuality. Vol. 2. The Use of Pleasure*. Trans. By R. Hurley. New York: Penguin Books.

Foucault, M. (1986[1984]). *The History of Sexuality. Vol. 3. The Care of the Self*. Trans. By R. Hurley. New York: Penguin Books.

Gardner, A. (2013). "Thinking about Roman Imperialism: Postcolonialism, Globalisation and Beyond?", *Britannia*, 44: 1–25.

Gordon, A. (1726). *Itinerarium Septentrionale: Or, A Journey Thro' Most of the Counties of Scotland, and Those in the North of England*. London.

Greene, E.M. (2011). *Women and Families in the Auxiliary Military Communities of the Roman West in the First and Second Centuries AD*. Unpub. PhD dissertation, University of North Carolina at Chapel Hill.

Greene, E.M. (2012). "Sulpicia Lepidina and Elizabeth Custer: A Cross-Cultural Analogy for the Social Role of Women on a Military Frontier", in M. Duggan, F. McIntosh and D.J. Rohl (eds), *TRAC2011: Proceedings of the Twenty First Annual Theoretical Roman Archaeology Conference, Newcastle 2011*. Oxford: Oxbow, 105–14.

Greene, E.M. (2013). "Female Networks in the Military Communities of the Roman West: A View from the Vindolanda Tablets", in Hemelrijk and Woolf (2013), 369–90.

Greene, E.M. (2015a). "*Conubium Cum Uxoribus*: Wives and Children in the Roman Military Diplomas", *Journal of Roman Archaeology*, 28: 125–59.

Greene, E.M. (2015b). "Roman Military Pay and Soldiers' Families: The Household Contribution to Subsistence", in N. Sharankov and L. Vagalinski (eds), *Proceedings of the 22nd International Congress of Roman Frontier Studies, Ruse, Bulgaria, September 2012*. Bulletin of the National Institute of Archaeology 42. Sofia: Bulgarian Academy of Science, 495–99.

Greene, E.M. (2016). "Identities and Social Roles of Women in Military Settlements in the Roman West", in S. Budin and J. Turfa (eds), *Women in Antiquity: Real Women across the Ancient World*. London: Routledge, 942–53.

Greene, E.M. (2017). "The Families of Roman Auxiliary Soldiers in the Military Diplomas", in Hodgson et al. (2017), 23–26.

Halperin, D. (1998). "Forgetting Foucault: Acts, Identities, and the History of Sexuality", *Representations*, 63: 93–120.

Halperin, D.M. (2015). "Not Fade Away", in Blondell and Ormand (2015), 308–28.

Halperin, D.M., Winkler, J.J. and Zeitlin, F.I. (1990). "Introduction", in D.M. Halperin, J.J. Winkler and F.I. Zeitlin (eds), *Before Sexuality. The Construction of Erotic Experience in the Ancient Greek World*. Princeton, NJ: Princeton University Press, 3–21.

Hemelrijk, E. and Woolf, G. eds, (2013). *Women and the Roman City in the Latin West*. Mnemosyne Journal Supplement. Leiden: Brill.

Hingley, R. (2005). *Globalizing Roman Culture: Unity, Diversity and Empire*. London: Routledge.

Hodgson, N. (2014). "The Accommodation of Soldiers' Wives in Roman Fort Barracks – On Hadrian's Wall and Beyond", in R. Collins and F. McIntosh (eds), *Life in the Limes: Studies of the People and Objects of the Roman Frontiers*. Oxford: Oxbow, 18–28.

Hodgson, N., Bidwell, P. and Schachtmann, J. eds, (2017). *Roman Frontier Studies 2009. Proceedings of the XXI International Congress of Roman Frontier Studies (LIMES Congress) held at Newcastle Upon Tyne in August 2009*. Archaeopress Roman Archaeology 25. Oxford: Archaeopress.

Holmes, B. (2012). *Gender. Antiquity and Its Legacy*. Oxford: Oxford University Press.

Hubbard, T.K. ed, (2014). *A Companion to Greek and Roman Sexualities*. Malden, MA: Blackwell Publishing.

Insoll, T. (2007). "Introduction. Configuring Identities in Archaeology", in T. Insoll (ed.), *The Archaeology of Identities: A Reader*. London: Routledge, 1–18.

Ivleva, T. (Forthcoming). "(In)visible Women and Children: Epigraphic and Archaeological Evidence for 'British' Migrant Families in the Roman Army", in L. Brice and E. Greene (eds), *Present but Not Accounted For: Women and the Roman Army*. Cambridge: Cambridge University Press.

James, S.T. (2006). "Engendering Change in Our Understanding of the Structure of Roman Military Communities", *Archaeological Dialogues*, 13/1: 31–36.

Johns, C. (1982). *Sex or Symbol. Erotic Images of Greece and Rome*. London: British Museum Publications.

Juntunen, K. (2018). "'Married with Children'–The Marital Patterns of Roman Auxiliary Soldiers in the *Diplomata Militaria*", in Sommer and Matešić (2018), 1039–45.

Kamen, D. and Levin-Richardson, S. (2015a). "Revisiting Roman Sexuality. Agency and the Conceptualization of Penetrated Males", in Masterson et al. (2015b), 449–60.

Kamen, D. and Levin-Richardson, S. (2015b). "Lusty Ladies in the Roman Imaginary", in Blondell and Ormand (2015), 231–52.

Klein, M.J. (2017). "Women and Children in Military Inscriptions from Northern Germania Superior", in Hodgson et al. (2017), 34–42.

Knapp, A.B. (1998). "Boys Will Be Boys. Masculinist Approaches to a Gendered Archaeology", in K. Hayes-Gilpin and D.S. Whitley (eds), *Reader in Gender Archaeology*. London: Routledge, 365–74.

Le Bohec, Y. (2017). "Des Femmes dans les Camps?", *Bonner Jahrbücher*, 217: 95–112.

Leitao, D.D. (2014). "Sexuality in Greek and Roman Military Context", in Hubbard (2014), 230–44.

Lister, K. (2019). "Sexing Up History: How to Study and Tell the History of Sex", *Historyextra: The official website for BBC History Magazine and BBC World Histories Magazine* [www.historyextra.com/period/georgian/history-sex-why-important-harris-list-covent-garden-ladies-historian/; accessed 16.03.2019].

Lyons, A.P. and Lyons, H.D. (2011a). "Introduction: Problems in Writing About Sex in Anthropology", in Lyons and Lyons (2011b), 1–7.

Lyons, A.P. and Lyons, H.D. eds, (2011b). *Sexualities in Anthropology: A Reader.* Chichester: Wiley-Blackwell.

Masterson, M., Sorkin Rabinowitz, N. and Robson, J. (2015a). "Introduction", in Masterson et al. (2015b), 1–12.

Masterson, M., Sorkin Rabinowitz, N. and Robson, J. eds, (2015b). *Sex in Antiquity: Exploring Gender and Sexuality in the Ancient World.* London and New York: Routledge.

Matić, U. (2012). "To Queer or Not to Queer? That is the Question: Sex/Gender, Prestige and Burial no. 10 on the Mokrin Necropolis", *Dacia*, LVI: 169–85.

Mattingly, D. (2004). "Being Roman: Expressing Identity in a Provincial Setting", *Journal of Roman Archaeology*, 17: 5–25.

Mattingly, D. (2006). *An Imperial Possession. Britain in the Roman Empire.* London: Penguin History of Britain Series.

Mattingly, D. (2011). *Imperialism, Power and Identity Experiencing the Roman Empire.* Princeton, NJ: Princeton University Press.

Moral, E. (2016). "Qu(e)erying Sex and Gender in Archaeology: A Critique of the 'Third' and Other Sexual Categories", *Journal of Archaeological Method and Theory*, 23: 788–809.

Morgan, D. (2018). *Images at Work: The Material Culture of Enchantment.* Oxford: Oxford University Press.

Naerebout, F.G. (2014). "Convergence and Divergence: One Empire, Many Cultures. Integration and Romanization", In G. de Kleijn and S. Benoist (eds), *Integration in Rome and in the Roman World. Proceedings of the Tenth Workshop of the International Network Impact of Empire (Lille, June 23–25, 2011).* Leiden: Brill, 263–81.

Ormand, K. and Blondell, R. (2015). "One Hundred and Twenty-Five Years of Homosexuality", in Blondell and Ormand (2015), 1–22.

Parker, A. (2015). "The Fist-and-Phallus Pendants from Roman Catterick", *Britannia*, 46: 135–49.

Phang, S.E. (2001). *The Marriage of Roman Soldiers (13 BC–AD 235): Law and Family in the Imperial Army.* Leiden: Brill.

Pilcher, J. and Whelehan, I. (2017). *Key Concepts in Gender Studies.* London: Sage.

Pitts, M. (2007). "The Emperor's New Clothes? The Utility of Identity in Roman Archaeology", *American Journal of Archaeology*, 111: 693–713.

Pitts, M. and Versluys, M.-J. eds, (2015). *Globalisation and the Roman World. World History, Connectivity and Material Culture.* Cambridge: Cambridge University Press.

Revell, L. (2009). *Roman Imperialism and Local Identities.* Cambridge: Cambridge University Press.

Revell, L. (2010). "Romanization: A Feminist Critique", in A. Moore, G. Taylor, E. Harris, P. Girdwood and L. Shipley (eds), *TRAC2009. Proceedings of the Nineteenth Annual Theoretical Roman Archaeology Conference.* Oxford: Oxbow books, 1–10.

Revell, L. (2015). *Ways of Being Roman: Discourses of Identity in the Roman West.* Oxford: Oxbow books.

Revell, L. (2016). "Footsteps in Stone: Variability Within a Global Culture", in S.E. Alcock, M. Egri and J.F.D. Frakes (eds), *Beyond Boundaries: Connecting Visual Cultures in the Provinces of Ancient Rome.* Los Angeles, CA: Getty Publications, 206–21.

Rubin, G. (1975). "The Traffic in Women: Notes towards a Political Economy of Sex", in R. Reiter (ed.), *Toward an Anthropology of Women.* New York: Monthly Review Press, 157–210.

Schörner, G. ed, (2005). *Romanisierung-Romanisation: Theoretische Modelle und praktische Fallbeispiele.* Oxford: Archaeopress.

Scott, E. (1993). "Introduction: TRAC (Theoretical Roman Archaeology Conference) 1991", in E. Scott (ed.), *Theoretical Roman Archaeology, First Conference Proceedings.* Aldershot: Avebury/Ashgate, 1–4.

Skinner, M.B. (1997). "Introduction. *Quod multo fit aliter in Graecia* ... ", in J.P. Hallett and M.B. Skinner (eds), *Roman Sexualities.* Princeton, NJ: Princeton University Press, 3–29.

Skinner, M.B. (2014). *Sexuality in Greek and Roman Culture.* Second edition. Malden, MA: Wiley.

Sommer, C.S. and Matešić, S. eds, (2018). *Limes XXIII – Proceedings of the 23rd International Congress of Roman Frontier Studies Ingolstadt 2015. Akten des 23. Internationalen Limeskongresses in Ingolstadt 2015.* Beiträge zum Welterbe Limes Sonderband 4. Mainz: Nünnerich-Asmus Verlag.

Stoll, O. (2006). "Legionäre, Frauen, Militärfamilien. Untersuchungen zur Bevölkerungsstruktur und Bevölkerungsentwicklung in den Grenzprovinzen des Imperium Romanum", *Jahrbuch des Römisch-Germanischen Zentralmuseums Mainz*, 53(1): 217–344.

Surtees, A. and Dyer, J. eds, (2020). *Exploring Gender Diversity in the Ancient World.* Edinburgh: Edinburgh University Press.

Tomas, A. (2011). "Reading Gender and Social Life in Military Places", *Światowit: Annals of the Institute of Archaeology of the University of Warsaw*, 8(Fasc. A): 139–53.

Tomas, A. (2015). "Female Family Members of the *Legio I Italica* Soldiers and Officers: A Case Study", in L. Mihailescu-Bîrliba (ed.), *Colonisation and Romanisation of Moesia Inferior. Premises of a Contrastive Approach.* Parthenon: Kaiserslautern and Mehlingen, 93–125.

van Driel-Murray, C. (1995). "Gender in Question", in P. Rush (ed.), *Theoretical Roman Archaeology: Second Conference Proceedings.* Aldershot: Avebury, 3–21.

van Driel-Murray, C. (1997). "Women in Forts?", *Jahresbericht der Gesellschaft Pro Vindonissa*, 1997: 55–61.

van Driel-Murray, C. (1998). "A Question of Gender in a Military Context", *Helinium*, 34: 342–62.

van Driel-Murray, C. (2008). "Those Who Wait at Home: The Effect of Recruitment on Women in the Lower Rhine Area", in Brandl (2008), 82–91.

van Enckevort, H. (2017). "Some Thoughts about the Archaeological Legacy of Soldiers' Families in the Countryside of the *Civitas Batavorum*", in Hodgson et al. (2017), 16–23.

Vanhoutte, S. and Verbrugge, A. (2017). "Women and Children at the Saxon Shore fort of Oudenburg (Belgium)", Hodgson et al. (2017), 48–52.

Versluys, M.-J. (2014). "Understanding Objects in Motion. An *Archaeological* Dialogue on Romanisation", *Archaeological Dialogues*, 21(1): 1–20.

Voss, B. and Schmidt, R.A. (2000). "Archaeologies of Sexuality: An Introduction", in R.A. Schmidt and B. Voss (eds), *Archaeologies of Sexuality.* London: Routledge, 1–35.

Webster, J. (2001). "Creolizing the Roman Provinces", *American Journal of Archaeology*, 105(2): 209–25.

Weston, K. (2011[1998]). "The Bubble, the Burn, and the Simmer: Introduction: Locating Sexuality in Social Science", in Lyons and Lyons (2011b), 7–27. Reprinted from Weston, K. 1998, *Long Slow Burn: Sexuality and Social Science.* London: Routledge, 1–27.

Whittaker, C.R. (2004). *Rome and its Frontiers: The Dynamics of Empire.* London: Routledge.

Williams, C.A. (2010). *Roman Homosexuality: Ideologies of Masculinity in Classical Antiquity.* Oxford: Oxford University Press.

Part I
Seeing (beyond) sex

2 On a knife-edge

An image of sex and spectacle from Roman north-west Europe

John Pearce

Introduction

In 2009 a metal detectorist reported the discovery of a copper-alloy Roman knife handle at Syston, Lincolnshire, a findspot 25 km from the Roman *colonia* at *Lindum*/Lincoln (Figure 2.1). This artefact is one of many hundreds of thousands recorded by the Portable Antiquities Scheme (PAS), a project established in 1997 to document archaeological finds made by members of the public in England and Wales (Worrell 2008: 358–9; Bland et al. 2017). It was subsequently acquired for Lincoln Museum where it is now displayed (Lee 2012). The handle carries a group of three figures modelled in the round and engaged

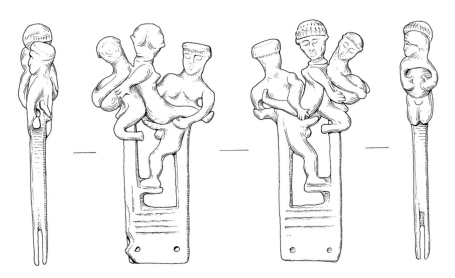

Figure 2.1 The Syston knife handle, 6.4 cm long (LIN-536F87)

(Drawn by D. Watt, © D. Watt and Lincolnshire County Council, used under a Creative Commons Licence)

in a precarious sex act. A naked male stands, his erect penis about to penetrate (or simulate penetration of) either a female who balances on the back of a smaller kneeling male or more likely the kneeling male himself. The latter figure holds an enigmatic spherical object. When discovered the handle was thought to have few parallels, but further research shows at least 25 surviving examples of this and similar objects from north-west Europe between German Rheinland-Pfalz and the English Midlands. Using selected examples, this chapter describes the scene presented, a new addition to the repertoire of Roman sexual images, and discusses potential inspirations for it among other representations of sex as well as provincial spectacles. Rather than emphasising the authority of a single interpretation, the chapter explores diverse potential ancient responses to the scene which, it argues, must be embedded in the material experience of making sense of the scene as encountered in use on a small three-dimensional object. As for terminology, this image is described as a scene of sex rather than of lovemaking, since it neither suggests intimacy or affection. It is not described as erotic, since it is not clear if arousal is its primary purpose (cf. Clarke 1998: 14–15).

In the study of Roman visual representations of sex, small portable objects from the northern provinces, such as the Syston handle, have played little part. If the destruction of such objects or their closeting in restricted collections mainly characterise an earlier era, some circumscriptions around their dissemination and study persisted well into the twentieth century (Johns 1982; Clarke 2003; Thüry 2009). However, in the last two decades exhibitions across continental Europe have drawn attention to a substantial surviving corpus of textual references to and visual representations of sex from Rome's northern provinces (e.g. Baude and Dumas 2005 (Les Baux de Provence), Faust et al. 2007 (Trier), and Thüry 2009 (Avenches)). The publicity attached to individual finds also illustrates the shift in perspective; the Syston handle, for example, was chosen as one of "Britain's Secret Treasures" for a UK primetime TV series of 2013 based on the PAS (Ochota 2013: 40–2). Yet even if recent literature on Roman sexuality and its visual representations has paid further attention to provincial examples, prompted by Clarke's advocacy of the potential interpretive richness of this material, the lion's share of scrutiny continues to fall on Pompeii and Rome, and on provincial objects which have affinities with Mediterranean images (Dierichs 1997; Clarke 1998, 2003, 2014; see also Chapter 1). Despite the consuming academic interest in provincial responses to Roman culture, sexuality has received little attention as a dimension of this, notwithstanding appeals for greater scrutiny (Matthews 1994). Study has been mainly limited to considering the topoi around the sexual mores of the "Other" (Roisman 2014) or the sexual dimension of Roman military violence (e.g. Phang 2004).

The Syston knife handle and its parallel pieces represent an instance of that isolation. Other sexual subjects on knife handles have been briefly considered in the discussion of Roman images of sex, but these have more direct affinities with the wider corpus, especially among Pompeian wall paintings (e.g. Johns 1982: 135–6). The involvement of three individuals in a sexual act and the occurrence of a masturbating figure differentiate this scene from most of the latter. Although it has some affinities with other scenes, it does not obviously derive from a known source. This chapter's aim is therefore to establish this scene as a new source for the study of Roman representations of sex by outlining the characteristics of these knife handles and their iconography. This will require a description of the scene and a comparison to potential visual and textual parallels, in order better to comprehend the scene by identifying the actors and acts. In doing so the chapter follows a traditional pathway for the analysis of small bronzes in figural form. As well as enabling the scene to be placed in a tradition of visual representations, it can also be assessed as evidence for social and cultural history, since it may represent a performance at a public spectacle. Other images on small-scale objects are commonly exploited in this way as a source for reconstructing spectacle culture in a provincial setting (e.g. Wilmott 2008: 173–8), and these knife handles may offer further insights in this respect for Britain and Gaul. However, this approach risks overlooking the character of such images as representations with a likely complex relationship to any social realities. In order to consider their roles as representations, it is essential to consider when and where images such as this were created, by and for whom, and above all how they were seen and experienced, in order to establish how they were comprehended (Clarke 1998: 9, 2007: 9–10). This approach is more easily applied to some media than others, for example wall paintings, and will require some adaptation in this case. As is explained below, there is considerable uncertainty concerning the use to which these objects were put and thus the context in which they were experienced. It is also likely that they were used by individuals of diverse backgrounds. However, acknowledging the likelihood of viewers with diverse reference points and varying understandings presents an opportunity rather than an impediment, since it mitigates the risk of assuming the existence of an omniscient viewer with encyclopaedic reference materials to hand (Hughes 2009). This approach also encourages attention to the small-scale and the three-dimensional quality of the image, since in this case, as in that of other portable decorated artefacts, image and object form are integrally connected (Swift 2009). For the knife handles it will be argued that viewing from different angles not only enables comprehension but also changes a viewer's perspective on the object in terms of identification with actors in the scene. This too is conditioned by the context of use, likely to be shaving and related grooming.

The chapter thus begins with an overview of the object type on which this scene appears, this being one of many decorated small knife handles of this kind. This establishes some characteristics of the social, cultural, and functional contexts in which the object circulated and was used. A description of the scene will follow, with discussion of the identity of the participants, perhaps spectacle performers, and the nature of the act. The relationships to possible sources of inspiration and the possible insights into sex as part of spectacle culture in a provincial setting will then be explored, followed by a consideration of potential responses to the image. While the scene can be read as normative, for example embodying a construction of Roman sexuality dominated by a penetrating male, handling the object also arguably subverted such a reading, prompting instead an impression of incongruity and jokiness which better fits a likely context of use, a maintenance of vulnerable bodily boundaries.

On a knife-edge: decorated toilet knives

The scene on the Syston handle is one example of diverse figural and other decoration found mainly on short-bladed pocket knives, objects found in large numbers in provinces north of the Alps. The Syston handle fits a fixed-blade knife, but most other surviving decorated handles are for folding knives. Their iron blades are typically about 6 cm long, sometimes shorter, and rarely exceed about 8 cm in length. The handles are of a similar length to accommodate folding blades, which slot into them along one side. A groove in the end of the handle allows for the blade to attach to it; the blade is held in place by a fixing pin through the collar (sometimes also within a ferrule) around which it pivots. Blades occasionally survive but are more often seen only in traces of iron corrosion products. The object type originates in the late Iron Age, but decorated handles were probably made throughout the Roman period (Schenk 2008: 50). Surviving examples are documented in antler, ivory, jet, and occasionally in amber and chalcedony, but bone and copper alloy predominate among the raw materials from which they were made. Decorated examples comprise a minority of all the knife handles of this form: at Augusta Raurica/Augst, for example, only 11 decorated examples derive from depositional contexts of the second to fourth century A.D. among more than 100 bone handles (Deschler-Erb 1998: 129–31). The first and only synthesis was published almost 80 years ago (von Mercklin 1940). The focus of subsequent studies on particular sites, materials, or motifs (e.g. Deschler-Erb 1998; Bertrand 2008; Fries 2008; Hoss 2009; Bartus 2010) means that the decorative repertoire as presently documented can only be sketched. This repertoire, as Rusch notes, knows no bounds in its variety, being matched in this respect by no other portable artefact type (*"Ihr Formenreichtum kennt keine Grenzen"*: Rusch 1981: 548).

On both types, folding and fixed-blade (albeit in fewer instances), the figural decoration is manifested as full figures, heads on terminals, or as herms. Among the anthropomorphic images are divinities and mythological beings, including Hercules, Venus, Apollo, Marsyas, Pan, Amores, a Kriophoros, as well as humans, including gladiators, wrestlers, actors, philosophers, parasites, and sexual athletes, as in this case. Zoomorphic forms include horses, large felines, eagles, dolphins, birds, horses, monkeys, and hounds chasing hares. Plant forms occur occasionally, most memorably the knife handles in the form of asparagus shoots from *Augusta Treverorum*/Trier and environs (Hoss 2009). Other decoration includes phalluses, trapezophoric pieces, human legs, pigs' trotters, balusters, and scabbards (von Mercklin 1940; Crummy 2011: 111–12). Inscriptions are rare, being mainly names of gladiators and of horses and charioteers on the scabbard shape that is preferred for circus souvenirs (Landes

2008; Bartus 2010). The hare and hound handles far outweigh other forms in terms of popularity, more than 70 examples having been reported to the PAS (Pearce and Worrell 2015). As well as serial production of these types the medium also witnesses considerable inventiveness for occasional pieces, requiring virtuoso carving and casting. This includes adaptation of images from larger three-dimensional representations, for example of the *Venus Pudica* and "crouching Venus" types, the "thorn puller" and the Kriophoros (Rusch 1981; Fries 2008), the compression of complex animal figures into the quasi-rectangular space of the handle (McSloy 2003), and even, in the case of the asparagus-shoot handles, casting directly from nature itself (Hoss 2009).

A consensus on the knives' purpose is lacking. Size would dictate that handles could have only been held between the thumb and the index and middle fingers (though a child's hand could have gripped the whole handle). Some favour their use in toilet routines, partly because the keeled or angled back of the blade would enhance control during shaving or manicure (Riha 1986: 28–32; Boon 2000: 346, no. 81; Crummy 2011: 111–12). Others see them as multi-purpose small knives (Jackson and Friendship-Taylor 2001; Hoss 2009: 27; Jackson, personal communication). Fries (2008: 25) posits a size-dependent use, identifying smaller knives as razors, larger examples as cutting tools. Not all knives should be considered as primarily utilitarian, especially those with fragile protruding decoration. The Heracles–Telephus combination on a bronze handle from the Titelberg (Gaeng 2010: 29–30), the Kriophoros image on a bone handle from Bondorf, Baden-Württemberg (Rusch 1981), or the asparagus-shoot handles mentioned above exemplify the delicate projections which must have inhibited use in some cases. The richness and virtuosity of figural decoration, and the need to turn the handle in order fully to appreciate its details, suggests that some were intended to be seen as much as to be used, perhaps being exchanged as gifts, like the Saturnalia presents listed by Martial (*Epigrams* 14; Bartus and Grimm 2010). If a connection to shaving is correct, it might be that the gift was especially appropriate for the first shave as a highly visible rite of passage (Toner 2015: 97–8). Direct evidence for such gift-giving is lacking but close connections with the biographies of owners may explain occasional finds of knives with decorated handles as grave goods; in some cases these are however with female individuals (see below).

Selected examples demonstrate the distribution of knives of this type. von Mercklin (1940) proposed the Rhineland as a likely centre of production, given the wealth of examples in the region's museums, but the many findspots across the northern provinces and beyond make it likely that there were multiple production centres, especially for handles in bone and copper alloy. In the absence of a recent study of provenances, only anecdotal observations can be made concerning the socio-spatial contexts in which these objects circulated. Findspots of gladiator handles reveal a distribution across many site categories, albeit with some predominance of urban and military settings (Bartus 2010). The many examples of handles from Britain documented by the PAS, most probably derived from non-villa rural settlements, show a more extended distribution

(Pearce and Worrell 2015). On the other hand the likely major variation in cost, depending on materials and craftsmanship, makes the specific form of individual knives a potential marker of social difference. Examples such as the ivory modelled on portraits of the philosopher Chrysippus or the Kriophoros could serve as symbols of elite *virtus*, the former epitomising intellectual cultivation, the latter *philanthropia* (Rusch 1981). The association in funerary contexts with large grave good assemblages suggests the higher social status of some knife owners (e.g. Lemoine et al. 2008; Höpken and Liesen 2013: 393, 459–60; Gottschalk 2015: 332–3). The burial of an ivory-handled knife in leopard form in a richly furnished third-century grave of an adolescent girl from London illustrates both this status context and the potential for establishing gendered associations for the object type (Redfern et al. 2017). This London case and others undermine an exclusive association with male *cultus*.

Knife handles showing scenes of sex: a summary of form and context

Among the figural scenes on knife handles (all made in copper alloy) are sex acts of varied forms (see Appendix).[1] Some are paralleled in Pompeii and beyond. For example, a handle of unknown provenance now in the British Museum features a *symplegma* familiar from Pompeian paintings and other portable objects in which a naked male figure reclines behind a female, penetrating from behind but shown in side view (no. 1). Another metal-detected find from Britain documented by the PAS from Askham Bryan, North Yorkshire (Figure 2.2; see also Appendix 2.1, no. 2), shows a reverse *mulier equitans* ("woman riding") scene, a coupling paralleled on a handle from the Haddad

Figure 2.2 The knife handle from Askham Bryan, 5.9 cm long (SWYOR-374234)

(© West Yorkshire Archaeology Advisory Service, used under a Creative Commons Licence)

collection (no. 3) as well as on other representations of sex. A scene of three figures, one hooded male standing behind a kneeling figure entering the embrace of a reclining figure on a metal-detected find from northern France also finds parallels in the repertoire of sex scenes on terra sigillata (no. 4). On the handle of an unprovenanced fixed blade knife in the collection of the Römisch-Germanisches Museum in Cologne, a standing hooded figure lifts (with his teeth) the tunic of a standing female figure with her back to him so as to penetrate her (no. 5). She holds a large rod-like object which Franken (1996: 127–8, no. 164) interprets as a (Priapic?) herm. However, it seems more likely, on analogy with a similar stamped motif on terra sigillata from Trier's workshops that she may be turning a rotary quernstone with a long handle (Huld-Zetsche 1972: 77–8, type 98).

All these scenes are however less significant numerically than the distinctive scene shown on the Syston handle, described above. In the absence of comparanda, Faider-Feytmans (1979: B27) included the first published example of this scene, on a handle from Liberchies (no. 6), among the *objets douteux* in her corpus of Belgian bronzes (1979: 212). Her laconic description ("*un personnage masculin* [...] *presse le corps d'une femme nue*") evades the specifics of the image. Catherine Johns documented four (probably) British examples when publishing a knife handle found during the 1930s excavations from Verulamium/St. Albans (Johns 1984: 56–9). The largest collection of examples so far in print is to be found in Sabine Faust's (2005: 190–3) publication of three handles from Trier's hinterland. She has subsequently identified several further unprovenanced examples sold on the antiquities market (personal communication). Further instances almost certainly exist unrecognised in public and private collections; at Corinium Museum, for example, conversation with Amanda Hart, the curator, revealed the existence of an unpublished example in the Bathurst collection, probably found in or around *Corinium*/Cirencester (no. 7). A small number of similar scenes modelled in the round but probably not on knife handles are also known, for example a handle or terminal from the villa at Borg, Saarland (Miron 1997: 34, abb. 19; Faust 2005: 191), a possible pendant, though lacking a suspension loop, from the theatre at Verulamium (Johns 1984: Plate IIIc) and a fragmentary unprovenanced bronze in the Römisch-Germanisches Museum in Cologne (Franken 1996: 127–8, no. 164, abb. 247).

In order to interpret the scene, it is first necessary to describe it more fully. Since the Syston example is atypical in several respects, the description focuses on a more regular instance from Liry (Ardennes) (Figure 2.3; see also Appendix 2.1, no. 8) in eastern France, following which some variations will be outlined drawing on other examples. The better modelling of the Liry and related pieces allows for key detail on poorly preserved or more schematically rendered handles, such as those from Britain, to be more precisely understood.[2] The Liry handle is a surface find from a small town in the *civitas* of the Remi (B. Lambot, personal communication). The 5.8-cm-long handle comprises a collar with moulded bands decorated with diagonal hatching and a terminal in the form of three figures, a standing and a kneeling male and a female suspended

Figure 2.3 The knife handle from Liry, 5.8 cm long

(Private collection, drawn by Bernard Lambot, reproduced with kind permission of B. Lambot)

between the two. The woman is naked save for a breastband (*mamillare*), armlet on her right arm, and boots, of which the hobnails are rendered as small raised points on the soles. She has an elaborate coiffure. Her hair falls in waves on either side of her head and is raised as a diagonally braided plait from the neck to the top of her head, the detail being cold worked. She lifts herself with her arms extended from the shoulders of the kneeling figure, her buttocks resting on the top of his back. Her disproportionately short legs are supported by the standing figure, the right leg resting on his shoulder and upper arm, and gripped by his left hand, the left being tucked under his right arm. She faces the standing male figure, also booted, who wears a short garment beneath a hooded cloak (*cucullus*), of which the hood is rolled down; his clothes are hoisted to reveal an erect phallus (nearer his knees than his groin), on the point (?) of penetrating her. Like the woman his portrait features (hair, eyebrows, and beard) are cold worked in a schematising manner. The hair is separated from the face by a groove, perhaps to accentuate the cap-like quality of the coiffure which parallel short incisions show as swept back. The beard is rendered as punched dots. The smaller male figure kneels with his right knee on the ground and his left leg bent. With both hands he holds a disproportionately large erect penis. The heads of all three figures are large, that of the kneeling man especially so, and facial features are crudely rendered. Traces of a rivet survive on the handle collar where the blade pivoted within the handle. The blade does not survive, but when folded would have slotted into a groove running between the legs and up the back of the standing male.

The rendering of the Liry figures is closely paralleled by others from eastern Gallia Belgica in a cluster roughly centred on Trier, including two from Trier's own rural hinterland at Altrich and Kusel (nos 9–10) and one from the small town of *Ricciacum*/Dalheim, Luxembourg (no. 11). They bear such a strong mutual resemblance that they must derive from the same or closely related workshops; the location of one such workshop is suggested by discovery at Dalheim of a mis-cast fragment from a handle of this type (Faust 2005: 190–3). Variations of position, gesture, dress, hair, and style can also be identified. The slightly larger Trier Viehmarkt handle (6.5 cm long) (no. 12), the most accomplished when judged from the perspective of naturalism, illustrates these most visibly. In this case the standing male's hood is pulled up, and the woman, without ornaments, is dressed in a short-sleeved tunic; she too wears hobnailed shoes. Unlike the Liry figure her face is framed by a ridged wave of hair which is gathered in a bun at the back of her head. The kneeling figure wears a short tunic, hoisted to reveal his penis, but he is not masturbating and his arms are crossed, perhaps better to support the weight on his shoulders. Examples from Britain are more highly schematised; on a find from Over Wallop, Hampshire (Figure 2.4), and its near twin from Verulamium, for example, the hands, feet, hair, and dress are reduced to parallel grooves and the masturbating figure cannot easily be identified for what it is (nos 13–14). The resemblance of the distinctive extended headdresses (an exaggeration of the often pointed *cucullus*?) on examples from Lambourn (Berkshire) (no. 16) and the unprovenanced instance from the Bathurst collection (Figure 2.5; see also Appendix 2.1, no. 7) likewise suggest derivation from a common or related source. In another variant, attested in very similar examples from Hertfordshire and Yvelines, all the figures appear to be naked (nos 16–17). The Syston handle with which the chapter began (no. 15) also differs in key attributes and arrangement from any other surviving examples, including the apparent nudity of all three figures and the turning of their heads outward from the scene, as well as the highly schematised cap-like hair. The standing male also appears to penetrate the kneeling male, placed in an elevated position on the openwork frame of the handle, rather than the female. The kneeling figure may not be aroused, though it is difficult to be certain on this point. Most unusually, he grips a large near-spherical object which has been interpreted as a possible severed head because of an apparent "cap-line" of hair on it (Worrell 2008: 358–9). Alternatively, it is a performance prop, rendered unidentifiable through wear. Finally, the handle from the small town of

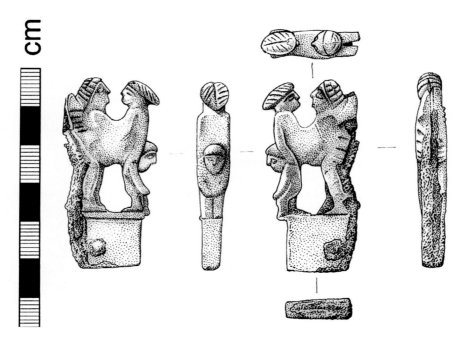

Figure 2.4 Folding knife handle from Over Wallop, Hants, 5.6 cm long (PAS HAMP-4D3135)

(Drawn by Alan Cracknell, © Winchester Museums Service, used under a Creative Commons Licence)

Liberchies (no. 6) carries a short punched inscription set out on both sides: *qui fecit/memoro//pone au(t)/pedico* ("Who did this I remember: put me down or I bugger you").[3]

Limited context information frustrates the establishing of a precise milieu for knife handles of this type. From Britain and Gallia Belgica: the exiguous provenance information suggests the knives circulated on urban, rural, and small town sites. The instances recorded by the PAS, from Over Wallop, Hampshire (Figure 2.4; see also Appendix 2.1, no. 13), Monk Soham, Suffolk (no. 19), and Syston (no. 15) exemplify the rural findspots. With the exception of the handle from the Verulamium theatre (no. 14), all the others are surface or metal-detected finds or lack information on their contexts. This limited contextual data is typical for decorated knife handles in general, since so many derive either from recent metal-detecting or from older collections with little or no provenance information.

The absence of stratigraphic information removes one potential source of evidence for dating these objects, and the excavated example from Verulamium was found in dark earth deposits overlying the abandoned theatre (no. 14).

Figure 2.5 Folding knife handle, Bathurst Collection, Cirencester, Corinium Museum (© Corinium Museum)

While the more schematised representations are otherwise undatable, in some cases coiffure helps date manufacture, especially for the Liry handle (Figure 2.3; see also Appendix 2.1, no. 8) and those like it (nos 9–11). The plait gathered in braids at the neck and pulled over the top of the head of the female figure is best paralleled in imperial portraits of the mid-third century A.D., for example those of Furia Tranquillina or Otacilia Severa (empresses respectively in A.D. 241–4 and 244–9) (Kleiner 1992: 378–81). From their hair and beard the standing males on this and related handles might be construed as having Antonine or Severan portrait features (Faust 2005: 191). The punched decoration used to render the beard may mimic the curls produced by the use of the drill on imperial portraits of these periods. The hairstyles of the female on the Trier Viehmarkt handle (no. 12), perhaps closer to Julio-Claudian examples, however may suggest an earlier date for some (Faust 2005: 190). From the affinity of the scene to Oswald's terra sigillata figure type Z (Oswald 1937, plate XC) Catherine Johns (personal communication) suggests a second-century date. This affinity is discussed further below.

Reading the scene: a public sexual performance?

In the following section I discuss the identification of the main participants and the scene, drawing mainly on the better-preserved and more clearly modelled scenes, beginning with the female figures. Where dress is identifiable these are usually naked but for armlets and breastbands. These attributes are associated with other representations of both mortal and divine women. Many women represented as participants in sex in Pompeian wall paintings and related images are similarly depicted, sometimes only with jewellery, sometimes also with the *mamillare* and with elaborate hair styles. Opinions differ as to whether or not such figures should be identified as prostitutes (Dierichs 1997: 121–4; Clarke 2003: 44, fig. 18). Deities are sometimes similarly figured, for example the famous "Venus in a bikini" found at Pompeii (National Archaeological Museum, inv. no. 152798) with a *mamillare* and arm ornaments. A find from Hinzerath, that is near the small town of *Belginum*/Wederath and close to Trier, a finely made bronze statuette of a near nude female deity with *mamillare* echoes this iconography but is difficult to identify specifically as Venus or a nymph (Menzel 1966: 37, no. 79). Thus, the elaborate coiffure, dress, and jewellery did not by themselves enable the viewer easily to differentiate between divinities who embody sexual attraction, or mortal women presented with similar attributes of *cultus* and *luxus*. In other media, not only wall painting but also small-scale representations on lamps and terra sigillata, such attributes are sometimes extended by the presence of other toilette objects as well as comfortable domestic interiors (Clarke 1998). However, the hobnailed boots (*caligae*) worn by the woman on the Liry handle (Figure 2.3; see also Appendix 2.1, no. 8) make for an incongruous contrast with her *mamillare* and armlets; on the Trier Viehmarkt (no. 12) handle the boots are more in keeping with the woman's tunic. The *caligae* point to a lower social status context, and perhaps an outside setting, that is not a well-furnished bedroom but a bucolic encounter.

It is also difficult to pin a particular identity on the standing male since hooded figures without further specific attributes have an extraordinarily wide connotative range (Deonna 1955). Nonetheless, two broad groups, human and divine, can be identified as likely candidates for association in the minds of ancient viewers. Examining first (probable) human figures, males, naked save for (sometimes hooded) cloaks, appear among stamped motifs showing sex on terra sigillata, documented by Oswald on two plates he devoted to sex scenes in his publication of figure types on terra sigillata (types H and K, these being untitled and omitted from the subject index; Oswald 1937: plates XC, XCI). In another scene on a cake mould from Winden am See, Burgenland, with echoes of the knife handle image, a bearded male, his hood lowered and the cloaks folds hoisted, approaches a woman on a couch (Thüry 2010: 5). The implied secrecy of the hood might evoke adulterous activity, but alongside the tunic and boots/gaiters, the cloak may rather recall representations of rural working people (*"les gens du peuple … et … tous ceux qui s'adonnent à de rudes labeurs"*: Deonna 1955: 9). The best known examples are the *cucullati* who animate the foreground of a wall painting from Trier showing a villa facade (Hoffmann 1993) and a famous figurine, again from Trier, of a beardless man in hooded cloak and tunic, his legs and feet bound with garter-like wrappings, who may be a lantern carrier (Menzel 1966: 41, no. 86). A countryman of similar type is a common figure in hunting scenes on terra sigillata vessels made in Trier, carrying a horn and *pedum* (Huld-Zetsche 1972: 137, M64–M65, 1993: 85, no. M130).

The association with rural activity partially explains the use of cloaked figures as seasonal personifications or as other divinities in various media and contexts. Among the personifications of the seasons, winter sometimes wears a hooded cloak, for example on the mosaic from Chedworth, Gloucestershire (Cosh and Neal 2010: 54–9). More widely documented are the hooded figures, manifested in small stone sculptures and occasional bronzes, of the *genii cucullati*, diminutive hooded figures with a possible fertility connection, their body swathed in the folds of the garment extending to the knees or feet, with little else visible but the face (Deonna 1955; Durham 2012: 3.9). Alternatively, the image recalls the *Priapus anasyromenos* type, sometimes met in small bronzes in which the often cloaked and hooded god lifts his cloak which cradles piles of fruit in its folds to reveal the phallus rising from his groin (e.g. LIMC VIII.1. 1034–6; Durham 2012: 3.17). Perhaps closer in spirit are two hooded and bearded priapic figures, one found in a later first century burial from Rivery, Picardie, the other unprovenanced (Bayard and Mahéo 2004: 148–9, no. 212; Kronberg Frederiksen 2015). In both cases a statue of a male bearded figure with a short-hooded cloak and a short tunic and *caligae* has a detachable upper body which, when lifted, reveals a phallus on slender legs. The inscription on the Liberchies handle also recalls the sexual aggression of the god in the Priapeia (see further below).

The kneeling figure has fewer attributes to allow identification. He substitutes for the couch seen in other sex scenes and as a human counterpart to an inanimate possession serving a basic physical function, his role is thus archetypally servile. Being a diminutive figure, present but not participating, he joins the occasional subordinate figures sometimes featured in sex scenes. Provincial examples include onlookers from a part-opened door at a couple having sex on a bed on a terra sigillata stamp (type W, Oswald 1937: plates XC, XCI) or from a window above the bed figured on a ceramic *oscillum* from Augst (Thüry 2009: fig. 24). If that were not enough, he is also demeaned by his exposed and/or erect outsize genitals. This characteristic is often part of a wider "othering" alongside caricatured and grotesque portrait traits (Clarke 1998: 128). Smaller bronzes and related objects from the northern provinces drew more widely on such figure types derived from the genre conventions established for Hellenistic art (Thüry 2009: 2, 13–16). The masturbation is difficult to parallel, auto-eroticism being rare in Roman representations of sex and indeed, in discussion of Roman sexuality, scarcely featuring, for example in the index to a recently published volume on ancient sexuality (Hubbard 2014). Its peripheral character is likely due in large part to exploitation of slaves as sexual objects

(Harper 2013: 26–7). Martial, for example, illustrates his poverty relative to his friend, Candidus, by comparing the latter's throng of Ganymede-like attendants with his own reliance on his own hand (*Epigrams* 2.43.14). The resort to masturbation in itself might thus be a servile trait. In another epigram (11.104, 13–22) slaves masturbate outside the door while Hector and Andromache make love (Richlin 2006: 351; Williams 2010: 34). The same interpretation as marking servile status can be applied to a unique scene moulded in relief on a second-century central Gaulish beaker where a seated figure holding a lamp masturbates amidst other sex scenes involving couples (Johns 1982: 141–2).

On the Syston handle (Figure 2.1; see also Appendix 2.1, no. 15) the kneeling figure holds an enigmatic object, interpreted in its first publication as a severed head (Worrell 2008: 358–9). Developing this suggestion further, Collins (2013: 36–7) identifies the standing male as a *pileus*-wearing soldier and the woman as a native because of a possible torc around her neck. He reads the figure as a joking comment on the local British population, the stereotyped Celtic head hunter here subject to degradation by a representative of Roman power. This works against the visual conventions of Roman art seen elsewhere, both on public monuments and on individual funerary monuments, where head-taking is a token of triumph by Romans over barbarians, and where one would expect a Roman soldier to be more clearly distinguished from his adversaries (Ferris 2009: 131–48). The possibility cannot be dismissed, especially given the incongruities on which this scene seems to play, but the object may be better interpreted as one of the props of uncertain character which appears in related scenes in other media (see below).

On one level what is shown is clear: allowing for the variation outlined above, the scene shows sexual activity or simulated sexual activity on the part of three people in a precarious configuration. Previous commentators have suggested that the scene recalls a public performance. Johns (1984: 58–9) for example emphasises "the strenuous role of the kneeling figure, and the somewhat athletic pose represented", while to Faust et al. (2007: 52) the grouping suggests an "*akrobatisches Liebesakt*". Unlike scenes on ceramics there are no framing elements or furniture to indicate the setting. However, the dress elements of the male (often) for travel and for heavy weather, the boots of some females, and the improvised "couch" evoke a bucolic rather than domestic setting. The varying representation of the figures, especially the standing male, may suggest that they could be identified as a range of stock characters rather than as performers or imaginary protagonists.

Unlike other scenes on knife handles showing more conventional *symplegmata* (see above), this scene is not straightforwardly related to other surviving representations. Pompeian wall paintings offer no close specific parallel. Groups of three are uncommon in the Pompeian corpus; the main exceptions, from the Suburban Baths, have been cast as humorously transgressive means of marking bath lockers (Clarke 1998: 237: "a steady crescendo of increasingly comic representations of sexual depravity") and do not resemble in detail the knife handle scene. Some closer parallels in spirit and, occasionally, in the details of composition may be identified in portable media from the north-west provinces, especially decorated bowls made in Gallic samian (Webster and Webster 2011) as well as lamps (Vucetic 2014) and Rhône valley ceramic appliqué medallions dated to the second and third centuries A.D. (Wuilleumier and Audin 1952; Clarke 1998: 257–61). All such media, especially the Rhône valley medallions, include some representations of sex which combine an acrobatic and hazardous character, sometimes enhanced by props, for example the lamps often held aloft by lovers on the medallion images (Clarke 1998: 224–5).

Two individual scenes have further affinities with the knife handle combination. The first is a terra sigillata motif occurring on vessels made in eastern Gaul in the second century A.D. (Figure 2.6; Oswald's figure Type Z (1937 plate XC); Delort's "*quator libertin*" (1933: 205)). In this scene three figures are in the same arrangement as on the knife handle, although all the participants are naked, and the kneeling man on the left reaches for a rectangular object, a likely prop of some kind. Unlike the knife handle, a fourth figure kneels behind the standing man; his role, as on an Arles lamp, may be to push against the buttocks of the standing figure to augment the degree of penetration (cf. Clarke 2007: 222). In a scene known only from a single example, a Rhône valley ceramic appliqué medallion shows a very similar arrangement to the knife handle; a naked woman sits on the back of a man, holding up a lamp, while the kneeling figure holds an object (Figure 2.7; Wuilleumier and Audin 1952: 133, no. 233). Clarke argues that this may be a public sex act as part of a spectacle performance, suggesting that the object being held by the kneeling figure is a prop, perhaps a pail or

Figure 2.6 A sex scene from terra sigillata vessels made in eastern Gaul in the second century A.D., Type Z

(Redrawn from Oswald 1937, plate XC)

Figure 2.7 Ceramic medallion with erotic scene, middle Rhône valley
(Redrawn from Wuilleumier and Audin 1952, no. 233)

lantern. He suggests that the woman is gripping the man around the waist, rather than being penetrated, although this is difficult to assess because of the bowdlerised drawings, the male genitals having been omitted (Clarke 2007: 224–5, 2014: 530–1).

Manuals incorporating illustrations of complex sexual positions composed in the Hellenistic period are often invoked as potential sources of surviving images of sex (e.g. Dierichs 1997). References in Latin literature suggests that manuals associated with almost certainly pseudonymous authors such as Philaenis and Elephantis were well enough known for allusion to them to be understood. Fragments of such a manual discovered at Oxyrhynchus suggests their circulation beyond the metropolis (Parker 1992). Since it is not obviously dependent on a specific surviving composition, the scene discussed here might have originated in a lost exemplar of this kind. However, Clarke's (1998: 244–50) proposal that sex scenes on lamps and ceramic finewares owed their form mainly to the adaptation of existing scenes to new media and new patrons seems better to characterise the knife handles which are clearly adapted to their medium, and continue to develop during the period in which they are produced.

An alternative or complementary source for inspiration may be found in festival and spectacle in the northern provinces. Performance with a sexual content, whether in words, gestures, nudity, or narrative, is a component of Roman spectacle culture, both in the metropolis and beyond, often as the filler or warm-up acts in a "paratheatrical" tradition (Denard 2007: 139). This characterised the festival of the Floralia, especially in the form of the *nudatio mimarum*, involving the performance by actors of short pieces with sexual themes, especially adultery. Performances may have included sex itself, simulated or real. Sexual elements may also have been present in other aspects of Roman spectacle, perhaps including some punishments of criminals, as well as in street theatre (Clarke 1998: 206–12; Webb 2008: 107; Florence 2014: 366–7). However, documenting the specific character of any spectacle performance is a challenge even at the centre of the empire, since texts typically describe the exceptional rather than the normal, take for granted knowledge of the performance, and focus on the responses of spectators, in order to serve political, moral, or religious points (Parker 1999). This indirect and ambiguous quality also characterises the few references to representations of sex in the context of spectacles; in particular, literary texts offer ideologically laden stereotypes of female performers which artificially emphasise their affinity to the prostitutes with whom they shared legal *infamia* (Webb 2002). Some representations which combine sex with physical ingenuity and/or risk have nonetheless been interpreted as portraying public spectacles of this type, in particular the wall painting from the Caupona of the Street of Mercury, Pompeii, which shows a woman naked but for a breast band, bending over to put down a jug while she raises a glass to her lips as a man, also raising his glass and hoisting his tunic, attempts to penetrate from behind (Clarke 1998: 206–11). Clarke's interpretation of some Rhône valley ceramic appliqués as showing public performance, real or simulated, has been noted above. Similarly, we might read the knife handles as showing a performance of this kind, an acrobatic display of strength and dexterity, combining a very carefully contrived balancing act, requiring amusingly indecorous exertion, with titillation. The participants might be identified as performers, for example mimes, whose dress embodies the porous boundaries between performer and prostitute, or actors who embody comic archetypes, or whose appearance is risible. The contrast between bedroom luxury, present in the dress of the woman, and rusticity in the traveller's cloak, hobnailed boots, improvised "couch", and so on, might allude to some comic scenario with human stock characters or divine participants (Denard 2007). The hooded cloak offering the standing male a means of concealment, as well as other dress elements or props which suggest an encounter taking place outside the bedroom, may allude to an adultery story, one of the most popular mimes (Webb 2008: 105–9). Other scenes showing sex involving women at work may similarly suggest non-conjugal liaisons. These include the unprovenanced knife handle from the Römisch-Germanisches Museum in Cologne showing a standing hooded figure having sex with a woman with her back to him (no. 5), perhaps turning a rotary quernstone (see above), or the Trier ceramic medallion on which a standing male penetrates a woman who bends forward to decant wine from a barrel into a jug on the floor (Faust et al. 2007: 51, no. 25).

On this argument the knife handles join the evidence for performances which took place in the many spectacle buildings scattered across Rome's northern provinces. The principal evidence for the nature of performances in these venues is visual, occasionally in larger format such as mosaics, wall-paintings, and funerary sculpture, more commonly on portable objects identified as souvenirs of local performances, now supplemented by artefact assemblages from spectacle buildings and more nuanced understanding of structural functions (Landes 2008; Wilmott 2008; Bateman 2011). Dependence on such sources carries obvious risks, since the point of reference for images on imported and locally made ceramics, lamps, glass "sports cups", and so on is not easily determined: are they provincial or metropolitan spectacles, or other images, rather than the spectacle itself? Even for seemingly individualised pieces, for example the well-known vase from Colchester depicting individual bouts for named gladiators and *venatores*, the theoretical distinction between generic references and objects created as mementoes for specific local performances can rarely be applied (Landes 2008; Wilmott 2008: 169–70). Among northern provincial cities Trier, at the centre of a cluster of findspots of several knife handles showing this scene (nos 6, 8–12), is the most likely candidate for hosting spectacles of a richness and diversity likely to include mime and related performances with sexual content. The city possessed multiple spectacle buildings, including two theatres associated with the Irminenwingert and Altbachtal sanctuaries, respectively to the west and east of the city. The structural, epigraphic, and ritual evidence from these sanctuaries, especially the latter, reveals the translation of indigenous deities into a fundamentally Roman structure for public cults (Scheid 1995). A festival calendar accommodating performances such as mime seems therefore entirely plausible here, especially when mosaic evidence for detailed knowledge of Roman literary and theatrical culture in the city is added (e.g. Hoffmann et al. 1999: 110, 134, 138 (nos 56, 98, 103)). Circumstantially, other urban centres where knife handles of this kind have been found, namely Verulamium and Dalheim, offer architecturally sophisticated theatres where a diverse spectacle programme might also be imagined and where mementoes might be sold; at Verulamium, it will be recalled, the handle (no. 14) was found on the site of the theatre proper (Niblett and Thompson 2005: 99–101; Henrich 2011). That Dalheim provides the only evidence for the making of knives of this type has already been noted.

Responses to the scene

An exclusive preoccupation with the genealogy of the object may limit our understanding of its potential resonance in use, since it is not necessary to think that a single identification (as a specific spectacle scene, for example) was made by Roman viewers. Rather viewers will have understood it through the context knowledge on which they drew, of other images, texts, and unconscious frameworks for interpreting dress and attributes. Some proposed understandings of this object are sketched in the following paragraphs, including consideration of how engagement with the object in use may have conditioned the possible readings of it.

It has become a commonplace to interpret domestic decoration in terms of the *paideia* of its commissioners. In this model the commissioning of images inspired by Greco-Roman myth and literature or allusions to civic life display the cultivation of the patron and spawn further competitive manifestations of learning or intellectual virtuosity in symposium-type contexts. In a provincial setting this has been extensively argued for mosaics, the main surviving decorative form (e.g. Scott 2000). Similar arguments have been extended to portable objects, in particular precious metal vessels (Swift 2009). Whatever its specific derivation, the knife handle decoration offered similar possibilities for displaying elite cultural capital, perhaps as knives passed from hand to hand in an exchange of gifts (see above). This might take the form of connecting the scene to knowledge of the sexual manuals suggested above as the possible inspiration for this image. Others might have found within the scene echoes of the epigrammatic tradition, for example the mobilisation of Priapic personae in verse, using obscenities for sex acts and organs in violent invective by Catullus, Martial, or in the Priapeia themselves. In the latter verses, Priapus as a speaking herm threatens rape against those who breach the integrity of the garden or orchard he defends, the specific act graduated according to the perpetrator using the same lexicon (Richlin 1983). The evidence for familiarity with varied verse genres in Gaul (Woolf 1998: 72–5), and occasionally provincial echoes of the Priapeia (Thüry 2008: 297), suggest such a scenario is not completely fanciful, if unprovable.

So far, however, none of the knife handles showing this scene has been found in more costly materials, and it seems implausible to restrict responses to the image only to a small circle of provincial elites. Assuming that the object has a connection to spectacles, as argued above, then we might further consider the significance of these objects as embodiments of the "fan culture" associated with performers and spectacles. Fagan (2011) has demonstrated how such partisanship is not a marginal aspect of Roman "life and leisure" but a fundamental building block of socialisation, whether into imperial or civic communities or sub-groups based on neighbourhood, work, or age, through the collective experience of watching spectacles. How partisanship, whether for a particular style of fighting or individual performer, was mobilised not only on the terraces but also extended beyond the arena into the wider fabric of urban life has received less attention. It is perhaps best demonstrated in Pompeian graffiti, for example where fans of the pantomime Actius Anicetus and his troupe scratched their acclaim on tombs around the Porta Nocera and elsewhere (Franklin 1987). The occurrence of most spectacle images (and also texts naming performers) on vessels used probably for serving and consuming alcohol shows a possible extension of partisanship into key spaces for non-elite sociability such as the tavern. In such settings, objects bearing this decoration contributed to creating a shared material signature for groups of fellow drinkers, foregrounded when prompting explicit discussion of performance, offering opportunities for display of expertise through commentary (Toner 1995: 67–88). In this context it matters less whether the objects were created as mementoes of specific performance or generic images, since both could contribute in these respects. Given their possible association with shaving (see above), we might seek another site of male non-elite sociability for knife handles to be visible and play a similar role, namely the barber's shop, where their ambiguity could also prompt conversation as to how they should be understood. Caution is necessary here, since a barber would probably use his own tools rather than those brought by his customers. Nonetheless Toner's (2015: 102–6) reconstruction of these spaces evokes a tavern-like picture where men became urbane, not only through modification of their appearance but by assimilating group dispositions on their social environment learned, as in the tavern, through competitive banter.

Performers such as gladiators and charioteers embodied key values in Roman popular culture, dexterity, speed, quick-wittedness, aggression, and so on (Toner 2009). In the case of knife handles bearing the sex scene discussed here, we might anticipate fans aligning themselves with the "protagonist" of the scene, the standing male figure. This figure might have been construed as presenting another aspect of popular (and elite) culture, a hypersexual Priapic persona, anticipating or realising the penetration of the other participants whose positions exemplify their passive subordination. Normative gender and status differences in Roman discourse about sex are established by the roles played as penetrator or penetrated, the dominant figure of the free adult male always playing the insertive role (vaginally, anally, orally) (Williams 2010: 17–19; see Chapters 8 and 11). This can also be identified as a facet of provincial culture in the Roman north from the miscellany of inscribed *instrumenta*, graffiti, and (occasionally) monumental inscriptions. The lexicon of these is quite wide, and the tone varies from badinage to the direct celebration of sexual conquest; in the painted plaster of a *domus* at Limoges, Quintus scratched a record that he had "fucked on the *nones* of Mars" (Bost 1993: 53–7; Barbet and Fuchs 2008: 139–51). The commonest occurring term is *pedico/pedicare* ("to bugger"), threatening or celebrating anal penetration (Kamen and Levin-Richardson 2015: 451–2; also Soproni 1990; Thüry 2008: 298–300; Williams 2014). In this sense it occurs as a threat on "speaking objects" which is unwittingly activated by reading the text. For example the reader of a post-cocturam graffito on a beaker found at Meaux makes her or himself the butt of the joke by turning the vessel through its entire circumference to reveal the text: *ego qui lego pedicor* (CIL 13, 1001740: "I who read (this) am buggered"). The only knife of the kind discussed in this chapter carrying an inscription, from Liberchies (no. 6), bears a text which draws on invective of this type. As noted above, the inscription extends over both sides of the handle (*qui fecit/memoro//pone au(t)/pedico*). The lines referring to recall ("Who did this I remember)" lack clear parallels, and might refer to the scene itself, that is referencing the object's possible purpose as a souvenir of a spectacle. However, the companion text on the other side ("put me down or I bugger you") suggests that the act of picking up the object through injudicious curiosity is remembered and will be met with sexual violence unless the perpetrator desists. Whose voice is expressed is ambiguous: is it the knife's owner, the object itself, or perhaps even the standing figure on the handle?

Whichever candidate is preferred, the same humiliating retribution is promised for an offence (theft) which will not go unforgotten. The text articulates and complements the Priapic disposition which could be read into the figural scene.

It would be easy, however, to overemphasise the scene as culturally normative. The degree to which a male viewer might identify with the standing figure is open to question. In this performance, all three participants, whatever their relative positions, are demeaned by being on show. Naked or not, they form the objects of pleasure beneath the gaze of others, all are likely to suffer from *infamia* or some related impairment, exacerbated by the danger of embarrassment or injury in case of failure. The form of the knife further undermines identification with this actor. When closed the knife blade folds into a slot between the standing male's buttocks, turning him into the "penetrated" figure. Discussion above has noted how turning the handle reveals different aspects of its jokiness or incongruity, the hobnailed boots of the woman, the masturbation by the kneeling figure, and so on, but it also confuses the identifications proposed above between viewer and participants. Participants in sex scenes in Roman art rarely face the viewer, their gaze being mostly directed into the scene itself, especially at sexual partners, even if this requires anatomically unlikely contortions. Clarke (1998: 231–6) has argued that where participants look out from the scene then they invite the viewer to identify with them. One such category is the male figure who penetrates another while signalling to a viewer external to the scene, as in some images from the Suburban Baths at Pompeii. Another is the subordinate figure, not participating; for example an attendant by the bed in one of the *cubiculum* paintings from the Villa Farnesina who looks out from the scene and makes the viewer a subordinated voyeur (Clarke 2003: 30–2). On the knife handles discussed here the standing male and female normally look at one another while only the kneeling figure looks out, as whoever holds the handle realises as they turn it. Meeting the gaze of the kneeling figure leaves the viewer on the sidelines, ascribed a demeaning onanistic role, like the slave who can only watch or listen. The Syston handle offers a further expression of unstable affinities as all three figures look outwards, the female and kneeling male in one direction, the standing male in another, changing the connection between viewer and participants as the handle turns. The inscription on the Liberchies handle (no. 5) also places the viewer of the scene and reader of the text in a non-dominant role. Through curiosity, prompted by the small size of the object and text, reading the inscription animates the threat of humiliation, whatever its source.

Thus, the knife handle image offers a further potential example of joking commentary on sexual norms rather than their direct reproduction (cf. Clarke 1998). The "unbecomingness" of this image accumulates from multiple elements, laughable participants, absurd and risky actions, and visual incongruities. A further incongruity arguably lies between the threat made on the Liberchies piece and the diminutive form of its mouthpiece, unlike some other "speaking objects" which threaten sexual violence, for example the Visegrád staff terminal with its multiple phallic projections (Soproni 1990). To complete the discussion this incongruity is returned to the context of use of the image, that is to the knife's functions. Its potential purposes as a toilet knife, that is for shaving or other grooming, or as a multi-purpose knife are not mutually exclusive. Both uses involved risk, a mortal risk inherent in the application of a blade to a vulnerable body region and the general risk to the integrity of bodily boundaries and the associated misfortune, real or metaphysical, which their breach might entail by creating a conduit for invidious powers. In this respect knife handle decoration as a whole is self-referential, alluding both to these threats and apotropaic powers against them. The chasing and biting animals on knife handles or the gladiators, for example, regularly reference the cutting blade. The handles on which the terminal takes the form of a stylised dog's head, open-mouthed with a long curling tongue, provide an example of a directly prophylactic image, canine saliva being thought to heal (Boon 2000; Pearce and Worrell 2017: 452–3, no. 22). Crummy reads the ivory knife handle carved in the form of mating dogs from Silchester as being similarly apotropaic by opposing risk with an emblem of natural fecundity (Crummy 2011: 111). The knife handles under discussion here can be argued also to have an apotropaic potency in various ways. Like other handles showing sex scenes or in phallic form, they echoed the protective symbolism of male and female genitalia on innumerable amulets for humans and animals (e.g. Nicolay 2007: 52–9; Parker 2015; see Chapters 4 and 5). Against a malign gaze, the phallus presented a talismanic assertion of fertility and prosperity (Clarke 2007: 63–72).

Conclusion

Within the repertoire of Roman representations of sex, the scenes of three on these knife handles from Britain and Gaul are neither entirely novel nor entirely familiar. Although comprehensible on a general level as a representation of sexual acrobatics, real or simulated, in detail they prompt uncertainty and ambiguity. Various sources have been posited for this scene, including other representations of sex, surviving or lost, or mime or related performance as witnessed in the theatre at Trier or in other spectacle buildings. None of these offers a direct model for the scenes in question, which like others on knife handles of this kind are adapted from a wide iconographic repertoire to the three-dimensional and small-scale medium on which they appear. Future finds of representations of sex may clarify the sources from which these images derive, but in order to consider how provincial Romans responded to them a genealogical approach, that is the detection of antecedents, is not sufficient. The evidence at our disposal is too limited to determine a precise context for who made and who owned such objects and how they were used. However, it is enough to develop some observations on how the images might have been read from varied perspectives, for example through a prism of connoisseurship of epigrams, an appreciation of public spectacle, or from a dominant male insertive discourse about sexuality. Where elite or popular responses began and ended is difficult to determine (cf. Toner 2015). It is acknowledged that all these suggestions for how the scene was understood risk reproducing the biases towards metropolitan elite male dispositions concerning sexuality, though such dispositions are also attested in (some) provincial settings. Consideration of the object in three dimensions and in its likely context of use, for shaving or grooming, suggests an alternative function as an apotropaic image, not only by embodying Priapic aggression but also by prompting laughter or mockery through its incongruities and "unbecomingness", augmenting its ability to deflect *invidia*.

Acknowledgements

For their generous help with images, access to museum finds, publications, and discussion of individual objects, I am especially grateful to Sabine Faust (Rheinisches Landesmuseum Trier) and also to: Francis Grew (Museum of London); Amanda Hart and Heather Dawson (Corinium Museum, Cirencester); Catherine Johns; Bernard Lambot; Günther Thüry; and my colleagues Henrik Mouritsen and Akrivi Taousiani. For their helpful comments I also thank the editors and the participants at seminars and conferences in London, Southampton, Lampeter, Wrocław, and Rome where I discussed these scenes. The responsibility for any errors is wholly mine.

Appendix 2.1: Knife handles with sex scenes: selected examples

Nos 1–5 are miscellaneous scenes, nos 6–19 scenes with three participants comprising standing and kneeling males and a female balancing between the two. For the PAS finds, the reference is unique to each object. For the Artefacts database the reference number (all prefixed by CNF) is for a type represented by one or more examples, for which details on individual finds are reported.

Number	Provenance	Publication reference	PAS/ Artefacts
1	Unprovenanced (British Museum)	Johns 1982: 134–6, fig. 113; von Mercklin 1940: 160 (BM Accession number Greek and Roman 1856.1226.874)	
2	Askham Bryan N. Yorks, UK	Worrell and Pearce 2012: 362, fig. 5	SWYOR-374234/ CNF-4031
3	Haddad collection, possible British provenance	Haddad Collection Sale no. 9050 Christie's 1998.	
4	Northern France		CNF-4028

(Continued)

(Cont.)

Number	Provenance	Publication reference	PAS/ Artefacts
5	Unprovenanced (RGM Cologne)	Faust 2005: 193; Franken 1996: 127–8, no. 164	
6	Liberchies, Hainaut (B)	Faider-Feytmans 1979: B27	
7	Unprovenanced, possibly Cirencester (Corinium museum)	Bathurst Collection, unpublished, museum accession no. B636	
8	Liry (La Côte Vitlet), Ardennes (FR)	Lambot 1998; B. Lambot personal communication	
9	Altrich, Rheinland-Pfalz (DE)	Faust et al. 2007: 52, fig. 26b	CNF-4004
10	Kusel, Rheinland-Pfalz (DE)	Faust et al. 2007: 52, fig. 26c	CNF-4004
11	Dalheim, Luxembourg	Faust 2005: 192	
12	Viehmarkt, Trier (DE)	Faust et al. 2007: 52, no. 26, fig. 26a	CNF-4003
13	Over Wallop, Hants (UK)		HAMP-4D3135/ CNF-4004
14	Verulamium/St Albans, theatre, Herts (UK)	Johns 1984: 56–9, Plate III	CNF-4004
15	Syston, Lincs (UK)	Worrell 2008: 358–9, fig. 12	LIN-536F87/ CNF-4035
16	Lambourn, Berks (UK)	Johns 1984: 56–9, Plate III	
17	Baldock, Herts (UK)	Mills 2000: 87, ref. RB259 (M146).	
18	Boinville-en-Mantois Yvelines (FR)	Barat 2007: 117, fig.89	
19	Monk Soham, Suffolk (UK)		SF-A23522

Notes

1 The bracketed numbers after the following discussion of some individual finds of knives refer to entries in the Appendix 2.1 where further bibliographic information is given.

2 A publication of a corpus of these knives and related objects, outside the scope of the present chapter, is currently in preparation with Sabine Faust, Rheinisches Landesmuseum Trier, which will document the typological diversity in full.

3 Schwinden's suggested reconstruction of *pone au(t)/pedico* is preferred here to *Ponem pedico* (Brulet et al. 2002: 187, no. 117), since it is both the most plausible reading of the surviving letters and closely echoes a formula found on other objects (Faust 2005: 192; Thüry 2008: 298–300).

Bibliography

Barat, Y. (2007). *Cartes Archéologiques de la Gaule.78. Les Yvelines*. Paris: Éditions de la Maison des sciences de l'homme.

Barbet, A. and Fuchs, M. (2008). *Les Murs Murmurent: Graffitis Gallo-Romains: Catalogue de L'Exposition Créé au Musée Romain de Lausanne-Vidy, 2008*. Gollion: Infolio.

Bartus, D. (2010). "Les Manches de Couteau à Représentation de Gladiateur de L'Époque Romaine", in L. Borhy (ed.), *Studia Celtica Classica et Romana Nicolae Szabo Septuagesimo Dedicata*. Budapest: Pytheas, 27–50.

Bartus, D. and Grimm, J. (2010). "A Knife Handle from Caerwent (*Venta Silurum*) Depicting Gladiators", *Britannia*, 41: 321–24.

Bateman, N. (2011). *Roman London's Amphitheatre*. London: Museum of London Archaeology.

Baude, J.-M. and Dumas, C. (2005). *L'Érotisme des Gaules*. Les Baux de Provence: Musées des Baux.

Bayard, D. and Mahéo, N. (2004). *La Marque de Rome: Samarobriva et Les Villes du Nord de la Gaule*. Amiens: Musée de Picardie.

Bertrand, I. (2008). "Le Travail de L'Os et du Bois de Cerf à Limonum (Poitiers, F)", in I. Bertrand (ed.), *Le Travail de L'Os, du Bois de Cerf et de la Corne à L'Époque Romaine: Un Artisanat En Marge?* Montagnac: Mergoiil, 101–44.

Bland, R., Lewis, M., Pett, D., Richardson, I., Robbins, K. and Webley, R. (2017). "The Treasure Act and Portable Antiquities Scheme in England and Wales", in G. Moshenska (ed.), *Key Concepts in Public Archaeology*. London: UCL Press, 107–21.

Boon, G. (2000). "The Other Objects of Copper Alloy", in M. Fulford and J. Timby (eds), *Late Iron Age and Roman Silchester Excavations on the Site of the Forum-Basilica, 1977, 1980–86*. London: Society for the Promotion of Roman Studies, 338–57.

Bost, J.-P. (1993). "Exploits Amoureux à Limoges au 3ième Siècle Après J.-C.: Trois Graffiti de la 'Maison des Nones de Mars'", *Travaux d'Archéologie Limousine*, 13: 53–57.

Brulet, R., De Longueville, S. and Vilvorder, F. (2002). *Liberchies Entre Belgique et Germanie: Guerres et Paix en Gaule Romaine*. Morlanwelz: Musée Royal de Mariemont.

Christie's. (1998). *Sale 9050 Christie's New York: Ars Amatoria: The Haddad Family Collection of Erotic Art*. www.christies.com/LotFinder/lot_details.aspx?intObjectID=1404030

Clarke, J. (1998). *Looking at Lovemaking*. Berkeley, CA: University of California Press.

Clarke, J. (2003). *Roman Sex 100 BC – AD 250*. New York: Harry N. Abrams.

Clarke, J. (2007). *Looking at Laughter: Humor, Power, and Transgression in Roman Visual Culture, 100 B.C.– A.D. 250*. Berkeley, CA: University of California Press.

Clarke, J.R. (2014). "Sexuality and Visual Representation", in Hubbard (2014), 509–33.

Collins, R. (2013). "Artefacts in the Limelight: Recording Britain's Secret Treasures", *Current Archaeology*, 284: 34–39.

Cosh, S. and Neal, D. (2010). *Roman Mosaics of Britain. Vol. 4. Western Britain*. London: Society of Antiquaries.

Crummy, N. (2011). "The Small Finds", in M. Fulford and A. Clarke (eds), *Silchester: City in Transition. The Mid-Roman Occupation of Insula IX c. AD 125–250/300*. London: Society for the Promotion of Roman Studies, 100–32.

Delort, E. (1933). *Vases Ornés de la Moselle*. Nancy: Société d'Impressions Typographiques.

Denard, H. (2007). "Lost Theatre and Performance Traditions of Greece and Italy", in M. McDonald and M. Walton (eds), *Cambridge Companion to Greek and Roman Theatre*. Cambridge: Cambridge University Press, 139–60.

Deonna, W. (1955). *De Télesphore au «Moine Bourru»: Dieux, Génies et Démons Encapuchonnés*. Brussels: Collection Latomus.

Deschler-Erb, S. (1998). *Romische Beinartefakte aus Augusta Raurica*. Augst: Römermuseum.

Dierichs, A. (1997). *Erotik in der römischen Kunst*. Mainz: Zabern.

Durham, E. (2012). "Depicting the Gods. Metal Figurines in Roman Britain", *Internet Archaeology*, 31. doi:10.11141/ia.31.2.

Fagan, G. (2011). *The Lure of the Arena. Social Psychology and the Crowd at the Roman Games*. Cambridge: Cambridge University Press.

Faider-Feytmans, G. (1979). *Les Bronzes Romains de Belgique*. Mainz: Zabern.

Faust, S. (2005). "Figürliche Bronzen und Gegenstände aus anderen Metallen aus Stadt und Bezirk Trier in Privatbesitz III", *Trierer Zeitschrift*, 67/68: 157–212.

Faust, S., Seewaldt, P. and Weidner, W. (2007). "Erotische Kunstwerke im Rheinischen Landesmuseum Trier", *Funde und Ausgrabungen im Bezirk Trier*, 39: 39–62.

Ferris, I. (2009). *Hate and War. The Column of Marcus Aurelius*. Stroud: History Press.

Florence, M. (2014). "The Body Politic: Sexuality in Greek and Roman Comedy and Mime", in Hubbard (2014), 366–80.

Franken, N. (1996). "Die antiken Bronzen im Römisch-Germanischen Museum Köln. Teil 3. Fragmente von Statuen. Figürlicher Schmuck von architektonischen Monumenten und Inschriften. Hausausstattung, Möbel, Kultgeräte, Votive und verschiedene Geräte", *Kölner Jahrbuch*, 29: 7–203.

Franklin, J.L. (1987). "Pantomimists at Pompeii: Actius Anicetus and his Troupe", *American Journal of Philology*, 108: 95–107.

Fries, A. (2008). "Figürliche Klappmessergriffe aus Bein im Rheinischen Landesmuseum Trier", *Funde und Ausgrabungen im Bezirk Trier*, 40: 24–36.

Gaeng, C. (2010). "Héraclès et Télèphe. Un Bronze Énigmatique du Titelberg", *MNHA Empreintes*, 3: 25–31. http://issuu.com/mnha/docs/empreintes_3_2010_lr [accessed 04.07.17].

Gottschalk, R. (2015). *Spätrömische Gräber im Umland von Köln*. Darmstadt: Zabern.

Harper, K. (2013). *From Shame to Sin. The Christian Transformation of Sexual Morality in Late Antiquity*. Cambridge, MA: Harvard University Press.

Henrich, P. (2011). "Das gallo-römische Theater von Dalheim (Großherzogtum Luxemburg)", *Études de lettres*, 1–2. http://edl.revues.org/109; doi:10.4000/edl.109 [accessed 04.07.17].

Hoffmann, P. (1993). "Das Bild einer Villa Rustica auf einer Wandmalerei aus Trier?", *Trierer Zeitschrift*, 56: 123–34.

Hoffmann, P., Hupe, J. and Goethert, K. (1999). *Katalog der römischen Mosaike aus Trier und dem Umland*. Mainz: Zabern.

Höpken, C. and Liesen, B. (2013). "Römische Gräber im Kölner Süden II. Von der Nekropole um St. Severin bis zum Zugweg", *Kölner Jahrbuch*, 46: 369–571.

Hoss, S. (2009). "A Delicate Vegetable: An Asparagus Knife-Handle from the Fort of Laurium (Woerden, NL)", in H. van Enckevoort (ed.), *Roman Material Culture. Studies in Honour of Jan Thijssen*. Zwolle: SPA, Foundation for the Promotion of Archaeology, 25–30.

Hubbard, T.K. ed, (2014). *A Companion to Greek and Roman Sexualities*. Oxford: Wiley/Blackwell.

Hughes, J. (2009). "Personifications and the Ancient Viewer: The Case of the Hadrianeum 'Nations'", *Art History*, 32: 1–20.

Huld-Zetsche, I. (1972). *Trierer Relief-Sigillata: Werkstatt I*. Bonn: Habelt.

Huld-Zetsche, I. (1993). *Trierer Relief-Sigillata: Werkstatt II*. Bonn: Habelt.

Jackson, R. and Friendship-Taylor, R. (2001). "A New Roman Gladiator Find from Piddington, Northants", *Antiquity*, 75: 27–28.

Johns, C. (1982). *Sex or Symbol. Erotic Images of Greece and Rome*. London: British Museum Press.

Johns, C. (1984). "Folding Knife", in S.S. Frere (ed.), *Verulamium Excavations III*. Oxford: Clarendon Press, 58–59.

Kamen, D. and Levin-Richardson, S. (2015). "Revisiting Roman Sexuality: Agency and the Conceptualization of Penetrated Males", in M. Masterson, N. Rabinowitz and J. Robson (eds), *Sex in Antiquity: Exploring Gender and Sexuality in the Ancient World*. London: Routledge, 449–60.

Kleiner, D. (1992). *Roman Sculpture*. Yale: Yale University Press.

Kronberg Frederiksen, N. (2015). "Venus Priapus", *Archives of The Thorvaldsen Collection: Related Articles*. http://arkivet.thorvaldsensmuseum.dk/articles/venus-Priapus [accessed 20.03.16].

Lambot, B. (1998). "Scène de Groupe", *Bulletin Instrumentum*, 7: 28.

Landes, C. (2008). "Le Circus Maximus et Ses Produits Dérivés", in J. Nélis-Clément and J.-M. Roddaz (eds), *Le Cirque Romain et Son Image*. Bordeaux: Ausonius, 413–30.

Lee, A. (2012). "A Roman Erotic Knife Handle from Syston, Lincolnshire", *Lincolnshire Past and Present*, Spring 2012: 14.

Lemoine, Y., Bertrand, I. and Martos, F. (2008). "Un Canif à Manche Anthropomorphe Découvert à Forum Voconii (F. Cannet-des-Maures, Var)", *Bulletin Instrumentum*, 28: 29–30.

Matthews, K. (1994). "An Archaeology of Homosexuality? Perspectives from the Classical World", in S. Cottam, D. Dungworth, S. Scott and J. Taylor (eds), *TRAC 94. Proceedings of the Fourth Theoretical Roman Archaeology Conference*. Oxford: Oxbow, 118–32.

McSloy, E. (2003). "A Zoomorphic Clasp Knife Handle from Gloucester", *Lucerna*, 26: 6–8.

Menzel, H. (1966). *Die römischen Bronzen aus Deutschland: Trier*. Mainz: Zabern.

Mills, N. (2000). *Celtic and Roman Artefacts*. Witham: Greenlight Publishing.

Miron, A. (1997). *Das Badegebäude der römischen Villa von Borg*. Merzig: Kulturstiftung für den Landkreis Merzig-Wadern.

Niblett, R. and Thompson, I. (2005). *Alban's Buried Towns. An Assessment of St Albans' Archaeology up to AD 1600*. Oxford: Oxbow.

Nicolay, J. (2007). *Armed Batavians: Use and Significance of Weaponry and Horse Gear from Non-Military Contexts in the Rhine Delta (50 BC–AD 450)*. Amsterdam: Amsterdam University.

Ochota, M.-A. (2013). *Britain's Secret Treasures*. London: Headline.

Oswald, F. (1937). *Index of Figure Types on Terra Sigillata*. Liverpool: Liverpool University Press.

Parker, A. (2015). "The Fist-And-Phallus Pendants from Roman Catterick", *Britannia*, 46: 135–49.

Parker, H. (1992). "Love's Body Anatomized: The Ancient Erotic Handbooks and the Rhetoric of Sexuality", in A. Richlin (ed.), *Pornography and Representation in Greece and Rome*. Oxford: Oxford University Press, 90–111.

Parker, H.N. (1999). "The Observed of All Observers: Spectacle, Applause and Cultural Poetics in the Roman Theatre Audience", in B. Bergmann and C. Kondoleon (eds), *The Art of Ancient Spectacle*. Newhaven, CT: Yale University Press, 163–79.

Pearce, J. and Worrell, S. (2015). "Detecting Roman Britain: The Portable Antiquities Scheme and the Study of Provincial Material Culture", *Anales de Arqueología Cordobesa*, 25/26: 19–48.

Pearce, J. and Worrell, S. (2017). "Roman Britain in 2016. II. Finds Reported under the Portable Antiquities Scheme", *Britannia*, 48: 427–56.

Phang, S. (2004). "Intimate Conquests: Roman Soldiers' Slave Women and Freedwomen", *Ancient World*, 35.2: 207–37.

Redfern, R.C., Marshall, M., Eaton, K. and Poinar, H.N. (2017). "'Written in Bone': New Discoveries About the Lives of Roman Londoners", *Britannia*, 48: 253–77.

Richlin, A. (1983). *The Garden of Priapus. Sexuality and Aggression in Roman Humour.* Oxford: Oxford University Press.

Richlin, A. (2006). "Sexuality in the Roman Empire", in D.S. Potter (ed.), *A Companion to the Roman Empire*. Oxford: Blackwell, 327–53.

Riha, E. (1986). *Römisches Toilettgerät und medizinische Instrumente aus Augst und Kaiseraugst*. Augst: Römermuseum.

Roisman, J. (2014). "Greek and Roman Ethnosexuality", in Hubbard (2014), 398–416.

Rusch, A. (1981). "Römische Klappmesser aus Kongen und Bondorf", *Fundberichte aus Baden-Württemberg*, 6: 541–49.

Scheid, J. (1995). "Les Temples de l'Altbachtal à Trèves: Un 'Sanctuaire National'?" *Cahiers Gustave Glotz*, 6: 227–43.

Schenk, A. (2008). *Regard sur la Tabletterie Antique. Les Objets en Os, Bois de Cerf et Ivoire du Musée Romain d'Avenches*. Avenches: Musée Romain.

Scott, S. (2000). *Art and Society in Fourth-Century Britain: Villa Mosaics in Context*. Oxford: Oxford University School of Archaeology.

Soproni, S. (1990). "Satyr-Silen Bronzekopf mit Meistername aus Visegrád", *Folia Archeologica*, 41: 43–51.

Swift, E. (2009). *Style and Function in Roman Decoration*. Aldershot: Ashgate.

Thüry, G.E. (2008). "Die erotischen Inschriften des Instrumentum Domesticum: Ein Überblick", in M. Hainzmann and R. Wedenig (eds), *Instrumenta Latina II. Akten des 2. Internationalen Kolloquiums Klagenfurt Mai 2005*. Klagenfurt: Verlag des Geschichtsverein für Kärnten, 295–304.

Thüry, G.E. (2009). *Amor au Nord des Alpes: Sexualité et Érotisme dans l'Antiquité Romaine*. Avenches: Association Pro Aventico.

Thüry, G.E. (2010). *Amor zwischen Lech und Leitha: Liebe im römischen Ostalpenraum*. Wels: Stadtmuseum.

Toner, J. (2009). *Popular Culture in Ancient Rome*. Cambridge: Polity Press.

Toner, J. (2015). "Barbers, Barbershops, and Searching for Roman Popular Culture", *Papers of the British School at Rome*, 83: 91–109.

Toner, J.P. (1995). *Leisure and Ancient Rome*. Cambridge: Polity Press.

von Mercklin, E. (1940). "Römische Klappmessergriffe", in V. Hoffiller (ed.), *Serta Hoffilleriana: Commentationes, Gratulatorias Victori Hoffiller Sexagenario Obtulerunt Collegae, Amici, Discipuli A.D. 11. kal. mar 1937*. Zagreb: Zaklada tiskare Narodnih novina, 339–52.

Vucetic, S. (2014). "Roman Sexuality or Roman Sexualities? Looking at Sexual Imagery on Roman Terracotta Mould-made Lamps", in H. Platts, C. Barron, J. Lundock, J. Pearce and J. Yoo (eds), *TRAC 2013: Proceedings of the Twenty-Second Annual Theoretical Roman Archaeology Conference, London 2013*. Oxford: Oxbow, 140–58.

Webb, R. (2002). "Female Entertainers in Late Antiquity", in P. Easterling and E. Hall (eds), *Greek and Roman Actors*. Cambridge: Cambridge University Press, 282–303.

Webb, R. (2008). *Demons and Dancers. Performance in Late Antiquity*. Cambridge, MA: Harvard University Press.

Webster, P. and Webster, J. (2011). "'Is Your Figure Less Than Greek?' Some Thoughts on the Decoration of Gaulish Samian Ware", in D. Bird (ed.), *Dating and Interpreting the Past in the Western Roman Empire. Essays in Honour of Brenda Dickinson*. Oxford: Oxbow, 195–215.

Williams, C. (2010). *Roman Homosexuality: Ideologies of Masculinity in Classical Antiquity*. Oxford: Oxford University Press.

Williams, C. (2014). "Sexual Themes in Greek and Latin Graffiti", in Hubbard (2014), 493–508.

Wilmott, T. (2008). *The Roman Amphitheatre in Britain*. Stroud: Tempus.

Woolf, G. (1998). *Becoming Roman: The Origins of Provincial Civilization in Gaul*. Cambridge: Cambridge University Press.

Worrell, S. (2008). "Roman Britain in 2007. II. Finds Reported under the Portable Antiquities Scheme", *Britannia*, 39: 337–67.

Worrell, S. and Pearce, J. (2012). "Roman Britain in 2011. II. Finds Reported under the Portable Antiquities Scheme", *Britannia*, 43: 355–93.

Wuilleumier, P. and Audin, A. (1952). *Les Médaillons D'Applique Gallo-Romains de la Vallée du Rhône*. Paris: Les Belles Lettres.

3 More than just love and sex
Venus figurines in Roman Britain

Matthew G. Fittock

Introduction

Pipeclay figurines of Venus may reflect Classical ideas about love and sex or provincial concepts that might relate to fertility and protection. This chapter explores the provincial beliefs and religious practices of the different social groups of people associated with the 401 pipeclay figurines of Venus that have been found in Britain through a study of their typology, chronology, distribution, and context. In doing so it shows that, in pipeclay at least, there was much more to this "Roman" goddess than the traditional conceptions we usually have of her.

The meaning of Venus imagery in Roman Britain and beyond

In her usual guise, Venus was the popular Roman goddess of love and sex whose image is often seen throughout the Classical world. Iconographically, she is based on Aphrodite—the Greek goddess embodying similar qualities—who, like Venus, was often depicted in the form of life-sized stone and marble statues in public spaces and temples as well as in small terracotta figurines that were mainly used for private worship in homes and domestic tombs (Havelock 1995: 103–11). The close connection between these two goddesses is particularly demonstrated by the general iconography they share, with both goddesses usually depicted standing nude or semi-nude—as if rising from the sea or bathing—with their heads facing forward or tilted slightly to one side, and one leg—typically the left, but sometimes both—bent at the knee. In this sense Aphrodite can be compared to several Roman types of Venus. The first is "Venus Anadyomene", most versions of which appear standing nude and pressing her hair with one or both hands, sometimes standing on or surrounded by shells and/or with drapery either around her body, held to one side, or positioned nearby. The other recognisable form is the "Venus Pudica" type where the goddess is typically depicted standing nude with her hands covering her breasts and her abdomen, either with or without a garment around her waist that covers her legs and feet. Venus bathing nude, crouched and covering herself, is perhaps one of the other most recognisable and iconic Classical depictions of the goddess but is not depicted in pipeclay. As we will see, most of the pipeclay figurines of Venus found in Britain and across the Continent are a distinctive variation of "Venus Anadyomene", while a smaller number appear to take inspiration from the "Venus Pudica" type that, in pipeclay form at least, is much less common overall (e.g. van Boekel 1987: 162–9). However, there are also a small number of other pipeclay types of Venus with their own distinctive stylistic traits too.

Aphrodite's embodied qualities of love, lust, and sexuality generally appear to be expressed in Roman Venus. As a popular Roman goddess she was evidently a central part of public and private religious life for many people throughout the Roman world. Overall however, she does not appear to have been as popular as other gods and goddesses of the Roman pantheon, where evidence of her reverence is comparatively rare (Webster 1997: 332). Despite this she is still often referred to in her various epithets, including epigraphs and monumental sculpture, as well as imperial coinage. She was likewise a popular subject for artwork from monumental sculpture to the smaller clay and metal figurines that occupied household shrines (Lloyd-Morgan 1986), while emperors even tried to associate themselves with the goddess, with Caesar and Augustus, for example, maintaining the story that the Julii family were directly descended from her (Beard et al. 1998: 144–5; Orlin 2007: 67–9). Such dedication is evidenced at many sites. In Pompeii, for example, Venus was not only revered in the city's public temples and shrines but was also one of the most popular deities depicted in domestic spaces where she was portrayed in wall paintings, reliefs, and mosaics, as well as in metal and terracotta figurines associated with domestic *lararia* (e.g. Brain 2016). Similarly, portable metal forms of the goddess are well known from Germany (Menzel 1966, taf. 38, no. 80), the Netherlands (van Boekel 1987: 902–3; see also Lloyd-Morgan 1986: 183, fig. 15 for one from Krefeld-Gellep), and Switzerland (Kaufmann-Heinimann 1977, taf. 71–3, no. 69), yet these too are relatively rare.

In fact, one of the best ways in which we can gauge the reverence of Venus throughout the western provinces is by the number of pipeclay figurines of her that have been found in each region. Produced mainly in the Allier Valley region of central France,[1] pipeclay figurines of Venus were exported in various quantities to several Roman provinces. In France, for example, over 300 figurines from what are now relatively out-of-date museum catalogues (e.g. Rouvier-Jeanlin 1972: 91–120; Vertet and Vuillemot 1973; Rouvier-Jeanlin 1986; Bémont et al. 1993) show that Venus was not only the most common deity depicted in pipeclay in this region, but also that she had a relatively stronger following here than elsewhere. In other regions the numbers seem to confirm that she was not as popular, with roughly 155 figurines from Belgium (Beenhouwer 2005: 426–528) and fewer still (36) from the Netherlands (van Boekel 1987: 496–551) and (28) Switzerland (von Gonzenbach 1995: 101–30). Although up-to-date catalogues incorporating all the pipeclay figurines of Venus from museums and excavated sites in all of these regions would be useful, what the existing evidence does broadly show is that the popularity of Venus, in pipeclay form at least, varied between the provinces. It also shows that she was evidently more popular in the regions that are closest to Britain where people probably shared closer or similar beliefs.

The concept of Venus and her qualities were facets that evidently resonated with some Romano-British people. Generally speaking she does not seem to have been as popular here as in Gaul, but she was occasionally worshipped through the media of epigraphy and stone reliefs, as on: a commemorative slab by the Sixth Legion at Croy Hill, East Dumbartonshire, for example (RIB 2163); mosaics (Lloyd-Morgan 1986: 185, figs 18–19); statuary (e.g. Durham 2012: 3.31, 2014: 216; see also Jones and Mattingly 2002: 282–5 for her distribution on non-military sites); as well as on occasional objects, such as silver or bronze pins (e.g. Johns 1996: 140). However, her popularity in Britain once again seems to have been most commonly expressed in the form of pipeclay figurines where there are now 401 examples from the province. By and large these are the same types that we see in Gaul and are probably associated with a similar set of religious beliefs and practices. But what exactly do these objects mean and can they be directly linked with the Classical goddess of love and sex? Furthermore, what other additional nuances of belief might they express in Britain?

Questions like these have been at the centre of discussions about the significance of Venus figurines in Britain and beyond for the past 50 years, during which time several alternative suggestions have been put forward about who they are meant to characterise and why they might do so. Most of the original and subsequent ideas put forward about this are focussed on the symbolic meaning of Venus figurines and incorporate wider ideas about how the process of cultural transmission impacted on the symbolic representations and roles of Classical "Roman" gods and goddess in the provinces. Jenkins (1958), for instance, was one of the first to suggest that pipeclay figurines of Venus may not in fact depict the Classical form but instead a provincialised, in this case primarily "Gaulish", version of her. In this sense Jenkins consequently refers to these pipeclay figurines as a form of "Pseudo-Venus" to try and clearly differentiate them from other Classical depictions of the goddess. However, in my opinion this is an unnecessarily confusing term considering that he only applies it to the most common pipeclay Venus types. Moreover, they are already inherently distinguishable from other non-pipeclay depictions by their generally cruder style and the very distinctive type of yellowish-white clay that they are made of. Webster (1997: 332–4, 2001: 220–1) later developed this argument to suggest that pipeclay figurines of Venus therefore reflect a process of cultural amalgamation and uses them to evidence her theoretical framework of creolisation. In doing so she, firstly, argues that such pipeclay figurines are indeed hybridised "Celtic" forms of the Classical goddess Venus, and, secondly, points out the complex cultural and social ideas and interactions of the people that they embody. As such, these figurines are indeed overall a specifically "Gaulish" take on a Classical form but one that reflects a mix (i.e. creolised form) of Classical and "indigenous" religious beliefs about fertility in Roman Gaul. As wholly imported objects, Webster further argues that the very presence of these figurines (and any other pipeclay gods and goddesses) in Britain subsequently reflects the cultural transmission of religious beliefs and practices from Gaul, and that this directly influenced the beliefs and practices of Romano-British people.

Other ideas about the identity and cultural significance of such figurines have been suggested. Jenkins (1958) himself postulates that they could alternatively be a completely different type of Gaulish deity altogether, or possibly even a simple sexualised representation of a woman. Another idea is that they might be some sort of "water-nymph" based on their frequent occurrence at some sacred spring sites in Britain (e.g. Springhead, see Jarrett 2008: 71–2, tab. 1(1), 264–5, fig. 81, 71–2, fig. 29, tab. 1(8–10), 267) and Gaul (e.g. Vichy, see Green 1986: 95). Nevertheless, the underlying and universally agreed position is that, through her commonly attributed name, pose, and features (i.e. rounded breasts, hips, and buttocks) and analysis of the contexts in which they are usually recovered (i.e. occupation deposits, temples, and burials), these figurines probably do depict some form of Venus and are, at the very least, fundamentally linked to the idea of the mother-goddess and their strong associations with fertility, abundance, and good health throughout the western provinces where they were probably used as religious and votive objects. One of the subsequent ideas often put forward, given the prominence of their inherently female imagery, is that this type of figurine was either mainly or even exclusively used by women (Jenkins 1958: 70; van Boekel 1987: 238; Bristow 2012: 16), though this has so far not been proven by detailed contextual analysis.

While Drakeman (2008) agrees that these figurines are evidence of what she calls a "syncretic process" combining aspects of Roman and "Celtic" religious expression, her analysis of iconographic, production, and distributional evidence importantly reveals much more about the multiple ritualistic (native cult activity) and funerary (burials) ways in which they were used. Highlighting the range of contexts and interpretations with which they are associated, Drakeman shows, for instance, that many of these figurines were indeed used in households for protection and fertility, and to safeguard expectant mothers during pregnancy and childbirth, though also that they were used as dedications for protection at temples, sanctuaries, and in graves—the latter possibly to accompany as well as guard both dead adults and children in the afterlife (see also Green 1986: 94–5). Their occasional recovery from sanctuaries and sacred spring sites like Vichy in France has additionally been taken to mean that they might have had some kind of votive role, possibly linked with healing, medicine, and even magic (Ferris 2012: 60–76, 121). The problem is that such studies only include a small proportion of the British finds in their surveys and analyses, while evidence for magical use is still ambiguous and hard to identify, although certainly not beyond the realms of possibility.

Assessing the possible meaning of pipeclay Venus figurines in Britain and comparing them to other depictions of the goddess in other media usefully highlights interesting differences that may well reflect the alternative cultural ideas and beliefs that some people had about her. For example, although the aforementioned commemorative slab at Croy Hill depicts Venus in a similar pose to pipeclay figurines, she is arguably executed in a more "Classical" style with her head tilted to the left, crossed legs, and holding her hair and drapery in opposite arms than the front facing and straight legged pipeclay depictions. At the other end of the scale, the images of the goddess in mosaics are potentially more "Romano-British" in terms of their style, with their even more overly pronounced body parts and additional non-Classical features. A good example of this is the caped Venus in the Low Ham mosaic who, as well as her elaborate hairstyle, also has distinctive flowing, expansive hair, especially rounded hips, and is accompanied by small cupids either side of her (Lloyd-Morgan 1986: 185, figs 18–19). Another is the Venus depicted in the Rudston mosaic which wears a cape and has what appears to be a mirror nearby (Smith 1980: 134–6, pl. XII). There are likewise also important differences between pipeclay figurines of Venus and the images of "water-nymphs" that are occasionally depicted in stone reliefs at sites such as Conventina's Well (e.g. Allason-Jones and McKay 1985: 13–14, pls V–VI, nos 1 and 4). Although the carved figures at this site do share some stylistic characteristics with pipeclay depictions of Venus (their hairstyles are broadly similar and both are often depicted with robes or drapery), they are subtly different in many ways. For example, most, if not all, of the "water-nymphs" are generally shown reclining rather than standing, and are also usually robed from the waist down and over one arm, whereas most of the pipeclay figurines of Venus stand upright and either hold drapery to one side or with it arranged around their waist with their arms uncovered. Although subtle, these kinds of stylistic distinctions are culturally significant and probably reflect important differences in how people revered the goddess. Indeed, what we appear to have in pipeclay form therefore is the Classical motif of Venus executed in a provincial, specifically Gaulish, style that probably represents a different set of beliefs than the other depictions of the same and similar goddesses that are also known across Britain.

Perhaps the best way to highlight this is to briefly compare the collections of pipeclay and metal Venus figurines that are known from Britain.[2] Although comparable in form and proportion, in stylistic terms, metal figurines of Venus are not only finer and higher in quality, but also more anatomically proportioned than pipeclay figurines, with smaller bodies and less pronounced buttocks and hips. This is especially showcased by the "Classical" bronze figurine of Venus from St Albans (Durham 2012, ID 132) that, with its outstretched arms and flailing drapery around her waist, is regarded as one of the most finely executed examples of the goddess in all of Britain. Some metal figurines are alternatively regarded as being more "provincial" in style (suggesting that they may even have been made in Britain), but these again maintain their characteristic quality and stylistic distinctiveness against the pipeclay examples. This group includes an undraped figurine from Colchester, Essex, that holds a lock of hair in one hand and covers her breast with the other (Durham 2012, ID 136), and another from Southwark, London, that this time shows Venus with one hand placed on her torso and the other covering her breast (Durham 2012, ID 144).

As well as their visual differences, a brief look at the quantities, distributions, and contexts of metal Venus figurines, as well as all other metal figurine types, from Britain suggests that their meaning and use differed to pipeclay figurines as well. Analysing metal figurines like this is complicated by the probability that they are much more likely to have survived than pipeclay figurines, and because metal ones may equally have been more frequently recycled rather than discarded. The value placed on metal objects by antiquarians and modern excavators additionally means that metal figurines are more likely to have been published. Nevertheless, there are some notable trends. For example, although their cheaper material and wider availability is typically taken to mean that pipeclay figurines may well have belonged to people of a lower social and economic status than the perceived rarer, "more luxurious", metal figurines that were probably owned by higher-status people (Jenkins 1977: 418; van Boekel 1987: 902), the recorded quantities of each not only suggests that pipeclay figurines (946 including all types) are just as rare as metal figurines (996), but also that the types and numbers of depictions differ as well. In the case of deities (Figure 3.1) where those in pipeclay are not only overwhelmingly of goddesses, and metal figurines mainly depict gods, it is also significant that Venus (401) is most common in pipeclay and Mercury most common in metal (21). Such differences once again suggest that the figurines in each of these materials probably had subtly different meanings and uses for different groups of people throughout the province (Fittock 2017: 180–94 and 288–316 for a fuller account of this).

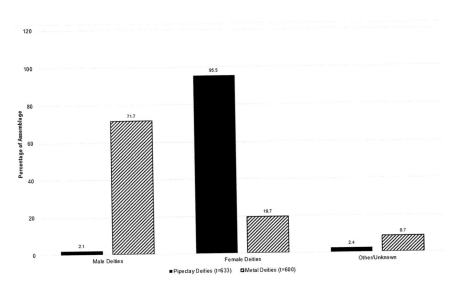

Figure 3.1 The proportional gender of all pipeclay and metal deity figurines in Britain

More specific differences between the use of metal and pipeclay figurines of Venus, as well as the practices they are associated with, are evident from their varying spatial and contextual distributions (Figure 3.2). Useful contextual information for metal figurines is generally lacking but the available data do suggest a mixed urban and rural use from the second century onwards, much like pipeclay figurines. Here, a site-type analysis not only shows that most metal figurines of Venus mainly derive from southern Britain, but also that they have a social profile more associated with what can be broadly called "higher-status" urban sites like *civitas* capitals than "lower-status" urban and rural sites more typically associated with pipeclay figurines.[3] The 107 pipeclay figurines from London stand out here, but this is something that probably reflects the settlement's position as a focal point for pipeclay importation from Gaul. In contrast, metal figurines of Venus are not as closely linked with military and rural populations as pipeclay examples, with only one metal Venus coming from a possible military site in Colchester, Essex (Durham 2012, ID 137) and another from a villa at Compton Grove, Gloucestershire (Durham 2012, ID 618). Elsewhere, metal figurines of Venus, as well as all other types, were used much less than pipeclay figurines for religious purposes, with a residual find from Woodeaton, Oxfordshire (Durham 2012, ID 141) being the only example of a metal Venus figurine from a temple site. Likewise, only five metal figurines have been found in hoards while none are known from burial contexts. Combined, all of the evidence from just this brief summary seems to affirm the higher material, if not cultural, value of metal figurines over pipeclay, and that figurines in each material were used in slightly different ways by different economic and social groups.

In summary, this chapter examines the collection of 401 pipeclay figurines of Venus that are now known from Roman Britain. This is one of the largest under-assessed such groups from any of the Roman provinces and also one of the largest collections of Venus-related material culture from the western provinces to date. It analyses them to determine if they had more to do with Classical traditions of love and sex or provincial ideas about fertility and protection in Roman Britain. To do this, this new study has collected all of the known figurines of this kind from the province along with a rich array of detailed contextual information that can tell us much more about their possible meaning and use in Roman Britain as the last comprehensive study of this material was carried out over 40 years ago (e.g. Jenkins 1958, 1977). Significantly, these pipeclay figurines constitute the main way in which Venus was depicted in Roman Britain overall, but unfortunately previous studies have not revealed exactly what the meaning of these objects was, let alone precisely who used them and in what ways. These questions will therefore be directly addressed throughout the rest of this chapter by analysing the collection through typology, distribution, chronology, and context to reveal the practices they were for and the cultural groups that used them.

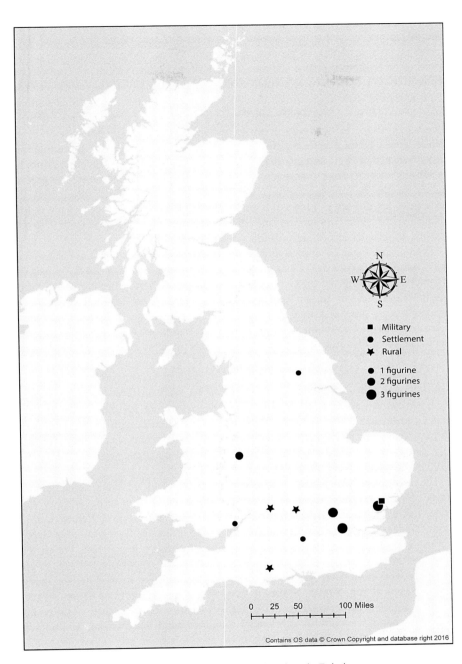

Figure 3.2 The social distribution of metal Venus figurines in Britain

The assemblage

The 401 pipeclay Venus figurines come in nine different types. While each type varies slightly in detail, in general they depict Venus nude or semi-nude, either wearing or holding drapery, standing on a hollow hemispherical or square base. As well as her thin waist and small breasts, she is usually shown with an elaborate hairstyle with long strands draped over her shoulders, basic facial features such as large eyes and thick lips, rounded hips and buttocks, and enlarged hands held close to her body or up to her head (occasionally holding objects). While Types 1 and 2 are very similar visually, the iconography of the remaining seven types may well suggest that they have slightly different specific symbolic meanings and therefore that, even within the scope of this one deity, the precise nature of the beliefs surrounding her probably varied slightly throughout the province, as did their respective popularities. Each type is described below according to their production in either Gaul or the Rhine–Moselle,[4] while images of selected types are provided in Figure 3.3.

Type 1 and Type 2 Venus figurines are the most common types in Britain and the Continent (Figure 3.3, T1 and T2). Both types depict a form of "Venus Anadyomene", showing the goddess standing on a small hemispherical plinth holding her right hand up to her head (or hair) and her left hand by her side holding drapery—arm positions that distinguish them somewhat from the "standard" form of "Venus Anadyomene" with often two hands pressing the hair and drapery nearby to one side. These two very similar pipeclay types are differentiated by how the goddess holds this drapery: on Type 1 figurines it is draped over her left wrist and on Type 2 figurines it is held in her fingertips. A range of different garment designs and hairstyles can be seen on both types but overall in fewer varieties than on the Continent (e.g. Rouvier-Jeanlin 1972: 91–120; von Gonzenbach 1995: 101–13). Parallel moulds of each type on the Continent suggest that both were mainly produced in Allier (France) where they are usually found in first and especially second-century contexts (van Boekel 1987: 499; Beenhouwer 2005: 426–83).

The rarer types of Venus produced in Central Gaul all have some general traits of either "Venus Anadyomene" and "Venus Pudica" in terms of how they pose, but all have distinctive features. In full form, the Type 3 Venus figurine from Wroxeter (Figure 3.3, T3), like the Type 1 and 2 figurines, also depict Venus holding her hair with her right hand and drapery in her left, but in this case her drapery hangs above an eagle perched by the goddess's left leg, a type that may well have been produced as early as the mid-first century (Beenhouwer 2005: 521, cat. nr. 5069). Similarly, the two Type 4 figurines from London (Figure 3.3, T4) and Brougham (Cumbria) likewise do not cover their bodies with their hands and hold a garment in their left hand but, instead, additionally hold a jug or *patera* in the right hand down by their right side (Cool 2004: 122, no. 11, fig. 4.95). The London find appears to be Gaulish in style with a domed hemispherical base (Beenhouwer 2005: 506), but the Brougham figurine with its square base may well be a product of Cologne instead (Cool 2004: 122). There

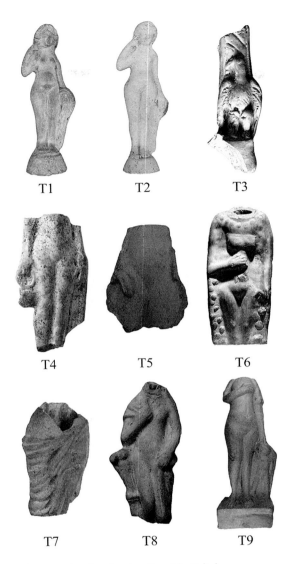

Figure 3.3 Types of Venus pipeclay figurine found in Britain

T1 and T2—examples of Type 1 and Type 2, both from London (© and reproduced by courtesy of Museum of London); T3—example of Type 3 from Wroxeter (SHYMS: 2013.00072, image supplied by Shropshire Council, Shropshire Museums); T4—example of Type 4 from London (© and reproduced by courtesy of Museum of London); T5—example of Type 5 from Caerwent (2007.35H/ 7.6 SF85, by permission of the National Museum of Wales); T6—example of Type 6 from London (1928,0713.10, © The Trustees of the British Museum); T7—example of Type 7 from London (2096, © and reproduced by courtesy of Museum of London); T8—example of Type 8 from York (YORYM: H81, © York Museums Trust (Yorkshire Museum)); T9—example of Type 9 from Colchester (COLEM 1908.1619 © Colchester Museums) are only a couple of broadly similar Continental parallels that might stylistically date the London figurine from the late first to early second centuries (e.g. Beenhouwer 2005: 506), while the Brougham figurine may be similar in date, if not slightly later. Alternatively, the Type 5 figurine from Caerwent (Monmouthshire) poses in a covered way in a style to some extent reminiscent of "Venus Pudica" with her right hand on her right thigh and left hand covering her left breast, and drapery hanging down her side over her left shoulder to her feet (Figure 3.3, T5). Continental parallels have a suggested date of between the late-second and early-third centuries (Beenhouwer 2005: 488–9, Serie 111–13). The Type 6 (*Vénus-à-Gaine*) figurine from London (Figure 3.3, T6), meanwhile, appears to be a slightly different, likely earlier, take on this covered stance, with the right hand positioned over the abdomen and left hand by the goddess's left side, though with no visible garment. Instead, the figure is backed by a rectangular panel decorated with rosettes and circular studs on either side and is probably a first century type (Jenkins 1969: 318–19).

The remaining Venus figurine types were all produced in the Rhine–Moselle region and are all variations of "Venus Pudica". The first of these is the Type 7 figurines. When complete these would have depicted the goddess standing and supporting drapery around her waist with her left hand and covering her breasts with her right hand, or some other combination of hand placement. These were found at Caerleon (Monmouthshire), Dover (Kent), London (Figure 3.3, T7), and Springhead (Kent) and were probably made in the second to third centuries (see van Boekel 1987: 514–23; Beenhouwer 2005: 490–500). The Type 8 figurine from York (Figure 3.3, T8), meanwhile, is a slightly different version of Venus with the goddess this time holding a cloak draped around her back supported by the left hand at her abdomen and right hand as it covers her right breast; there is also a small figure, possibly an Amor or Cupid, on her right side. All date to the mid- to late-second century (van Boekel 1987: 547–8; Beenhouwer 2005: 511–12, Serie 151). Finally, the Type 9 Venus figurine from St Osyth, Essex (Figure 3.3, T9) is also accompanied by an Amor or Cupid as she alternatively covers both of her breasts with her right arm and hand, but this time there is no visible drapery and the Amor or Cupid is by her left leg. This type is stylistically attributable to a slightly later date than the Type 8 figurine, from the late-second to mid-third centuries (Beenhouwer 2005: 508–10).

In total there are 22 Type 1 figurines, 100 of Type 2 (by far the most common type in Britain), five of Type 7, two of Type 4, and one each of Types 3, 5, 6, 8, and 9. There are also 231 fragments that depict general attributes of Venus but cannot be ascribed a specific type, and 36 finds that have not been seen by the author but are identified as Venus in site reports or by Jenkins (1977). Although all of these types are slightly different it is likely that they only represent small, if any, differences in the meaning of the goddess and the beliefs being generally expressed by them. But what they do show is that people did revere Venus in slightly different symbolic ways within this wider belief system. Indeed, this is perhaps indicated best by the Type 6 figurine from London with its rosette and stud style decoration that mimics other sun-related imagery often documented on objects throughout Gaul (e.g. Green 1986: 33–71).

At the same time, the different quantities of each type also tell us about how they were traded and supplied to Britain, as well as their availability here, and what this might mean. In terms of importation, the first interesting aspect is that while over 400 appears to be quite a large number of figurines, this actually amounts to an average of just two per year imported to Britain over the 200 years of the second and third centuries. This is a very small number of overall imports, although many more figurines may remain lost and yet to be discovered. In terms of availability this might mean that most Romano-British people who wanted a pipeclay figurine of Venus likely only had access to the most commonly imported types (i.e. Types 1 and 2). Most of these probably arrived via London where there is a concentration of the most common Type 1 and Type 2 figurines that were probably imported through the port on the River Thames (Fittock 2015: 119–22, figs 6–7 for a distribution map of some of these). Most of these people may not have known of, cared about, or had access to the wider range of rarer types of Venus figurine that were available elsewhere on the Continent and thus settled for what was most widely available. Yet, there was also evidently a small proportion of the Romano-British population who could access these rarer Venus types and did so. This especially appears to be the case later in the Roman period when, significantly, these rare types tend to appear, as the more common types were less widely available and popular as they once were. These people were perhaps not as indiscriminate and uncaring in their selection of figurine and possibly made more specific choices about the type(s) they wanted and acquired. Exactly who these people were is a question that is addressed further below.

Chronology

The most useful way to establish a chronology of Venus figurines in Britain is to examine the dates of the contexts in which they are found rather than attempt to employ purely stylistic criteria. Overall, the assemblage is relatively well dated with 126 out of 401 figurines coming from dated deposits but regrettably a significant proportion of finds (245) are from residual or undated contexts. One of the major concerns with this dating method is that it only provides a date for the last use of a figurine when many objects were evidently produced a lot earlier and stayed in use for many years before they were deposited. The number of dated finds and types per century is illustrated in Figure 3.4. Again, many of the rarer Venus types (i.e. Types 3, 6, 8, and 9) in Britain are from poorly recorded or undated deposits. In these cases, better dated Continental parallels can suggest when a British find was made and used but these are often prone to similar problems, though none conflict with any of the dated British material.

Overall, the dated material shows the limited but mixed use of Venus figurines in the first century, a peak in the second century before a decline in the third century, and a small rise in the fourth century: the number of types per century has a similar profile. The earliest finds include two Type 1/2

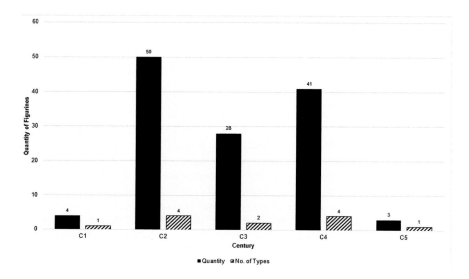

Figure 3.4 The quantity of dated pipeclay Venus figurines and number of types in Britain per century

figurines from a drain at Chichester (Sussex) and a levelling deposit at Bloomberg (London) dated A.D. 60–75 and A.D. 65–70/80 respectively (Down 1989: 213, no. 3, fig. 27.15 (Chichester) and M. Marshall, personal communication (London)), and a Type 1 figurine in an *in situ* destruction layer from the site of One Poultry, London dated A.D. 90–100 (Rayner et al. 2011: 407). All of these are from habitation sites in two of Britain's largest urban centres, indicating an early association with civilian religious beliefs and practices. Two other figurines may also be associated with this period: firstly, the Type 6 Venus from the Bank of England site in London (Jenkins 1978: 152–5, no. 9, fig. 3), the rarity of which is probably a general result of its early production date, and, secondly, a Type 1/2 figurine from the small settlement at Orsett (Essex) tentatively dated to the first century that highlights the early influence of Venus figurines in rural religious practice too (Carter 1998: 101–2, fig. 66). Overall then, the early supply of figurines to Britain broadly reflects the small range of Venus types being produced during the earlier stages of this particular industry in central Gaul.

The peak of finds in the second century (50) alongside the increased number of types available suggests a greater popularity of Venus figurines in this period to some extent. However, this figure might be more related to the general growth of the Gaulish as well as Rhineland industries that were by now supplying more types to British markets, albeit in fewer varieties and numbers than seen elsewhere on the Continent. In Britain, the Type 1 and 2 figurines that continued circulating were joined by the first Type 7 figurines. This can be evidenced by the figurine from Springhead (Kent), the earliest figurine to directly reflect ritual practices at a temple (Jarrett 2008: 71–2). Interestingly, this was in a rural setting, but the temple complex here was probably one that people travelled to specifically for such a purpose. A similar example of this early temple-based ritual activity is the Type 1 Venus figurine from Heybridge, Essex (Atkinson and Preston 2015: 2.4 and 3.7). Additionally, the initial use of Venus figurines for funerary practices, this time on urban sites, is evidenced by the Type 2 figurine from a cremation burial in St Albans (Jenkins 1958: 73, no. 52, 1977: 329, no. 4). Other rare types started to circulate in habitation areas of urban centres at the same time. This is demonstrated, for example, by the Type 4 Venus figurine from a Trajanic pit found near to a building in Southwark (London) that was probably made in central Gaul and exported to the settlement during broadly the same period (Jenkins 1977: 342, no. 38).

The decreased number of dated finds (28) suggesting a fall in circulation in the third century can probably be linked to the general decline of the Gaulish industry in this period. The fact that these are only common types (i.e. Types 1 and 2) would also suggest a scaling back of the range that was now being exported to Britain, where circulation was primarily at large urban sites. The other important change that we see during the third century, and extending into the fourth, is the increased occurrence of Venus figurines in funerary contexts. Many of the figurines were by now very old (some up to 200 years, based on their typology) and might have been curated, possibly as heirlooms (see below). There is also evidence of the first Venus figurine-related graveside rituals in the form of the Type 4 Venus from Brougham that was probably burnt on a pyre (Cool 2004: 122, no. 11, fig. 4.95).

Interestingly, the number of dated figurines (41) and types increases in the fourth century, but this is probably due to increased discard as their importance dwindled. There is also a greater likelihood that some of these later finds were disturbed or redeposited and actually reflect earlier activity. This is especially the case for the rare Type 5 and Type 7 Venus figurines from Caerwent (E. Chapman, personal communication) and Caerleon (Evans 2000: 301, no. 7, fig. 72.7) that are both from disturbed or mixed contexts.[5] Yet some of the Type 1 and Type 2 figurines from more secure contemporary contexts could have been retained and passed down by their owners, possibly with greater importance as old objects.

Spatial and social distribution

Pipeclay figurines of Venus were clearly very important social and symbolic objects that reflect the personal beliefs and practices of individuals as well as different social groups, and to understand this better it is important that their contexts are studied in detail. In order to do this a social distribution analysis recording contextual information in two stages has been carried out (Eckardt 2002, 2005; Eckardt and Crummy 2008). The first stage assesses the type of site a figurine is from (e.g. military, urban, or rural). Military sites include mainly forts; urban sites include *coloniae*, *municipia*, and large and small towns; and rural sites include small settlements and villas. On this occasion *civitas* capitals and London are listed separately to highlight the proportion of figurines from these sites. The second stage records specific details about the type of deposit the figurines were found in (e.g. habitation contexts, burials, or sanctuaries). In addition to the obvious concern that the distribution of these objects may reflect little more than which sites have been excavated and published, there are a number of other well documented problems with classifying sites in this way. It includes often oversimplifying the complexities of site morphology and legal status, whether *civitas* capitals should be a separate category or grouped with large or small towns, and how small towns and rural settlements can be clearly differentiated (Smith et al. 2016). Quantifying sites with both military and civilian (urban) populations can also be problematic, especially when there is no clarifying dated contextual information. In such cases a find's value is split between the relevant categories (Eckardt 2002: 29–30; Eckardt and Crummy 2008: 96). Yet despite its problems this approach still highlights many useful patterns about the kind of people that used Venus figurines in Britain.

Figure 3.5 illustrates that Venus figurines are widely distributed across Britain but with a dense distribution in the south-east, especially in London (107 finds) where they likely arrived from Gaul and were redistributed to the rest of Britain (Fittock 2017: 253–6, figs. 7.19–21). Across the rest of the country they are found on a variety of different site types, indicating a widespread use across the social strata (Figures 3.6–3.7). A significant proportion of Venus figurines comes from military sites (forts) on the south coast, though the densest grouping of such sites is along the Hadrian's Wall corridor. Significantly, the majority of the figurines were found in fort *vici* as opposed to barrack blocks (see Fittock 2017: 648–52; for discussions about the character of the military *vici* populations see Mason 1987; Franzen 2006; Birley 2016).

A closer look at the site-type distribution shows that pipeclay figurines of Venus were overwhelmingly used by urban populations across the province. Some of these are from *civitas* capitals like Silchester (10) and Canterbury (6) and the *municipium* of Verulamium (7), but most are from large urban centres, including Colchester (6), York (6), and, especially, London (107) (Fittock 2017: 652–63). Differences in recording and publication to some extent account for the large number of finds from these sites compared to others like Dorchester where only one figurine is recorded. The urban group may be even larger given that many finds are from *vici*, but again, the composition of such populations is difficult to determine. Nevertheless, *vici*, as well as urban populations, would have included men, women, and children.

A smaller number from rural and villa sites show that Venus figurines were also being used by some people in the countryside. As well as those from Hawkedon (Suffolk) and Mucking (Essex), this group also includes single finds from a number of southern villas including Fishbourne (Sussex), Gestingthorpe

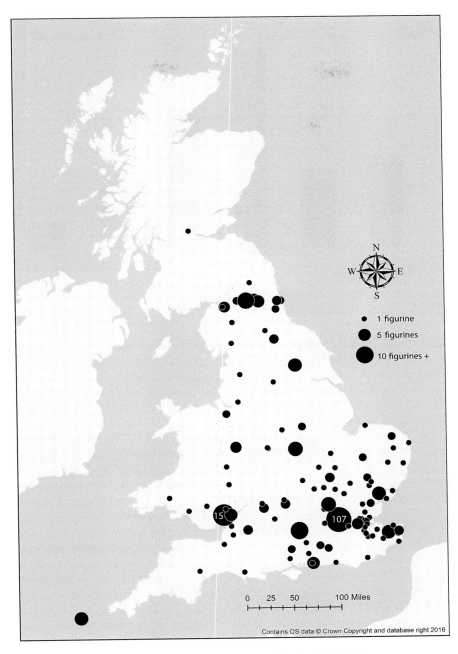

Figure 3.5 The spatial distribution of pipeclay Venus figurines in Britain

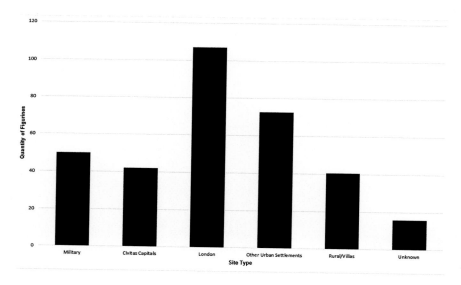

Figure 3.6 The social distribution of pipeclay Venus figurines in Britain

(Essex), and Wilcote (Oxfordshire), with two figurines specifically associated with villa structures from Gorhambury (Hertfordshire) and Chiddingford (Surrey) (Fittock 2017: 664–9). Some of these finds are from sites and contexts indicative of ritual use in rural areas. This includes one find from a temple complex at Heybridge (Essex) and six from Nor'Nour (Isles of Scilly), recently reinterpreted as a ritual site (Butcher 2000–1).

The other figurines that are part of this group are the 69 fragments of Venus from the site of Ruxox Farm in Bedfordshire, an assemblage that also includes as many as eight fragments of Dea Nutrix figurines, six of Minerva, a single head of Bacchus, and several unidentifiable fragments (Fadden 2010). Examination of the assemblage by Fadden (2010: 2) suggests that it equates to at least 72 different objects, most of which are of Venus, meaning that roughly a sixth of the total number of Venus figurines found in Britain are from this single site. This is quite unusual in that it is the largest from a Romano-British rural site and is starkly at odds with the wider pattern of lower Venus figurine use on rural/villa sites throughout the rest of the province, although she was evidently still quite popular amongst some of the countryside population. Nevertheless, Ruxox throws up some other possibilities. One idea already put forward based on the presence of the figurines and small amount of structural remains identified in an adjacent field is that Ruxox may well have been the site of a temple, shrine, or villa near to a now dried up river within the vicinity of a nearby small Roman settlement (Simco 1984: 31–2, 56; Dawson 2004: 18–33; James 2009: 58; Fadden 2010: 10). Indeed, a large waterlogged timber plank and

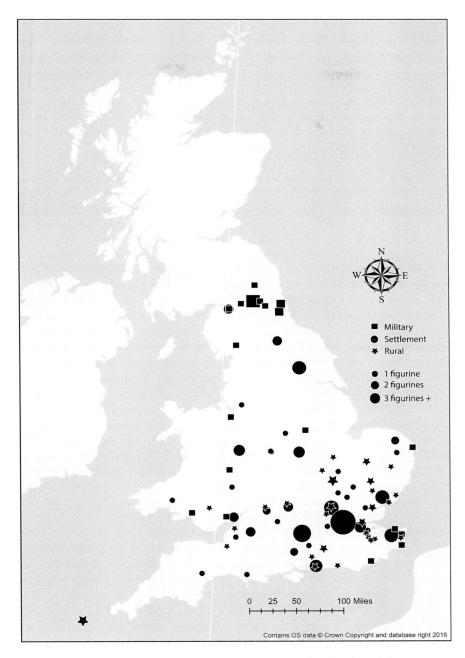

Figure 3.7 Map of the social distribution of pipeclay Venus figurines in Britain

a sandstone wall were discovered in the 1950s, which at the time were interpreted as the possible foundations of a wooden bridge that once crossed the old river course (Dawson 2004: 18), or the footings of a ritual platform to make votive offerings (e.g. James 2009: 60). It is hard to know exactly what is going on at Ruxox Farm without a more detailed investigation of the structural remains, other finds, and figurines from the site and whether the fragments were deposited all at once, maybe as a hoard, or over time. It does, however, seem that the pipeclay assemblage is a significant collection that may well reflect a more unusual practice than those more commonly associated with these objects in both the urban and rural areas of Britain.

Chronologically, although both datasets from the first/second centuries and third/fourth centuries are small and the number of residual finds increases over time, Figure 3.8 shows that most first- and second-century finds are located in the south-east on urban sites, with few from military, rural, and villa sites. In the third and fourth centuries finds from military sites are better represented but most are still from *vici*. Meanwhile, finds are widely distributed across southern Britain from contexts spanning the second and third centuries. In contrast, use by rural populations remained confined to the south-east throughout the Roman period, but this could be under-represented due to the general lack of figurines from dated contexts from rural sites rather than rural excavations in Britain overall (see Smith et al. 2016).

Contextual evidence can tell us much more about use of Venus figurines in private or domestic settings in Britain even if their exact symbolic meaning is not clear in such contexts. The vast majority of finds from military, urban, and rural sites are from what can be broadly defined as occupation deposits (e.g. pits, ditches, dumps, floor levels, drains, or general occupation layers), many of which were near to military (barrack blocks and ramparts) or civilian (e.g. houses/workshops) buildings. Most of these deposits are generally interpreted as refuse but some were probably used in nearby domestic shrines. Indeed, a small number of finds from urban (as well as rural) sites included broad groups of objects ranging from broken pottery to items of adornment but none are confidently attributable to specific genders. It is therefore entirely possible that pipeclay figurines of Venus and others represent the beliefs of both men and women. Other figurines are from deposits that might reflect ritual activity, like wells and associated fills, as at South Shields (Allason-Jones and Miket 1984: 341, nos 9.63–4), Brampton (Rankov et al. 1982: 370, pl. 36), and Wickford (Jenkins 1977: 325, no. 8), as well as possibly the Walbrook in London, for example, but in most cases these are probably nothing more than discarded refuse too (Merrifield 1995: 38; Crummy with Pohl 2008; Wardle 2011: 347). This is emphasised by the fact that most of the figurines from military and urban sites are fragmentary body parts with breaks in multiple places (e.g. the neck, waist, knees, and/or the ankles). Experimental work with replica Venus figurines has shown that removing heads was most likely the only deliberate,

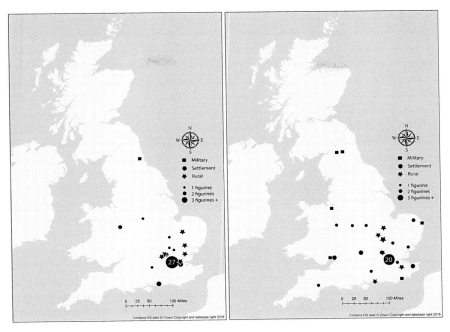

Figure 3.8 Social distribution of pipeclay Venus figurines from the first and second (left) and third and fourth centuries (right)

possibly ritual, practice, and other breaks are more likely accidental, wear, or discard (Fittock 2015: 129, 2017: 394–415, forthcoming).

The figurines from religious contexts like temples and graves not only tell us about the ritual and funerary role of Venus figurines but also give us a better insight into their possible meaning. Those from temples (Figure 3.9) are only partially useful for this, given that they were only occasionally used for this kind of public worship. Indeed, out of these 21 finds, only 5 are definitely from temple sites, while 16 come from possible temple contexts. Their recovery from mainly small urban towns (6) and rural sites (12) in the south-east suggests that such temple-related use was either carried out by these populations or, more likely, that people specifically travelled to these remoter locations to do so. It is not clear who was worshipped at many of these sites. Bronze figurines from Heybridge (Henig 2015) suggest a mix of gods were venerated including Mercury (goat and cockerel figurines), Venus (two bronze heads of the goddess), and hunting deities like Diana or Silvanus (a silver boar and bronze stag). Some other sites, such as Baldock, Roxton, and Springhead, are closely associated with natural springs and rivers. This group may well also include the 69 Venus fragments from Ruxox Farm as discussed above, as well as the six finds from the coastal site of Nor'Nour

(Isles of Scilly) that is now regarded as a religious site (Butcher 2000–1). The other three figurines from known temples or possible temples on military and urban sites are the ones from Richborough (Jenkins 1977: 322, no. 7), the town at Corbridge (Allason-Jones 1988: 214, no. 24), and a fragment of Venus from a "rubbish pit" overlaying a timber drain near the south-west corner of London's Mithraeum that is not directly associated with the temple but does broadly correspond to its use from A.D. 240 (Shepherd 1998: 221–2; Wardle 1998: 111 and 178; Fittock 2015: 122).

The only evidence of direct ritual activity comes in the form of a Type 7 Venus figurine at Springhead that was found on the first to second century *cella* floor of Temple 1 (Penn 1959: 55–6) and the six fragments from Nor'nour, Isles of Scilly, that were also found with three fragments of Dea Nutrix figurines inside what was probably a temple structure (Fulford 1989; Butcher 2000–1). All of the other Venus figurines from Springhead and other temple sites are actually from deposits close to temples or possible structures rather than within temple or temple-related structures, though it is often difficult to tell how they were used on these sites. At Springhead, this includes three Venus figurines found in the vicinity of the temple complex: an unknown type near Temple VII, a Type 1/2 figurine from a temple ditch near an oven building, and a Type 2 figurine from a second century "temple ditch fill" close to a nearby building (see Jarrett 2008: 70–8, 264–9 for all the pipeclay figurines from Springhead). Elsewhere, there is a Type 1 figurine from a mid-second-century pit located outside of the temple entrance at Heybridge, Essex (Atkinson and Preston 2015: 2.4, fig. 81, Group 409); a Type 2 Venus figurine from a late first to early second-century pit located close to a possible shrine at Baldock, Hertfordshire (Stead and Rigby 1986: 168, no. 688, fig. 73); three Type 1/2 figurines from second-to-third-century pits and ditches in field enclosures at Roxton in Bedfordshire (Taylor and Woodward 1983: 20, nos 1–3, fig. 4), another from Shenstone in Staffordshire (Burnham et al. 2002: 309), and two Type 1/2 figurines from the area around the possible temple site at Hawkedon, Suffolk (Franks 1888: 10–12; Jenkins 1977: 353, nos 1–2). All of these could have been offerings of some kind at some point, much like several other figurines from Springhead both in pipeclay (three of Dea Nutrix) and bronze (a dog) that, like the pipeclay figurines at Heybridge found with personal objects, were probably personal offerings as well (Jarrett 2008: 225–7, 264–70).

An insight into the funerary use and meaning of Venus figurines is provided by the 11 finds from cemetery and burial contexts. Like temples, these are mainly located in the south-east (Figure 3.10) with northerly outliers in Brougham and Carlisle; most are associated with urban populations on large and small sites (seven figurines) rather than small rural settlements (four). Unfortunately, five of these figurines are either residual finds or from poorly recorded or undated deposits in cemeteries that tell us little more about exactly how they were used here.[6] There are, however, four figurines from dated cremation and inhumation burials that broadly highlight the continuity of Venus figurine use in changing Romano-British burial practices. The first, and earliest, find

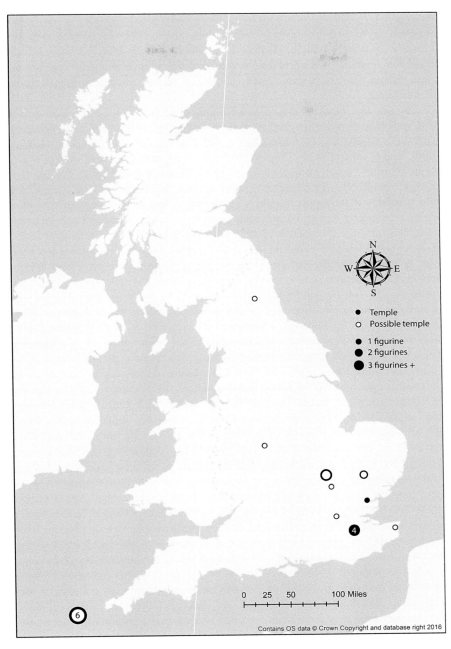

Figure 3.9 The distribution of pipeclay Venus figurines from temple sites in Britain

is a Type 2 Venus from a Hadrianic–Antonine cremation burial in St Albans (Jenkins 1977: 329, no. 4). The other three were found together in an *in situ* mid-third to mid-fourth-century child inhumation (B392) in London's eastern cemetery at Tower Hamlets (Wardle et al. 2000: 188–9, 263). This burial contained the remains of a child inside a lead coffin with a wooden exterior containing a range of other grave goods and three Venus figurines arranged around the head-end.

Although few pipeclay figurines of Venus have been found in child graves, other pipeclay types have, as at Arrington (Taylor 1993), Baldock (Burleigh et al. 2006), possibly Brighton (Kelly and Dudley 1981), Colchester (Eckardt 1999), and Godmanchester (Taylor 1997). It is, of course, difficult to know why Venus figurines were put in the graves of children. One way to shed some light on this would be to consider the genders of these children, but this is unachievable because of the poor condition of the surviving skeletal remains in these burials. Analysing the grave goods in these burials has likewise been inconclusive, with only the cremations at Brighton and Godmanchester tentatively identified as being females based on the limited presence of female-related jewellery such as bangles, beads, and chains accompanying the poorly preserved skeletal remains (see Chapter 7).

Other ideas can be put forward based on the life course of the child, as well as the position of the figurines in the grave and their state of preservation. Crummy (2010), for instance, argues that the position of mother-goddess figurines, as well as other amuletic objects, around the head and body of children in Romano-British graves was an important way of protecting them in the afterlife. This may well have been the sentiment being expressed in the Claudio-Neronian cremation burial in Colchester where 13 figurines (10 "comic and reclining figures", 1 Hercules, a child bust, and a bull) and 10 animal vessels that surrounded the remains of a child could represent the deceased's family unit and the numerous sacrificial animals that guard the family in life and, here, the child in the afterlife (Eckardt 1999: 60–8). Meanwhile, the mid-second-century grave in Godmanchester with figurines of a horse and a bull found either side of a child cremation, as if guarding it, are both sacred animals that were possibly put in the grave as sacrifices to protect the dead infant (Taylor 1997: 390–1). Similar sentiments are also potentially expressed in the fourth-century inhumation burial at Baldock in Hertfordshire where a Dea Nutrix figurine interpreted as prominently positioned on top of a deceased child's chest may well have been placed there to protect them in the afterlife (Burleigh et al. 2006). The intact and unworn condition of the three Venus figurines arranged around one end of burial B392 in London could be interpreted in a similar way, while their age at the time of burial—as much as 200 years old—could also indicate that they may have been regarded as even more important objects, possibly curated heirlooms.

One important aspect that stands out from some of the pipeclay figurines positioned in graves in Britain is the close link they have with sick or diseased children. The remains of the young child in burial B392 in London, who was

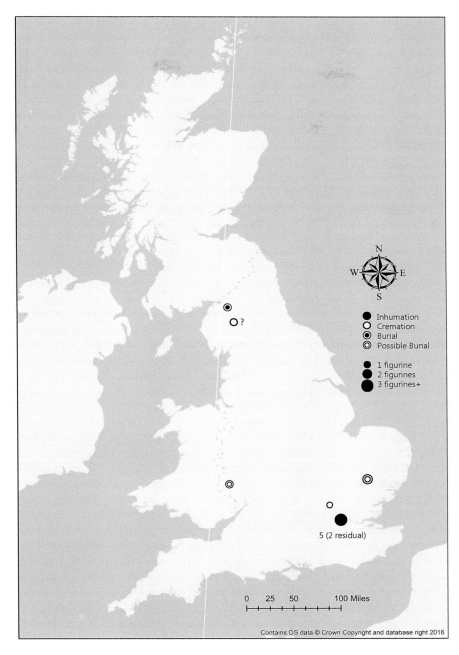

Figure 3.10 The distribution of pipeclay Venus figurines from burials in Britain

approximately six years old upon dental evidence, experienced otherwise stunted skeletal growth (rickets), suggesting that they suffered a significant amount of nutritional and environmental stress (Conheeney 2000: 286). Although no other *in situ* child graves with Venus figurines are known from Britain, there is another grave with other whole and relatively well-preserved pipeclay figurine types positioned prominently around a deceased, diseased, or sick child in the same way. This grave is the mid-second-century inhumation at Arrington in Cambridgeshire where a large selection of figurines including a *Matronae*, a bald-headed infant, a long-haired child, a seated figure, a cloaked figure, two rams, and a bull or ox were placed inside a wooden box on top of a lead-lined wooden coffin, inside of which were the remains of a child with hydrocephalus, otherwise known as water on the brain (Taylor 1993: 194 and 202). It is possible that some of the other child graves with pipeclay figurines in Britain are also those of sick or diseased children, but their poorly surviving osteological evidence makes it hard to know for sure. Nevertheless, the two graves from Arrington and London do indicate that some pipeclay objects found in south-east Britain, including those of Venus, are indeed closely associated with protecting sick children in the afterlife (Fittock 2015: 123–4).

The other important aspect regarding the pipeclay figurines from burials in Britain, that are again mainly in the south-east, is their close association with not just higher-status activity, but also foreigners. This is indicated not just by the structures of these burials but also the relatively opulent grave good assemblages some of them contain. For example, burial B392 in London consisted of a relatively ornate wooden lead-lined coffin with an elaborate decoration made of sea shells that included the Venus figurines and several other objects of Gaulish origin that included a glass dish, a miniature glass bowl, two glass bottles, a pair of gold earrings, a bone pyxis, a gold coin, and an ivory figurine (Wardle et al. 2000: 188–9). Other high-status burials with non-Venus figurines but still types made in Gaul, and other grave goods deemed Gaulish in origin in Britain, include the Colchester Child's Grave with its large object assemblage that included a samian plate, a Gaulish lead-glazed cup, 3 flagons, a feeding bottle, a Lyon ware cup, 2 coarse ware cups, a clay lamp, 2 or 3 glass vessels, 1 bronze patera, 36 coins, and *c*.600 fragments from an ornate funerary couch (Eckardt 1999: 68–78). Another is the mid to late-second-century cremation burial in Brighton, Sussex, containing a selection of pottery and glass vessels, a bronze brooch and box fittings, an iron oil-lamp holder and various iron implements, and vessels (Kelly and Dudley 1981: 83, pls 1A–B, fig. 9). The burial in Godmanchester can also be added to this list because of the position of the cremation within the town's walls and its relative wealth, with its vessels, jewellery, casket, and bull and horse figurines standing out as an importation of Gallo-Belgic traditions into this part of south-east Britain (Taylor 1997: 393). Some Romano-British graves are less opulently adorned but they are still of high status and culturally unusual in composition. For example, the inhumation burial at Arrington is generally considered to be exotic for Cambridgeshire with its mix of Gaulish and Rhine–Moselle-made figurines, its wooden lead-lined coffin, fabrics, and an expensive aromatic resin, possibly incense (Taylor 1993: 203–5 and 207–8); while at Baldock, Hertfordshire, although the grave good assemblage only consists of three small wooden caskets, hobnails, and a pair of leather shoes, it was the only one of 1800 graves in the cemetery to include a pipeclay figurine and was surrounded by a wooden structure that may have publicly displayed the body before it was lowered (Burleigh et al. 2006: 278–82, fig. 8). Consequently, some of the Venus figurines from other residual or uncertain funerary contexts in Britain could therefore have belonged to higher-status foreigners as well.

Graveside rituals inspired by high-status foreign practices are additionally possibly evidenced by the rare Type 4 Venus from Brougham, Cumbria. This figurine was burnt all over and found with a collection of other personal objects including a gold chain and two glass beads, which might have been burnt on a pyre before being deposited as a possible cremation burial in the third or fourth century (Cool 2004: 122, no. 11, fig. 4.95). In her analysis Cool (2004: 464) points out that the rare figurine probably made in Cologne, as well as the relatively rich character of the grave goods found with it, are all suggestive of higher-status Pannonian culture, particularly noting that putting pipeclay figurines on pyres was not a regular Romano-British practice but one that occurred much more often in provinces such as Raetia. Indeed, only a small number of other pipeclay figurines displaying evidence of burning are known from Romano-British cemeteries, affirming the rarity of this practice. This includes the Venus fragment from burial B156 as well as the rare but residual depiction of Juno with soot on its back from the same cemetery (Wardle et al. 2000: 263; Fittock 2015: 115–6, fig. 4d). However, it is unclear as to when or why this burning took place or whether it was a deliberate act or not.

Reconsidering the meaning of pipeclay figurines of Venus in Britain

Overall, not only does the number of pipeclay figurines of Venus in Britain suggest that they were more popular there than other forms and epigraphic mentions of the goddess, but their distribution and the contexts of these "provincialised" objects indicate that their meaning and use also differed from these other "Classical" representations. The latter are rarely found in Britain and are probably more closely associated with her traditional ideas about love and sex than those concerning beliefs about fertility and protection. In this sense, the social and contextual distribution of pipeclay figurines of Venus in Britain suggests that this particular form of the goddess was broadly revered throughout the social spectrum but more generally on urban and rural sites that are typically regarded as being towards the lower end of the social hierarchy. Most of these figurines are from habitation contexts such as pits, ditches, and rubbish deposits before which they may well have been used in domestic shrines, perhaps to protect the household overall, or to encourage fertility (i.e. the conception of children) within it. No pipeclay figurines of Venus have ever been found *in situ* within a household shrine, but this is not to say that these small portable objects could not have been placed around the home and moved between different rooms of a house depending on what they were required for. However, their common recovery from pits, ditches, and refuse deposits on such sites does suggest that many were discarded at some point. This might have occurred once they had fulfilled or failed in their intended purpose, but the higher number from later contexts indicates that the popularity of these figurines markedly declined from the third century. Unfortunately, these contexts provide no detailed information as to the sex and gender of the people who used them, meaning a possible association with men, women, and children.

Although "Classical" depictions and epigraphic dedications to Venus are most often found in religious or ritual contexts in Britain, the distribution of pipeclay figurines in temples and burials contrastingly suggests that their use for such purposes was quite a rare occurrence, and that this practice was mainly concentrated in the south-east of the province. Here, pipeclay figurines of Venus appear to have been dedicated mainly at rural temples that some people probably travelled to specifically to make a dedication, either in temples or near them. Unfortunately, contextual evidence provides little indication of what this practice involved or exactly why people used Venus figurines in this way. I suggest that they were perhaps more formal public votive offerings that people dedicated to the goddess as thanks to her for fulfilling a vow or vows (e.g. Derks 1998: 218–31) and that such vows were probably based on fertility or protective concerns relating to the general health of either individuals or groups of people within families and households.

Furthermore, this analysis has also shown that a relatively small number of pipeclay figurines of Venus were occasionally used by some people for funerary practices in Britain. While most of these figurines are from poor quality residual or disturbed deposits, one burial from London (B392) does offer an unusual insight whereby this assemblage is indicative of how one individual or family used Venus figurines as a way to protect a deceased child with rickets in the afterlife as part of a more personal kind of practice. Other small groups used other pipeclay figurine types for similar purposes in other parts of Britain. Given the usually poor and varied quality of object assemblages from urban and rural sites, the London burial, as well as others in Britain, at the same time offer a useful way to examine further the social status of people that occasionally used pipeclay figurines of Venus and other types in this way. Specifically, these were probably a small group of higher-status Gaulish foreigners who mainly lived in south-eastern Britain.

At this point it is also worth emphasising the contrasting ways in which the Venus figurines from Britain are preserved in funerary and non-funerary contexts and what this might mean. While previous studies have suggested that fragmented figurines may well have been deliberately broken for use as anatomical *ex votos* at sites such as temples (e.g. Ferris 2012: 121, 2014), closer examination of the assemblages from London (Fittock 2015: 125–9) and, more generally, from Britain (Fittock 2017: 394–402) has provided a more detailed picture. As well as highlighting that Venus fragments from whole figurines contrast with the specially made individual limbs that are typically associated with *ex voto* use on the Continent and in Britain, these studies specifically show that most figurines are broken and comprise body parts like the torso and legs. Some of these fragments might be anatomically related to the practices they were used for; some are indeed from temples that may be related to ritual practices. Yet, most are actually from the urban and rural occupation deposits associated with refuse disposal (e.g. pits and ditches) that probably have little to do with ritual activity. The most striking findings, however, are the notable under-representations of heads amongst the assemblage, suggesting that these particular body parts were either being used, or disposed of, in a different way. Moreover, the few whole Venus figurines from the province come exclusively from burials or funerary related contexts, accentuating their significance as possible heirlooms. Further work is needed to determine if there are any significant variations in fragmentation patterns (and practices) between Britain and Continental regions (e.g. Fittock 2015: 128), but experiments on replica figurines have demonstrated that the heads of Venus figurines are more likely to have been deliberately broken off than any of the other lower-body parts found, highlighting their general significance as well (Fittock 2017: 402–14, forthcoming). Consequently, we should arguably now include these absent heads as part of the anatomical *ex voto* discussion, even though we do not yet know exactly what their use was, and consider the possibility that they were used for practices that do not leave strong archaeological traces.

"Whose Venus?" Gaulish origins of Romano-British practice

Having identified the various practices for which pipeclay figurines of Venus were used in Britain, there is significant evidence to suggest that their origins mainly lay in the closer cross-channel connections that Britain had with Gaul than any other province. The most obvious indication of this is that most of the figurines found in Britain are types that were made in and are regularly found in Gaul (i.e. Types 1, 2, 3, 5, and 6, as well as one of the Type 4 figurines). Another indication of this comes in the form of the overall number of finds from other Continental regions whereby the 401 figurines from Britain are most closely matched by those from France (275 as per Rouvier-Jeanlin 1972), while far fewer figurines have been found in Belgium ($t = 155$, Beenhouwer 2005: 426–528), the Netherlands ($t = 36$, van Boekel 1987: 496–551), and Switzerland ($t = 28$, von Gonzenbach 1995: 101–30). Overall, the much higher number of 401 figurines from Britain therefore suggests that Venus may well have been relatively more popular there than anywhere else. In addition, although they all probably generally relate to similar beliefs, the number of each respective type in each region—and the possible slight variances in beliefs they might reflect—also suggests that the popularity of these differed in each region, even between Britain and Gaul. Here, for instance, not only are Type 1 figurines more common in France and Type 2 figurines more common in Britain, but the low numbers of Types 3, 4, 5, and 6 in Britain generally suggest that they were much less popular there. This is also true of the small selection of types made in the Rhine–Moselle region that are likewise rare in Britain (Types 7, 8, 9, and the one Type 4 figurine from Brougham), as well as the region in which they were produced.

Such cross-channel connections in practice can also be seen though the similar contexts in which pipeclay figurines of Venus are generally found throughout Britain and the Continent. Although there are very few comprehensively up-to-date studies of the site types and deposits they come from, a general review of the data available from the aforementioned Continental catalogues shows that, by and large, pipeclay figurines of Venus mainly are from the same kind of sites and deposits, and were therefore used in similar ways, as they were in Britain. In France, the Netherlands, Belgium, and Switzerland, the highest proportion are from the occupation of settlements with deposits mainly in pits, ditches, and refuse suggesting use in household shrines, and a smaller proportion of finds from religious contexts such as temples and, least often, burials. It is this burial evidence, however, which provides us with some evidence that Venus figurines were perhaps used slightly differently for funerary practices on the Continent. Significantly, this appears to show that they, as well as other mother-goddess types associated with protection and healing, such as Dea Nutrix, were found in burials and tombs of both adults and children (e.g. Rouvier-Jeanlin 1972: 32; Allain et al. 1992: 170–2; Burleigh et al. 2006: 286) rather than just the latter. There also seems to be a further distinction within the context of children specifically, whereby although several figurines of Venus have been found placed prominently around the head of the deceased in a protective manner in France, this practice appears to apply more to new-born infants rather than older children (Carroll 2018: 114–16). A good example of such practice are the three graves with figurines of Venus and Dea Nutrix found in the Roman cemetery at Argenton in France that was in use from the second century (Allain et al. 1992: 52–3, 170, figs 36, 64, and 95, fig. 27). The health status of many Continental graves is unclear, but it is therefore possible that the small group of people who buried pipeclay figurines of Venus and other depictions with sometimes sick and diseased post-newborn children in the second and third centuries in London, Arrington and the south-east did so as part of a more individualised or even regionalised practice, but one still based on religious beliefs and funerary rites originating in Gaul.

Conclusion

This chapter shows that an analysis of typology and context can shed light on the nature of religious practice and hint at both gendered and provincial beliefs. Although popular in Classical contexts as the goddess of love and sex, the occurrence and meaning of classicising Venus imagery is relatively rare in Roman Britain where she most commonly occurs in the form of pipeclay figurines. Symbolically, the origins of and inspiration for these figurines may well lie in the Classical monumental, artistic, and figurative depictions of

Venus that traditionally associate the goddess with love and sex but importantly, the depictions of Venus in pipeclay generally appear to be more "provincial" in style than the other depictions of the goddess in regions such as Britain, Gaul, and the Rhine–Moselle where, given their contexts, they probably reflect a slightly different set of beliefs associated with fertility and protection. However, there are several typological varieties that might reflect the slightly different beliefs of some people in Britain, some of which are rare types from Gaul and the Rhine–Moselle region that are more likely to have been brought to the province by individual incomers. The various quantities of these different types in Britain and across the Continent also suggest that the figurines, as well as the beliefs and practices of the people associated with them, had closer cultural and religious connections with Gaul than any other western province.

The detailed analysis examining the chronology, social distribution, and contexts of Venus figurines in this chapter reveals more about how and why they were used in Roman Britain. This has shown that these figurines were mainly used by civilians and only rarely by military and rural populations throughout the province. They appear to have been used most often in habitation settings where they were probably used in household shrines to protect family members (whether young or old) and encourage fertility before they were thrown away into the pits, ditches, and rubbish deposits they are now most commonly found in. However, there is no strong indication from these contexts or the broad range of goods sometimes found with them that they were used primarily or exclusively by women, and I would suggest that they could represent the beliefs and practices of both men and women. The popularity of Venus figurines increased over time, peaking in the third century when their involvement in religious practices became more prevalent in that they appear more often in temples where some may be deliberately broken *ex votos*. Whole figurines also began to appear more rarely as protective funerary symbols for guarding and protecting the deceased in the afterlife, and many could have been heirlooms. An examination of grave goods suggests that this was quite a high-status practice mainly carried out by foreigners from Gaul and occasionally the Rhine–Moselle region. Further study of this particular practice on the Continent is still needed, but comparison with Continental graves does further suggest that some Venus figurines in Britain were part of a regionalised south-eastern Romano-British practice of using them in the graves of sick or diseased children.

Finally, comparing the different styles and contextual distributions of pipeclay and metal figurines of Venus in Britain has the potential to reveal further nuances in their symbolic meaning and social status. As well as being more "Classical", finely executed depictions in more valuable material, the limited social distribution of metal Venus figurines on mainly *civitas* capitals, compared to the wider distribution of pipeclay figurines, overall highlights that metal figurines of the goddess were probably higher-status objects than their pipeclay counterparts. Both appear to have been used in similar ways on such sites, but the overall rarity of metal Venuses and their scarcity in temples and burials does point towards their higher value.

Acknowledgements

Greatest thanks, of course, goes to the editors for the invitation to write this contribution and for their comments, as well as those of the reviewer, that improved the final piece. I extend special thanks to Dr Hella Eckardt (University of Reading) who commented on an earlier draft of this text and has supported my studies over many years, as well as the numerous museum curators, assistants, and archivists who provided access to the figurines themselves and gave permission to use images of them. A grant kindly provided by the Roman Finds Group contributed towards photography of some Venus types. Finally, this chapter includes work carried out as part of a PhD on the pipeclay figurines from Roman Britain that was kindly funded by the AHRC South, West and Wales Doctoral Training Partnership and additionally supervised by Dr Martin Pitts (University of Exeter), to both of whom I offer gratitude for their support.

Notes

1 A small range of different types was also made in the Rhine–Moselle region from the mid-first to third centuries. See van Boekel (1987: 203–16) for a useful summary of these production regions, as well as the respective growth and decline of these industries, as well as Higgins (1976) and again van Boekel (1987: 216–31) for descriptions of the manufacturing processes including moulding techniques.
2 See Durham (2012) for the full collection of *c.*1000 metal figurines found in Britain, specifically section 3.31 on Venus figurines, as well as Durham (2014: 197–8), fig. 2, no. 1; see also Fittock (2017: 180–94 and 288–316) for a detailed analysis of this topic with regards to all of the metal and pipeclay figurine types in Britain.
3 See Durham (2012) for the metal figurines from *civitas* capitals: ID 1181 (Caerwent), IDs 132–4 (St Albans), IDs 686, 397, and 400 (Wroxeter), ID 338 (Silchester); for *colonia* IDs 136, 138–40 (Colchester), ID 305 (York)). Interestingly, only three metal Venus figurines are known from London (Durham 2012, IDs 131, 144, and 339).
4 In a slightly different configuration than my unpublished PhD (Fittock 2017) in order to account for this.
5 We can even add to this the Type 4 Venus from Brougham (Cumbria) that also comes from an area that was disturbed to some extent by later activity.
6 A Type 2 Venus at Kenchester, Herefordshire, see Jack and Hayter (1926: pl. 35) and Jenkins (1977: 328, no. 1); the two Type 1/2 figurines from Hawkedon, Suffolk; an unknown type from Carlisle, see Haverfield (1900: 504, pl. 1) and Jenkins (1977: 322, no. 2); and two Type 1/2 Venuses from London: one at Clare Street and another from the residual fill of inhumation burial B156 at Tower Hamlets, see (Wardle et al. 2000: 262–3).

Bibliography

Allain, J., Fauduet, I. and Tuffreau-Libre, M.E. (1992). *La Nécropole Gallo-Romaine du "Champs de l'Image" à Argentomagus (Saint-Marcel, Indre)*. Mémoire du Musée d'Argentomagus 1. Saint-Marcel: Revue Archéologique Centre France supplément 3.

Allason-Jones, A. and McKay, B. (1985). *Coventina's Well. A Shrine on Hadrian's Wall.* Gloucester: Alan Sutton Publishing.

Allason-Jones, L. (1988). "The Small Finds", in M.C. Bishop and J.N. Dore (eds), *Corbridge: Excavations of the Roman Fort and Town, 1947–80*. London: Historic Buildings and Monuments Commission for England, Archaeological Report 8, 159–218.

Allason-Jones, L. and Miket, R. (1984). *The Catalogue of Small Finds from South Shields Roman Fort*. Newcastle upon Tyne. Tyne and Wear: Society of Antiquaries of Newcastle upon Tyne Monograph Series.

Atkinson, M. and Preston, S.J. (2015). "Heybridge: A Late Iron Age and Roman Settlement. Excavations at Elms Farm 1993–5. Volume 2", *Internet Archaeology*, 40 doi:10.11141/ia.40.1 [accessed 17.05.2016].

Beard, M., North, J. and Price, S. (1998). *Religions of Rome, Volume 1. A History*. Cambridge: Cambridge University Press.

Beenhouwer, J. (2005). *De Gallo-Romeinse Terracottastatuetten van Belgische Vindplaatsen in het Ruimer Kader van de Noordwest-Europese Terracotta-Industrie*. Leuven: Katholieke Universiteit.

Bémont, C., Lahanier, C. and Rouvier-Jeanlin, M. (1993). *Les Figurines En Terre Cuite Gallo-Romaines*. Paris: Éditions de la Maison des sciences de l'homme, Documents d'archéologie française 38.

Birley, A.R. (2016). "The Complexity of Intramural and Extramural Relationships on the Northern Frontier of Roman Britain—A Vindolanda Case Study", in S. Hoss and A. Whitmore (eds), *Small Finds and Ancient Social Practices in the Northwest Provinces of the Roman Empire*. Oxford: Oxbow Books, 146–73.

Brain, C. (2016). "Venus in Pompeian Domestic Space: Decoration and Context", in R. Cascino, F. de Stefano, A. Lepone and C.M. Marchetti (eds), *TRAC 2016. Proceedings of the Twenty-Sixth Annual Theoretical Roman Archaeology Conference, Rome 2016*. Oxford: Oxbow Books, 51–66.

Bristow, J. (2012). "Evidence for Small-Scale Religious Practices in Roman Hampshire? Using Pipe-Clay Figurines as Disposable Devotional Objects", *Hampshire Field Club and Archaeological Society Newsletter*, 57: 15–16.

Burleigh, G., Fitzpatrick-Matthews, K. and Aldhouse-Green, M.J. (2006). "Dea Nutrix Figurine from a Romano-British Cemetery at Baldock, Hertfordshire", *Britannia*, 37: 273–94.

Burnham, B.C., Hunter, F., Fitzpatrick, A.P., Hassall, M.W.C. and Tomlin, R.S.O. (2002). "Roman Britain in 2001", *Britannia*, 33: 275–371.

Butcher, S. (2000–1). "Roman Nornour, Isles of Scilly: A Reconsideration", *Cornish Archaeology*, 39–40: 5–44.

Carroll, M. (2018). *Infancy and Earliest Childhood in the Roman World*. Oxford: Oxford University Press.

Carter, G.A. (1998). *Excavations at the Orsett 'Cock' Enclosure, Essex, 1976*. Chelmsford: Essex County Council.

Conheeney, J. (2000). "Inhumation Burials", in B. Barber and D. Bowsher (eds), *The Eastern Cemetery of Roman London: Excavations 1983–1990*. London: Museum of London Archaeology Service Monograph 4, 277–97.

Cool, H.E.M. (2004). *The Roman Cemetery at Brougham, Excavations 1966–67*. Britannia Monograph Series, 21. London: Society for the Promotion of Roman Studies.

Crummy, N. (2010). "Bears and Coins: The Iconography of Protection in Late Roman Infant Burials", *Britannia*, 41: 37–93.

Crummy, N. and With Pohl, C. (2008). "Small Toilet Instruments from London: A Review of the Evidence", in: J. Clark, J. Cotton, J. Hall, R. Sherris and H. Swain (eds), *Londinium and Beyond: Essays for Harvey Sheldon*. York: Council for British Archaeology Research Report 156, 212–25.

Dawson, M. (2004). *Archaeology in the Bedford Region*. British Archaeological Reports British Series 373. Oxford: Archaeopress.

Derks, T. (1998). *Gods, Temples and Ritual Practices*. Amsterdam Archaeological Studies 2. Amsterdam: Amsterdam University Press.

Down, A. (1989). *Chichester Excavations 6*. Chichester: Phillimore, for Chichester District Council.

Drakeman, C. (2008). *Portable Goddesses: The Use and Significance of Pipeclay Figurines of Venus in the Northern Roman Provinces from the First-Third Centuries CE*. Unpublished PhD Thesis, University of Oxford.

Durham, E. (2012). "Depicting the Gods: Metal Figurines in Roman Britain", *Internet Archaeology*, 31. http://intarch.ac.uk/journal/issue31/durham_index.html [accessed 08.01.2014].

Durham, E. (2014). "Style and Substance: Some Metal Figurines from South-West Britain", *Britannia*, 45: 195–221.

Eckardt, H. (1999). "The Colchester Child's Grave", *Britannia*, 30: 57–90.

Eckardt, H. (2002). *Illuminating Roman Britain*. Monographies Instrumentum 23. Montagnac: Instrumentum.

Eckardt, H. (2005). "The Social Distribution of Roman Artefacts: The Case of Nail-Cleaners and Brooches in Britain", *Journal of Roman Archaeology*, 18: 139–60.

Eckardt, H. and Crummy, N. (2008). *Styling the Body in Late Iron Age and Roman Britain. A Contextual Approach to Toilet Instruments*. Monographies Instrumentum 36. Montagnac: Instrumentum.

Evans, E. (2000). *The Caerleon Canabae: Excavations in the Civil Settlement 1984–90*. London: Society for the Promotion of Roman Studies.

Fadden, K.J. (2010). *Report on Romano-British Artefacts Found on the Surface of Ruxox Farm in the County of Bedfordshire*. Ampthill and District Archaeological and Local History Society. www.adalhs.mooncarrot.org.uk/reports.php [accessed 12.01.2015].

Ferris, I. (2012). *Roman Britain through its Objects*. Stroud: Amberley.

Ferris, I. (2014). "A Pipeclay Pseudo-Venus Figurine from Binchester Roman Fort, County Durham", in R. Collins and F. McIntosh (eds), *Life in the Limes: Studies of the People and Objects of the Roman Frontiers*. Oxford: Oxbow Books, 105–08.

Fittock, M.G. (2015). "Broken Deities: The Pipeclay Figurines from Roman London", *Britannia*, 46: 111–34.

Fittock, M.G. (2017). *Fragile Gods. Ceramic Figurines in Roman Britain*. Unpublished PhD thesis, University of Reading.

Fittock, M.G. (forthcoming). "Off with their Heads! Broken Figurines and Religious Practice in Roman Britain", in L.A. Graña Nicolaou, T. Ivleva and B. Griffiths (eds), *The Role of Experimentation in Roman Archaeology: Methods and Approaches to Testing Theoretical Hypotheses*. Sheffield: Equinox.

Franks, A.W. (1888). "Remarks upon an Amphora and Two Figures, Found at Hawkedon, January, 1880", *Proceedings of the Suffolk Institute of Archaeology*, 6: 10–12.

Franzen, P. (2006). "The Nijmegen Canabae Legionis (71–102/105 AD). Military and Civilian Life on the Frontier", in Á. Morillo, N. Hanel and E.M. Hernández (eds), *Limes XX. Roman Frontier Studies*. Leon: Anejos de Gladius, 13, 1271–83.

Fulford, M. (1989). "A Roman Shipwreck off Nornour, Isles of Scilly?", *Britannia*, 20: 245–49.

Green, M.J. (1986). *The Gods of the Celts*. Gloucester: Alan Sutton.

Havelock, C.M. (1995). *The Aphrodite of Knidos and Her Successors. A Historical Review of the Female Nude in Greek Art*. Ann Arbor, MI: The University of Michigan Press.

Haverfield, F. (1900). "Romano-Gaulish Statuette Found in Carlisle", *Transactions of the Cumberland and Westmorland Antiquarian and Archaeological Society*, 15: 503–5.

Henig, M. (2015). "Figural Bronzes", in M. Atkinson and S.J. Preston (eds), Heybridge: A Late Iron Age and Roman Settlement, Excavations at Elms Farm 1993–5, *Internet Archaeology*. 40. doi:10.11141/ia.40.1.henig1 [accessed 17.05.2016].

Higgins, R.A. (1976). "Terracottas", in D. Strong and D. Brown (eds), *Roman Crafts*. Hampshire: Duckworth, 105–09.

Jack, G.H. and Hayter, A.G.K. (1926). *Excavations on the Site of the Romano-British Town of Magna, Kenchester, Herefordshire, 2: 1924–5*. Transactions of the Woolhope Naturalist's Field Club Report of the Excavations at Kenchester. Hereford: Jake and Carver.

James, A. (2009). *The Field of Figurines. How Significant is the Assemblage of Roman Pipeclay Figurines in the Interpretation of Occupation from a Farm at Ruxox in Bedfordshire?* Unpublished BA thesis, University of Reading.

Jarrett, R. (2008). *Reappraising Penn and Harker: A Reassessment of the Finds from Excavations at Roman Springhead, Published between 1957 and 1984, and Interpretations Made about Their Use in Past Activities*. Unpublished PhD Thesis, University of Durham.

Jenkins, F. (1958). "The Cult of the 'Pseudo-Venus' in Kent", *Archaeologia Cantiana*, 72: 60–76.

Jenkins, F. (1969). "Romano-Gaulish Clay Figurines Found in London", *Latomus*, 103: 312–27.

Jenkins, F. (1977). *Clay Statuettes of the Roman Western Provinces*. Unpublished PhD Thesis, University of Kent.

Jenkins, F. (1978). "Some Interesting Types of Clay Statuettes of the Roman Period Found in London", in J. Bird, H. Chapman and J. Clark (eds), *Collectanea Londiniensia: Studies in London Archaeology and History Presented to Ralph Merrifield*. London: London and Middlesex Archaeological Society, 148–62.

Johns, C. (1996). *The Jewellery of Roman Britain: Celtic and Classical Traditions*. London and New York: Routledge.

Jones, B. and Mattingly, D.J. (2002). *An Atlas of Roman Britain*. Oxford: Oxbow Books.

Kaufmann-Heinimann, A. (1977). *Die Römischen Bronzen der Schweiz I. Augst und das Gebiet der Colonia Augusta Raurica*. Mainz: Zabern.

Kelly, E. and Dudley, C. (1981). "Two Romano-British Burials", *Sussex Archaeological Collections*, 119: 65–88.

Lloyd-Morgan, G. (1986). "Roman Venus: Public Worship and Private Rites", in M. Henig and A. King (eds), *Pagan Gods and Shrines of the Roman Empire*. Oxford University Committee for Archaeology Monograph 8. Oxford: Oxford University Committee for Archaeology, 179–88.

Mason, D.J.P. (1987). "Chester: The Canabae Legionis", *Britannia*, 18: 143–68.

Menzel, H. (1966). *Die Römischen Bronzen aus Deutschland. II Trier*. Mainz: Zabern.

Merrifield, R. (1995). "Roman Metalwork from the Walbrook—Rubbish, Ritual or Redundancy?", *Transactions of the London and Middlesex Archaeological Society*, 46: 27–44.

Orlin, E. (2007). "Urban Religion in the Middle and Late Republic", in J. Rüpke (ed.), *A Companion to Roman Religion*. Malden, MA: Blackwell, 58–70.

Penn, W.S. (1959). "The Romano-British Settlement at Springhead; Excavation of Temple I, Site C1", *Archaeologia Cantiana*, 73: 1–61.

Rankov, N.B., Hassall, M.W.C. and Tomlin, R.S.O. (1982). "Roman Britain in 1981", *Britannia*, 13: 327–422.

Rayner, L., Wardle, A. and Seeley, F. (2011). "Ritual and Religion", in J. Hill and P. Rowsome (eds), *Roman London and the Walbrook Stream Crossing: Excavations at 1 Poultry and Vicinity, City of London*. London: Museum of London Archaeology Monograph 37, 404–08.

Rouvier-Jeanlin, M. (1972). *Les Figurines Gallo-Romaines en Terre Cuite au Musées des Antiquités Nationales*. Paris: Éditions du Centre National de la Recherche Scientifique.

Rouvier-Jeanlin, M. (1986). *Figurines Gallo-Romaines En Terre Cuite. Musée Archéologique Dijon Tentoonstellingscataloog*. Dijon: Musée archéologique.

Shepherd, J. (1998). *The Temple of Mithras, London. Excavations by W.F. Grimes and A. Williams at the Walbrook*. London: English Heritage.

Simco, A. (1984). *Survey of Bedfordshire: The Roman Period*. Bedford: Bedfordshire County Council.

Smith, A., Allen, M., Brindle, T. and Fulford, M. (2016). *The Rural Settlement of Roman Britain*. Britannia Monograph 29. London: Society for the Promotion of Roman Studies.

Smith, D.J. (1980). "Mosaics", in I.M. Stead (ed.), *Rudston Roman Villa*. Leeds: Yorkshire Archaeological Society, 131–38.

Stead, I.M. and Rigby, V. (1986). *Baldock: The Excavation of a Roman and Pre-Roman Settlement, 1968–72*. Britannia Monograph 7. London: Society for the Promotion of Roman Studies.

Taylor, A. (1993). "A Roman Lead Coffin with Pipeclay Figurines from Arrington, Cambridgeshire", *Britannia*, 24: 191–225.

Taylor, A. (1997). "A Roman Child Burial with Animal Figurines and Pottery, from Godmanchester, Cambridgeshire", *Britannia*, 28: 386–93.

Taylor, A. and Woodward, P. (1983). "Excavations at Roxton, Bedfordshire, 1972–74: The Post-Bronze Age Settlement", *Bedfordshire Archaeology*, 16: 7–28.

van Boekel, G.M.E.C. (1987). *Roman Terracotta Figurines and Masks from the Netherlands*. Groningen: Rijksuniversiteit te Groningen.

Vertet, H. and Vuillemot, G. (1973). *Figurines Gallo-Romaines En Argile d'Autun*. Autun: Musée Rolin.

von Gonzenbach, V. (1995). *Die römischen Terracotten in der Schweiz: Untersuchungen zu Zeitstellung, Typologie und Ursprung der mittelgallischen Tonstatuetten, Band A*. Basel: Bern.

Wardle, A. (1998). "The Small Objects", in J. Shepherd (ed.), *The Temple of Mithras, London. Excavations by W.F. Grimes and A. Williams at the Walbrook*. London: English Hertitage, 110–207.

Wardle, A. (2011). "Finds from the Walbrook Deposits", in J. Hill and P. Rowsome (eds), *Roman London and the Walbrook Stream Crossing. Excavations at 1 Poultry and Vicinity, City of London, Part II*. Museum of London Monograph 37. London: Museum of London, 329–49.

Wardle, A., Shepherd, J., Symonds, R., Riddler, I., Lloyd-Morgan, G. and Hammerson, M. (2000). "Catalogue", in B. Barber and D. Bowsher (eds), *The Eastern Cemetery of Roman London: Excavations 1983–1990*. Museum of London Archaeology Service Monograph 4. London: Museum of London, 142–263.

Webster, J. (1997). "Necessary Comparisons: A Post-Colonial Approach to Religious Syncretism in the Roman Provinces", *World Archaeology*, 28: 3, 324–38.

Webster, J. (2001). "Creolizing the Roman Provinces", *American Journal of Archaeology*, 105: 209–25.

4 His and hers

Magic, materiality, and sexual imagery

Adam Parker

A magical introduction

The expansion of the Roman Empire into north-west Europe brought with it many things social, religious, economic, and material—and all at different speeds in differing locations. The material culture of the Roman world included types of objects depicting disembodied sexual parts, both male and female, which were largely absent from the material culture of the Late Iron Age communities they encountered. From the earliest days of its expansion into the north-west and across the sea into Britannia these objects became present in the archaeological record of the areas which would become the north-west provinces. Focussing on the Roman material culture of these periods, largely in the Imperial period, offers an opportunity to discuss the nature, use, and materiality of these enigmatic, understudied, and sometimes challenging objects.

The focus of this chapter is to discuss the broad nature, range, and implications of sexual imagery in Roman Britain in terms of its apotropaic functionality and some of the important contextual interpretations, observations, and speculations regarding connections between materials and magical practices.

The potential benefits that could be gained by an application of material-focused approaches to the study of Roman magic are vast. Curse tablets, phallic amulets, inscribed gemstones, and other magical objects were all ascribed with agency by those who used them, in that these objects were believed to have the ability to influence the real world, for better or for worse (McKie and Parker 2018: 5). At its absolute core, materiality is an analysis of things: tangible, substantial objects that existed in the real world. It is concerned with how and why things are made, the materials that constitute them, the technology required to produce them, and the manners in which things relate to people, places, ideas, memories, social structures, and so on (Tilley et al. 2006: 4). The field of material culture studies, which had its genesis in the dialogue between archaeology, anthropology, and a number of social sciences, has grown out of a central concern for the place. The implications of materiality for the study of Roman magic is based on the importance of the materials and their connections to context; the times, places, and ways in which they were used mattered a great deal for their efficacy (McKie and Parker 2018: 5). Thus, these issues should also matter a great deal for their modern interpretation.

The study of Roman magical theory and thought, certainly since its re-emergence on the academic scene in the latter part of the twentieth century, has become entrenched in the study of Classics and literature (Otto 2013: 308), with artefactual studies often given only a cursory or secondary role in the interpretation of Roman magic (McKie and Parker 2018: 1). There are a wide range of modern approaches to take in order to define what "magic" is, its relationship to religion, and how this might affect our interpretations of material culture in the Roman world. There is definitely a trend towards rejecting rigid conceptual definitions in favour of promoting a general holistic definition of "magic", helpfully linking it to the allied areas of religion and medicine (e.g. Merrifield 1987: 6–9; Bailliot 2015: 94; Bremmer 2015: 11; Chadwick 2015: 37–8; McKie 2016: 23). Coming at the fore of the material turn of magic, Merrifield's (1987: 6) definition is one of the widest used and most utilitarian:

> Religion is used to indicate the belief in supernatural or spiritual beings; "magic", the use of practices intended to bring occult forces under control and so to influence events; "ritual", prescribed or customary behaviour that may be religion if it is intended to placate supernatural beings, magical if it is intended to operate through impersonal forces of sympathy or by controlling supernatural beings.

Influenced by this and the theoretical work of Versnel (1991: 178), I have previously proposed my own definition of magic which does define the concept and incorporates many of its functionalist, theoretical elements into a more technical form (Parker 2016: 109).

This definition is used implicitly throughout the following discussion. For the sake of clarity though, if one were to distil the nature and essence of what is here described as "magical", the end result would be a wide-ranging series of objects, materials, images, and words, which are used in both simple and complex ritual practices throughout the Roman world in order to achieve one main goal: protection. Protection of the self, of the family, of a place, of social interests, either in life or in death, is the central concept to what magic was. This was, perhaps, best exemplified in the depiction of sexual imagery. Both phallic and vulvate imagery, as human sexual parts depicted divorced from the rest of the body, were potent and efficacious amulets. These sexual images could be worn upon the body as pendants or finger rings, upon harnesses for both people and animals, and were available in a range of materials. They could be scribbled or carved onto stone, used to decorate the home, or adorn cutlery or weapons. Phallic and vulvate imagery clearly held a place of significance in the Roman world, but this was not a single cohesive expression of magical practice. It was a context specific, individualised, and variable practice constituting many everyday aspects of material culture.

Ladies and gentlemen

To begin then, this section provides a general outline to the types of such objects which may be encountered.

Phallic forms

The evidence for phallic imagery serving a protective or apotropaic function comes to us from both Classical sources (Varro *De Lingua Latina* 7.97; Aristophanes *Achanians* 241; Pliny the Elder *Natural History* 28.7) and from the material evidence. Most clearly, the phallus was depicted as one of the main enemies of the Evil Eye (Turnbull 1978: 199–200). The Eye is the Roman embodiment of bad luck and was both feared and respected (Plutarch *Quaest. Conv.* 5.7); any object, image, act, or ritual designed to deflect or nullify its effects aims to promote good luck or good health (as the antithesis to the negative effects of the Eye) and may thus be called apotropaic. There are two slightly differing representations of the Eye, and in both cases it is under attack from its "enemies" (otherwise describable as "apotropaic symbols"). The most common depiction of the Eye and phalli together is when it is under attack as part of the "all suffering eye" scene, for example on a mosaic from the *House of the Evil Eye* at Antioch, a carved stone relief from Leptis Magna (Johns 1982, fig. 77), and a gold earring from Norfolk (Worrell and Pearce 2014, no. 20, fig. 20)—all these examples include a phallus as one of the enemies of the Evil Eye. The second type of representation shows only the phallus attacking an Evil Eye one-on-one and often in a very biological way, involving the phallus ejaculating over or towards an Eye (Figure 4.1). These visual topoi can be seen throughout the Roman world, demonstrating a shared cultural understanding in both the dangers posed to human health by the Eye and the imagery by which it may be deflected.

An issue of this narrative was best described by Johns (1982: 66): "It is often completely ambiguous in cases where both eyes and phallus are represented, whether the phallus is supposed to be overpowering the Evil Eye, or whether the eye motif is itself performing an apotropaic function". As a case in point, a second-century gold figurine depicting Phthonos, the Greek personification of Envy (an alternative personification of the qualities of the Evil Eye according to Dasen (2015: 184, pl. 9)), was depicted with a large, stylised phallus. In this example it is unclear whether the phallus was defending or supporting the figure of Phthonos in a positive way or somehow working together with the deity.

Turning to the province in hand, the most frequently encountered representation of the phallus in Roman Britain is when it was used as an icon on an object of personal adornment. Varro (*De Ling. Lat.* 7.97) and Pliny (*Nat. Hist.* 28.7) described it as an image designed to be worn or suspended, and by the time it reaches Britain this use of the phallic imagery is something with a historic pedigree to it. We know that it was also used in similar ways during

Figure 4.1 A carving from Leptis Magna depicting a zoomorphic phallus ejaculating towards ("attacking") a disembodied eye

(© Sasha Coachman via Wikimedia Commons [CC By Attribution SA 3.0])

the Republican period (Johns 1982: 62; Deschler-Erb and Božič 2002). It is worth noting that whilst we have very little secure chronological dating for the development of the phallic image in its various forms, the depiction of a flaccid phallus in bone appears to be something which has become unfashionable by the time the northern frontiers of the Empire are firmly established (see Chapter 11). Thus, in the vast majority of depictions in its imperial-era form, the phallus is ithyphallic (erect), with flaccid examples much rarer.[1]

On objects of personal adornment phallic imagery appears as pendants with suspension loops (an amorphous grouping not yet broken up by typological discussion) made from gold (PAS: SWYOR-E56143; ESS-0CDDC1), copper alloy (PAS: LIN-9DF6E7; SF-5B3285), and bone (PAS: SF-EE7435). It is used on harness pendants (PAS: NLM-AABF51) and strap fittings (PAS: LVPL1746), hair pins (PAS: DUR-6FDBA2), finger rings (Johns 1982, pl. 10), and seal box lids (PAS: HAMP-069741; Andrews 2012: 102–3), in amber (Johns 1982, pl. 10), or on deer antler pendants (Greep 1994: 81–2). What these myriad examples show, as a group, is that there were multiple ways of physically suspending an apotropaic phallus about a body (Figure 4.2). Perhaps the one shared quality of all of these object types is that they were overt, physical

Figure 4.2 Variability in the form and medium of phalli, as depicted on objects of personal adornment. Clockwise from top left: copper alloy mount from Brough St.Giles, North Yorkshire (PAS: DUR-F4D1F7); gold pendant from Knaresborough, North Yorkshire (PAS: SWYOR-E56143); gold finger ring with a phallus on the bezel from Wing, Buckinghamshire (PAS: BUC-C9CEE4); winged phallus from Wetheringsett-cum-Brockford, Suffolk (PAS: SF-EE7435); seal-box lid with riveted and enamelled phallus from Kings Worthy, Hampshire (PAS: HAMP-069741); antler roundel with stylised phallus carved into front face from Dowgate, City of London (PAS: LON-791EC5)

things—visibility was an important quality for the efficacy of the apotropaic phallus. Indeed, this idea stands to reason when we consider its enemy, the Evil Eye: it was a human-shaped eye with the ability to fix its gaze on the unwary so, logically, whatever device deflects it also needed to be seen.

The same logic applied to phalli carved and incised in stone (e.g. Coulston and Phillips 1988, nos 405–7, 447, 457, 529) or shown in barbotine relief on ceramics (Webster 1989: 9) because these too were overt, publicly visible spaces. Whilst there are no examples of the (in)famous *tintinnabula* from a secure Romano-British context (though there is one tentative candidate: see

Parker 2018: 63), these objects are found elsewhere in the Empire (Blazquez 1985). This extensive variation in the phallic form is incredibly important in understanding its role in the apotropaic toolkit of Roman Britain because it was an image that could easily be adapted onto different types of objects.

Thinking semiotically about the phallus, at its most simple or abstract it may be represented by a single line and two circles. Even as a three-dimensional object it may be simply represented by a cylindrical tube with two globular appendages at one end, or, even, just as a cylindrical tube. The artistic addition of a glans, foreskin, or urinary meatus (themselves, potentially, only by the addition of simple incised lines) onto such an object removes any doubt as to what it represented, but such additions are not necessarily required for an understanding of the image or symbol to be transferred to its viewer (see Chapter 5, Appendix 5.1 and Figure 5.1).

One problem that we may encounter when discussing phallic imagery is the question of whether depictions of phalli in their usual anatomical positions upon the mammalian body share this protective quality, or whether it is only disembodied phalli that can provide protection. For example, in the former category we might consider an incised graffito of an ithyphallic horse from Birdoswald (Wilmott 1997: 319) and depictions of the god Priapus, who is depicted in stone at Vindolanda (Birley 2007: 142) and wooden statuary (Johns 1982: 50) as well as in small metal figurines (Durham 2012, 3.17). In these examples there is no clear relationship of the good versus evil narrative, and the anatomical correctness, perhaps, removes some of the supernatural efficacy of the totemic, disembodied phallus. Were all phallic images simply an avatar of Priapus and his prominent appendage or does Priapus himself simply harness the protective power of the phallus? We cannot be sure, but the material evidence reveals that the ithyphallic, disembodied phalli were more commonly encountered as small finds than their anatomically embodied cousins. Priapus was a fertility god, particularly responsible for the fecundity of nature, and was associated with gardens and farms (Johns 1982: 50). His function was primarily associated with protecting organic growth rather than supernatural protection of people, but there is clearly a relationship between the two concepts.

Varro's description of the object type as being hung around the necks of boys presents the phallic image as being associated with both the male sex and the protection of youth and to these two temporal categories we can add a social one—a circumstantial relationship with the military in the north-west provinces. The archaeological evidence from Britain that supports Varro's comments regarding infancy includes: a group of six fist-and-phallus pendants associated with the grave of an un-sexed infant from Catterick, North Yorkshire (Parker 2015); a very small, winged phallic pendant included as one of a number of grave goods from a child (probably infant) inhumation at Butt Road, Colchester (Crummy 1983: 58; Crummy 2010: 46–7); a casket burial, also from Colchester, including a phallic pendant amongst other personal ornaments (Philpott 1991: 161). Phallic pendants are also known from a child's inhumation in a lead coffin from St Albans and the grave of an (adult?) male at Guilden Morden,

Cambridgeshire (Philpott 1991: 161). The use of phallic images on military dress accessories and fittings (see Chapter 5; PAS: NLM-AABF51) and the inclusion of carved phalli on walls within and around military sites (see Chapter 9), on a window voussoir at Birdoswald (Wilmott 1997: 65, fig. 39), and the fortress curtain wall at York for example (RCHME 1962: 114) are clear evidence of a "military" relationship, though we should not consider it limited to these people or spaces.

Vulvate forms

Vulvate imagery was much less common than its male counterpart in the Roman north-west, but it is considered to have fulfilled a similar apotropaic function (Johns 1982; Chapter 5). Importantly I should point out that the Classical literature, patriarchal through and through, is somewhat less forthcoming of the apotropaic uses of this image.

The most common form this decoration takes in the north-western provinces was, undoubtedly, the vulvate mount. Identification of this object has been hampered by the application of the unhelpfully anachronistic description "coffee-bean mount" in modern literature (e.g. PAS: PUBLIC-7AF296; LANCUM-693772). The vulva was primarily depicted as a raised, ovate dome with a single incision (usually cast, occasionally hand-incised) along its length as a representation of a pudendum (Lloyd-Morgan 1995: 378–9; Kovač and Koščević 2003: 23). This motif most commonly appeared on copper alloy mounts in which it is backed by a hexagonal plate containing a pair of rivets on its reverse (e.g. PAS: YORYM-F157B0). The interior of the decoration in these cases is hollow. Whilst no typological or contextual assessments of this image in Roman material culture are currently available, there is clear variance within the type. For example, the backing may be lozenge-shaped and attached by four rivets (PAS: SUF-64BF83), the same pudendum shape also appeared on harness pendants with integral suspension loops (PAS: HAMP3503; NMS-128B64), strap slides (PAS: PUBLIC-7AF296), a mount with oak-leaf backing (PAS: NMS-30C9B2), a finger ring (PAS: SWYOR-3794D6), and a tinned vessel handle (PAS: NMS-6B16C2). A variation on the rounded ovoid shape is an elongated ellipsoid with pointed ends which has a raised, rather than incised or depressed, line along its length. This lesser-known form is used as a mount (PAS: SF4173; LIN-666197), as a brooch (PAS: SWYOR-FFF684), and as a button-and-loop fastener (PAS: YORYM-BA9A5D).

A small group of harness pendants may depict a vulva from a different visual profile: full frontal. In these examples, it appears as a pair of raised, moulded lines emanating from the edge of an object. In the case of the harness pendants they separate a fist and phallus (Bishop 1988: 152, type 8l; Chapter 5, Figure 5.10).

With the vulvate form, it is largely the type of object where variance in its representation can be found, although as mentioned above, stylistic differences in the actual pudendum do exist, largely whether the longitudinal marking is incised or a raised moulding (see Chapter 5). A single example of one such longitudinal incision being cross-marked by a lateral incision is known from Britain (Dearne 2017) and demonstrates the potential for more variations to have existed than have been identified. The "coffee-bean"/vulvate form is quite a simple image to represent, particularly in cast metal products. In all the vulvate examples listed above, and their variants, the objects were made from copper alloy and this was unlike the additional prevalence of lead, silver, gold, and bone for phallic objects used for personal adornment (Figure 4.3).

Figure 4.3 Variability in the form and medium of the vulvate pudendum, as depicted on objects of personal adornment. Clockwise from top left: copper alloy mount with hexagonal-shaped backing from Norton-on-Derwent, North Yorkshire (PAS: YORYM- F157B0); copper alloy mount with lozenge-shaped backing from Charing, Kent (PAS: SUR-64BF83); copper alloy finger ring from Folkton, North Yorkshire (PAS: SWYOR-3794D6); copper alloy button-and-loop fastener from Preston, East Riding of Yorkshire (PAS: YORYM-BA9A5D); copper alloy, riveted mount with pendant hanger from Upham, Hampshire (PAS: HAMP3503)

Multiplication

Multiplication of sexual imagery, particularly of phalli, was a popular motif in the Roman world. Duplication, triplication (and beyond) of a single image, or its contextual or literal connection to another similar apotropaic image is particularly interesting to consider when attempting to understand the function of such objects.

Perhaps the most famous examples of multiplication of a phallic image ("polyphallism") within a single object are found amongst the *tintinnabula*. The central figure is usually a macrophallus, sometimes itself zoomorphic in form, and often polyphallic. As an example: a *tintinnabulum* from Pompeii in the British Museum depicts a large, winged phallus with leonine legs (Figure 4.4). It has a smaller, erect phallus between the thighs, and a curled tail which has a glans at its terminal. Human figures incorporated as part of such fantastical designs are less common, but known examples include a macrophallic Mercury with a quad-phallic hat (Museo Archaeologico Nazionale di Napoli), a grotesque figure with both forward and rearward facing macrophalli (British Museum, no. 1814, 0704.1595), and a macrophallic dwarf gladiator who is fighting his own penis, which has become a teeth-and-claw baring tiger at its end (Museo Archaeologico Nazionale di Napoli, no. 27853).

To the modern viewer these images are challenging—a mix of the humorous, offensive, and eye-poppingly bizarre, resulting in a lack of contextualised research into the objects (Parker 2018). A compounding factor in our understanding of *tintinnabula* is the fact that antiquarian collections were hidden from public view; the selective access into the Victorian era *Secretum* of the British Museum is a case in point (Gaimster 2000; see also Chapters 2, 5, and 8). Multiplied phalli were too unorthodox for an Early Modern audience. The antiquarian impact on these objects may also have resulted in the loss of context because the majority of *tintinnabula* in museum collections are unprovenanced. Those with a secure provenance are overwhelmingly from Pompeii or Herculaneum, but at least one example is recorded from Trier (Williams 1999, pl. 9) and another was probably from Colchester (Parker 2018: 63). The *tintinnabula* appear to be an object type where particularly fantastical representations achieved through the multiplication of phalli were common, quite unlike the individual sexual parts of men and women otherwise worn upon the body. Wilburn's (2012: 15–16) framework for identifying magical practices within the Roman archaeological record promotes the idea that exoticism—the incorporation of the weird, wonderful, and unusual—is prevalent within the materials and rituals of Roman magic. The same idea was characterised in the 1930s by Malinowski (1935: 221–2) as "the coefficient of weirdness", and it is perhaps through this lens that the *tintinnabula* and the idea of multiplication should be viewed. They were deliberately incorporating additional supernatural elements to drive the visual narrative to become less human, less biological, less mundane, in an attempt to make the objects more supernatural, more exotic, and thus more magical.

Figure 4.4 Copper alloy *tintinnabulum* from Pompeii depicting a zoomorphic phallus. In the British Museum (BM 1856, 1226.1086)

Tintinnabula primarily multiply phalli with more phalli, but phalli may, instead, be multiplied with different apotropaic images (see Chapter 5). A hand or fist, clenched or depicting the *mano fico* through holding the forefinger beneath the thumb, was also an apotropaic symbol; its significance relates to a complex understanding of the symbolic importance of hands. Eckardt (2014: 167–70) explored this significance and indicates a number of situations where the representation of hands is important: as a symbol of marriage; as a gesture in oratory; the medium through which gods bestow blessings; and as a votive object in its own right. Like phalli and vulvae, the hand was also disembodied. Thus, one prominent amuletic object which multiplied its protective symbols in one space was the fist-and-phallus amulet—one end a fist, the other a phallus (Figure 4.5). These two images were, perhaps, chosen both for reasons of disembodiment but also because they could be simply joined together on portable objects by means of a cylindrical shaft (merging wrist/forearm with phallus).

Greep (1983a: 286–7) defined three prominent types of fist-and-phallus in bone, all of which were first or second century A.D. in date. In addition to these, metal fist-and-phallus depictions may project from an upwardly curved bar (Bishop 1988: 98; PAS: NLM863) or be stylised and joined together by a rectangular plate (Cool et al. 1995: 1538, no. 6322; Kovač and Koščević 2003: 56, nos 120–1). In all cases the two elements were at opposing ends. A unique group of six fist-and-phallus pendants from Catterick, North Yorkshire (Wilson 2002: 66–70, fig. 260, no. 244) incorporate fist-and-phallic elements, but have three left-handed and three right-handed fists, each joined together with its requisite phallus by a scallop-shell moulding interpreted as a female symbol (Parker 2015: 142). In comparable, earlier, harness pendant variants this central image is quite clearly a vulva (Bishop 1988: 152, type 8l; Parker 2015:

Figure 4.5 Fist-and-phallus harness pendant from York
(© York Museums Trust (Yorkshire Museum) [CC by SA 4.0])

140, fig. 6) and may have inspired a subtler artistic representation in the latter group.

With depictions of sexual imagery, we must question why there is such a trend towards multiplication of the images. Perhaps it is because it, paradoxically, both reflects and opposes the anatomical reality of the human form. It reflects the human form because it clearly draws upon human genitalia as the source of this imagery and, as Johns (1982: 62) suggested, remains recognisable when divorced from the rest of the body. Conversely it opposes the normality of the human form by the very fact that it is multiplied. Wilburn (2012: 17–18) suggested that unusual or exotic images were particularly important as *materia magica*. Does this multiplication then create a more supernaturally relevant image? Something more exotic? Was it a simple application of logic: one is good, but more are better?

Multiplication did not have to be achieved by this rather ballistic, visual method; the apotropaic image may have been combined with other ritual elements. As a magical device, the repetition of speech or images was incorporated into a number of spells of the *Papyri Grecae Magicae* (a collection of spells, incantations, and do-it-yourself ritual guides from second century B.C. to fifth century A.D. Egypt; see Betz 1992). The repetition of a single phrase as part of the ritual, or its repetition on multiple days, is a running theme in the papyri (e.g. *Papyri Grecae Magicae* III.409; III.411–12; IV. 209; XII.306–7). The magical act of writing a curse tablet also incorporated a number of physical gestures which had significance to the petitioner, such as turning the curse tablet whilst writing, and folding it up afterwards (McKie 2016: 21–3); movements which may be habitually or necessarily repeated. These brief examples serve to demonstrate a point—that the "magical" nature of a singular apotropaic image (in this case, the sexual images) may be otherwise combined with other protective, magical, or medicinal words, sounds, images, movements, gestures, or objects.

Male and female: sexual or magical?

Images depicting scenes of orgies and sexual pleasure amongst a group are well known from the Roman world: on ceramic drinking vessels (Johns 1982: 94; Dumas 2012: 16–18), oil lamps (Dumas 2012: 16–18; Fedele and Labate 2013; Vucetic 2014), floor mosaics (Dumas 2012: 17), intaglios/gemstones (Ogden 2002: 263, fig. 13.1; Dumas 2012: 11) and finger rings (PAS: LIN-336,194), statues and sculpted reliefs (Johns 1982, pl. 15, 21–3), knife handles (Chapter 2; PAS: LIN-536F87), and *spintriae* (PAS: LIN-536F87), though not all of these may be found in Roman Britain. Can the multiplication of sexual imagery ever actually be regarded as "magical"? Roman artefacts include many representations of intercourse which seem to have no hidden meaning or purpose beyond representing the sexual act (Johns 1982: 10) and it should not be a surprise to discover this artistic relationship with sex and sexuality in the Classical period. However, for the most part these depictions of sex were things designed to encourage or represent love and lust or, more prosaically, the mundane, biological concerns of mortal creatures rather than supernaturally charged images protecting those who viewed them.

Returning to the province of Britain specifically, there are a small number of case studies which we may highlight which present both male and female sexual imagery in the same space. We have no evidence in the north-west provinces of the elaborate sexual frescoes that are prevalent on walls in first century Pompeii (e.g. Clarke 1998, 2003; Puccini-Delbey 2012). Depictions of couples or groups mid-coitus were, however, available on portable objects. A small group of copper alloy knife handles in Britain, for example, all depict erotic scenes (Downes and Griffiths 2016: 40, see also Chapter 2). The example from Grantham is fairly typical of this form: a tall male figure is standing and penetrating a woman, whose legs he holds at his waist (Lee 2012). Her back is propped up against a smaller male figure facing the opposite direction, who is squashed against the edge of the frame and her back and otherwise fulfils no sexual role. Do images of genitalia "in action" have the same connotations as the disembodied genitals? As far as we can tell the answer to that question is "no". Perhaps this is due to the sheer, banal, human normality of sex in the face of other supernatural images?

There are, however, a small number of objects which *may* incorporate both male and female sexual parts in a disembodied form (and are thus magical?). In very few artefacts was there a secure relationship between a phallic element and a vulvate element within a single object. A type of harness pendant, mentioned above, contains both phallic and vulvate elements (Figure 4.5; Bishop 1988: 152, type 8l; Parker 2015: 140, fig. 6), but the location of these on this single object prevents the possibility that these individual elements could biologically interact in any kind of participatory sexual act because they were represented at either end of a singular bar or shaft. They instead, it may be argued, coexisted in a hermaphroditic state.

A carving recently discovered in Lincolnshire (UK) and reported to the Portable Antiquities Scheme (Figure 4.6, no. 1; PAS: LIN-CFA375) serves to highlight the problems in interpretation. The carving depicts a phallus in low relief, pointing upwards to a secondary figure which could be variously interpreted as either vulvate or representing an Evil Eye. The PAS report argued the former, though the author has opted, in print, for the latter (Parker 2017a). The stylistic interpretation is difficult as both vulva or Evil Eye, if represented in this abstract form, are visually very similar: both involve an ovate panel with a single incised line. The author's argument, at the time of writing, is based on an assessment that no other securely Roman carvings exist which incorporate these two elements, but that at least three other secure "phallus and the Evil Eye" carvings are known: two from Chesters (Coulston and Phillips 1988, nos 404 and 407) and one from Maryport (Bailey and Haverfield 1915: 158, no. 86). One carving which may throw this interpretation into question is a recently discovered phallic and clearly vulvate carving from Derbyshire, found reused in a property now owned by the National Trust (Figure 4.6, no. 3; Rachel Hall,

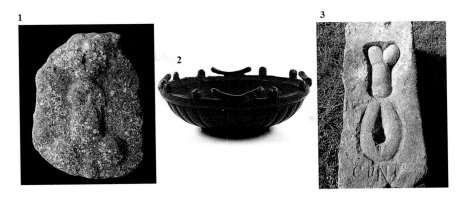

Figure 4.6 Objects where it is unclear whether the phallus is pointing towards an Evil Eye or a vulva: 1—Phallic carving recorded with the Portable Antiquities Scheme (PAS: LIN-CFA375); 2—Roman(?) phallic bowl from Trier; 3—Roman(?) carving from Derbyshire, reused in a National Trust Property

(1—© Portable Antiquities Scheme [CC BY 2.0]; 2—© York Museums Trust (Yorkshire Museum) [CC BY SA 4.0])

personal communication). In this carving, the more familiar "ovate" outline was tapered and left open at the shortened edge, creating a tear-drop shape profile. The lateral incision was instead deeply carved and also tear-drop shaped. The phallus pointed towards the "open" part of this figure, and both were inscribed below with the Latin phrase *cuni*. Whilst the authenticity of this carving remains questionable, it has the potential to devalue the previous interpretation that phalli are not depicted with vulva when inscribed on stone media in Roman Britain. Assuming, for the sake of argument, that it was authentically Roman, the depiction of a phallus and vulva in this manner is a complicated narrative and it would appear to straddle the divide between normal human sex and the disembodied, supernatural images.

Also lacking secure authenticity, but worthy of tentative mention in this capacity, is a copper alloy bowl in the collection of the Yorkshire Museum, originally from Trier, in which pudenda-like mouldings project above the lip of the bowl, each with its own end of a dual-ended phallus pointing directly at it (Figure 4.6, no. 2; Parker 2017b). In this example the "lateral incised line" motif is surrounded by radial lines which could represent human tissue (and thus be vulvate) or the lines of an iris (and thus be Evil Eyes). If either or both of these examples prove to be post-Roman in date, then the depictions of sexual imagery in this way reveal more about how Roman sexual imagery was *thought* to be presented by antiquarian forgers than they do about Roman attitudes.

Materia magica and the importance of materials

The Latin phrase *materia magica* is a somewhat anachronistic modern invention which references the "substances" referred to in Greek magical texts (as ουσία), but it has been appropriated for the material study of magic in Roman archaeology by Wilburn (2012, ch. 2). For Wilburn, the *materia magica* ("the magical materials") refers to an undefined corpus of magical objects and it is in this capacity that the innumerable individual objects depicting male and female sexual imagery may be considered.

Given that the sexual images do not represent a single, cohesive corpus of evidence, it should come as no surprise that there was a huge range of materials which the images could be made from. The association between apotropaic images and explicitly chosen materials is, in theoretical terms, one of the defining features of how "magic" functioned (Versnel 1991; Wilburn 2012). Many materials are thought to have been used for their inherent medicinal or magical qualities—drawn, perhaps, from a mixture of their visual appearance, their physical properties, their availability, and their cost. In this category we may, for example, place jet and amber. Jet is a form of coal, which may be found geologically throughout the north-west provinces—the primary Roman source of which was from the East Yorkshire coastline where it could be collected from the foreshore (Allason-Jones 1996: 5–6). Amber is a form of fossilised resin, primarily traded west from the Baltic (Eckardt 2014: 105). Both stones are lightweight, electrostatic when rubbed, and generally only sourced in small pieces; the electrostatic quality is of particularly interest and may, at least in a small group of jet pendants depicting the Medusa, have been deliberately manipulated in order to "activate" its magical qualities (Parker 2016: 107–8).

The majority of apotropaic sexual images in the Roman world were made from much more familiar materials. Pliny the Elder argued that gold had inherent apotropaic qualities: "gold is efficacious as a remedy in many ways, being applied to wounded persons and to infants, to render any malpractices of sorcery comparatively innocuous that may be directed against them" (*Nat. Hist.* 33.25). Its most prominent use as a medium for magical or medicinal practices in the Roman world is as a material used for phylacteries (see Kotansky 1994 for a catalogue), the creation of which are correlated in the instructional spellbooks of the Greek Magical Papyri (e.g. *PGM* III. 282–409 and *PGM* IV.1167–1226). These phylacteries invoke supernatural beings to provide explicit protection for an individual. As an example, a gold *lamella* from Berkshire (PAS: BERK-0B6771; Tomlin 2008) included 16 lines of Greek text which invoked various supernatural characters to protect Fabia, daughter of Terentia, during childbirth. The *lamella* was folded and, presumably, held in a cylindrical amulet case in order to be worn around the neck during childbirth. Gold is strongly associated with other Roman examples, deliberately chosen as the medium for such magical and medicinal texts. The combination of this material with the phallic image was, thus, particularly efficacious.

Gold was, however, relatively rare in the material culture of the Roman north-west. We might speculate that copper presented a cheaper alternative. Visually, the originally bright and brassy copper alloys used for pendants are far removed from the green patina-covered examples that are available to the modern viewer—in their original context, the copper alloy objects would provide many of the same sensory stimuli as the gold objects, being visually shiny, metallic, and reflective, on the same yellow–orange colour spectrum, but also a conductor of heat (thus warmed to the touch from bodily contact and, potentially, colder when first picked up and put on). The copper alloys may have created a more robust object which was less liable to bending or damage than gold. Speculating further, copper alloy could have been a deliberate choice, ahead of malleable gold, for phallic charms if they were designed to be used in situations where structural stability was necessary; horse-harness pendants are one such example.

The few examples of gold phallic pendants known from Roman Britain, from Braintree, Essex (Johns and Wise 2003), Hillington, Norfolk (PAS: NMS-94CA46), and Knaresborough, North Yorkshire (PAS: SWYOR-E56143), are all ithyphallic pendants and all are small: 28 mm, 21.5 mm, and 19.98 mm in length and weighing 3.86 g, 2.44 g, and 1.86 g respectively. These are in contrast to copper alloy pendants which may be both much larger and heavier (e.g. PAS: KENT-D23DE1—38.4 mm in length, weighing 12.3 g—and PAS: LIN-9DF6E7—45.41 mm in length, weighing 11.6 g). The small, gold pendants may be more appropriately sized for children. Certainly, this association with children is furthered by the discovery of a number of tiny gold finger rings with a simple, ithyphallic decoration on the bezel, inappropriate for use by adults (Johns 1982: 63, pl. 10). In all cases the gold pendants are formed from hollow tubes with soldered, applique decoration whereas the copper alloy pendants are single-piece cast objects. A hollow gold tube is much more likely to become accidentally damaged than a solid copper object of similar proportions. The additional weight, if not the size, of the copper alloys could be due to the relative cost of the materials in that the expensive gold is hollow and the cheaper copper is solid. Gold was more likely to be reused or recycled than the copper materials, perhaps limiting the visibility of this object type in the archaeological record.

Although the phallic form, when used as an item of personal adornment, was readily visible in a range of materials, when appearing as a *tintinnabulum* it was almost always copper alloy (e.g. Johns 1982, pl. 13; fig. 1; Blazquez 1985, figs 1–2). Of more than 30 known to the author, only a single example incorporates another material: an unprovenanced, zoomorphic, phallic alabaster in the Wellcome Collection (no. A67895) and admittedly even this has copper alloy wings. Largely, this material exclusivity may be related to their function as wind chimes with the incorporation of bells beneath a phallic figure—they are required to create a noise and copper alloy was the obvious choice of a durable, castable material with resonant auditory properties.

Interestingly, this material exclusivity is also applicable to vulvate objects when used as items of personal adornment. Cast depictions of the ovate pudendum with a single central incision, mentioned above, appear exclusively as copper alloys. Clearly many of the harness mounts and fittings come from military contexts and were worn by men; although depicting vulvae, they were not inherently "female" objects. An example of an apotropaic image designed explicitly for women may be the silver *lunulae* which, when was worn as a pendant, had a strong female association in the archaeological record (Cleland et al. 2007: 118; Dasen 2015: 190). With regard to vulvae, there were at least two alternative forms in which they were depicted in ceramic. One is a type of ceramic oil lamp with vulvate decoration on a widened handle, strongly associated with the first century (e.g. an example from Naukratis, Egypt, dating to the late first century A.D. (Villing et al. 2013–15) and Corinth, Greece, from the mid-first century A.D. (Slane 1990: 11). The second is a small group of *antefixae* from York with stylised vulvate borders framing a female bust (Johns 1982: 74). This minimal variation is in stark contrast to depictions of male sexual imagery.

In addition to gold, phalli are also recorded in lead (PAS: SWOY-B3F86F) and in silver (e.g. in a chest of objects associated with the grave of a one-year-old from the Apt region of France (Dasen 2003: 286, fig. 10a)). All phalli were not, however, represented in metal. Antler roundels are known from across the north-west provinces (Greep 1994; Chapter 5, Figure 5.17); they always utilised the crown and usually were made from naturally shed antlers. A sub-type of the commoner undecorated form of the antler roundels included a phallic carving in the centre of the roundel face. The use of antler exclusively for this form of object is intriguing. The morphological variance and distribution is well presented by Greep, but the nuances of the connection between these objects and magical practices is much under-studied. Pliny, again, discussed the medicinal properties of stag horn as a cure for epilepsy (*Nat. Hist.* 8.50.112–19) and there was, equally, a wider mythological basis for the importance of antler adorning, for example, the heads of Faunus and Cernunnos (Johns 1982: 64), themselves at least partially nude. The major outstanding question is, perhaps, where were these objects intended to be suspended? Were they for people, for places, or for other objects? Until a contextual spatial relationship between object and place is established our understanding of phallic antler roundels will remain minimal and we are left to speculate on the potential sympathetic magical link expressed between the strength and aggression of stags fighting for mating rights, and these roundels.

The inclusion of a gold *bulla* as one of the other objects in the Apt region grave group is particularly interesting. *Bullae* were worn by freeborn male children, the material of which is a visible clue to the social status of the child and the family he comes from (Cleland et al. 2007: 26; Dasen 2015: 195), with gold representing individuals with the highest status in Roman society. Through the lens of materiality, this grave group may offer an insight into the connection between apotropaic imagery and social status.

There was no such material importance evident for phallic imagery carved into stone. A study by the author of the phallic carvings in the north of Roman Britain has shown that the vast majority, where petrological information is available, were from local sources (Parker 2017c) and, where they remain *in situ* in the built environment, are the same types of stones as those surrounding them. In these examples there is no prerequisite to acquire a different or exotic material to incorporate into the building scheme; the imagery is efficacious in itself and is utilised in liminal places where its visible prominence is more important than the nuances of its shape or the stone upon which it was built. Perhaps a supernatural connectivity to the surrounding liminal spaces was better exemplified through this means?

Some of the contexts in which sexual images were used, for example away from static, fixed positions, were thus rather ephemeral and liable to temporal or spatial changes. So too, perhaps, could the material have been ephemeral—there is no reason to believe that organics could not have substituted metals for such objects, or have been the media upon which images were drawn. Wooden phallic pendants, hewn from sticks and branches already bearing a passing resemblance, are not beyond the scope of possibility. Whilst there is no evidence, at least as far as the author is aware, that this may have been the case, certain Roman magical and medicinal practices may be entirely lost to us because their component were entirely organic and thus ephemeral in the archaeological record in any number (Parker 2019). We should thus continually be cautious due to this fact. We are probably seeing only part of the complete corpus of the range of materials used to bear sexual images because of archaeological recovery biases and taphonomic processes favouring inorganic, durable metals and stone over organics.

Ephemerality may also be linked to manufacturing processes because we do not know where such objects were made. Clearly it took a level of professional skill to create a *tintinnabulum* and access to precious metals for the gold pendants, but bespoke or non-professional designs can be seen in graffiti or in the simply incised stone phalli (see Chapter 9). There were also numerous forms and shapes of phallic and vulvate objects; whilst close similarities in forms amongst the copper alloy examples (especially with the hexagonally backed vulvate mounts) allude to a shared knowledge or shared expectations of the forms, there is not yet evidence to suggest a centralised manufactory for these objects. I suggest that the myriad differences suggest opportunities for "off-the-shelf" products, bespoke commissions, and individual creations. Certainly, they did not require any particularly esoteric knowledge to produce.

Beyond the discussions of materials and materiality, we must interrogate the contexts in which magical objects have been encountered (e.g. Chadwick 2012; Wilburn 2015) because it is through such contextual analysis that connections may be made between objects, people, and ritual practices. Nuance is so often lost by looking at magical objects through a wide lens—the investigation of single contexts and micro-processes is an alternative avenue of valuable investigation (see Garland 2018). As a case in point, we may return to the unique group of fist-and-phallus pendants from Catterick, North Yorkshire (Wilson 2002: 66–70, fig. 260, no. 244) which incorporate fist-and-phallic elements and have three left-handed and three right-handed fists joined together by a scallop moulding. There was a strong contextual association between phallic imagery and the military (Turnbull 1978: 199; Greep 1983b: 139–40), but this specific group is unusual, not only in being a set, but because it forms the grave goods of an infant inhumation. There is a strong literary discussion of the sympathetic magical function of phalli representing power, strength, virility, and fertility—none of which were properties immediately required by an infant (Parker 2015). There are very few other burials from Roman Britain which incorporate phallic objects (Philpott 1991: 161), and only 12 others from the Roman world that are directly associated with children's graves (Whitmore 2017: 51, table 1; Chapter 10). In the specific context at Catterick the pendant group is unique, the association with children rare, and the interpretative narrative open for debate. This context thus provides an opportunity for questioning a traditional interpretation of what phallic images were intended for.

Individual objects devoid of archaeological context, such as those found through metal detecting, have lost their direct spatial and temporal associations. Thanks to recent research by Whitmore (2017), they may not be devoid of interpretative context. Whitmore's theoretical approach to wearing a phallic charm utilised an experimental reconstruction to argue that specific activities, in combination with specific materials used to suspend the pendant, could result in variations in the physical movement of the object around a person. Such insights into the individual use of phallic pendants offer an opportunity to view the objects as individual artefacts, which may have been designed for specific uses as items of personal adornment, or applicable for specific age or social groups. In the case of the reconstructed phallus, it was based on an example from excavations at Piercebridge and was clearly designed to be self-supporting and remain pointing directly outwards from the body whilst being worn. Writing some years before his seminal work on material approaches to Roman magic, Ralph Merrifield (1969: 170) described the phallic image as "a kind of lightning conductor for bad luck". Considering this interpretation, the desire or need for a phallic charm to continually point outwards, to where malignant influences may be intercepted and nullified and thus not interfere with the wearer, seems somewhat obvious. The material expression of using phalli as pendants highlights the importance of individuality in their use—clearly there was a limit to the efficacy of a phallic charm. If the phallus was an all-powerful lightning conductor, the Roman world would have been full of giant representations throughout towns and cities the Empire over. Clearly this is not the case. Phalli were found on a single person, on a single door, or room, or building, or on an individual cup, seal box, or harness; they were explicitly used in small-scale spatial contexts informed by liminal concerns.

Conclusions

This chapter has attempted to present the wide-ranging forms and materials in which sexual imagery was presented in the Roman world, and to discuss some of the material and interpretative concerns relating to these. The focus in this chapter has been a discussion on the broad nature, range, and implications of sexual imagery in Roman Britain. The imagery is often problematic and much work is yet to be done, on the provincial scale, to firmly establish some key aspects of interest to the archaeological discipline—chronology, forms, and contexts. However, it can be shown that objects designed for apotropaic purposes, in this case sexual images, were informed by their materials. Thus, stone phalli were static supernatural guardians of permanent, physical spaces constructed in stone. Objects designed to adorn the body were overt in nature, linked to their apotropaic efficacy and the desire to deflect the Evil Eye. This facet is also linked to the choice of materials. When made in metals, the phallic and vulvate adornments were overwhelmingly made from copper alloys or gold, as bright, noticeable things. Beyond these there may be conceptual links between the choices of materials—gold may have had medicinal properties and animal remains may have sympathetically linked the wearer of the amulet to the physical properties of the animals. Sexual imagery, of both male and female sexual parts, was a common icon encountered throughout Romano-British material culture; its function was not erotic, but protective.

Acknowledgements

This chapter is informed by research undertaken as part of the author's PhD in Classical Studies at the Open University. I thank my supervisors Helen King, Emma-Jayne Graham, and Ursula Rothe for both their challenging discussions and constant improvements of my work. I heartily thank the editors of this volume both for inviting and accepting my contribution and for their deft editorial input into earlier versions of this chapter, and to the peer reviewer who suggested valuable changes.

Note

1 Of over 270 phallic pendants and mounts known to the author from Roman Britain, 13 may be described as flaccid rather than ithyphallic and are all metal rather than bone.

Bibliography

Allason-Jones, L. (1996). *Roman Jet in the Yorkshire Museum*. York: Yorkshire Museum.
Andrews, C. (2012). *Roman Seal-Boxes in Britain*. British Archaeology Reports 567. Oxford: Archaeopress.
Bailey, J.B. and Haverfield, F. (1915). "Catalogue of Roman Inscribed and Sculptured Stones, Coins, Earthenware, etc. Discovered in and Near the Roman Fort at Maryport

and Preserved at Netherhall", *Transactions of the Cumberland and Westmorland Antiquarian and Archaeological Society*, 2nd Ser., 15: 135–172.

Bailliot, M. (2015). "Roman Magic Figurines from the Western Provinces of the Roman Empire: An Archaeological Survey", *Britannia*, 46: 93–110.

Betz, H.D. ed, (1992). *The Greek Magical Papyri in Translation (Including the Demotic Spells)*. 2nd Edition. Chicago, IL and London: University of Chicago Press.

Birley, P. (2007). "The Sculpted Stone", in A. Birley and J. Blake (eds), *Vindolanda Excavations 2005–2006*. Hexham: Vindolanda Trust, 138–143.

Bishop, M. (1988). "Cavalry Equipment of the Roman Army in the First Century AD", in J.C. Coulston (ed.), *Military Equipment and the Identity of Roman Soldiers. Proceedings of the Fourth Roman Military Equipment Conference*. British Archaeological Reports International Series 394. Oxford: Archaeopress, 67–195.

Blazquez, J.M. (1985). "Tintinabula de Merida y de Sasamon (Burgos)", *Zephyrus*, 38: 331–335.

Boschung, D. and Bremmer, J.N. eds, (2015). *The Materiality of Magic*. Morphomata 20. Paderborn: Wilhelm Fink.

Bremmer, J.N. (2015). "Preface: The Materiality of Magic", in Boschung and Bremmer (2015), 7–20.

Chadwick, A.M. (2012). "Routine Magic, Mundane Ritual – Towards a Unified Notion of Depositional Practice", *Oxford Journal of Archaeology*, 31(3): 283–315.

Chadwick, A.M. (2015). "Doorways, Ditches and Dead Dogs – Excavating and Recording Material Manifestations of Practical Magic Amongst Later Prehistoric and Romano-British Communities", in C. Houlbrook and N. Armitage (eds), *The Materiality of Magic: An Artifactual Study Investigation into Religious Practices and Popular Belief*. Oxford: Oxbow, 37–64.

Clarke, J.R. (1998). *Looking at Lovemaking: Constructions of Sexuality in Roman Art 100 B.C.–A.D. 250*. Berkeley, CA: University of California Press.

Clarke, J.R. (2003). *Roman Sex: 100 BC to AD 250*. New York: Harry N. Abrams.

Cleland, L., Davies, F. and Llewellyn-Jones, L. (2007). *Greek and Roman Dress from A to Z*. London and New York: Routledge.

Cool, H.E.M., Lloyd-Morgan, G. and Hooley, A.D. (1995). *Finds from the Fortress*. Archaeology of York, Series 17, Fascicule 10. York: Council for British Archaeology.

Coulston, J.N.C. and Phillips, E.J. (1988). *Corpus Signorum Imperii Romani: Volume I, Fascicule VI. Hadrian's Wall West of the North Tyne, and Carlisle*. London: British Academy.

Crummy, N. (1983). *Colchester Archaeological Report 2: The Small Finds from Excavations in Colchester1971–9*. Colchester: Colchester Archaeological Trust.

Crummy, N. (2010). "Bears and Coins: The Iconography of Protection in Late Roman Infant Burials", *Britannia*, 41: 37–93.

Dasen, V. (2003). "Les Amulettes d'enfants dans le monde grec et romains", *Latomus*, 62: 275–289.

Dasen, V. (2015). "Probaskania: Amulets and Magic in Antiquity", in Boschung and Bremmer (2015), 177–204.

Dearne, M.J. (2017). "A Crossed Line: A Slightly Different (?Military) Harness Mount", *Lucerna: Newsletter of the Roman Finds Group*, 52: 9.

Deschler-Erb, E. and Božič, D. (2002). "A Late Republican Bone Pendant from the Münsterhügel in Basel (CH)", *Instrumentum Bulletin*, 15: 39–40.

Downes, A. and Griffiths, R. (2016). *Fifty Finds from Yorkshire: Objects from the Portable Antiquities Scheme*. Stroud: Amberley.

Dumas, C. (2012). "L'Art Érotique de la Mythologie au Spiritual", *Sexe á Rome: Au-del á des Idées Reçues*. *Dossier d'Archéologie*, 22: 14–19.

Durham, E. (2012). "Depicting the Gods: Metal Figurines in Roman Britain", *Internet Archaeology*, 31. http://intarch.ac.uk/journal/issue31/durham_index.html [accessed 20.03.2017].

Eckardt, H. (2014). *Objects and Identities: Roman Britain and the North-Western Provinces*. Oxford: Oxford University Press.

Fedele, A. and Labate, D. (2013). "Una Rara Lucerna Con Scena Erotica E Iscrizione Da Forum Popilii", *Forlimpopoli: Documenti e Studi*, 24: 65–78.

Gaimster, D. (2000). "Sense and Sensibility at the British Museum", *History Today*, 50(9). www.historytoday.com/david-gaimster/sex-and-sensibility-british-museum [accessed 20.03.2017].

Garland, N. (2018). "Linking Magic and Medicine in Early Roman Britain: The 'Doctor's' Burial, Stanway, Camulodunum", in Parker and McKie (2018), 85–102.

Greep, S. (1994). "Antler Roundel Pendants from Britain and the North-Western Provinces", *Britannia*, 25: 79–97.

Greep, S.J. (1983a). *Objects of Animal Bones, Antler, and Teeth from Roman Britain*. Vol I. Unpublished PhD thesis: University College Cardiff.

Greep, S.J. (1983b). "Note on Bone Fist and Phallus Pendants", in N. Crummy (ed.), *The Roman Small Finds from Excavations in Colchester 1971–79*. Colchester Archaeology Report 2. Colchester: Colchester Archaeological Trust, 139–140.

Johns, C. (1982). *Sex and Symbol? Erotic Images of Greece and Rome*. London: British Museum Press.

Johns, C. and Wise, P.J. (2003). "A Roman Gold Phallic Pendant from Braintree, Essex", *Britannia*, 34: 274–276.

Kotansky, R. (1994). *Greek Magical Amulets: The Inscribed Gold, Silver, Copper, and Bronze Lamellae. Part I, Published Texts of Known Provenance*. Papyrologica Coloniensia, Vol. 22/1. Westdeutscher Velag.

Kovač, D. and Koščević, R. (2003). *The Phallus vs The Curse: The Archaeological Collection of Dr. Damir Kovač*. Zagreb: Muzei Grada Zagreba.

Lee, A. (2012). "A Roman Erotic Knife Handle from Syston, Lincolnshire", *Lincolnshire Past and Present*, 87: 14.

Lloyd-Morgan, G. (1995). "Roman Non-Ferrous Metalwork", in D. Phillips and B. Heywood (eds), *Excavations at York Minster Volume I, Part 2 The Finds*. London: Royal Commission on the Historical Monuments England, 378–390.

Malinowski, B. (1935). *Coral Gardens and Their Magic: A Study of the Methods of Tilling the Soil and of Agricultural Rites in the Trobriand Islands. Volume II: The Language of Magic and Gardening*. London: George Allen and Unwin Ltd.

McKie, S. (2016). "Distraught, Drained, Devoured or Damned? The Importance of Individual Creativity in Roman Cursing", in M. Mandich, T. Derrick, S. Gonzalez Sanchez, G. Savani and E. Zampieri (eds), *TRAC 2015: Proceedings of the Twenty-Fifth Annual Theoretical Roman Archaeology Conference*. Oxford: Oxbow, 15–27.

McKie, S. and Parker, A. (2018). "Introduction: Materials, Approaches, Objects, Substances", in Parker and McKie (2018), 1–8.

Merrifield, R. (1969). *Roman London*. London: Cassell.

Merrifield, R. (1987). *The Archaeology of Ritual and Magic*. London: BT Batsford.

Ogden, D. (2002). *Magic, Witchcraft and Ghosts in the Greek and Roman World: A Sourcebook*. Oxford: Oxford University Press.

Otto, B.-C. (2013). "Towards 'Historicizing' 'Magic' in Antiquity", *Numen*, 60: 308–347.

Parker, A. (2015). "The Fist-and-Phallus Pendants from Roman Catterick", *Britannia*, 46: 135–149.

Parker, A. (2016). "Staring at Death: The Jet *Gorgoneia* of Roman Britain", in S. Hoss and A. Whitmore (eds), *Small Finds and Ancient Social Practices in the Northwest Provinces of the Roman Empire*. Oxford: Oxbow, 98–117.

Parker, A. (2017a). "A New Perspective on a Roman Phallic Carving from South Kesteven, Lincolnshire", *Lincolnshire History and Archaeology*, 49: 91–98.

Parker, A. (2017b). "A Copper-Alloy Bowl with Phallic Decoration from Trier, in the Collection of the Yorkshire Museum", *Lucerna: Newsletter of the Roman Finds Group*, 52: 5–8.

Parker, A. (2017c). "Protecting the Troops: Phallic Carvings in the North of Roman Britain", in A. Parker (ed.), *Ad Vallum: Papers on the Roman Army and Frontiers in Celebration of Dr. Brian Dobson*. Oxford: Archeopress, 117–130.

Parker, A. (2018). "The Bells! The Bells! Approaching *Tintinnabula* in Roman Britain and Beyond", in Parker and McKie (2018), 57–68.

Parker, A. (2019). "Curing with Creepy Crawlies: A Phenomenological Approach to Beetle Pendants in Roman Magical and Medicinal Practice", *Theoretical Roman Archaeology Journal*, 2(1): doi:10.16995/traj.363

Parker, A. and McKie, S. eds, (2018). *Material Approaches to Roman Magic: Occult Objects and Supernatural Substances*. TRAC Themes in Roman Archaeology 2. Oxford: Oxbow.

Philpott, R. (1991). *Burial Practices in Roman Britain: A Survey of Grave Treatment and Furnishing AD 43–410*. British Archaeological Reports British Series 219. Oxford: Archaeopress, 117–130.

Puccini-Delbey, G. (2012). "La Prostitution À Rome", *Sexe á Rome: Au-del á des Idées Reçues. Dossier d'Archéologie*, 22: 58–63.

Royal Commission on Historic Monuments England (RCHME). (1962). *Eburacum, Roman York*. London: RCHME.

Slane, K.W. (1990). *Corinth. Results of Excavations Conducted by the American School of Classical Studies at Athens, Volume XVIII, Part II, The Sanctuary of Demeter and Kore: The Roman Pottery and Lamps*. Princeton, NJ: The American School of Classical Studies at Athens.

Tilley, C., Keane, W., Küchler, S., Rowlands, M. and Spyer, P. (2006). "Introduction", in C. Tilley, W. Keane, S. Küchler, M. Rowlands and P. Spyer (eds), *Handbook of Material Culture*. London: SAGE Publications, 1–6.

Tomlin, R.S.O. (2008). "Special Delivery: A Graeco-Roman Gold Amulet for Healthy Childbirth", *Zeitschrift fur Papyrologie und Epigraphik*, 167: 219–224.

Turnbull, P. (1978). "The Phallus in the Art of Roman Britain", *Bulletin of the Institute of Archaeology, University of London*, 15: 199–206.

Versnel, H.S. (1991). "Some Reflections on the Relationship Magic-Religion", *Numen*, 38 (2): 177–195.

Villing, A., Bergeron, M., Bourogiannis, G., Johnston, A., Leclère, F., Masson, A. and Thomas, R. (2013–15). "Oil Lamp, Ref: AN11169670 01001", *Naukratis: Greeks in Egypt*. British Museum Online Research Catalogue. www.britishmuseum.org/research/online_research_catalogues/ng/naukratis_greeks_in_egypt.aspx [accessed 15.07.2016].

Vucetic, S. (2014). "Roman Sexuality or Roman Sexualities? Looking at Sexual Imagery on Roman Terracotta Mould-made Lamps", in H. Platts, J. Pearce, C. Barron, J. Lundock and J. Yoo (eds), *TRAC 2013: Proceedings of the Twenty-Third Annual Theoretical Roman Archaeology Conference, King's College, London 2013.* Oxford: Oxbow, 140–158.

Webster, G. (1989). "Deities and Religious Scenes on Romano-British Pottery", *Journal of Roman Pottery Studies*, 2: 1–28.

Whitmore, A. (2017). "Fascinating *Fascina*: Apotropaic Magic and How to Wear a Penis", in M. Cifarelli and L. Gawlinksi (eds), *What Shall I Say of Clothes? Theoretical and Methodological Approaches to the Study of Dress in Antiquity.* Boston, MA: Archaeological Institute of America, 47–65.

Wilburn, A.T. (2012). *Materia Magica: The Archaeology of Magic in Roman Egypt, Cyprus, and Spain.* Ann Arbor, MI: University of Michigan Press.

Wilburn, A.T. (2015). "Inscribed Ostrich Eggs at Berenike and Materiality in Ritual Performance", *Religion in the Roman Empire*, 1(2): 263–285.

Williams, C.A. (1999). *Roman Homosexuality: Ideologies of Masculinity in Classical Antiquity.* Oxford and New York: Oxford University Press.

Wilmott, T. (1997). *Birdoswald. Excavation of a Roman Fort on Hadrian's Wall and its Successor Settlements: 1987–92.* English Heritage Archaeological Report 14. London: English Heritage.

Wilson, P. (2002). *Cataractonium – Roman Catterick and its Hinterland: Excavations and Research 1958–1997, Part II.* CBA Research Report 128. York: Council for British Archaeology.

Worrell, S. and Pearce, J. (2014). "Roman Britain in 2011. II: Finds Reported under the Portable Antiquities Scheme", *Britannia*, 45: 397–429.

Part II

Representations and performance of the feminine (or is it?)

5   Barbie-bodies and coffee beans

Female genital imagery in the Mediterranean and the north-west provinces of the Roman Empire

Stefanie Hoss

Introduction

Depictions of male genitalia or their disembodied symbols (phalli) are common in both Greek and Roman imagery (see Chapters 4, 9, and 10). They are regularly encountered in both the Mediterranean and the north-west provinces, and were often used as *apotropaia*. In contrast, depictions of female genitalia are surprisingly rare, especially when considering the omnipresence of their male counterparts and the comparatively high frequency and seemingly untroubled manner in which the sexual act was unambiguously pictured in these societies. For a long time this curious absence was only noted or commented on very occasionally and never reached scholarly common opinion. The first large-scale study of the subject is Monika Gsell's (2001) overview on the (non-)representation of female genitalia in Western art. She found that "uncovered, non-metaphorical and detailed representations" (Gsell 2001: 13–14) of the outer, visible, female genitalia (including the mons pubis, outer and inner labia, clitoris, vulval vestibule, urinary meatus, and the vaginal opening) are extremely rare in all of Western art, from antiquity until today. In her opinion, the scarcity of depictions of female genitalia was occasioned by a taboo prohibiting them, which was in place in Graeco-Roman society as well as throughout the following centuries and is still present today.

This chapter seeks to investigate the depiction of female genitalia in Graeco-Roman societies both in the Mediterranean and the north-west provinces, and to summarise the scholarship on this subject. In order to do this, I will first outline a number of basic premises shaping the investigation, such as the connection between the taboo and the depiction of female genitalia, technical difficulties in depicting the vulva, and societal views on the vulva in general. In the next part, I will examine female genitalia as depicted on women in Mediterranean cultures, starting in Greece and moving on to the Roman Mediterranean culture. This is followed by a part which looks at similar representations in the north-west provinces. The chapter concludes with a discussion of the possibility of disembodied (symbolic) depictions of female genitals used as *apotropaia* analogous to the phalli.

Basic premises

Terminology: vulva and taboo

Because both the terms "vulva" and "taboo" are often used with slightly differing implications, it seems useful to define them for the purpose of this study. The word used in most of the scholarship on female genitalia in ancient art is "vulva", but this is actually the Roman term for the uterus, while the outer genitals were named *cunnus*. The word was seen as obscene in the Roman period, as is its modern cousin ("cunt"). The genital meaning of "vagina" is also modern; in antiquity, the word indicated a sword scabbard (Adams 1990: 80–1). The word is only used once in a sexual sense in ancient literature: in the comedy *Pseudolus* (4.7:80), Plautus uses the word "vagina" together with "sword" in reference to the lovemaking of male lovers—the term "vagina" thus describes a different organ here. As a note aside, a recent article in the British newspaper *The Guardian* also emphasises the importance of calling the outer genitals "vulva", while only the tube leading to the cervix is called "vagina" (Enright 2019b; see also, 2019a).

"Taboo" is understood here as an implicit social rule that prohibits a practice in a given society. There is an important difference between taboos and the explicit prohibitions of codified laws, but a practice can be forbidden by both a taboo and explicit laws (e.g. murder, incest). In contrast to most explicit laws, the power of the taboo lies in the fact that it is unquestioned and unconditional; it is seen as "natural" in that society (Barnard and Spencer 2010: 683; Freud 2014[1913]: 29). This ensures that a forbidden practice is removed from any possibility to question or criticise it. The expectation is that the violator of a taboo will be punished by supernatural forces with misfortune. This is supposed to occur to the violator him/herself and in some cases to those associated with him/her (family, village, tribe, people, etc.). However, these penalties do not completely exclude the violation of any given taboo for varying reasons and motivations. Anthropological research has linked taboos to objects and actions significant for the social order and generated by ambivalence about them. Taboos thus belong to the social control system of a society.

The implicit nature of many taboos makes it very difficult to prove their existence, as most people in the societies concerned can/will not acknowledge a particular taboo as being a social construct. To them, the avoidance of the practice prohibited by the taboo seems "normal" and "natural", even to a point where a violation can cause spontaneous physical reactions (e.g. disgust or fear). While it is generally more difficult to discover the absence than the presence of a practice, it is even more challenging to relate a particular absence to a taboo, since the implicit nature of taboos prevents discussion of them in the society concerned. Because of this, taboos generally only attract attention when an outsider comments on them. As our access to Graeco-Roman societies is mainly through the writings of its own members and through artefacts, the existence of a taboo prohibiting the depictions of female genitals can never be conclusively proven. However, it can be inferred by a number of written sources and by the fact that depictions of female genitalia are generally absent or limited, while male genitalia are depicted often and quite accurately.

Some taboos are very widespread and occur in many, or even in the majority of, societies, for instance the prohibition of cannibalism, in-group murder, and incest (Barnard and Spencer 2010: 683). Consequently, it cannot be excluded that we share certain taboos with Roman society. In fact, according to Gsell (2001), the taboo prohibiting the depiction of female genitalia is one that modern Western societies share with Greek and Roman cultures. This is supported by the non-depiction of female genitalia (with the exception of pornography), which is still a normative practice, a case proven by several studies in the social sciences (Heiland 2015: 31–41; also Braun 1999). These demonstrate that important parts of the female genitalia (mainly the labia minora) are not pictured correctly in today's media (Bramwell 2002) and that most women have only "limited access to sources of information about genital appearance other than the [pornographic] media" in which "an unnatural genital appearance has become normative" (Schick et al. 2009). This can induce significant anxiety in women about the normality of their own genitals, which in turn may lead to elective genital surgery, mostly to reduce the size of the labia minora (Smith et al. 2016). In other words, even in modern audiences with access to a wide range of media there is no consensus on the appearance of a "normal" vulva, or the diversity of appearance among vulvae (Laan et al. 2016). The problematic nature of the normative almost-non-depiction and/or the depiction of just one physical version of the vulva has recently also been acknowledged and challenged by several photobooks portraying a number of vulvae, in order to demonstrate the natural variation (Atalanta 2019; Dodsworth 2019). In addition to these, other forms of disseminating this information, such as the "Vulva Art Print" or the "Vulva Quartet Game", also aim to improve sexual health education (Atalanta 2019).

Therefore, if ancient and modern societies share the taboo inhibiting depictions of female genitalia, it is possible that this also influences scholars of Roman (Provincial) Archaeology, who experience the absence of depictions of female genitalia as "normal", and, consequently, are blind to the scarcity of these depictions in the societies under investigation.

Technical difficulties in depicting female genitalia

When the depiction of both male and female genitalia in Roman art was discussed in scholarship in the 1980s, the scarcity of depictions of female genitalia was often reasoned to stem from the difficulty of representing them (Johns 1982: 72; Heiland 2015: 42–3). Male genitals are (almost) "all out there" and are visible in most positions when the man in question is naked. Because they are largely external, they have a defined shape, which gives them a very recognisable form. This makes them relatively easy to depict, even if the organ is shown in schematic representations separate from the body. In contrast, female genitals could anatomically as well as metaphorically be described as being turned inward and externally unobtrusive. They are normally not fully visible to their owner and only visible to an external viewer when the legs are relatively wide apart, especially when the pubic hair is neither shaved nor trimmed. Because of their inward nature, their shape seems less well defined and difficult to reproduce and their small outer surface makes picturing them independent of the body they are attached to even more difficult (Johns 1982: 72; Heiland 2015: 42–3).

However, the "technical difficulties" often cited as hampering the correct depiction of the vulva with the outer labia open, while existent, can be overcome. An example of this can be found in Japanese erotic woodblock prints (*shunga*), which depict couples during lovemaking. Although the couples are usually dressed, their genitals are not only visible, but pictured both with extreme fidelity and in exaggerated size (Buckland 2010; Clark and Gerstle 2013). European examples that picture female genitalia are *The Origin of the World* by Gustave Courbet (1866) or Egon Schiele's *Black-Haired Girl with Lifted Skirt* (1911).

While these examples are all two-dimensional depictions, the majority of the depictions of female genitalia that have come down to us from antiquity are three-dimensional. However, the small number of two-dimensional depictions from antiquity on Greek vases and Roman wall paintings rarely depict the vulva correctly either.

It is readily understandable that an organ that can be likened to a (shallow) cave is more difficult to correctly depict than one that juts out. In order to see whether this artistic difficulty rather than a taboo is the reason for the scarcity of the depictions, it helps to look at parts of the body of which we can assume no prohibitions to have existed on their depiction in either the Roman or our societies. A good example is the face, which is depicted often in both cultures. Noses jut out and in this are comparable to penises; and mouths are cave-like and in this are similar to vulvas. There are not many depictions of open mouths from the front in ancient art, which is probably linked to the challenge of picturing them correctly. However, the outer characteristics of the mouth when closed—the lips—are relatively easy to picture and are often shown (more or less) correctly in ancient art. Consequently, if there had been no taboo on the depiction of female genitalia, we could expect that at least the outer characteristics of the vulva when closed (the outer *labia*) would be correctly illustrated in Greek and Roman art, but as will be shown below, they generally are not. This indicates that there are additional forces at work here and not just a simple artistic difficulty in the correct representation of a body part.

Another important point is that most phalli are not faithful portraits of human penises. While there are elaborate and very accurate versions, usually of a larger size, the vast majority and especially the smaller examples are highly stylised and schematised, consisting in their most simple form of a rounded shaft with two spheres next to one end. Consequently, a phallus is not truly a depiction of a penis, but rather a "shorthand" or symbol for it. A phallus is recognisable as "shorthand" for a penis in the same manner that an outline in the shape of an almond with a dark circle in the middle is readily recognised as a symbol for an eye. Yet, while resembling the almond shape sufficiently to be identifiable, eyes in fact look quite dissimilar and are very difficult to properly capture in either two or three dimensions. In both Roman and modern art, schematic versions of many parts of the body (nose, mouth, head, hands, feet, etc.) exist. It may, therefore, be possible that the main reason why the vulva was and is so difficult to represent is the lack of a readily recognisable, simplified, and schematic version that can be used as a model or "shorthand" for the depictions. The fact that there was such a schematic depiction model for male genitalia, the phallus, while there is a lack of a similar schematic depiction model of female genitalia, when at the same time there are models for other body parts equally difficult to depict (like the eye), is a good indication that a taboo must be the reason for the non-depiction. In a similar manner, there are no good schematic depiction models of the human anus, probably for similar reasons.

The discrepancy is also apparent in the results of an experiment detailed in Appendix 5.1. The experiment, conducted with 61 individuals, was aimed at testing the hypothesis that the depictions of the genitals can be compared to that of the mouth and nose in the respective difficulty of correctly drawing them. The participants were asked to draw three images: a penis, a vulva, and a human face showing only nose and mouth (Figure 5.1). The results showed a high variability in the depiction of the vulva. Mouths and noses were also depicted in various ways, but it was still possible to group them in types. It was

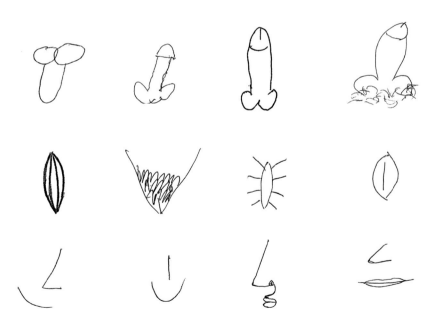

Figure 5.1 A selection of drawings of phalli, vulvae, and human noses and mouths from the 61 participants in the survey

surprising how extreme the similarity and schematic character of the phallus drawings were. The much higher variability and degree of ambiguity of the depictions of the vulva in this experiment led to the tentative conclusion that most people do not know any simplified "shorthand" depictions of this organ. Conversely, "shorthand" depictions of phalli seem to be so frequent that everybody had a "model phallus" they could follow. Another explanation can be sought in the level of artisanship. Most of the participants were inexperienced or indifferent draughtsmen, while two sets of depictions that were more faithfully lifelike in both the rendering of the penis and the vulva showed a high degree of draughtsmanship (Figure 5.2). The variation of type-models in noses and mouths may be the result of the common knowledge of several schematic "shorthand" types for each of them in modern Western society. It is thus probable that the existence of such "shorthand" types makes the phallus form easy to render and to recognise. While it would probably have been possible to develop a similarly schematic model for the vulva, which would have made both drawing it and recognition easier, this was not done, neither in antiquity nor today. The only possible explanation for this is a society-wide taboo inhibiting the correct presentation of the vulva.

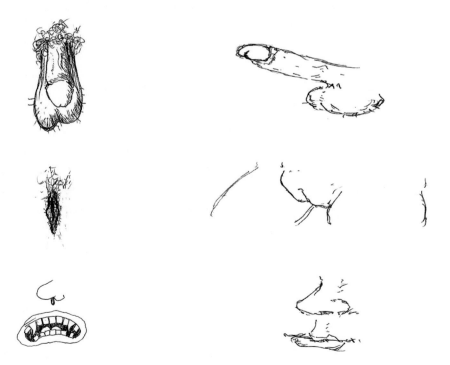

Figure 5.2 Drawings of phalli, vulvae, and human noses and mouths by two highly skilled participants

Roman societal positions on female genitals: the background of the taboo

In Roman polemics and satire, direct and non-symbolical references to female genitalia are almost without exception derogatory, and the genitals are described as objects of disgust (Richlin 1992: 26, 68–9, 109, 276). Only rarely are they referred to in any other way, the one consistent exception being Ovid, who is unusually positive about them (Richlin 1992: 158–9). The derogatory nature of most descriptions of female genitals becomes especially apparent in the vicious comments on older women who are perceived as sexually active and thus acting "inappropriately". A remarkably offensive example is a description forming a part of a poem from the Late Antique collection of first century A.D. poems called *Appendix Vergiliana*. In the poem, called *Priapeum*, the poet threatens his obstinate penis with having to enter the vagina of a "very old" woman, harshly describing it as a cold and wet cave with an entrance full of cobwebs. In one epigram, Martial describes the female genitalia as loose "like a pelican's foul gullet" (*Epigrams* XI.21.1, 10: *tam laxa ... quam turpe guttur onocrotali*). In another (*Epigrams* X: 90), he compares the genitalia of Ligeia to a *bustum* full of ashes. The poem's derogatory comments centre on the fact that a vagina is only a vagina if a penis uses it, and there is a very definite (and quite early) age limit to this use. Curiously, the genitalia of young and attractive women are never described in any of these writings.

The furious contempt of these descriptions is meant to hide male cultural anxieties about the active sexuality of women threatening the legality of their offspring and thus male positions of power (Richlin 1984: 75). Accordingly, all active female sexuality is seen as abnormal: a viewpoint that also explains the disgust of Roman authors with lesbian relationships, which do not endanger legal succession (Clarke 1998: 228; Johnson and Ryan 2005: 4 and 8). Defamation of the vulva, the female seat of lust and thus active sexuality, is a way of ensuring control over it.

Female genitals in the art of the Mediterranean

In this second part, we try to get an impression of the depictions of female genitals on women from the Classical Greek and Hellenistic cultures, before looking at the same subject in Roman culture. It must be stated at the outset that, generally, it is assumed that the body ideal for women in Graeco-Roman culture forbade all body hair, especially pubic hair, which was supposed to be plucked in sexually active women (Greek culture: Slater 2014[1968]: 12–13; Roman culture: Clarke 1998: 216). However, some doubt has been cast on the totality of the practice, at least in Greek women (Seaman 2004: 553). Some written sources indicate that grooming rather than removing all pubic hair is meant. However, as it will be shown in this section, images on Greek vases depict both women with no indication of pubic hair as well as with some remains of it, so perhaps there were differences in grooming in place, time, class, fashion, or taste.

Ancient Greek art

The vast majority of men and women on Greek erotic vases are depicted from the side, which in the case of the women mostly precludes any view of the genital organs, occasionally showing the slight rise of the mons Veneris. When showing the vulva, the images typically picture the pubic hair as a single black spot, or in some rarer cases with small black spots representing stubble (Kilmer 1993: 151–9, figs R20, R73, R93, R114, R144, R192, R207, R212, R309, R318, R507, R528, R543, R531, R970, R1196). A small number of pictures show the mons Veneris from the front with the cleft indicated by a line on "white" skin with the pubic hair removed or groomed to show just a little tuft or two strips on either side of the parting of the outer labiae (Figure 5.3, left, and Kilmer 1993: 147–51, figs R321, R370, R476, R462, R490, R531).

There are only a few cases of possible depictions of the labia. One example is from a red-figured drinking bowl dated to around 500 B.C. showing a naked woman inserting a dildo into her vagina and mouth (Figure 5.3, right), and another example is a *stamnos* dated to around 430 B.C. with a scene of two men holding a woman by her spread legs and lowering her on the erect penis of a man lying outstretched on a table (Kilmer 1993: R1151; Beazley Archive, no. 15807). These depictions suggest that the inner labia are only depicted when a penis or dildo is actively inserted into the vagina. This may be the case because, at that time, the vaginal opening framed by the labia is wide open or perhaps we only get to see the labia of "bad" women, who are depicted as so insatiable that they are either fellating a dildo or are having

Figure 5.3 Drawings of red-figured drinking bowls, dated to between 500 and 450 B.C. On the left: a naked woman urinating into a krater; on the right: a naked woman inserting a dildo into her vagina and mouth (Beazley Archive, nos 204391 and 201043

(Drawings by A. Smadi, Archäologisches Institut, Universität zu Köln)

sex with more than one man.[1] While it is not clear whether the women depicted here are prostitutes—Kilmer (1993: 159–67) and Vout (2013: 120) rightly warn of making simplistic assumptions on the depicted personae's station in life—what can be easily deduced from many of the scenes on Greek vases picturing both women and men is that, quite often, the treatment the women receive does not indicate respect, kindness, or love.[2] On the contrary, most of these depictions objectify women and depict them as lasciviously pleasuring their male partners or themselves.

A depiction described as "evoking" the pubes on a reused rectangular slab inscribed with the name of a well-known fourth-century B.C. *hetaira* found just outside a bathing area on the exterior of the Aphrodiseion at Merenda shows a shape that could be interpreted as representing the space between the legs of a female (Glazenbrook 2016: 191–3, figs 8.6). This space is marked in small picks, giving the impression of hair or stubble. Because of the probability of a social rule compelling women to depilate their pubic hair, this depiction may either show a woman outside the societal order or simply show the differences in grooming fashions.

An Attic marble votive plaque to Zeus Hypsistos,[3] in the Warren collection at the Boston Museum of Fine Art (no. RES.08.34b), also depicts a vulva. The lower part is a smooth triangle stood on its point, with a slight cleft from the point upward, ending in a shallow line. The upper part is irregular and shows an inscription with a circle above it and a star below it. The inscription reads: "to the highest [Zeus Hypsistos], Daphnis dedicated this". The form of the letters dates the plaque to the Roman imperial period. Stone votives of vulvae are rare, but smaller clay versions from the same period are more common (Wellcome Collection, no. A 63 60 58). Their depiction is quite similar in that they consist of a rounded smooth triangle stood on its point, with a line or slight cleft from the point upward. Across the wide upper part runs a double line or an indention. The vulva is thus depicted in a quite stylised form in both cases.

Strangely, even the figurines depicting Baubo do not display a reasonably realistic vulva. Baubo is an ancient mythical figure of the Eastern Mediterranean. A Greek myth relates how Baubo was able to make Demeter laugh for the first time after the abduction of her daughter: she lifted up her skirts and showed Demeter "everything" (Olender 1990). Figurines of Baubo often depict a naked headless torso with a face on the belly and the vulva hinted at by a cleft in the chin of the face (Gsell 2001: 54–5, figs 3–5; see also *Online Datenbank, Antikensammlung der Staatlichen Museen zu Berlin*, inv. nr. TC 8616). In a different type mainly found in Asia Minor and Egypt, Baubo, or Omphale, spreads her legs wide, with her hand either on her knees or touching the vulva with one hand. The genitals themselves are either represented completely flat (i.e. not present) or reduced to a cleft or a hole (Gsell 2001: 55–8, figs 6–8; see also the online collection of the British Museum, no. 1975,1103.1 and *Online Datenbank, Antikensammlung der Staatlichen Museen zu Berlin*, inv. nr. TC 4875).

Hellenistic art

Hellenistic depictions of Aphrodite also seem to be reluctant in depicting the vulva (Neumer-Pfau 1982: 106–9). As an example, the vulva of the Cnidian Aphrodite could aptly be described as "Barbie-like", consisting only of a lightly rounded, smooth triangle (Neumer-Pfau 1982: 108; Barrow and Silk 2018: 44–5). Seaman (2004: 551–7) has stated that many statues, when examined closely, exhibit faint remains of paint in the pubic area. This led her to argue that pubic hair was painted onto statues of females and young boys, in contrast to the statues of grown men, which have plastically rendered pubic hair. Both women and young boys are supposed to be passive sexual partners in the Greek ideal, and both are supposed to have groomed pubic hair, which is less three dimensional. Seaman (2004: 553–7) also lists a number of female statues that show either painted or incised lines separating the labia; in some cases a combination of incised lines and painted pubic hair can be (faintly) seen. If her observations are correct, pubic hair that is not groomed would have been seen as a sign of virility and active, not passive, sexuality, and, therefore, as unfitting for women and boys.

In Hellenistic art, the visual representations of sexual intercourse change drastically in comparison to earlier Greek models. While the earlier Greek vases mainly showed scenes in which men used women to engage in sexual intercourse for their own sexual satisfaction, the typical Hellenistic portrayal of sex depicts a beautiful male–female couple in a luxuriously appointed bed chamber engaged in sexual acts as equals (Clarke 2014: 511). A famous piece is a bronze mirror cover (partly silvered) now at the Boston Museum of Fine Art (Plate 1; Johns 1982: 134–5, figs 95 and 112; Clarke 1998: 22–6, figs 2 and 3), which is supposed to have been made in Corinth around 340–320 B.C. On the outer side, worked in bas-relief, a naked human (as opposed to god-like) couple is pictured on a bed, with a winged Eros flying above them. The woman lies on her left side, frontal to the viewer, with the man behind her. He is entering her from behind, while she opens up for him with her left leg angled forward and her right leg lifted high by her lover. Here, the vulva is shown as an open triangle, with the outer labia clearly delineated and framing the penis. Unfortunately, a large amount of crusty green patina blurs the picture here, but the faithfulness of the genital representation can also be deduced from the fact that the man's scrotum, which is seen from the underside, shows the scrotal raphe. The inside of the cover is silvered, with an incised decoration also showing a sexual act in a bed chamber (Figure 5.4). Here, the couple stand next to the bed, with the female raising her buttocks high, while bending her torso low, supporting herself only with her left hand and left leg. Raising her right leg, she takes her right hand to guide the penis of the man between her forefinger and middle finger into her vagina. The body and the genital area are clearly separated from both of the legs, but nothing more than a slight triangular bulge is visible from the vulva, and again, no pubic hair is indicated. The scene on the outside of the mirror cover supports the theory

Figure 5.4 Engraving with erotic scene on the silvered inside of a bronze mirror cover. Museum of Fine Arts, Boston, inv. no. RES.08.32c.2

(Drawing by A. Smadi, Archäologisches Institut, Universität zu Köln)

put forward earlier, namely that the vulva is pictured with the inner labia if something is inserted into the vagina. The inside depiction does not show the labia, but this may be owed at least in part to the position of the woman, which makes the labia difficult to see. However, it is noteworthy that the precision in the representations of the vulva (and the penis) of the outer depiction is greater than in earlier depictions. In addition, both the outside and the inside depiction portray the women as more equal partners in a relationship that is at least somewhat loving and respectful, rather than as objectified satisfiers of male desire.

Another depiction of lovers during intercourse can be found on a small fragment of a *rhyton* from Delos (second century B.C.) in which, again, the male lover sits behind the woman (Clarke 1998: 30, fig. 5). Here no bed is visible, the woman squatting on the man's lap. The couple lean back to gaze into each other's eyes and kiss, which again stresses that this is a fairly loving relationship in difference to most of the earlier Greek depictions. Her vulva is represented rather schematically as a hairless triangular slit. His penis, which is at the point of entering, is quite small, and no details such as the foreskin or the glans are recognisable. One could thus argue that both the penis and the vulva are depicted quite schematically.

Summary of Greek and Hellenistic art

We can thus summarise that the early Greek representations display the vulva only in depictions that show objectified women, who are on the point of inserting a dildo or penis into the vagina. Later Hellenised depictions show the vulva also in scenes that might be described as lovemaking because of the care with which the man handles the body of the woman. The women depicted here seem wealthier too, because of the rich jewellery they wear and the lavish appointment of the bed chambers. These images at least depict the vulva a bit more realistically than the earlier Greek art by showing the outer labiae. While the outer labiae are rendered somewhat schematically in these depictions, this is also true of the penis. Votive depictions generally show the vulva as a smooth triangle with a slit, one exception seemingly also depicting pubic hair, if this is what the picked area is supposed to picture (e.g. Wellcome Collection, no. A 63 60 58).

Roman art

Moving onto Rome and Italy, a major difference between Greek and Roman erotic art seems to be its use. In contrast to Greece, the numerous Pompeian wall paintings showing scenes of copulation suggest that they were not reserved for orgies with men and prostitutes/objectified women. While a small number come from a brothel, many were also found in bathhouses or in small, isolated *cubicula* in the well-appointed houses of the rich (Meyerowitz 1992: 132–3). Interestingly, the erotic frescoes of the brothels, bathhouses, and elite houses are stylistically quite similar; moreover, in their pairings and the manner of lovemaking both resemble the scenes on cheap oil lamps with erotic subjects mainly produced for the common people (Strong 2016: 120). Together, they demonstrate that similar representations of sex were used in different social settings for a number of different audiences. Of these, the erotic paintings in elite houses are the most surprising to us, as they may be supposed to have been produced for the wealthy married couples who owned these houses. Erotic subjects appear in the wall paintings of private rooms as well as in publicly frequented ones, but the depictions in the public sphere differed from those in the private sphere: in the publicly frequented rooms, erotic art tended to be mythological, while images of human lovemaking were more likely to be found in the private *cubicula*. However, the body positions and the manner of lovemaking were similar in both the mythological and human couples (Strong 2016: 120–1).

A picture from an unknown location within Pompeii shows a fairly common erotic scene in Roman culture: a man, seen from behind, is reclining on a bed, while the woman (often naked, but sometimes still wearing a breastband) is in the process of lowering herself to straddle his body and take his penis into her vagina (Clarke 1998, pl. 8). In this picture, the pubic hair is absent, but the vulva is only seen as a slightly triangular slit, despite the fact that the legs are often parted relatively wide. Another painting in Pompeii (the eastern picture on north wall of room f in the house at IX, 5, 16), dated to A.D. 62–79, originally probably also showed the woman's vulva (Clarke 1998: 184, fig. 72). The woman is depicted as kneeling above the man's lap, with her left hand going towards her genitals, most likely to guide his penis into her vagina. Unfortunately, the picture is much damaged by paint loss on this spot, and the depiction of the vulva is uncertain. In contrast to Greek art, where this manner of copulating never appears, similar scenes are quite frequent in Roman erotic art, which is probably connected to its possibilities of picturing both the act of penetration and the woman's body in full—a similar objective to the depiction on the Hellenistic mirror cover (Clarke 1998: 217–18).

Interestingly, the "catalogue" of erotic scenes of the *apodyterium* of the Suburban Bath in Pompeii also features some scenes rare in Roman erotic depictions, such as a scene of a woman fellating a man, a man performing cunnilingus on a woman, and other scenes involving several partners doing both (Clarke 1998: 219–40, pls 11–16). Because of their concern for the purity of the mouth, elite Romans saw both fellatio and cunnilingus as demeaning for the person using their mouth. Both sexual acts are presented in the writings of the elite as infamous: it is the province of male and female prostitutes and slaves (Clarke 1998: 220–2, 224). Free men performing this act were seen as "being fucked by women" (Parker 1997: 50–2), a very grave violation of the male (upper class?) norm of being the penetrator.

The cunnilingus scene in the Suburban Baths shows a woman richly adorned with jewellery sitting on a bed with her legs spread wide; she grabs her right leg at the knee, while the left is lying on the edge of the bed (Clarke 1998, pl. 12). Between her legs, a fully dressed man is crouching, with his mouth open and his tongue out. Strangely, the woman's genital organs are represented by a hairless mons Veneris with a slit depicted by the single line. However, if a woman spreads her legs as wide as they are on the wall painting, it is physically impossible for her vulva to open as little as depicted here: at least a slight opening of the vulva should be visible. The discrepancy between the (for Roman morals) outrageous nature of the erotic scenes in the Suburban Bath in Pompeii and the fact that, even here, the vulva is depicted in this "sanitised" manner shows the strength of the taboo prohibiting a natural depiction of the vulva. Picturing the vulva adequately apparently is impossible even when the context is meant to titillate and amuse the viewers with scenes of shocking sexual couplings.

The countless graffiti of Pompeii may be seen as a fairly direct expression of the common people's ideas on sexuality. Unsurprisingly, many depictions of phalli in a number of variations were identified among the graffito drawings, but no depictions of a vulva (Langner 2001: 32, fig. 7). The written graffiti were also the subject of a study on sexual terms. Here, the terms *futuere* (to fuck) and *cunnum lingere* were studied in relation to the construction of the sexuality of the common people of Pompeii (Conde Feitosa 2013: 46–7). As mentioned earlier, the upper levels of Roman male society professed an abhorrence of *cunnum lingere* in their writings. In contrast, the lower-class men of Pompeii seem to have had a less strict view of it in their graffiti. In these, *cunnum lingere*, while also often used mockingly, seems to be condemned less severely (Conde Feitosa 2013: 46–7). Moreover, male prostitutes advertise their willingness to perform cunnilingus for prices that resemble those asked by female prostitutes for fellatio (Clarke 1998: 225–6). Cunnilingus is thus not seen as more demeaning than fellatio among them.

Returning to Roman art in general, the scene that we encountered on the outside of the Corinth mirror cover in the Boston Museum (Plate 1) is repeated with some variations several times in Roman art. Curiously, the Roman examples consistently change one detail: the depiction of the vulva is reduced to a slit, if it is at all present. The most elaborate of these is another bronze mirror cover from Rome dating to the first century A.D. (Johns 1982, fig. 113, colour fig. 35; Clarke 1998, fig. 60; Gsell 2001, fig. 21). The depiction is striking in its rich and detailed execution: the decoration of the bed chamber is pictured with an ornate hanging lamp and a painting of an erotic scene with wooden shutters half-closed is visible above the couple on the bed. The bed is likewise luxuriously decorated and surrounded by the various remains of a feast. The woman wears a decorative chain on her body, which crosses at the breasts. The man's small penis is again pictured with shaft and testes, but details such as foreskin or glans cannot be discerned. It can thus be described as somewhat schematic. The woman's genitals are again reduced to a slightly triangular slit, despite the fact that she opens her legs wide and that the penis is on the point of being inserted into her vagina. Here, size must have played a significant role in the schematic nature of this depiction. However, we can at least say that this simple depiction of the vulva does not contradict the impression gained before, namely that the vulva is usually represented schematically, in order "to sanitise" the female genitals. This is also true of other depictions of the same composition; these are simpler and on an even smaller scale, and include an undated knife handle (Johns 1982, fig. 113; Vout 2013, fig. 94), a fragment of a Samian vessel dated to the first to second centuries A.D. (Johns 1982: 125–6, 135, fig. 103; Vout 2013, fig. 94) as well as a fragment of a terracotta vessel from the second to first centuries B.C. (Clarke 1998: 116, fig. 40) and a wall painting from Ostia, dated to A.D. 250 (Clarke 1998: 272–3, fig. 106).

Summary of representations in Mediterranean art

After having looked at the representations of female genitalia in the Mediterranean, we can thus state that naturalistic representations of the vulva were not a normal part of the Graeco-Roman Mediterranean repertoire. In most depictions of women, the vulva was represented either by a smooth triangle ("Barbie-like"), probably representing the vulva with closed outer labia, or by a slightly triangular slit, probably representing the vulva with opened outer labia, when a penis was inserted or about to be inserted. Votive depictions usually show a smooth triangle with a slit. However, a small change can be observed, namely that, while still rare, all slightly more overt depictions of female genitalia on woman are Greek and Hellenistic. While the Romans inherited some of their artistic representations from the Greeks, they seem to have changed the pictures depicting female genitalia to suit their different cultural preconceptions by "sanitising" them even more and picturing the vulva either as non-existent or as a small triangular slit.

Female genitals in the art of the north-west provinces

When looking at the art of the Roman provinces, we have to keep in mind that the various peoples living in this vast area are likely to have had differing ideas about sexuality and its representation in various art forms from those of the Romans, and also from each other (see Chapters 6 and 8).

Unfortunately, our knowledge of the sexual mores of these various cultures is severely hindered by the almost total lack of written sources authored by members of these cultures themselves. We must therefore rely on the descriptions of the sexuality of these peoples as given by Greek and Roman authors, but no substantial research has yet been done on this subject (Roisman 2014: 418). The image that is drawn in these writings of most peoples living north of the Alps is one of them being monogamous or, if polygamous, then "not driven to it by lust" as Tacitus says of the Germans (*Germania* 17–19). The few notable exceptions are supposed to be living on the edges of the known world and thus farthest removed from civilisation: Caesar (*Bello Gallico* 5, 14) relates that some less civilised Britons share their wives among 10–12 men, especially if they are brothers or fathers and sons. Descriptions of unbridled lust also exist: Diodorus (5.32.7–8) describes the Celts as neglecting their beautiful women in order to have wild homosexual affairs. However, there is consensus among modern historians of the ancient world that most ancient authors use the description of the sexual lives of the "others" (non-Romans, whether living north of the Alps or elsewhere) as a foil to set off the supposedly depraved morals of their contemporary fellow Romans (Roisman 2014: 412). These descriptions are thus less illuminating of the people they claim to describe than they are of the various social conflicts in contemporaneous Roman society.

A further caveat is that detailed and comparatively naturalistic anthropomorphic representations were mainly introduced into north-west Europe through

Roman contacts from the Iron Age/Republican era onwards. Roman models of depiction came to dominate or at least strongly influence local art representing naked humans during the Imperial period (Wilson 2015: 508–25). Therefore, even if a local culture differed in their ideas on female genitalia and their depiction from Roman culture, the use of Roman models of illustration may have obliterated this difference.

Looking at the various depictions of females in the north-west provinces, we can state that the overwhelming majority of women are depicted dressed. When shown undressed, most figures follow well-known Mediterranean models such as the Venus pudica or the crouching Venus (see Chapter 3). Here, the female genitalia are either (as good as) invisible or rendered "Barbie-like", that is depicting a smooth, lightly rounded triangle. The pubic hair may have been painted on, as in the Mediterranean.

Apart from those on reliefs and figures in the round, depictions of naked women in the north-west provinces are most common in sex scenes on lamps (Vucetic 2014). These scenes derive from Roman models and we consequently encounter couplings similar to those from Pompeii already discussed. The most interesting for our concern with the depiction of the vulva is a terracotta appliqué medallion from the Rhône Valley, dated to the second to early third century A.D. (Clarke 1998: 257–8, fig. 99). It again shows a naked man lying on a bed, with a naked woman squatting over him in order to take his penis into her vagina. The latter is pictured only as an indented triangle, but the size of the depiction would have made any more detail impossible in any case. Of the many relief scenes on terra sigillata depicting couples having sex, some show scenes in which the woman spreads her legs wide to receive the man's penis (Figure 5.5). Although this would naturally open the vulva at least somewhat, and we might at the minimum expect a triangular slit, the vulva is only indicated by a meeting of the lines delineating the woman's legs. While the small

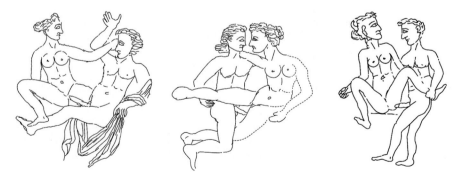

Figure 5.5 Decoration of terra sigillata bowls showing couples having sex
(Drawing by A. Smadi, Archäologisches Institut, Universität zu Köln, after Dierichs 1997: 140)

size of the representations, measuring only a few centimetres, makes an accurate depiction impossible, that on the right shows the man's penis with the glans set off by a line. If such a small part of the male anatomy can be depicted with this degree of accuracy, a more naturalistic depiction of the vulva would not have been technically impossible.

Nevertheless, a number of figures and reliefs from the north-west provinces show a slightly more life-like representation of the vulva, namely a smooth triangle with a cleft (Künzl 2001). Although the group has some outliers in Britain, southern France, the Bretagne, and on the Rhine, its centre is clearly in the eastern central region of Gaul, around the sources of the Seine (Figure 5.6). Whereas the depiction of the vulva within the group is consistent, the material and use of the objects differ: one group consists of 35 stone reliefs or figures in the round showing naked women, variously in the poses typical for Venus or Nymphs or dancers (Appendix 5.2, list 1). One of them, interpreted as *Dea Sequana*, is singular in having both curly pubic hair and a cleft. The second group consists of statuettes or small figurines of various practical uses (Künzl 2001). Five of them are bronze statuettes, while two more are clay moulds for such statuettes. Two others are

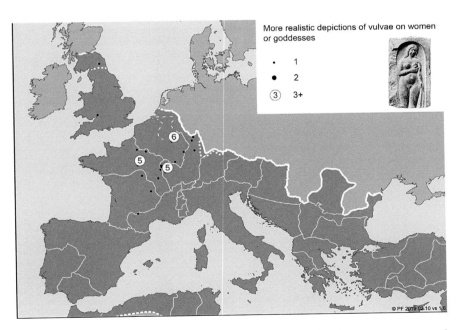

Figure 5.6 Distribution map of the more realistic depictions of vulvae on women or goddesses. As an example in the upper left: Altar with Dea Sequana, Dijon, Musée Archéologique, no. 994.1.59

(Map P. Franzen based on Appendix 2, list 1; data from Künzl 2001; altar: after Espérandieu XI 7681)

from bone, while the last is a stone foot of a pedestal table in the form of a column. All of them show the vulva on the body of a woman or goddess. The third group contains 15 rather flat and quite stylised depictions in stone that only show female bodies between the waist and the knees (Appendix 5.2, list 2). These are interpreted as anatomical votives, as some of them were found at the sources of the Seine, the forest of Halatte, and at other sanctuary sites (Figure 5.7). The last group is also composed of anatomical votives, but made from bronze and depicting the vulva only, in one case with an indication of pubic hair. The distribution of the anatomical votives (Figure 5.7) is similar to that of the full figures with vulva (Figure 5.6).

Künzl (2001) suggests that this manner of depicting the vulva was first used for anatomical votive offerings in stone or metal, and probably also in wood, although that must remain speculative. These votives were then used as an inspiration for similar depictions of female genitalia on naked goddesses, nymphs, or dancers. The slightly more realistic manner of depicting the vulva may indicate that a less rigid view on women and their sexuality existed in (at least) eastern central Gaul, the main distribution area of these depictions (Künzl 2001: 259–60).

In order to look to the east of Gaul, into the provinces on the Rhine and Danube, and northern Italy, I consulted the online database ubi-erat-lupa,

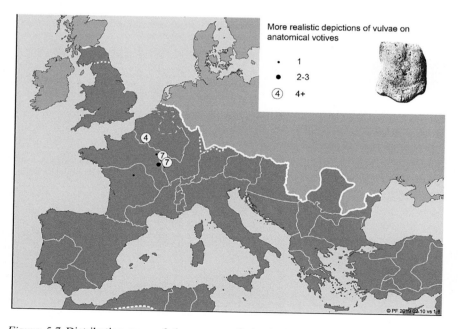

Figure 5.7 Distribution map of the more realistic depictions of vulvae on anatomical votives. As an example in the upper left: anatomical votive, Senlis, Musée d'art et Archéologie

(Map P. Franzen based on Appendix 2, list 2; data from Künzl 2001; altar: after Espérandieu V 3887 right)

which collects Roman stone monuments (lupa.at). I only found 23 depictions of naked women that include the genital region (Appendix 5.2, list 3). All of them comply with the Mediterranean manner of depiction showing either the pudica type, a slightly raised triangle, or an unmarked area ("Barbie-like"). As the collection of Gaulish reliefs and statues published by Espérandieu has already been searched for more naturalistic depictions of the vulva by Künzl (2001), it seems reasonable to assume that the depictions published in his paper are the only known ones in the north-west provinces differing from the Mediterranean model, and that only slightly.

In Britain, only two possible depictions of vulvae were discovered in the relevant collections, and these were shown as separate from the body. One of them is the fragment of an inscription (14 x 6 inches) found before 1912 at Maryport (RIB 872). It depicts a phallus aimed at a vaguely hexagonal shape and connected to it by a line. The other is on fragments of wall plaster found (82.5 x 82.5 mm) in the rubble tip outside of the villa of East Malling in Kent (RIB 2447.23 a–b). Here, two vaguely heart-shaped forms are depicted with a line running though the middle. Each of these can only tentatively be identified as a vulva.

Summary

We can thus conclude that the depiction of the female genitals on women in the north-west provinces was similar to that in the Mediterranean. Most vulvae are shown as smooth, slightly rounded triangles. There are exceptional cases, of course, such as the Gallic group of statues published by Künzl (2001), where the depiction of the vulva was enhanced with a cleft, and in some rare cases even with an indication of pubic hair.

Apotropaic depictions of female genitals in the north-west provinces

Basic premises

There is a notable discrepancy between the depiction of male and female genitalia as *apotropaia* in the north-west provinces. Male genitalia are represented disembodied, schematic, and simplified, essentially as a symbol, but one still resembling the actual appearance of human penises (and their scrota) sufficiently to be readily recognisable. Female genitalia, however, are not depicted disembodied; rather, with only a few exceptions, various objects have been chosen as symbols to act as "stand-ins" or substitutes for the female genitals. Among the common objects identified as substitutes for the vulva are the *manus fica*, the cowrie and scallop shells, the lunula, and other, less common, images. These all are symbolic substitutions for the vulva, as I argue below, and had been in circulation before the Roman period. Another discrepancy lies in the frequency of the different representations: while depictions of male genitalia as *apotropaion* are almost ubiquitous in both the Mediterranean and the north-west provinces, the depiction of the symbols for the vulva are comparatively rare in both regions. Faraone (2018: 72–3) explains the rarity of amulets using the vulva with the difficulty of depicting it in a small and easily recognisable form. This is the same argument we have seen earlier in the discussion of the depictions of the vulva on women. However, the argument can be countered in the same manner: if one had wanted to make such a schematic depiction, it would have been possible, just as it was possible for other body parts that are difficult to depict, for example the human eye.

In order to look at the use of the vulva symbols as *apotropaion*, it is essential to clarify why *apotropaia* were thought to be necessary in antiquity and how they were supposed to work. I base my discussion on the work of Elliott (2016b: 7–83, 121–266).

Antique scientific theory assumed that the human eye actively emitted invisible rays in order to see; it was also believed that some people, when charged or "energised" by negative feelings of hatred or jealousy, could harm with these rays, causing misfortune, illness, and death. As this power was not aimed or controllable, the people projecting these rays quite involuntary could even harm themselves. Anything and anybody that could evoke envy or jealousy by possessing health, beauty, success, or wealth could be the aim of the Evil Eye (on the Evil Eye, see Chapter 4). Counter-measures included protection through a great variety of protective words, gestures, and actions, which are now difficult to reconstruct. Another protective measure was the use of amulets, believed to exert power to the good of the person owning them when in contact or close proximity to him/her or his/her possession by warding off evil. Amulets derived this protective power either from their material or their form (or both), with the power of the form mainly lying in its ability to provoke (embarrassed) smiles or laughter. This was effected by using forms of a lewd or vulgar or otherwise "unbecoming" character: "beings with a funny appearance or in which some obscene details are accentuated are good *apotropeia*, as well as normal beings represented in indecent attitudes, making vulgar gestures or noise" (Levi 1941: 225). The desired effect was achieved by using the power of laughter to defuse the negative energy (envy, jealousy, or wrath) necessary to charge or "energise" the Evil Eye. At the bottom of this is the astute psychological observation that it is difficult to maintain a high level of negative energy during or after laughter.

Many amulets thus have a form that was perceived as lewd or vulgar in Roman times, but which was harnessed in order to drive away the Evil Eye. This explanation runs contrary to the idea that the depiction of male genitals was "unproblematic" for Romans: the apotropaic power of vulgar or lewd depictions only works if they are still able to provoke (embarrassed) laughter, at least in principle (Johns 1982: 63). It follows that the large amount of artefacts depicting disembodied male genitals or comically enlarged genitals on men are, contrary to common opinion, not proof of an open-minded view on male nakedness. Instead they demonstrate that male genital nakedness was still seen as embarrassing outside of the "correct" circumstances, such as socially permitted situations at the bathhouse or the gymnasium. Had this not been the case, they would not have provoked the laughter that was the whole point of the *apotropaion*.

In contrast to Elliott (2016b), Faraone (2018: 71–2) has suggested that the phallic amulets signal an aggressive attitude against the daemons, diseases, and evils that inhabit the outside world. While the phallus (like the raised middle finger) threatens penetration ("I will fuck you!"), the *mano fica* feminises the opponent ("You are a cunt!", which is going to be fucked). In a similar manner Bartsch (2006: 138–52) has argued that phalli are thought to work against the Evil Eye by penetrating it.

Romans used, therefore, the power of the male reproductive organs in the phallus not in order to venerate it, but in order to provoke laughter through its "unbecomingness" and grotesquely exaggerated size, as well as in order to threaten penetration, or, most likely, both at the same time. However, the fact remains that the power of the male reproductive organ was symbolised by a disembodied and schematic depiction of the male genitals. In contrast, the power of the female reproductive organ was hidden behind "substitutes" and it seems questionable whether they were seen as being aggressive.

Many Roman amulets consist of a combination of *apotropaia*. An amulet can combine several symbols, for instance a phallus and a *manu fica*, but it can also combine a symbol and a material, for example a phallus made from horn, to enhance the apotropaic power, or it may combine all of the above (see Chapter 4). While these multi-symbol amulets may often seem confusing to us, we have to remember that the people using these amulets in antiquity would not have needed to pick apart the various symbols and meanings. The symbols were embedded in the culture and, more importantly, their use and benefit had been conveyed to them by many routines and stories of their elders. This approach to amuletic objects is still true today: a modern example of an amulet unrecognisable to anyone not knowing its provenance is the Italian *cornicello* or *cornetto rosso portafortuna*, the modern incarnations of which resemble a small chilli pepper made from plastic (Elliott 2016b: 183–4, illus. 14). The modern form is a substitute for the miniature antelope horns used in previous centuries. The antelope horn, while being additionally powerful because of the material horn (apotropaic in itself, see below), was also a substitute for the phallus. However, most modern wearers of the *cornetto* use it without knowing the history behind it and only connect a vague sense of it "bringing good luck and averting evil" with it. An amulet may thus represent several things at the same time and it may use substitutes for symbols deemed unacceptable to wear or show openly. Over a given period of time, amulets can also go through various different substitutes in order to keep up with changes in social mores. Even more important, as long as their reputation to avert evil and bring good luck remains alive, amulets can be used without being understood by their users.

Apotropaia: their use and distribution

This section showcases the various apotropaic objects depicting "substitutes" for the vulva with a discussion on their use and distribution in the European north-west. However, before we turn our attention to these amulets, I would like to mention an unusual and, as far as I am aware, singular example of symbolic substitute for the vulva as an apotropaic measure in Mediterranean art. It can be found on a mosaic at the entrance to a caldarium in the bath complex of the House of Menander at Pompeii (Plate 2; Clarke 1998: 122, 129–33, fig. 44). The mosaic depicts two pairs of strigils arranged to look like the vulva's outer and inner labia. A hanging oil container between them might represent a clitoris or symbolise a penis (Clarke 1998: 122, 129–33). The latter would mean that both male and female genitalia are represented in a symbolic fashion, doubling the apotropaic power. Above this stands an "Ethiopian" servant, pictured in black and carrying two water jugs. He wears a laurel wreath on the head and a piece of cloth around his hips. The latter is riding up because of his (for Roman eyes) comically enlarged penis, pictured with the glans in a different colour (red). The intention governing the design of this mosaic was to avert the Evil Eye from the bathhouse and its visitors. As such, it belongs to a large corpus of threshold mosaics with the same purpose (Dunbabin 1989: 33–4). Yet, while they often picture symbols of male genitalia and other symbols of good luck, such as kantharoi, swastikas, peltae, and vines, among others (Dunbabin 1989: 38–40), this is the only known example depicting a vulva, even if the depiction is oblique and symbolic.

Mano fica

A common substitute for the vulva was the *mano fica*—literally, the fig-hand, a fist with the thumb inserted between the forefinger and the middle finger—representing the vagina with the penis inside. This gesture is very old and had already been used in amulets made from faience, jet, or gold foil during the Pharaonic age by the Egyptians (Faraone 2018: 71, fig. 2.10).

Amulets featuring only the *mano fica* (Figure 5.8) are rare in the north-west provinces: five are currently known (Cool et al. 1995: 1538–9, figs 716–17; PAS: LIN-2BE126 and NCL-7916E6). However, combinations of an erected phallus with a raised lower arm and hand in the gesture of the *mano fica* into a double horn shape are relatively common with 40 examples documented at present (Appendix 5.2, list 4). In this manner they combine the male (phallus) with the female principle (*mano fica*) and add a third layer of protection with the horn shape. Horns, the visible sign of the power and vitality of male animals, were used throughout antiquity as symbols of strength, sexual potency, and fertility (Elliott 2016b: 272, 297–300; Faraone 2018: 64–5). They were also used in the gesture, sometimes referred to as "horns-of-the-bull", whereby the forefinger and pinky are stretched straight out, while the other fingers are rolled into a fist (Elliott 2016b: 183–8). In the provinces, a variation of the *mano fica* gesture was also used, as it is generally acknowledged that a hand with the thumb tucked beneath the index finger represents the same *apotropaion* as the more common depiction of a thumb between forefinger and middle finger (Henig 1984: 166–7).

Finds of the phallus-cum-*mano fica* amulets (designed to be) worn by humans are recorded from both the Mediterranean (Johns 1982: 63–4,

Figure 5.8 Amulet with *mano fica* gesture designed to be worn by humans, from Wellingore, North Kesteven, Lincolnshire (PAS; LIN-2BE126)

colour fig. 10, lower bottom row, middle two) and the north-west provinces (Parker 2015, fig. 1; Chapter 4 in this volume). Their distribution in the north-west indicates their widespread use, even if the map is far from complete (Figure 5.9).

This type of pendant was also frequently used for the horse harness of the early first century A.D. (Figure 5.10; Bishop 1988, table 6, figs 47–9). However, the pendants seem to disappear completely during the course of the early second century, as they do not turn up among the ample collection of finds from the Upper Germanic-Rhaetian Limes dating into the latter half of the second and third centuries A.D. published by Oldenstein (1976). The combination of phallus and *mano fica* often also has a flaccid phallus hanging at the front between the two "horns", making the amulet even more powerful through the combination of several apotropaic images (see Chapter 4). In one rare instance from Sicily, an amulet with the combination of a phallus and a *mano fica* has what may be a vulva depicted in the same place (Manganaro 1996: 139, pl. XIV, fig. 21).[4]

As these pendants generally have an eyelet, they must have been used as a hanger, for which there are many possible places on the horse harness. However, it is generally unknown where precisely they hung on the horse: it is indeed likely that it was a matter of personal preferences or perhaps regional

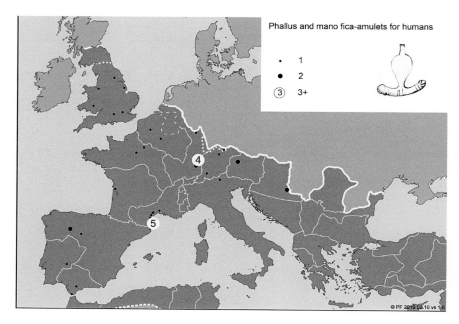

Phallus and mano fica-amulets for humans

·   1
●   2
③   3+

Figure 5.9 Distribution map of various types of amulets with a phallus and *mano fica* pointing upwards, designed to be worn by humans

(Map P. Franzen based on Appendix 5.2, list 4, picture of amulet: PAS, NLM863, © Portable Antiquities Scheme [CC BY 2.0])

use. Amulets have been found on the harnesses of horses for riding and those used to draw vehicles. Other finds indicate that they were also used for other equids such as donkeys and mules, and even other animals such as dogs.

Amulets of this form are extremely frequent finds in military installations in the north-west (Figure 5.11). This is probably due to the fact that military installations had a high concentration of horses. In addition, because of the relative wealth of the soldiers, a high proportion of these horses (both mounts and draught animals) had a decorated harness. We could even speculate that, at least in the cavalry, soldiers were more prone to use amulets for their horses, as they were completely dependent on their health and well being during battle. In the Mediterranean region, finds of horse harness amulets are rare: currently three examples from the Bay of Naples have been recorded (Ortisi 2015: 48, fig. 15, cat. nos D90–2, pls 36 and 87). The small number of these finds in Pompeii and its surroundings can be sought in the eighteenth and nineteenth-century excavation practice of only keeping a selection of finds and separating those perceived as being of a disreputable character into the *gabinetto segreto* (see Chapters 2 and 8). While indeed amulets of this type are only rarely mentioned in excavation reports from the Mediterranean, Roman metal finds are generally rarer in the Mediterranean, often caused by the drier soil conditions, which are unfavourable for metal preservation.

Figure 5.10 Amulets designed for horses with a *mano fica* combined with a phallus into a double horn shape, some with a flaccid phallus in front, some combined with a lunula (after Bishop 1988, figs 47–9: types 8l, 8o, 10a–k, 10m–o, 10q–t)

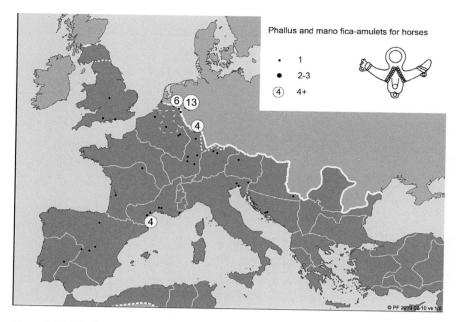

Figure 5.11 Distribution map of various types of horse amulets with a phallus and *mano fica* (Map P. Franzen based on Appendix 5.2, list 5)

Cowrie shell and coffee bean

Another object used to represent the vulva was the cowrie shell (first recognised by Jahn 1855: 79). Cowrie is the common name for a group of sea snails of the family *Cypraeidae*, which occur in many oceans around the world, with some species having their natural habitats in the Red Sea, the Mediterranean, and the Atlantic Ocean along the African coast as far south as Senegal. The word "cowrie" is often used to refer only to the shells of these snails, which are oval, rounded, with a flat underside surface that has a long, narrow, slit-like opening, often toothed at the edges. The surface of the shells is shiny and slightly translucent. Its underside resembles both a vulva (with the outer labia closed) and a half-closed eye at the same time (Hildburgh 1942: 179). Symbolising both of these body parts, a cowrie amulet could ensure fertility as well as warding off the Evil Eye simultaneously. In the Mediterranean they were frequently put into the graves of children, and in one instance one of them was found "in a residential district with the nail that apparently fixed it to a wall" (Faraone 2018: 73; also Elliott 2016a: 133).

In addition to actual cowrie shells, representations of the form of the shell in other materials were also in use. These representations have the form of an oval protuberance or dome incised lengthwise by a groove, looking like a coffee bean. We can thus identify several steps in the process of substitution: the cowrie shell is used as a substitute for the vulva because the vulva cannot be pictured. In a second step, and probably at least in part because of practical considerations, the form of the cowrie shell is then copied in other materials. These copies of cowrie shells in other materials first appear as jewellery in faience, semi-precious stones, or metal in Egypt during the Pharaonic age (Andrews 1994: 45, fig. 64; Dubiel 2008: 149–50). The continued use of this form in the Hellenistic period is proven by a necklace made from gold cowrie shells in the collection of the Getty Museum (Museum no. 92.AM.8.11, see also Pfrommer 2001: 100–1). The early use of this form in Italy may be represented by 20 bronze amuletic pendants for humans in the British Museum depicting a cowrie shell (British Museum, nr. WITT-434).[5] As they all originally were collected during the eighteenth and nineteenth centuries by private individuals in Italy, it seems very likely that they are Italian, but the dates given for them range from the sixth century B.C. to "Roman".

A type of bronze horse gear amulet, a mount consisting of a hexagonal plate with the coffee bean-shaped protuberance in the centre, is generally held to represent the vulva, even though it has commonly been named "coffee-bean" by scholars (Figure 5.12; Chapter 4). The reluctance of scholars to name the

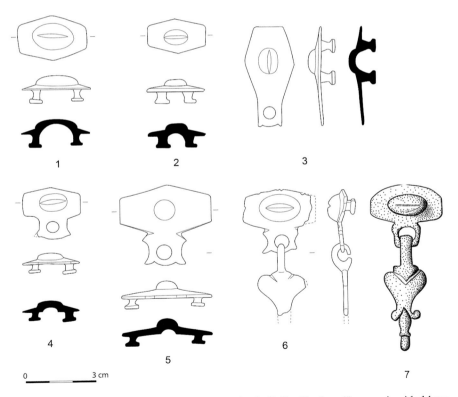

Figure 5.12 Amulets with depiction of a cowrie shell ("coffee bean") on a six-sided base plate, which could also represent a shield

Nos 1–6: after Nicolay (2007: 390, pl. 79); no. 7: drawing A. Smadi, Archäologisches Institut, Universität zu Köln, after Oldenstein (1976, Kat. Nr. 267)

female genitals by their Latin name, as they would the male, is an additional confirmation of Gsell's hypothesis mentioned above, namely that the taboo visualising the female genitals in word and pictures still exists today. These vulvate mounts usually have two or more rivets on their reverse, with small round platelets at the end to fix them onto leather. Some mounts also have a perforation or suspension loop on one side, to hang a pendant from. This type of mount dates into the second half of the third century A.D. (Höck 2006: 252–5, 266–7, find list 2, fig. 3). The distribution map shows that they appear in fairly high numbers in the north-west, with an even higher concentration in the border provinces in Britain and on the Rhine and Danube (Figure 5.13). This is probably connected to the fact that horse gear is more common in the garrisons of the Roman army, for the reasons mentioned above: the army had more horses, which were more often highly decorated. However, the distribution elsewhere in the north-west demonstrates that these decorative mounts were not reserved for the army. The sparse finds from the Mediterranean in their distribution resemble that of most other metal finds connected to horse gear. This makes it likely that the form was distributed Empire-wide. Similar cowrie-shaped protuberances were also found on other items of contemporary horse gear, such as rectangular strap fittings or round strap guides (Appendix 5.2, list 6). Items with this decoration not belonging to horse harnesses have only

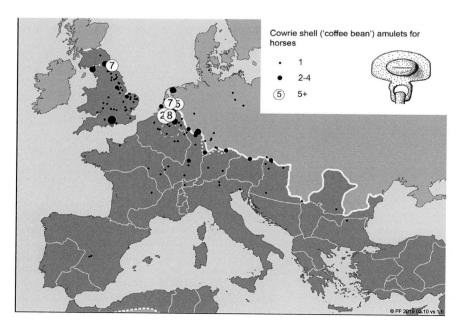

Figure 5.13 Distribution map of horse amulets with depiction of a cowrie shell/"coffee bean" on a six-sided shield

(Map P. Franzen based on Appendix 5.2, list 6)

been collected in Britain so far and include the bronze amuletic pendants mentioned above, a finger ring from Scarborough (PAS, no SWYOR-3794D6), a button-and-loop fastener with a square plate from Preston (PAS, no YORYM-BA9A5D), a vessel handle from Stoke Ferry (PAS, no NMS-6B16C2), and an unidentified object from the Isle of Wight (PAS, no IOW-AC2C04). While the "coffee-bean" type of mounts are generally accepted as representing a vulva, comparisons with other objects such as the jewellery mentioned above makes it clear that they also belong to the group of apotropaic images representing a cowrie shell, which was used as a substitute for the vulva itself.

Moreover, the mount plate has the same shape as a shield and the "coffee-bean" could also be seen as an enlarged shield boss with a central groove running from top to bottom. Shields of different forms are common *apotropaia*, especially from the second century A.D. onwards: while Celtic shield forms such as represented, for instance, by two rectangular brooches from Selby (PAS, nos SWYOR-54B456, SWYOR-FFF684; Hoss 2015: 201, fig. 3b) are infrequent finds, the pelta, a Greek shield form introduced to the north-west by the Romans, is common on elements of dress such as belts and brooches, but also incorporated into the chapes of knife and sword scabbards and sheaths (Hoss 2015: 201, 203–4, figs 3b and 6), and on horse harnesses (Hoss Forthcoming).

The vulvate mount as a combination of an allusion to a shield with the protrusion as a shield boss plus the cowrie as a substitute for the vulva demonstrates the difficulties in unambiguously identifying the various symbols that constitute an *apotropaion*. Indeed, a recognisable ambiguousness in order to maximise the protective powers of the amulet is often achieved through the combination of two or more *apotropaia* into a single amulet, as seen above with the *mano fica* amulets. The combination of as many protective images as possible on a single object may even be named a hallmark of Roman *apotropaia* (see Chapter 4). A similar combination of male and female genitalia is also present in the coffee bean mount with a perforation, from which a pendant hangs, whose form is mostly described as heart shaped (Gschwind 1998: 120–1, list of finds: 137–8, figs 7,6–7, also fig. 24.7). Contrary to this description, in my opinion this actually depicts a stylised phallus, with the lower part representing a flaccid phallus, while the upper heart shape represents a scrotum with the testes (Hoss Forthcoming). In their subject, these amulets thus are a successor of the amulets with flaccid phalli.

The rather late third century A.D. date of the coffee bean mount is curious. It is possible that the protection of horses with cowrie shell amulets or their representations in bronze only gained popularity in the later Empire. Another, rather speculative explanation *ex nihilo* may be that earlier *apotropaia* had used real cowrie shells. Some species of the true cowrie (*Cypraeidae*) occur naturally in the southern Mediterranean, the Red Sea, and the Indian Ocean, as well as on the coasts of Africa (Burton and Burton 1969–70: 556–7). Two different species (*Trivia arctica* and *monarcha*), whose lower sides look so similar to cowries that they were named "false cowries", have a natural habitat stretching from the Mediterranean to the Orkneys and thus could have been used in the north-west.

But even if cowries from the Red Sea or the Indian Ocean were preferred for the *apotropaia*, these shells are small, light, and hard, and are thus quite easily transportable over long distances. To my knowledge, there are no finds of cowrie shells in the European north-west, but it is possible that these have not been preserved or that their (broken) remains were overlooked or not recognised in excavations as being *apotropaia* on horse harnesses. If that was indeed the case, the question remains as to why the bronze form started to be used in the third century A.D. Did the soldiers start to prefer the gleaming brass versions to real ones? Or were real cowrie shells no longer readily available in the north-west? The latter argument is made more persuasive by the fact that, with the exception of some military settlements, such as Dura Europos and Volubilis, the type of horse harness decoration shown in Figure 5.13 has not been found in the Mediterranean, suggesting the possibility that real shells were used here. However, as mentioned above, this is a speculative explanation, which needs to be confirmed by finds of real cowrie shells in connection with horse harnesses. As to whom the cowrie shells protected, from what we know it seems likely that the real cowrie shells and their representations used in jewellery and dress accessories (necklaces with beads, finger rings, button-and-loop fasteners) were used by women. In contrast, the "coffee bean" mounts seem to be only used with horse gear. The susceptibility of horses and other equids like mules and donkeys to the Evil Eye was well known and greatly feared in antiquity, which may explain the profusion of protective amulets used on them (Hoss Forthcoming).

Scallop shell

The scallop shell is also often used as a substitute for the vulva, as it is a symbol of Aphrodite/Venus, who was born of the sea and floated ashore on a scallop shell. In antiquity, the most famous depiction of Aphrodite on a scallop was a painting by Apelles. Other versions abounded and statuettes showing Aphrodite covering her pubic area with a scallop shell make the connection quite clear. One version of this motif is the first to second centuries A.D. bronze statuette from the sanctuary of Apollo in Cyprus (British Museum, Nr. 1872,0816.87).

Scallops were already used as *apotropaia* for humans in amulet strings and as jewellery in the Mediterranean in pre-Roman graves and are also found in the Roman period (Faraone 2018: 64). In contrast, in the north-west a derivative of the scallop was used on horse harnesses. It has the same outer form as a scallop, but in most cases lacks the ribbing (Figure 5.14). On the back, these mounts usually have one or two squat pins with small round platelets at the end, demonstrating their use on leather (Gschwind 1998: 116–20, list of finds: 130–2, figs 1, nos 18–21; 2, no 7; 3; 4, nos 1–4; 6, no 5). The form is found all over the Empire (Figure 5.15), but only appears in contexts dating from the mid-third to the mid-fourth centuries A.D. Again, this may be connected to the fact that possible earlier examplars, which had been real shells, have deteriorated too much to be found or recognised as apotropaic amulets in excavations. It is equally possible that the form, together with the cowrie, only became popular at this late date. The dearth of well-dated finds from the first half of the third century A.D. may indicate that the form could have emerged earlier

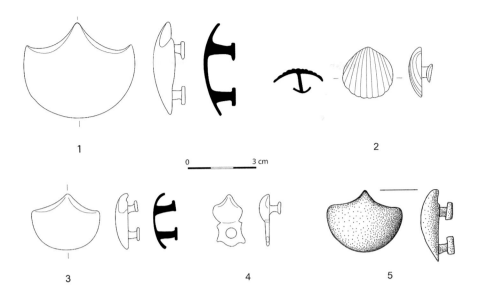

Figure 5.14 Amulets with depiction of a scallop shell

Nos 1–4: after Nicolay (2007: 384, pl. 73); no. 5 drawing A. Smadi, Archäologisches Institut, Universität zu Köln, after Oldenstein (1976, Kat. Nr. 698)

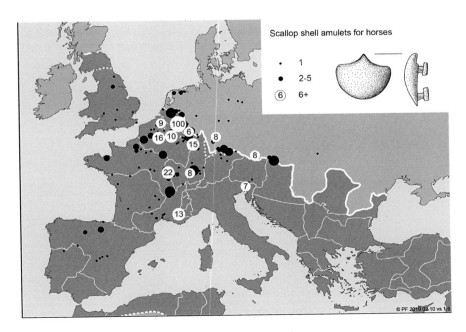

Figure 5.15 Distribution map of scallop shell horse amulets

(Map P. Franzen based on Appendix 5.2, list 7)

(Gschwind 1998: 116–20). The use of the scallop form on horse harnesses is confirmed by the finds in two third-century A.D. tumuli in Belgium which contained sets of horse harnesses: the Tombe de Saives near Celles-lez-Waremme (de Loë 1937; Massart 2000), which contained more than 100 scallop shell mounts, and the tumulus of Long-Pont near Thorembais-Saint-Trond (Mariën 1994). Very small scallop studs from Gaddesby and Thurcaston-and-Cropston are also mentioned by Parker (2015: 142, n. 23), but the size of those—the larger is 3 x 2.8 cm long—points to them being worn by humans as they would have been near impossible to see on a horse. Scallops are occasionally used as additions on other amulets, such as the six phallus-cum-*mano fica* amulets found at Catterick, where they form the common source from which the phallus and the arm spring (Parker 2015: 135–6, fig. 1 and 141, fig. 7). Like the flaccid phallus on other composite amulets, the scallops may have strengthened the apotropaic protection granted by the phallus and *mano fica*.

Almond shapes

Some decorative mounts have forms that may or may not depict a vulva. Two forms of horse harness decoration were sometimes described in the literature as depicting the vulva (Oldenstein 1976: 140): these types of mounts or hangers could best be described as almond shaped and they usually have two forms. The first form is a pointed oval, with one to two ridges on the inside, which follow the form, creating smaller ovals (Figure 5.16, no. 1). These were filled with enamel in the same manner in which the more common round buttons were, and probably are similar in date, namely the second to third centuries A.D. (Gschwind 2004: 173, Kat. Nr. C519–35, Taf. 52; Nicolay 2007, pl. 71, cat. nr. 79.24; 82.181; 170.18; 222.76; 242.71; 242.72). They would picture the vulva quite explicitly, with the inner labia represented by the smaller

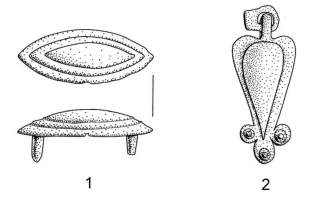

1   **2**

Figure 5.16 Horse harness decoration that may possibly picture a vulva

(Drawing A. Smadi, Archäologisches Institut, Universität zu Köln, after Oldenstein 1976, Kat. Nr. 280, 287)

ovals on the inside. But we have to take into account that both in the Mediterranean and the north-west the depictions of the vulva almost never get to be as explicit as that. Only Greek or Hellenistic depictions show the inner labia, but these never picture disembodied vulvae. Therefore, it seems very unlikely that the almond-shaped buttons are supposed to represent a vulva. Another form of similar date has an almond shape with a pointy end, where the hanger or mount is decorated with a trefoil or roundels, which often carry a circle-dot -decoration (Figure 5.16, no 2; Oldenstein 1976: 139–42, 248–9, Cat. Nr. 278–81, Taf. 35). Again, this form would depict an open vulva, which in my opinion makes it unlikely that a vulva is meant in these decorations. It is likely that both these forms refer to almonds rather than the vulva (Oldenstein 1976: 140).

Other objects with almond shaped decoration are a group of Mediterranean oil lamps, which are described as having vulva-shaped handles (Bailey 1963–96 cat. nos Q1025, Q1050 Q1947, Q2713, Q3010, Q3011, Q3021; see also Johns 1982, fig. 58). The handles are oval and domed and have an almond shaped slit that is often emphasised by colour. On one side (away from the lamp's body), these elements have a small roundish button. This button and the rather wide opening make it unlikely that a cowrie is meant here. They could indicate that these handles perhaps truly depict the vulva or, more likely, another substitute for the vulva, the pomegranate, with a slice cut out to reveal its interior, which is red and full of seeds, and an ancient symbol of fertility.

Only one case convincingly demonstrates an association between the almond shape and the vulva. This object is an exceptional amulet made as an antler-disc roundel with two decorated sides found in Cologne (Figure 5.17). One side displays a phallus in the middle, flanked by two almond shapes with a line going from tip to tip. On the other side is a double phallus between a rough lunula and a bean-like shape with a straight line across it (Greep 1994: 84 and 95, cat. nr. 153, pl. III a and c). The apotropaic function of antler-disc roundels has long been established and they are a common amulet group, often decorated with phalli (Greep 1994; Unz and Deschler-Erb 1997, cat. nr. 1663–89, pl. 60). Exceptional in this object is the combination of the phallus with the female symbols, the lunula, and both a schematic depiction of the vulva (the almond shape with a line) and the cowrie-like bean shape with a line. Antler-disc amulets are known from graves, but were also found connected to horse gear.

Lunula

A form that only alludes to the female is the lunula. While the lunula is not a substitute for the vulva as such, it ultimately represents the female power of reproduction. The linking of the moon with the female is a result of the idea that as both the menstrual and lunar cycles average around 29.5 days, they must be connected. This idea is quite old and probably one reason why the moon is a female deity in the Mediterranean world. Lunate amulets were used as protective imagery

a   b

Figure 5.17 Antler-disc roundel from Cologne (Römisch-Germanisches Museum Köln, Nr. N5128

(Photo Ph. Gross, Archäologisches Institut, Universität zu Köln)

from at least the fourth century B.C. onwards in Mesopotamia and from the first millennium on in Greece, but were also known in the European north-west before the advent of the Romans (Wrede 1975: 243; Zadoks-Josephus Jitta and Witteveen 1977: 168). They were common amulets for women, children, and animals in Roman times (Figure 5.18, upper row; Zadoks-Josephus Jitta and Witteveen 1977: 168; Riha 1990: 72–3, cat. nr. 714, 717–19, 2947; Johns 1996, fig. 6.4; Johns 1997: 113, nos 320–2; Massart 2002: 101–3; Crummy 2010: 51).

However, unlike other forms of protection connected to the feminine, lunulae were also worn by (one group of) men, and very manly men at that: lunular pendants were a typical decoration of the ends of the so-called "apron" of the military belt in the Rhineland from the Neronian to the Flavian period, as depicted on the gravestones of the soldiers and on official monuments (Figure 5.18, lower row; Bishop 1992, table 1; Wieland 2008: 32; Ortisi 2015: 35, cat. nr. 23–7, pl. 22; Hoss 2014a: 100, Graph VII.28). The form was also used for the military decorations of the soldiers (phalerae), as the Newstead and Lauersfort finds demonstrate (Maxfield 1981: 94–5, pl. 15, 16a).

The lunulae were also frequently used to decorate horse harnesses as supported by both the archaeological finds and the many depictions on stone monuments showing horses wearing them. These are mostly large examples worn on the breast and occasionally smaller ones hanging from the browband or the breeching strap, which runs along the haunch and under the tail of the horse (Bishop 1988: 69–84; Hoss Forthcoming). Lunulae are the only *apotropaion* that appears on horses in all known depictions, whether the gravestones of cavalrymen, official state monuments, or the equestrian statues of emperors. Lunulae were used on horse harnesses from the first to the third centuries A.D., making them the longest surviving *apotropaion* on such harnesses (Figure 5.19; Bishop 1988: 107–8, type 9, 153–5, figs 47–8; James 2004: 88–9, cat. nr. 193–8; Hoss Forthcoming). Finds of lunular horse pendants from Pompeii, Boscoreale, and Stabiae demonstrate that their scarcity in

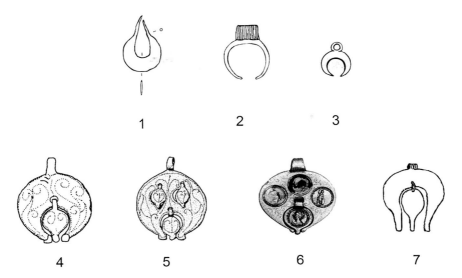

Figure 5.18 Lunate amulets for humans: upper row—lunate female jewellery: no 1: ear-
ring; nos 2–3: pendants; lower row—lunate pendants from the so-called
"apron" of the soldier's belt

(Nos 2–3: drawing S. Hoss after Riha 1990, Kat. Nr. 714, 717, 719; nos 4–7: from Hoss 2014, Kat.
Nr. F. 23, F. 29, F. 45, F. 47)

other excavations in the Mediterranean region is probably due either to
a publication bias or the recycling of material (Ortisi 2015: 36, 131–2, 137, cat. nr.
D 78–89, 163.c, pl. 36–7, 51 and 87). We can thus assume that the original distribution of these amulets was quite as wide in the Mediterranean as in the European
north-west (Fig. 5.20).

It is interesting to note that the lunulae designed for female jewellery are different from those meant for soldiers or horses: while the latter two almost uniformly
have a hole in the apex of the inner curve in order to attach a further pendant, often
leaf shaped and meant to fill the void of the crescent, this is never the case with
lunulae worn by women. Moreover, the first century A.D. lunulae for horse harnesses have a wide variety of possibilities in the design of the terminals: pointed,
each side terminating in a sphere or touching the same sphere (so that the whole
resembles a disc with a round hole), or with round tips that carry rings or other
decorations. Furthermore, horse harness lunulae were often combined with phalli in
various manners, thus representing "double purpose" amulets, where both the male
and the female genitals are combined (see Figure 5.10, nos 7, 10–11; also Artefact:
APH-4055, 4111–12). For instance, in addition to the common lunula with pointed
terminals, the terminals of lunulae could also be rounded, resembling two flaccid
phalli pointing downwards (as in Figure 5.10, no. 9 and Figure 5.19, no. 4). Sometimes this form was combined with another flaccid phallus with a scrotum hanging

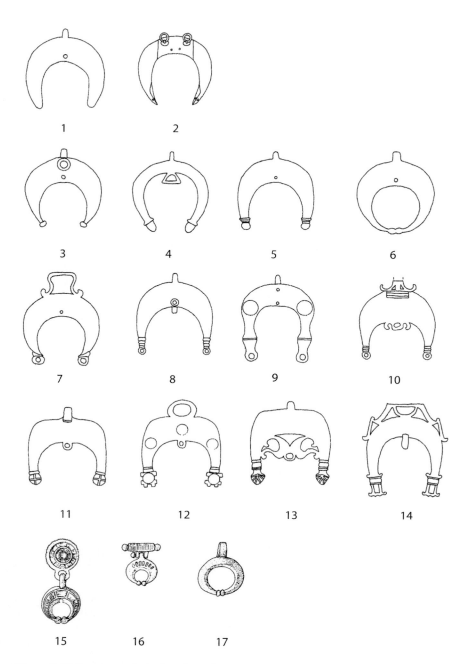

Figure 5.19 Lunate pendants from horse harnesses

Nos 1–14, first century A.D.: after Bishop (1992, figs 47–8); nos 15–17, second century A.D.: drawing S. Hoss after Oldenstein (1976, Kat. Nr. 444, 449, 450)

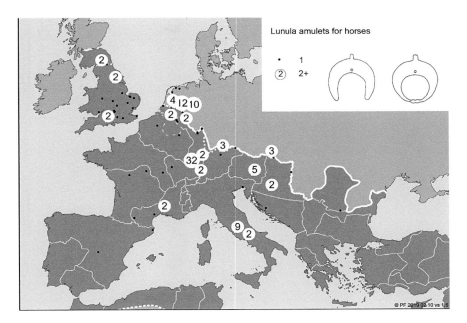

Figure 5.20 Distribution map of first to third centuries A.D. lunate horse amulets, with the lunula pointing downwards

(Map P. Franzen based on Appendix 5.2, list 8)

in the middle (Figure 5.21; Bishop 1988: 98, 146, 150, type 6, fig. 46; Hoss Forthcoming). These amulets were mostly found in military settlements of the early first century A.D. and seem to have fallen out of fashion rather quickly (Figure 5.22).

Summary

Summarising, we can state that, for apotropaic purposes, the vulva was replaced by a number of objects that physically resembled and symbolically represented either it or, more generally, the female principle. While the form and the exact execution of an amulet could vary between the Mediterranean and the European north-west, the objects that were used as substitutes for the vulva in the north-west were the same as in the Mediterranean. This is only to be expected if we consider that most of the ideas of the Evil Eye and the remedies used against it, including *apotropaia*, were probably imported from the Mediterranean. It is also interesting to note that, at least in the north-west, the majority of the substitutes for the vulva were used on horse harnesses and were not worn by people. In contrast to this, the lunula was not only the most common apotropaic decoration for a horse but also a very common form for female jewellery, and even used for a while as the decoration of the "apron" of the soldier's belt.

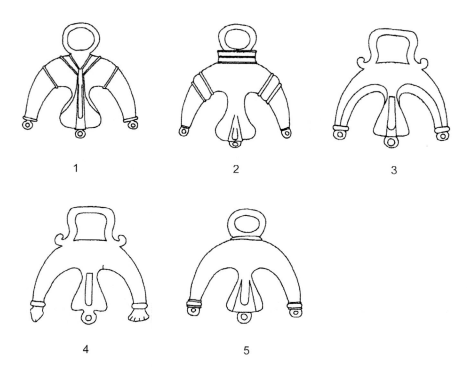

Figure 5.21 First century A.D. lunate pendants formed by two flaccid phalli pointing downwards

(After Bishop 1992, fig. 46)

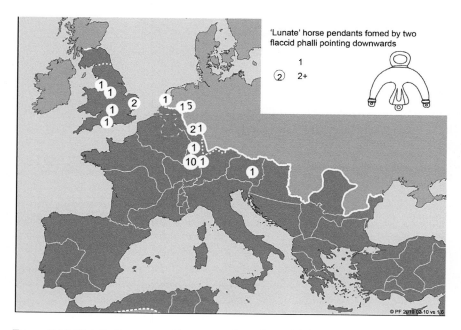

Figure 5.22 Distribution map of lunate pendants formed by two flaccid phalli pointing downwards

(Map P. Franzen based on Appendix 5.2, list 9)

Conclusion

This chapter started with a summary of the scholarship inquiring into the depictions of the vulva on women in the Mediterranean Graeco-Roman culture in order to compare them with the relevant depictions in the north-west provinces of the Roman Empire and determine whether we can see any similarities or differences.

In the Mediterranean we can see that, unlike the representations of male genitalia, depictions of female genitalia on women were not life-like, but at most showed a smooth triangle (representing the depilated vulva with closed outer labia) or a slightly triangular slit (representing the hairless vulva with opened outer labia). However, there are indications that pubic hair was not completely removed in Greek and Hellenistic culture: some vases depict it and some statues show remains that seem to be evidence of painted pubic hair and/or a line separating the outer labia. Seaman (2004) has suggested that the preference to paint the pubic hair of young boys and women in contrast to the three-dimensional rendition of the pubic hair of grown men may be in order to make it appear groomed. Un-groomed pubic hair would have been seen as a sign of virility and active sexuality, while groomed hair would be more fitting for the passive sexual role of young boys and women. Rare exceptions from these not very life-like depictions are highly erotic pictures from the Greek and Hellenistic cultures, which show the insertion of a penis/dildo. These depict the vulva somewhat more realistically, namely open to at least a triangular slit and in some early cases perhaps even showing the inner labiae. In contrast to this, Roman Mediterranean imagery universally presents female genitals with the pubic hair removed and the outer labia shown as closed. Here, a line separating the outer labiae represents the height of naturalism that is possible. In depictions that show a penis being inserted the line is, in some cases, slightly widened to a slim triangle, but in others, the labiae remain incongruously closed, even when the woman is shown with her legs spread wide to accept a penis into her vagina or a tongue into her vulva. That so little of the vulva has been naturalistically depicted, even with the hair removed, is a sign that the representation was "sanitised" and that a taboo was in place.

Most depictions of the vulva attached to a body either portray goddesses or mortal women; they rarely have an apotropaic purpose, the exceptions are those representing the Baubo, which are limited to Asia Minor and Egypt. Even here, the vulva of the Baubo is only represented in a "sanitised" version, namely (mostly) as a hole. Turning to the north-west provinces of the Roman Empire, most of the depictions of the vulva attached to a body are similar to those in the Roman Mediterranean, namely a smooth, "Barbie-like" triangular area. Only a handful of exceptional cases depict female genitalia in more detail, that is with an incised slit, and in one case even depicting pubic hair. These are geographically concentrated in the eastern part of central Gaul, and may be indicative that women in that region enjoyed a more equal status to men (Künzl 2001: 259–60; see Chapter 6 for similar cases in Romano-British society). A caveat has to be added here: just as in the Mediterranean, the depictions showing a smooth triangular area may originally have been painted.

In both the Mediterranean and the European north-west, the apotropaic depiction of "disembodied" female genitals almost always uses substitutes, such as the *mano fica*, the shells of cowrie and scallop, or the lunula. Differences in emphasis between the Mediterranean and the north-west can be distinguished in detail, but these are likely to result from differences in the amount of production and preservation rather than from differences in the acceptance or use of the depictions. The main use for most apotropaic substitutes for the vulva seems to be on horse harnesses, at least in the north-west. That the latter may be a distortion of ancient reality is shown by the finds from the Bay of Naples, which demonstrate that horse gear in that region resembles the contemporary finds from the north-west provinces to a high degree. Consequently, it seems possible that future publications of the metal finds of Mediterranean excavations will correct our impression of the distribution of horse gear amulets.

This also applies to the use of the vulva substitutes in the protection of humans. The lunula was not only the most common apotropaic decoration for a horse but also an extremely common form of jewellery for women and children, and was even used as the decoration on soldiers' belts. While lunulae were the *apotropaion* occurring with the highest frequency in female jewellery, pomegranates were also fairly frequent, as were representations of scallops and cowries. The reason for the lower amounts of finds of jewellery including depictions of cowrie and scallop shells could lie in the fact that many women may have worn the natural shells, perhaps on cords made from textile or leather, which would not have been preserved.

What has, I hope, become clear is that the depiction of the female genitals in both the ancient Mediterranean and the north-west provinces differs profoundly from the depiction of the male genitals. With the phallus, a schematic model of the human penis was developed that was easily recognisable, even in hastily drawn or small depictions. However, no such schematic model was successfully developed for the vulva. Instead, substitutes like the cowrie shell and the lunula were used. As the experiment above showed (Appendix 5.1; Figures 5.1 and 5.2), a number of schematic depictions of eyes and other body parts certainly existed and still exist, therefore it would have surely been possible to develop a schematic model for the vulva, had the societies in question wanted to. Moreover, the number of depictions of male genitals pictured on male figures or as disembodied phalli substantially exceed those of the vulva (see Chapters 4, 9, and 10). The most likely explanation for this is the existence of a taboo inhibiting the depiction of the female genitalia. This impression is strengthened by the "Barbie-like" non-depiction of female genitalia on most three-dimensional statues of women, where a more naturalistic depiction of at least the outer labia would have undoubtedly been within the reach of the sculptors. While one should take into account the possibility of a painted depiction of the outer labia on these statues, the wall paintings from the Roman Mediterranean show depictions of vulvas without hair and only delineated by a painted line. This convincingly demonstrates that the likelihood of the existence of a more naturalistic depiction of the vulva in Roman imagery is slim.

The taboo inhibiting the correct representation of the vulva is a society-wide phenomenon in the Roman Empire from the Mediterranean to the European north-west. Like the written defamations of this female organ, the visual non-representation, and probably also verbal defilements in daily life, were meant to control this female seat of lust and, thus, active sexuality. This is particularly visible in the depictions of Aphrodite/Venus *pudica*, the Graeco-Roman ideal of feminine beauty and female identity. The statue type is defined by the goddess covering her "shame" (genitalia) with her hand. The Latin *pudicus* covers both the word fields of chaste/modest/virtuous as well as bashful/shamefaced/ashamed and it is quite revealing of Roman cultural attitudes that this is the appellation for a woman covering her genitals.

The ideal woman was one that was ashamed of her genitals and subordinated herself both socially and sexually to the male. The basis for this need for control was formed by male cultural anxieties about the legality of their offspring and, consequently, about the active sexuality of women threatening male positions of power (Langlands 2006: 21). One can argue that the anatomically correct portrayal of the vulva would be a symbol of female "shamelessness", of a perverse, socially unacceptable, active sexuality. The consequence of this is that a representation of the vulva in its full glory was, and still is, not possible. The vulva is non-existent; the phallus is omnipresent.

Acknowledgements

I thank Tatiana Ivleva and Rob Collins for suggesting this interesting subject to me, and both them and the anonymous peer-reviewer (m/f) for many improvements on the original chapter; the latter especially for suggesting the experiment described in Appendix 5.1. I also thank the passengers of the bus on the Serbian Limes Congress for participating in the said experiment. Similar thanks are due to Martijn Wijnhoven for shamelessly exploiting his colleagues for the same experiment. I owe many thanks to all the people who helped me getting the pictures that explain my argument, especially Mike Bishop, Eckhard Deschler-Erb, Philipp Gross, Sophie Hay, and the incomparable Amira Smadi. But my biggest thanks go to Paul Franzen, who sacrificed many hours of his time to generate the maps.

Appendix 5.1

In order to test the hypothesis that the depictions of the sexual organs can be compared to the mouth and nose in the respect to the difficulty of accurately drawing each anatomical feature, one of the anonymous peer reviewers suggested an experiment. In this experiment a range of people (colleagues and friends) of both sexes were asked to draw both male and female genitals and a nose and mouth each, as well as providing basic information about their gender, age bracket (by decade), and their country of origin.

A 2018 LIMES/Roman Frontier Studies Congress held in Serbia with long bus excursions offered the chance to complete the experiment. There were 42 participating Roman archaeologists (28 male, 14 female) with ages ranging from the 20s to the 60s, whose nationalities included North Americans and diverse Europeans in a relatively even fashion (from Scandinavia and the British Isles, Germany, Austria, Hungary, and Romania, but excluding Mediterranean countries, with the largest group of a single nation being eight Germans). The sample thus seems quite representative—of Roman archaeologists. Because of this, a control sample of non-archaeologists was asked to participate as well. This consisted of 19 Dutch people with ages ranging from the 30s to the 60s, of which 12 were male and 7 female. Surprisingly, the greatest difficulties were apparently experienced by the participants in drawing a mouth and nose, with many opting for very simple single line sketches.

Anatomy	Perspective		Position (independent of perspective)		Anatomy	Perspective		Detail	
Nose	From side	37	Located on face	22	Mouth	Open	18	Lips present	5
	From front	23	Disembodied	37		Closed	40	Lips present	26
Phallus	From side	58	Located on body	5	Vulva	Open	24	Lips present	23
	From front	1	Disembodied	54		Closed	31	Lips present	7

The pictures were arranged in different groups by their manner of depiction. It is interesting to note the consistency of the depiction of phalli from the side, with only one depiction (the most natural depiction, demonstrating superior draughtsmanship, see Figure 5.2) from the front. The vast majority of the phalli were also depicted as disembodied, while the vulvae were drawn considerably more contextualised in their position on the body.

Noses were pictured from the front more often than the phalli, but the majority of these depictions consisted of a single straight line. The mouth was drawn as closed about twice as often as depicted as being open, but lips were mostly drawn on closed mouths, often in the typical heart or bow shape. In contrast to this, drawings of the vulva were slightly more often drawn open (56.3 per cent) than closed (43.6 per cent), and here the lips were more often pictured with an open vulva than with a closed one.

The diversity of representation was the greatest with female genitalia, followed by noses and then mouths. In contrast, male genitalia were depicted with extreme similarity, almost always from the side and often very schematic. As a high number of noses and mouths were also depicted in a fashion that was quite similar, it seems very likely that most people used depictions they had seen before as models for their own pictures rather than actual images of the organs in question. With female genitals, many opted for the easier mons pubis rather than the complicated vulva, and most depictions of the female genitalia had some degree of ambiguity. This may point to the fact that there are (almost) no preconceived models for this organ that the participants could use. This would strengthen the theory that depictions of the vulva are still rare in Western societies, while those of phalli seem to be so frequent that everybody has a "phallus model" in mind, which they can follow when drawing. The variation in noses and mouths is most likely connected to the fact that they are pictured very often in flat art and animation, and accordingly the participants had various models in their minds, which they could follow or refer to.

Appendix 5.2

The following lists give the references for the maps in the figures. The data were taken from Deimel (1987), Bishop (1988 and 2009), Deschler-Erb (1996 and 2012), Unz and Deschler-Erb (1997), Gschwind (1998), Waasdorp (1999), Künzl (2001), Müller (2002), Kovač and Koščević (2003), James (2004), Radman-Livaja (2004), Höck (2006), Lenz (2006), Aurrecoechea Fernández (2007), Nicolay (2007), Poulter (2007), Franke (2009), Hoss (2013), Ivčević (2013a and 2013b), Hoss (2014b), Maspoli (2014), Lewis (2016) and the internet-based databases Artefact, Portable Antiquities of the Netherlands (PAN), Portable Antiquities Scheme (PAS), and ubi-erat-lupa.

Despite the large amount of data collected in the databases and the fact that many large published collections of metal finds in the north-western provinces of the Roman Empire were consulted, the lists are of course far from complete. However, they give a good indication of the general distribution of the forms.

List 1

Distribution of the more realistic depictions of vulvae on women goddesses (after Künzl 2001).

Country	Place name	Title	Amount
B	Arlon	Dancers	6
D	Alzey	Venus	1
D	Karlsruhe	Venus?	1
D	Mainz	Venus	1
F	Alesia	Venus (knife handle)	1

(*Continued*)

(Cont.)

Country	Place name	Title	Amount
F	Bettwiler	Nymph	1
F	Bourges	Woman	1
F	Brémur-en-Vaurois	Dea Sequana	2
F	Châtillon-sur-Seine	Venus	1
F	Dijon	Woman	5
F	Escles	Dancer	1
F	Guiry-en-Vexin	Nymphs	2
F	Lezoux	Venus	1
F	Meaux	Venus	1
F	Mesvres	Venus	1
F	Orléans	Woman	5
F	Vieux	Venus	1
F	Villiers-le-Duc	Venus/Nymph	1
GB	High Rochester	Nymph	1
GB	Lydney Park	Woman (flat carving)	1
			35

List 2

Distribution of the more realistic depictions of vulvae on anatomical votives (after Künzl 2001).

Country	Place name	Amount
F	Alesia	1
F	Argenton-sur-Creuse	1
F	Châtillon-sur-Seine	7
F	Dijon	7
F	Semur	2
F	Senlis	4
F	Troyes	1
		23

List 3

List of the depictions of vulvae on female bodies on ubi-erat-lupa.

Reference no.	Country	Place name	Description	Pudica	Unmarked	Triangle
16678	AU	Wien	Venus			1
26514	D	Kindenheim	Woman emerging from flower		1	
7627	D	Neuenhaus	Maenad ?		2	
7647	D	Oberriexingen	Diana	1		
26976	D	Pforzheim	Maenad		1	
24983	HR	Solin	Mythical figure		1	
2767	HU	Budapest	Season		1	
4520	HU	Budapest	Maenad		1	
10550	HU	Budapest	Venus		1	
3885	HU	Dunaújváros	Venus		1	
3943	HU	Dunaújváros	Venus			1
5922	HU	Dunaújváros	Season		1	
5224	HU	Nagytétény	Venus	1		
9985	HU	Now Budapest	Venus	1		
6054	HU	Szöny	?		1	
10455	HU	Tác	Venus		1	
4456	HU	Visegrád	Hesione ?		1	
18105	IT	Aquileia	Venus/Nymph	1		
18444	IT	Aquileia	Venus		1	
21597	IT	Aquileia	Venus			1
21597	RO	Istria	Mythical figure		1	
11447	SI	Zagrad pri Prevaljah	Spring nymph		1	
				4	**16**	**3**

List 4

Distribution map of various types of amulets designed to be worn by humans with a phallus and *mano fica* pointing upwards.

Reference	Country	Place name	Amount
Artefact AMP 4031	AU	Salzburg	2
Artefact AMP 4031	CH	Baden	2
Artefact AMP 4031	CH	Chur	1
Artefact AMP 4031	CH	Windisch (Vindonissa)	4
Artefact AMP 4031	D	Augsburg	1

(Continued)

(Cont.)

Reference	Country	Place name	Amount
Artefact AMP 4031	D	Mainz	1
Artefact AMP 4031	D	Oberstimm	1
Artefact AMP-4002	E	Acinipo, Rondo La Vieja	1
Artefact AMP-4002	E	Baelo Claudia (Cadiz)	1
Artefact AMP-4002, AMP-4028	E	L'Escala, Ampurias	5
Artefact AMP 4021	E	Mérida, La Corchera [prov. Badajoz]	1
Artefact AMP 4031	E	Rosinos de Vidriales	1
Artefact AMP-4019	E	Valladolid	1
Artefact AMP-4004	F	Aspiran, Les Gisses	1
Artefact AMP-4002	F	Baralle, La Chapelle des Morts	1
Artefact AMP 4021	F	Barzan, Moulin du Fâ	1
Artefact AMP-4002	F	Béziers,	1
Artefact AMP 4021	F	Chartres	1
Artefact AMP-4002	F	Château-Porcien, Nandin	1
Artefact AMP-4002	F	Fontès, Les Pradesses	1
Artefact AMP 4031	F	Gruissan, Saint-Martin-le-Bas	1
Artefact AMP-4002	F	Paris, Jardins du Sénat	1
Artefact AMP 4031	F	Villetelle, Le Sablas	1
Lewis (2016, fig. 8)	GB	Brecon Gaer	1
Artefact AMP-4002	GB	Chester	1
PAS, NLM863	GB	East Lindsay	1
Artefact AMP 4031	GB	London	1
Artefact AMP 4031	GB	Silchester	1
Artefact AMP-4002	GB	York	1
Artefact AMP-4002	HR	Osijek	2
Artefact AMP 4031	IT	Mechel, Tirol	1
			40

List 5

Distribution map of various types of horse amulets with a phallus and *mano fica*.

Reference	Country	Place name	Amount
Artefact PHD-4019	AU	Mondsee	1
Artefact PHD-4019	BE	Gand	1
Artefact PHD-4019	BE	Spontin	1
Bishop (1988)	CH	Baden	2
Unz and Deschler-Erb, taf. 58–9	CH	Windisch	20
Bishop, Artefact PDH-4048	D	Ailsingen	2
Bishop	D	Augsburg-Oberhausen	3
Bishop	D	Haltern	13
Bishop	D	Hofheim	1
Bishop	D	Mainz	4
Deschler-Erb (2012, D6, D7)	D	Moers (Asciburgium)	2
Bishop	D	Oberaden	1
Bishop	D	Rheingönheim	2
Bishop	D	Rottweil	1
Artefact PHD-4019	D	Trier	1
Lenz, kat. nr. 332, 333, 335	D	Xanten	3
Aurrecoechea Fernández, fig. 4.8	E	Albalate de Zorita	1
Artefact PHD-4019	E	L'Escala, Ampurias	4
Aurrecoechea Fernández, fig. 4.7	E	Maqueda (Toledo)	1
Artefact PHD-4019	E	Merida	1
Aurrecoechea Fernández, fig. 4.6	E	Ocaña (Toledo)	1
Artefact PDH-4048	E	Varea [Logroño]	1
Artefact PHD-4019	F	Beaucaire, Le Sizen	1
Artefact PHD-4019	F	Biesheim, Oedenburg	1
Artefact PHD-4019	F	Bordeaux	1
Artefact PHD-4073	F	Bourges	1
Artefact PHD-4019, AMP-4022	F	Fréjus	2
Artefact PDH-4048	F	Kembs	1
Artefact PHD-4019	F	Narbonne	2
Artefact PHD-4019	F	Nîmes	1
Artefact PHD-4019	F	Perpignan	1
Artefact PHD-4019	F	Valros, Les Combes	1
Bishop (1988)	GB	Baginton, The Lunt	1
Bishop (1988)	GB	Chicester	1
Bishop (1988)	GB	Hod Hill	1
Ivčević (2013a, kat. nr. 30-31)	HR	Salona	2

(Continued)

(Cont.)

Reference	Country	Place name	Amount
Kovač and Koščević, kat. nr. 90–2	HR	Sirmium	3
Ivčević (2013b, kat. nr. 33)	HR	Tilurium (Gardun)	1
Artefact PHD-4087	IT	Aquileia	1
Artefact PHD-4019	IT	Santa Maria di Sclaunicco	1
Artefact PHD-4019	LUX	Grevenmacher, Buerggruef	1
Bishop	NL	Nijmegen	6
Bishop	NL	Valkenburg	2
Artefact PHD-4019	SI	Ljubljana	1
			100

List 6

Distribution of horse amulets with depiction of a cowrie shell ("coffee bean") on a hexagonal base.

Reference	Country	Place name	Mount	On other horse gear
Höck, Fundliste 2	AU	Bad Deutsch-Altenburg (Carnuntum)	2	
Höck, Fundliste 2	AU	Bernhardsthal	1	
Höck, Fundliste 2	AU	Bregenz	1	
Höck, Fundliste 2	AU	Enns (Lauriacum)	1	
Höck, Fundliste 2	AU	Enzersfeld	1	
Höck, Fundliste 2	AU	Innsbruck	1	
Gschwind, Fundliste 1	AU	Lauriacum	1	
Gschwind, Fundliste 1	AU	Lichtenwörth	1	
Gschwind, Fundliste 1	AU	Lutzmannsburg	1	
Gschwind, Fundliste 1	AU	Zurndorf	1	
Gschwind, Fundliste 1	BE	Faimes (Celles-les-Waremme)	1	1
Gschwind, Fundliste 1	BE	Kruishoutem	1	
Artefact SPD-4008	BE	Mons	1	
Gschwind, Fundliste 1	BE	Wancennes	1	
Höck, Fundliste 2	BE	Waudrez	1	
Poulter, kat. nr. 2.152	BUL	Nikyup (Nicopolis ad Istrum)	1	
Höck, Fundliste 2	CH	Avenches	1	

(Cont.)

Reference	Country	Place name	Mount	On other horse gear
Artefact SPD-4008	CH	Martigny	1	
Höck, Fundliste 2	D	Bibelried	1	
Gschwind, Fundliste 1	D	Binningen (Kuhkeller)	1	
Gschwind, Fundliste 1	D	Dambach	1	
Gschwind, Fundliste 1	D	Eining	2	
Höck, Fundliste 2	D	Feldberg	1	
Gschwind, Fundliste 1	D	Froitzheim	1	
Höck, Fundliste 2	D	Gaukönigshofen-Acholshausen	1	
Gschwind, Fundliste 1	D	Gnotzheim	1	
Gschwind, Fundliste 1	D	Gommersheim	1	
Höck, Fundliste 2	D	Gross Behnitz	1	
Gschwind, Fundliste 1	D	Hedderheim	1	
Höck, Fundliste 2	D	Herzsprung	1	
Gschwind, Fundliste 1	D	Hontheim	1	
Gschwind, Fundliste 1	D	Jülich	1	
Höck, Fundliste 2	D	Klein Köris bei Grossjena	1	
Gschwind, Fundliste 1	D	Köngen	2	
Gschwind, Fundliste 1	D	Mainz und Umgebung	2	
Gschwind, Fundliste 1	D	Neuss	1	
Gschwind, Fundliste 1	D	Niederbiber	2	
Gschwind, Fundliste 1	D	Saalburg	3	
Höck, Fundliste 2	D	Soest-Ardey	1	
Höck, Fundliste 2	D	Stadtlauringen	1	
Höck, Fundliste 2	D	Thorsberg	1	
Gschwind, Fundliste 1	D	Tüddern	1	
Gschwind, Fundliste 1	D	Vettweis-Lüxheim	1	
Gschwind, Fundliste 1	D	Walldürn	1	
Gschwind, Fundliste 1	D	Zugmantel	1	
Höck, Fundliste 2	E	Ocaña	1	
Höck, Fundliste 2	E	Villasequilla de Ypes	1	
Gschwind, Fundliste 1	F	Autun	1	
Gschwind, Fundliste 1	F	Bayard-sur-Marne, Chaletet de Gourzon	1	
Artefact SPD-4007	F	Biesheim (Oedenburg)	2	
Höck, Fundliste 2	F	Caen	1	
Höck, Fundliste 2	F	Cosne-sur-Loire	1	
Artefact SPD-4008	F	Horbourg-Wihr	1	

(*Continued*)

(Cont.)

Reference	Country	Place name	Mount	On other horse gear
Artefact SPD-4008 Höck, Fundliste 2	F	Kembs	1	
Gschwind, Fundliste 1	F	Mâlain	1	
Gschwind, Fundliste 1	F	Selongey	1	
PAS, WAW-6507A6	GB	Alcester	1	
Höck, Fundliste 2	GB	Aldborough	1	
PAS, LANCUM-087A43, LANCUM-0F2FB1, LANCUM-0F23C9	GB	Allerdale	3	
PAS, HAMP-CF2DC7	GB	Appledram	1	
PAS, YORYM-9BD246	GB	Appleton-le-Moors	1	
PAS, NMS-4B7AD2	GB	Beeston	1	
PAS, BUC-47B447	GB	Boarstall	1	
Gschwind, Fundliste 1	GB	Brancaster	1	
Gschwind, Fundliste 1	GB	Brough-on-Humber	1	
PAS, NMS-128B64	GB	Burgh and Tuttington	1	
PAS, NMS-690EB4	GB	Burnham Market & Burnham Overy	1	
PAS, LIN-4CDD09	GB	Burton	1	
PAS, LVPL-617B96	GB	Buttercrambe	1	
Höck, Fundliste 2	GB	Caerleon	1	
PAS, NMS-FF7177	GB	Caistor St. Edmund	1	
PAS, NMS-4CE617	GB	Canteley	1	
PAS, SUR-64BF83	GB	Charing	1	
Gschwind, Fundliste 1	GB	Chesters	3	
Höck, Fundliste 2	GB	Colchester	1	
PAS, SWYOR-1779E1	GB	Collingham	1	
Gschwind, Fundliste 1	GB	Dalton Parlours	1	
PAS, WMID-EDEF42	GB	Elford (Lichfield district)	1	
PAS, NMS-01CB52	GB	Great Yarmouth		1
Höck, Fundliste 2	GB	Greta Bridge	1	
PAS, YORYM-170AB2	GB	Hambleton	1	
Gschwind, Fundliste 1	GB	Hexham (Vindolanda)	1	
Gschwind, Fundliste 1	GB	High Easters	1	
PAS, WILT-6D0403	GB	Hindon	1	
PAS, LVPL153	GB	Holme St Cuthbert	1	
PAS, LIN-666197	GB	Horncastle	1	

(Cont.)

Reference	Country	Place name	Mount	On other horse gear
PAS, NMS-F6C191, NMS-EA2E31	GB	King's Lynn	2	
PAS, ESS-317F52	GB	Little Laver	1	
PAS, LIN-B9E2E3	GB	Market Rasen	1	
PAS, LANCUM-693772	GB	Maryport	1	
Höck, Fundliste 2	GB	Newstead	1	
PAS, YORYM-F157B0	GB	Norton on Derwent	1	
PAS, BH-F094AD, BM-42E141, BM-8BA078, BM-8A9669, NCL-BFF114, NCL-92A846, NCL-916AA2	GB	Piercebridge	7	
PAS, PUBLIC-7AF296	GB	Raskelf		1
PAS, GLO-73B41A	GB	Rudford and Highleadon	1	
PAS, NMS-827A54	GB	Scole	1	
PAS, WAW-DEF284	GB	Shrawley	1	
PAS, LIN-688456	GB	Sleaford	1	
Höck, Fundliste 2	GB	South Ferriby	1	
Gschwind, Fundliste 1	GB	South Shields	2	1
PAS, SF-18D304	GB	St Edmundsbury		1
PAS, BUC-47A595	GB	Stoke Mandeville	1	
PAS, BERK-D4A06C	GB	Stonesfield	1	
PAS, SF3424	GB	Suffolk Somersham	1	
PAS, BH-18E5F3	GB	Uttlesford	1	
PAS, LIN-F8FAC6, LIN-3F5B88	GB	West Lindsey	2	
PAS, SUR-A8D2EA, SUR-873873, HAMP3503, HAMP867	GB	Winchester	4	
PAS, HAMP-FA01C3	GB	Wonston	1	
Gschwind, Fundliste 1	GB	Woodcock Hall (Little Cressingham)	1	
Gschwind, Fundliste 1	GB	York	1	
Radman-Livaja, kat. nr. 536	HR	Sisak	1	
Gschwind, Fundliste 1	HU	Környe	1	
Gschwind, Fundliste 1	IT	Aquileia	1	
Höck, Fundliste 2	IT	Mechel	1	
Höck, Fundliste 2	IT	Terlago-Dos Della Costa	1	

(Continued)

(Cont.)

Reference	Country	Place name	Mount	On other horse gear
Gschwind, Fundliste 1	LUX	Dalheim	1	
Gschwind, Fundliste 1	LUX	Titelberg	1	
PAN-00024826	NL	Aalburg	1	
Nicolay, pl. 79	NL	Aalst	1	
Höck, Fundliste 2	NL	Arnhem-Meijnerswijk	1	
PAN-00038246, PAN-00035426, PAN-00035425, PAN-00022410	NL	Bunnik	3	1
PAN-00040685-9, PAN-00025626, PAN-00025496, PAN-00020312, PAN-00018686	NL	Buren	7	
PAN-00011003	NL	Castricum	1	
PAN-00035934	NL	Cuijk	1	
PAN-00011980	NL	Delft	1	
Hoss (2014b, fig. II-5.64), Waasdorp (1999, kat. nr. 3.20)	NL	Den Haag	2	
Nicolay, pl. 79	NL	Empel	1	
PAN-00020177	NL	Ferwerderadiel	1	
Nicolay, pl. 79	NL	Gameren/Nieuwaal	1	
PAN-00043103	NL	Heerde	1	
Höck, Fundliste 2	NL	Herxen	1	
Nicolay, pl. 79	NL	Ijzerdoorn	1	
PAN-00019337, PAN-00042998	NL	Leeuwaarden	2	
PAN-00025735, PAN-00018372, PAN-00003222	NL	Maasdriel	3	
Nicolay, pl. 79	NL	Maurik	1	
PAN-00023203	NL	Neder-Betuwe	1	
PAN-00045052, PAN-00039420-1, PAN-00022305, PAN-00022298, PAN-00021123-4, PAN-00005071	NL	Neerijnen	8	
Nicolay, pl. 79	NL	Nijmegen	5	
PAN-00005093	NL	Nuenen	1	
Nicolay, pl. 79	NL	Ophemert	2	

(Cont.)

Reference	Country	Place name	Mount	On other horse gear
Nicolay, pl. 79	NL	Opijnen	1	
PAN-00011583, PAN-00005026, PAN-00002207	NL	Overbetuwe	3	
Nicolay, pl. 79	NL	Rumpt	1	
PAN-00036584, PAN-00036551-2	NL	Sittard	3	
Gschwind, Fundliste 1	NL	Ten Hoeve, Voerendaal	1	
Nicolay, pl. 79	NL	Tiel	2	
PAN-00033090-1, PAN-00011427, PAN-00007317	NL	Waadhoeke	3	
Gschwind, Fundliste 1	NL	Wange	1	
PAN-00043750, PAN-00043747, PAN-00039701. PAN-00039700, PAN-00012431, PAN-00022209, PAN-00018962, PAN-00012431, PAN-00010500, PAN-00010498, PAN-00010496, PAN-00010495, PAN-00010494, PAN-00010493, PAN-00008968, PAN-00008967, PAN-00007914, PAN-00007753, PAN-00004999, PAN-00004609, PAN-00004608, PAN-00004607.	NL	Zaltbommel	22	
Gschwind, Fundliste 1	RO	Romula (Reşca)	1	
Höck, Fundliste 2	RS	Singidunum (Belgrade)	1	
Höck, Fundliste 2	SY	Salhiyé (Dura-Europos)	2	
			223	**6**

List 7

Distribution of second and third century A.D. scallop shell horse amulets.

Reference	Country	Place name	Amount
Gschwind, Fundliste 2	AU	Bad Deutsch Altenburg (Carnuntum)	5
Gschwind, Fundliste 2	AU	Bruckneudorf	1
Gschwind, Fundliste 2	AU	Lauriacum	8
Gschwind, Fundliste 2	AU	Maria Saal (Virunum)	1
Artefact APH-4025	AU	Seebarn (Harmannsdorf)	2
Artefact APH-4025	BE	Blandain	1
Artefact APH-4025	BE	Claviers, Les Avins	3
Gschwind, Fundliste 2	BE	Faimes (Celles-les-Waremme)	100 (+)
Gschwind, Fundliste 2	BE	Halloy	1
Gschwind, Fundliste 2	BE	Kruishoutem	1
Gschwind, Fundliste 2	BE	Liberchies	1
Gschwind, Fundliste 2	BE	Long-Pont	9
Artefact APH-4025	BE	Pommeroeul	1
Gschwind, Fundliste 2	BE	Vodelée	1
Gschwind, Fundliste 2	BE	Wancennes	1
Gschwind, Fundliste 2	CH	Augst	2
Artefact APH-4025	CH	Avenches	8
Artefact APH-4025	CH	Bellach, Franziskanerhof	1
Gschwind, Fundliste 2	CH	Bubendorf	5
Artefact APH-4025	CH	Cham-Hagendorn	1
Gschwind, Fundliste 2	CH	Dietikon	1
Gschwind, Fundliste 2	CH	Gross Chastel	1
Gschwind, Fundliste 2	CH	Stein am Rhein	1
Gschwind, Fundliste 2	CH	Wittenauer Horn	1
Gschwind, Fundliste 2	D	Ahorn/Schillingstadt	1
Gschwind, Fundliste 2	D	Alteburg (near Zell)	4
Gschwind, Fundliste 2	D	Bergisch Gladbach	1
Gschwind, Fundliste 2	D	Berlin	1
Gschwind, Fundliste 2	D	Bitburg	1
Artefact APH-4025	D	Bruch (Lkr. Bernkastel-Wittlich)	1
Gschwind, Fundliste 2	D	Burghöfe, Mertingen	1
Gschwind, Fundliste 2	D	Bürgle near Gundremmingen	1
Gschwind, Fundliste 2	D	Ehingen-Dambach	2
Gschwind, Fundliste 2	D	Eining	4
Artefact APH-4025	D	Elsdorf, Hambach	5
Gschwind, Fundliste 2	D	Entersburg near Billingen	1
Gschwind, Fundliste 2	D	Froitzheim-Vettweiss	1
Gschwind, Fundliste 2	D	Gaukönigshofen	2

Reference	Country	Place name	Amount
Gschwind, Fundliste 2	D	Großjena, Naumburg	1
Gschwind, Fundliste 2	D	Hambuch, Burgberg	1
Gschwind, Fundliste 2	D	Hetzerath (Lkr. Bernkastel-Wittlich)	1
Gschwind, Fundliste 2	D	Hontheim, Entersburg (Lkr. Bernkastel-Wittlich)	6
Gschwind, Fundliste 2	D	Kaisersesch (Kuhkeller, near Binningen)	3
Gschwind, Fundliste 2	D	Katzenberg (near Mayen)	1
Artefact APH-4025	D	Klein-Schwechten	1
Gschwind, Fundliste 2	D	Konz	1
Gschwind, Fundliste 2	D	Krefeld-Gellep	1
Gschwind, Fundliste 2	D	Leverkusen	1
Gschwind, Fundliste 2	D	Lürken (near Aachen)	1
Artefact APH-4025	D	Mainz	1
Gschwind, Fundliste 2	D	Marktsteft, Michelfeld (Lkr. Kitzingen)	1
Gschwind, Fundliste 2	D	Mötsch	1
Gschwind, Fundliste 2	D	München	1
Gschwind, Fundliste 2	D	Nauen (Lkr. Havelland)	1
Gschwind, Fundliste 2	D	Neef, Petersberg (Lkr. Cochem-Zell)	1
Gschwind, Fundliste 2	D	Neuerburg, Neuerb. Kopf (Lkr. Eifel-Bitburg-Prüm)	1
Artefact APH-4025	D	Neunheilingen (Lkr. Unstrut-Hainich)	1
Gschwind, Fundliste 2	D	Neupotz	1
Gschwind, Fundliste 2	D	Niederbiber	4
Artefact APH-4025	D	Obermendig (Lkr. Main-Koblenz)	1
Gschwind, Fundliste 2	D	Ochsenfurt (Lkr. Würzburg)	8
Gschwind, Fundliste 2	D	Regensburg	1
Gschwind, Fundliste 2	D	Rheinzabern	1
Gschwind, Fundliste 2	D	Soest, Ardey	1
Gschwind, Fundliste 2	D	Thalmassing	4
Gschwind, Fundliste 2	D	Trier	1
Gschwind, Fundliste 2	D	Tüddern-Selfkant	1
Gschwind, Fundliste 2	D	Unterpfleichfeld (Lkr. Würzburg)	1
Gschwind, Fundliste 2	D	Westheim (Lkr. Weißenburg-Gunzenhausen)	2
Gschwind, Fundliste 2	D	Wörth	1
Lenz, Kat. Nr. 857-9	D	Xanten	3
Gschwind, Fundliste 2	D	Zugmantel (Taunusstein)	1
Artefact APH-4025	ES	Albalate de las Nogeras	1
Artefact APH-4025	ES	Albalate de Zorita	1
Artefact APH-4025	ES	Cabriana, Miranda de Ebro (prov. Burgos)	3
Artefact APH-4025	ES	Estremera	1
Artefact APH-4025	ES	Forua (Viscaya)	1

(*Continued*)

(Cont.)

Reference	Country	Place name	Amount
Gschwind, Fundliste 2	ES	Fuentespreadas	1
Artefact APH-4025	ES	Ocaña (Toledo)	1
Artefact APH-4025	ES	Pedrosa de la Vega (Palencia)	2
Artefact APH-4025	F	Aix-en-Provence	13
Artefact APH-4025	F	Alésia	3
Artefact APH-4025	F	Assay, La Croix de Bois	1
Artefact APH-4025	F	Autun	22
Artefact APH-4025	F	Bavay	16
Gschwind, Fundliste 2	F	Bayard-sur-Marne, Châtelet de Gourzon	1
Artefact APH-4025	F	Biesheim	1
Artefact APH-4025	F	Bliesbrück	15
Gschwind, Fundliste 2	F	Bolards	1
Artefact APH-4025	F	Chalon-sur-Saône	2
Gschwind, Fundliste 2	F	Combas, les Gravenasses	1
Artefact APH-4025	F	Corseul	3
Artefact APH-4025	F	Ecoust-Saint-Mein	2
Gschwind, Fundliste 2	F	Entrains-sur-Nohain	1
Artefact APH-4025	F	Famars	1
Gschwind, Fundliste 2	F	Genainville, Les Vaux de la Celle	1
Artefact APH-4025	F	Hérault	1
Artefact APH-4025	F	Lansargues, La Laure	1
Gschwind, Fundliste 2	F	Le Langon, Les Ouches	1
Artefact APH-4025	F	Le Mas-d'Agenais	1
Gschwind, Fundliste 2	F	Le-Vieil-Evreux	2
Gschwind, Fundliste 2	F	Les Gravenasses near Combas	1
Gschwind, Fundliste 2	F	Mailly-le-Camp	1
Gschwind, Fundliste 2	F	Mâlain	1
Gschwind, Fundliste 2	F	Meaux	1
Artefact APH-4025	F	Mer, Beaudisson	1
Artefact APH-4025	F	Mercey-le-Grand, La Cassière	1
Gschwind, Fundliste 2	F	Meyzieu, Le Dent	5
Artefact APH-4025	F	Montagnac	1
Gschwind, Fundliste 2	F	Nébian, Pichaurès	1
Artefact APH-4025	F	Nuits-Saint-Georges	3
Artefact APH-4025	F	Osselle	2
Artefact APH-4025	F	Parcey	1
Gschwind, Fundliste 2	F	Paris	1
Gschwind, Fundliste 2	F	Pichaurès near Nèbian	1
Artefact APH-4025	F	Pîtres	3
Gschwind, Fundliste 2	F	Poivres	4
Artefact APH-4025	F	Port-sur-Saône, Le Magny	1
Artefact APH-4025	F	Revelles, Le Trélet	4

(Cont.)

Reference	Country	Place name	Amount
Gschwind, Fundliste 2	F	Rezé	1
Artefact APH-4025	F	Rilly-sur-Vienne	1
Artefact APH-4025	F	Rodelle, Les Clapiès	1
Gschwind, Fundliste 2	F	Saint-Affrique, Rocher de Caylus	1
Artefact APH-4025	F	Sainte-Anastasi	1
Artefact APH-4025	F	Santes	1
Artefact APH-4025	F	Serre-les-Sapins	1
Artefact APH-4025	F	Tavaux, Les Charmes d'Amont	1
Artefact APH-4025	F	Thonon-les-Bains	1
Artefact APH-4025	F	Vaulx-Vraucourt	3
Gschwind, Fundliste 2	F	Vaux-de-da-Celle	1
Gschwind, Fundliste 2	F	Vienne	1
Gschwind, Fundliste 2	F	Vienne	2
Gschwind, Fundliste 2	F	Vireux-Molhain	10
Gschwind, Fundliste 2	GB	Colchester	1
Gschwind, Fundliste 2	GB	Dover	1
PAS, BM-764EFF	GB	Piercebridge	1
Artefact, APH-4025	GB	Silchester	1
PAS, GLO-E1D722	GB	Westbury-on-Severn	1
Gschwind, Fundliste 2	IT	Aquileia	7
Gschwind, Fundliste 2	LUX	Titelberg	1
Gschwind, Fundliste 2	LUX	Tossenberg	1
Artefact APH-4025	MA	Fertassa (Volubilis)	2
PAN-00044435	NL	Appingedam	1
PAN-00022714-5	NL	Buren	2
Hoss (2014b, fig. II-5.67)	NL	Den Haag	1
PAN-00023581	NL	Duiven	1
Nicolay, pl. 73	NL	Empel, De Werf	1
Gschwind, Fundliste 2	NL	Heerlen	1
Nicolay, pl. 73	NL	Lent	1
PAN-00043430	NL	Loppersum	1
PAN-00018507, PAN-00018371, PAN-00003223	NL	Maasdriel	3
Hoss (2013, fig. 14.18)	NL	Nijmegen	1
Nicolay, pl. 73	NL	Ophemert	1
Nicolay, pl. 73	NL	Opijnen	1
	NL	Overbetuwe	2

(*Continued*)

(Cont.)

Reference	Country	Place name	Amount
PAN-00030861, PAN-00010246			
Nicolay (2007, pl. 73)	NL	Rumpt	1
PAN-00038122, PAN-00033099	NL	Waadhoeke	2
Nicolay, pl. 73	NL	Wehl	1
PAN-00036128	NL	Winsum	1
PAN-00028688, PAN-00023015, PAN-00010501, PAN-00008986, PAN-00008971	NL	Zaltbommel	5
PAN-00035009, PAN-00032115	NL	Zuidhorn	2
Artefact APH-4025	PT	Coriscada, Vale do Mouro	1
Artefact APH-4025	SI	Hrušica	1
Gschwind, Fundliste 2	SK	Dúbravka	1
			347

List 8

Distribution of first to third centuries A.D. lunate horse amulets, with the lunula pointing downwards.

Reference	Country	Place name	Amount
Bishop	AU	Bad Deutsch-Altenburg (Carnuntum)	1
Deimel	AU	Magdalensberg	5
Maspoli, cat. nr. 202–4	AU	Wien	3
Artefact PDH-4066	B	Blicquy	1
Bishop	CH	Baden	2
Deschler-Erb, kat. nr. 340	CH	Oberwinterthur	1
Unz and Deschler-Erb, Taf. 48, Bishop	CH	Windisch (Vindonissa)	32
Bishop	D	Augsburg-Oberhausen	1
Franke, kat. nr. 570, 571, 950	D	Burghöfe	3
Bishop	D	Dangstetten	1
Bishop	D	Dormagen	1
Bishop	D	Friedberg	1
Müller, Taf, 48–9	D	Haltern	10
Bishop	D	Hüfingen	2
Bishop	D	Mainz	1
Deschler-Erb (2012, D10, D11)	D	Moers (Asciburgium)	2
Bishop	D	Rheinberg	1
Bishop	D	Rödgen	1
Bishop	D	Straubing	1
Bishop	D	Wiesbaden	1
Lenz, Taf. 26–8, 85	D	Xanten	19
Aurrecoechea Fernández, fig. 3.6	E	Estremera	1
Artefact PDH-4092	E	L'Escala, Ampurias	1
Artefact PDH-4066	F	Autun	1
Artefact PDH-4090	F	Biesheim	1
Artefact PDH-4066	F	Bourges	1
Artefact APH-4116	F	Margon	1
Artefact PDH-4089	F	Martres-Tolosane	1
Artefact PDH-4066	F	Mirebeau-sur-Bèze	1
Artefact PDH-4114	F	Naintré, Vieux-Poitiers	1
Artefact PDH-4089	F	Villetelle, Ambrussum	2
PAS, WAW-375525	GB	Brinklow	1
PAS, NLM-E9A225	GB	Burwell	1
Artefact PDH-4066	GB	Caerleon (Isca Silurum)	1

(Continued)

(Cont.)

Reference	Country	Place name	Amount
Bishop (2009)	GB	Carlisle	2
Bishop	GB	Castleford	2
PAS, SUR-80B2EB	GB	Charlwood	1
Bishop	GB	Colcester	1
Bishop	GB	Corbridge	1
PAS, HAMP-BEFA01	GB	Crondall	1
PAS, NMS-65D353	GB	Gayton	1
PAS, LIN-963591	GB	Great Hale	1
Bishop	GB	Hod Hill	2
PAS, LVPL-6E70B4	GB	Munch Wenlock	1
PAS, NARC3230	GB	Pottersbury (Northhamptonshire)	1
Bishop	GB	Richborough	1
PAS, NMS-ADC3E7	GB	Runhall	1
PAS, BERK-492437	GB	Sandford-on-Thames	1
PAS, BERK-DCEB17	GB	Warborough	1
PAS, NMS-0E81D5	GB	West Acre	1
PAS, SUR-F22F70	GB	West Ilsley (near Didcot)	1
Artefact PDH-4092	HR	Ivoševci (Brunum)	1
Artefact PDH-4066	HR	Sisak (Siscia)	2
Artefact PDH-4090	HU	Dunaújváros (Intercisa)	1
Artefact PDT-4020	IT	Aquileia	1
Artefact PDH-4066, PDH-4067	IT	Minturno	2
Artefact PDH-4092	IT	Rom	9
Artefact APH-4116	LUX	Diekirch	1
Artefact PDH-4143, PDH-4144,	MA	Fertassa (Volubilis)	2
PAN-00043404	NL	Bunnik	1
Bishop	NL	Burum	1
Bishop	NL	Ferwerd	1
PAN-00042002	NL	Geldermalsen	1
Bishop	NL	Heerlen	1
Bishop, Hoss (2013, fig. 14.19)	NL	Nijmegen	12
Bishop	NL	Piaam	1
PAN-00036413	NL	Sittard	1
Bishop	NL	Vechten	4
Bishop	NL	Voorburg	1
PAN-00043985, PAN-00025758	NL	Zaltbommel	2
Artefact PDH-4066	RO	Corabia (Sucidava)	1
James, fig. 41	SY	Salhiyé (Dura-Europos)	3
Total			**173**

List 9

Distribution of first century A.D. lunate pendants formed by two flaccid phalli pointing downwards.

Reference	Country	Place name	Amount
Deimel	AU	Magdalensberg	1
Deschler-Erb (1996, kat. nr. 341)	CH	Oberwinterthur	1
Bishop	CH	Windisch (Vindonissa)	10
Müller, Taf, 47–8, 51	D	Haltern	5
Bishop	D	Hofheim	1
Bishop	D	Mainz	2
Lenz, kat. nr. 340	D	Xanten	1
Bishop	F	Strasbourg	1
Bishop	GB	Chester	1
Bishop	GB	Chisbury	1
Bishop	GB	Colchester	2
Bishop	GB	Hod Hill	1
Bishop	GB	Wall (Staffordshire)	1
Bishop	NL	Valkenburg	1
Total			**29**

Notes

1 I thank Alissa Whitmore for pointing this out to me. Most sex scenes show couples copulating one on one.
2 Exceptions are Beazely Archive, nos 216500, 44984, and 41002; see Kilmer (1993: 164).
3 According to Schörner (2003: 163), Zeus Hypsistos is an Attic healing god, while according to Mitchell (2010: 168) the worshippers of this "highest god" were "quasi monotheistic". Both authors seem unaware of this votive and I have not found any explanation for its unusual depiction.
4 According to Faraone (2018: 72, n. 134), this exceptional combination is repeated on a stela in Leptis Magna, presumably to protect a building (see also Bernard 1991: 105).
5 British Museum nos 1772,0305.113*115*116*117*119*121; 1824,0498.64; 1856,1226. 687–8; 1865,1118.159–60; 1867,0508.159; 1872,0604.531*1093; 1975,1005.5; 1976,0818. 36–7; WITT 156; WITT.158; WITT.434.

Bibliography

Adams, J.N. (1990). *The Latin Sexual Vocabulary*, Charles Village (Maryland, USA): Johns Hopkins University Press.

Andrews, C. (1994). *Amulets of Ancient Egypt*, Austin: University of Texas Press.

Atalanta, H. (2019). *The Vulva Gallery, The Vulva Variations Art Print, The Vulva Quartet Game* www.thevulvagallery.com/shop [accessed 15.02.2019].

Aurrecoechea Fernández, J. (2007). "Arneses Equinos de Época Romana en Hispania", *Metalistería Romana en Hispania*, 13: 321–44.

Bailey, D.M. (1963–96). *A Catalogue of the Lamps in the British Museum*. London: British Museum.

Barnard, A. and Spencer, J. (2010). *Encyclopedia of Social and Cultural Anthropology*. London/New York: Routledge.

Barrow, R.J. and Silk, M.S. (2018). *Gender, Identity and the Body in Greek and Roman Sculpture*. Cambridge: Cambridge University Press.

Bartsch, S. (2006). *The Mirror of the Self: Sexuality, Self-Knowledge, and the Gaze in the Early Roman Empire*. Chicago, IL: University of Chicago Press.

Bernard, A. (1991). *Sorciers Grecs*. Paris: Fayard.

Bishop, M.C. (1988). "Cavalry Equipment of the Roman Army in the First Century AD", in J.C. Coulston (ed.), *Military Equipment and the Identity of the Roman Soldiers. Proceedings of the Fourth Military Equipment Conference*. Oxford: Archaeopress: 67–195.

Bishop, M.C. (1992). "The Early Imperial 'Apron'", *Journal of Roman Military Equipment Studies*, 3: 81–104.

Bishop, M.C. (2009). "The Body Armour", in C. Howard-Davis, *The Carlisle Millennium Project: Excavations in Carlisle, 1998–2001. Volume 2: The Finds*. Oxford: Oxford Archaeology, 687–705.

Bramwell, R. (2002). "Invisible Labia: The Representation of Female External Genitals in Women's Magazines", *Sexual and Relationship Therapy*, 17(2): 187–90.

Braun, V. (1999). "Breaking a Taboo? Talking (And Laughing) about the Vagina", *Feminism and Psychology*, 9(3): 367–72.

Buckland, R. (2010). *Shunga: Erotic Art in Japan*. London: British Museum Press.

Burton, M. and Burton, R. (1969–70). *The International Wildlife Encyclopedia*. New York: Marshall Cavendish.

Clark, T. and Gerstle, C.A. (2013). *Shunga: Sex and Pleasure in Japanese Art*. London: British Museum Press.

Clarke, J.R. (1998). *Looking at Lovemaking: Constructions of Sexuality in Roman Art 100 B.C.–A.D. 250*. Berkerly: University of California Press.

Clarke, J.R. (2014). "Sexuality and Visual Representation", in T.K. Hubbart (ed.), *A Companion to Greek and Roman Sexualities*. Oxford: Wiley Blackwell, 509–33.

Conde Feitosa, L. (2013). *The Archaeology of Gender, Love and Sexuality in Pompeii*. Oxford: Archaeopress.

Cool, H.E.M., Lloyd-Morgan, G. and Hooley, A.D. (1995). *Finds from the Fortress*. The archaeology of York: the Small Finds 17/10. York: York Archaeological Trust.

Crummy, N. (2010). "Bears and Coins: The Iconography of Protection in Late Roman Infant Burials", *Britannia*, 41: 37–93.

de Loë, A. (1937). *Belgique Ancienne: Catalogue Descriptif Et Raisonné Du Musées Royaux D'art Et D'historie À Bruxelles III: La Periode Romaine*. Brussels: Vromant.

Deimel, M. (1987). *Die Bronzekleinfunde vom Magdalensberg*. Kärntner Museumsschriften 71, Archäologische Forschungen zu den Grabungen auf dem *Magdalensberg* 9. Klagenfurt: Landesmuseum für Kärnten.

Deschler-Erb, E. (1996). "Die Kleinfunde aus Edelmetall, Bronze und Blei", in: E. Deschler-Erb (ed.), *Die Funde aus Metall. Ein Schrank mit Lararium des 3. Jahrhunderts. Ausgrabungen im Unteren Bühl*. Beiträge zum römischen Oberwinterthur—Vitudurum 7. Monographien der Kantonsarchäologie Zürich 27. Zürich: Egg, 13–139.

Deschler-Erb, E. ed., (2012). *Römische Militärausrüstung aus Kastell und Vicus von Asciburgium*. Funde aus Asciburgium 17. Duisburg: Faustus.

Dierichs, A. (1997). *Erotik in der Römischen Kunst*. Mainz: Philipp von Zabern.

Dodsworth, L. (2019). *Womanhood: The Bare Reality*. London: Pinter and Martin.

Dubiel, U. (2008). *Amulette, Siegel und Perlen. Studien zu Typologie und Tragesitte im Alten und Mittleren Reich*. Fribourg/Göttingen: Vandenhoeck und Ruprecht.

Dunbabin, K.M.D. (1989). "*Baiarum Grata Voluptas*: Pleasures and Dangers of the Baths", *Papers of the British School in Rome*, 57: 6–49.

Elliott, J.H. (2016a). *Beware the Evil Eye. The Evil Eye in the Bible and the Ancient World: Vol. 1: Introduction, Mesopotamia and Egypt*. Eugene: Cascade.

Elliott, J.H. (2016b). *Beware the Evil Eye. The Evil Eye in the Bible and the Ancient World: Vol. 2: Greece and Rome*. Eugene: Cascade.

Enright, L. (2019a). *Vagina: A Re-education*. London: Atlantic Books.

Enright, L. (2019b). "Why It Matters To Call External Female Genitalia 'Vulva' Not 'Vagina'", *The Guardian*, Tue 12 Feb 2019.

Faraone, C.A. (2018). *The Transformation of Greek Amulets in Roman Imperial Times*. Philadelphia, PA: University of Pennsylvania Press.

Franke, R. (2009). *Römische Kleinfunde aus Burghöfe III: Militärische Ausrüstungsgegenstände, Pferdegeschirr, Bronzegeschirr und –gerät*. Frühgeschichtliche und provinzialrömische Archäologie 9. Rahden/Westfalen: Leidorf.

Freud, S. (2014[1913]). *Totem und Tabu*. Hamburg: Nikol.

Glazenbrook, A. (2016). "Is There an Archaeology of Prostitution?", in A. Glazenbrook and B. Tsakirgis (eds), *Houses of Ill Repute. The Archaeology of Brothels, Houses, and Taverns in the Greek World*. Philadelphia, PA: University of Pennsylvania Press, 169–96.

Greep, S. (1994). "Antler Roundel Pendants from Britain and the North-Western Roman Provinces", *Britannia*, 25: 79–97.

Gschwind, M. (1998). "Pferdegeschirrbeschläge der zweiten Hälfte des 3. Jahrhunderts aus Abusina / Eining", *Saalburg Jahrbuch*, 49: 112–38.

Gschwind, M. (2004). *Abusina. Das römische Auxiliarkastell Eining an der Donau vom 1. bis 5. Jh. n. Chr.* Münchner Beiträge zur Vor- und Frühgeschichte 53. München: Beck.

Gsell, M. (2001). *Die Bedeutung der Baubo. Zur Repräsentation Des Weiblichen Genitals*. Frankfurt am Main: Stroemfeld.

Heiland, S. (2015). *Visualisierung Und Rhetorisierung Von Geschlecht. Strategien Zur Inszenierung Weiblicher Sexualität Im Märe*. Berlin/Boston, MA: De Gruyter.

Henig, M. (1984). *Religion in Roman Britain*. London: Batesford.

Hildburgh, W.L. (1942). "Cowrie Shells as Amulets in Europe", *Folklore*, 53(4): 178–95.

Höck, A. (2006). "Neues Militärisches aus Mechel", *Veröffentlichungen des Tiroler Landesmuseums Ferdinandeum*, 86: 245–76.

Hoss, S. (2013). "Metalen voorwerpen uit de Romeinse tijd", in E.N.A. Heirbaut (ed.), *De zuidwestelijke hoek van Ulpia Noviomagus in kaart gebracht. Resultaten van de opgravingen aan de Rijnstraat en Lekstraat in Nijmegen-West 2008–2010*. Archeologische Berichten Nijmegen—Rapporten 41. Nijmegen: Bureau Archeologie Gemeente Nijmegen, 195–276.

Hoss, S. (2014a). *Cingulum Militare. Studien zum römischen Soldatengürtel des 1. bis 3. Jh. n. Chr.* Unpubl. PhD Thesis, Leiden University.

Hoss, S. (2014b). "Metaal", in M.J. Driessen and E. Besselsen (eds), *Voorburg-Arentsburg: Een Romeinse Havenstad tussen Rijn en Maas*. Amsterdam: Amsterdams Archeologisch Centrum en Diachron, 613–77.

180   *Stefanie Hoss*

Hoss, S. (2015). "Zu einigen Dekorationsmotiven des 2. und 3. Jahrhunderts auf den Beschlägen von Soldatengürteln, Schultergurten und Fibeln", in P. Henrich, C. Miks, J. Obmann, and M. Wieland (eds), *NON SOLUM...SED ETIAM. Festschrift für Thomas Fischer zum 65. Geburtstag*. Rahden/Westfalen: Verlag Marie Leidorf, 199–206.

Hoss, S. (Forthcoming). "Hedging Your Bets—Sexual Imagery as Apotropaic Protection for Horses", *Journal of Roman Military Equipment Studies* 19.

Hubbard, T.K. ed., (2014). *A Companion to Greek and Roman Sexualities*. Chichester: Blackwell.

Ivčević, S. (2013a). "First Century Military Gear from Salona", in Sanader et al. (2013), 299–316.

Ivčević, S. (2013b). "Project Tilurium—Roman Military Equipment", in Sanader et al. (2013), 435–53.

Jahn, O. (1855). "Über den Aberglauben des bösen Blicks bei den Alten", *Berichte über die Verhandlungen der königlich sächsischen Gesellschaft der Wissenschaften zu Leipzig, Philiologisch-historisch Klasse*, 7: 28–110.

James, S. (2004). *The Excavations at Dura-Europos. Final Report, VII: The Arms and Armour and Other Military Equipment*. London: The British Museum.

Johns, C. (1982). *Sex or Symbol: Erotic Images of Greece and Rome*. London: British Museum.

Johns, C. (1996). *The Jewellery of Roman Britain*. Ann Arbor: University of Michigan Press.

Johns, C. (1997). *The Snettisham Roman Jeweller's Hoard*. London: British Museum.

Johnson, M. and Ryan, T. (2005). *Sexuality in Greek and Roman Literature and Society: A Sourcebook*. London: Routledge.

Kilmer, M.F. (1993). *Greek Erotica on Attic Red-Figure Vases*. London: Duckworth.

Kovač, D. and Koščević, R. (2003). *Falosom Protiv Uroka: Arheološka Zbirka Dr. Damir Kovač (The Phallus versus the Curse: The Archeological Collection of Dr. Damir Kovač). Exhibition Municipal Museum of Zagreb on the Occasion of the 75 Anniversary of the Croatian Numismatic Society*. Zagreb: Muzej Grada Zagreba.

Künzl, E. (2001). "Vulva: Zu einem gallorömischen Frauenbild", in T.A.S.M. Panhuysen (ed.), *Die Maastrichter Akten des 5. Internationalen Kolloquiums über das provinzialrömische Kunstschaffen im Rahmen des CSIR. Typologie, Ikonographie und soziale Hintergründe der provinzialen Grabdenkmäler und Wege der ikonographischen Einwirkung - Maastricht 29. Mai bis 1. Juni 1997*. Maastricht: Stichting Willem Goossens, 257–72.

Laan, E., Martoredjo, D.K., Hesselink, S., Snijders, N. and van Lunsen, R.H.W. (2016). "Young Women's Genital Self-Image and Effects of Exposure to Pictures of Natural Vulvas", *Journal of Psychosomatic Obstetrics and Gynecology*, 38(4): 249–55.

Langlands, R. (2006). *Sexual Morality in Ancient Rome*. Cambridge: Cambridge University Press.

Langner, M. (2001). *Antike Graffitizeichnungen. Motive, Gestaltung und Bedeutung*. Palilia 11. Wiesbaden: Reichert.

Lenz, K.H. (2006). *Römische Waffen, militärische Ausrüstung und militärische Befunde aus dem Stadtgebiet der Colonia Ulpia Traiana (Xanten)*. Bonn: Habelt.

Levi, D. (1941). "The Evil Eye and the Lucky Hunchback", in R. Stillwell (ed.), *Antioch-on-the-Orontes*. Princeton, NJ: Princton University Press.

Lewis, J. (2016). "Finds from the Frontier: Romans and Natives at Brecon Gaer Roman Fort", in X. Pauli Jensen and T. Grane (eds), Imitation and Inspiration. Proceedings of the 18th International Roman Military Equipment Conference held in Copenhagen, Denmark, 9th–14th June 2013. *Journal of Roman Military Equipment Studies*, 17: 235–42.

Manganaro, G. (1996). "Fallocrazia nella Sicilia Greca e Romana", *Zeitschrift für Papyrologie und Epigraphik*, 111: 135–39.

Mariën, M.E. (1994). *Quatre Tombes Romaines du IIIe siècle: Thorembais-Satin-Trond et Overhespen*. Monographie d'Archéologie National 8. Brussels: Musèes Royaux d'Art et d'Historie Bruxelles.

Maspoli, A.Z. (2014). *Römische Militaria aus Wien: die Funde aus dem Legionslager, den Canabae Legionis und der Zivilsiedlung von Vindobona*. Monografien der Stadtarchäologie Wien 8. Wien: Phoibos-Verlag.

Massart, C. (2000). "Éléments de Char et de Harnachement dans le Tumulus Tongres de IIIᵉ s. Les Deux Harnachements de Celles (Waremme), Belgique", *Kölner Jahrbuch*, 33: 509–22.

Massart, C. (2002). "Au-delà de Bijou, le Pouvoir de Symbole: Les Amulettes en Forme de Lunule et de Phallus", in K. Sas and H. Thoen (eds.), *Brilliance et Prestige: La Joaillerie Romaine en Europe Occidentale*. Leuven: Peeters, 101–103.

Maxfield, V.A. (1981). *The Military Decorations of the Roman Army*. London: Batsford.

Meyerowitz, M. (1992). "The Domestication of Desire: Ovid's *Parva Tabella* and the Theatre of Love", in A. Richlin (ed.), *Pornography and Representation in Greece and Rome*. New York: Oxford University Press, 131–58.

Mitchell, S. (2010). "Further Thoughts on the Cult of Theos Hypsistos", in S. Mitchell and P. van Nuffelen (eds), *One God. Pagan Monotheism in the Roman Empire*. Cambridge: Cambridge University Press, 167–208.

Müller, M. (2002). *Die römischen Buntmetallfunde von Haltern. Bodenaltertümer Westfalens 37*. Mainz: von Zabern.

Neumer-Pfau, W. (1982). *Studien zur Ikonographie und gesellschaftlichen Funktion hellenistischer Aphrodite-Statuen*. Bonn: Habelt.

Nicolay, J.A.W. (2007). *Armed Batavians. Use and Significance of Weaponry and Horse Gear from Non-Military Contexts in the Rhine Delta (50 BC to AD 450)*. Amsterdam Archaeological Studies 11. Amsterdam: Amsterdam University Press.

Oldenstein, J. (1976). "Zur Ausrüstung römischer Auxiliareinheiten", *Berichte der Römisch-Germanischen Kommission*, 57: 49–284.

Olender, M. (1990). "Aspects of Baubo: Ancient Texts and Contexts", in D. Halperin, J.J. Winkler and F. Zeitlin (eds), *Before Sexuality: The Construction of Erotic Experience in the Ancient Greek World*. Princeton: Princeton University Press, 83–113.

Ortisi, S. (2015). *Militärische Ausrüstung und Pferdegeschirr aus den Vesuvstädten*. Palilia 29. Wiesbaden: Reichert.

Parker, A. (2015). "The Fist-and-Phallus Pendants from Roman Catterick", *Britannia*, 46: 135–49.

Parker, H.N. (1997). "The Teratogenic Grid", in J.P. Hallet and M.B. Skinner (eds), *Roman Sexualities*. Princeton, NJ: Princeton University Press, 47–65.

Pfrommer, M. (2001). "Hellenistisches Gold und ptolemäische Herrscher", *Studia Varia from the J. Paul Getty Museum, Vol. II, Occasional Papers on Antiquities*, 10: 79–114.

Poulter, A.G. (2007). *Nicopolis ad Istrum. A Late Roman and Byzantine City*. London: Society for the Promotion of Roman Studies.

Radman-Livaja, I. (2004). *Militaria Sisciensia-Nnalazi Rimske Vojne Opreme iz Siska u Fundusu Arheološkog Muzeja u Zagrebu*. Zagreb: Arheološki Muzej.

Richlin, A.E. (1984). "Invective against Women in Roman Satire", *Arethusa*, 17: 67–80.

Richlin, A.E. (1992). *The Garden of Priapus: Sexuality and Aggression in Roman Humor.* Oxford: Oxford University Press.

Riha, E. (1990). *Der Römische Schmuck Aus Augst und Kaiseraugst.* Forschungen in Augst 10. Augst: Amt für Museen und Archäologie des Kantons Basel-Landschaft.

Roisman, J. (2014). "Greek and Roman Ethnosexuality", in Hubbard (2014), 405–37.

Sanader, M., Rendić-Miočević, A., Toninčinić, D. and Radman-Livaja, I. eds, (2013). *Weapons and Military Equipment in a Funerary Context. Proceedings of the XVIIth Roman Military Equipment Conference.* Zagreb: Arheološki Museju Zagrebu.

Schick, V.R., Rima, B.N. and Calabrese, S.K. (2009). "E*vulva*lution: The Portrayal of Women's External Genitalia and Physique across Time and the Current Barbie Doll Ideals", *The Journal of Sex Research*, 48(1): 74–81.

Schörner, G. (2003). *Votive Im Römischen Griechenland. Untersuchungen Zur Späthelle-nistischen Und Kaiserzeitlichen Kunst- Und Religionsgeschichte.* Altertumswissenschaftliches Kolloquium 7. Stuttgart: Franz Steiner.

Seaman, K., (2004). "Retrieving the Original Aphrodite of Knidos", *Atti della Accademia Nazionale dei Lincei. Rendiconti Classe di Scienze Morali, Storiche e Filologiche*, ser. 9, vol. 15: 531–94.

Slater, P.E. (2014[1968]). *The Glory of Hera. Greek Mythology and the Greek Family.* Princeton, NJ: Princeton University Press.

Smith, N.K., Butler, S., Wagner, B., Collazo, E., Caltabiano, L. and Herbenick, D. (2016). "Genital Self-Image and Considerations of Elective Genital Surgery", *Journal of Sex and Marital Therapy*, 43(2): 169–84.

Strong, A.K. (2016). *Prostitutes and Matrons in the Roman World.* Cambridge: Cambridge University Press.

Unz, C. and Deschler-Erb, E. (1997). *Katalog der Militaria aus Vindonissa. Militärische Funde, Pferdegeschirr und Jochteile bis 1976.* Veröffentlichungen der Gesellschaft Pro Vidonissa XIV. Brugg: Gesellschaft Pro Vidonissa.

Vout, C. (2013). *Sex on Show: Seeing the Erotic in Greece and Rome.* Berkeley, CA: University of California Press.

Vucetic, S. (2014). "Roman Sexuality or Roman Sexualities? Looking at Sexual Imagery on Roman Terracotta Mould-made Lamps", in H. Platts, J. Pearce, C. Barron, J. Lundock and J. Yoo (eds), *TRAC 2013: Proceedings of the Twenty-Third Annual Theoretical Roman Archaeology Conference, King's College, London 2013.* Oxford: Oxbow Books, 140–58.

Waasdorp, J.A. (1999). *Van Romeinse Soldaten en Cananefaten. Gebruiksvoorwerpen van de Scheveningseweg.* Den Haag: Gemeente Den Haag.

Wieland, M. (2008). *Ein neu gefundener römischer Soldatengrabstein von der Hohe Straße in Köln.* Unpublished M.A Thesis, University of Cologne.

Wilson, R.J.A. (2015). "The Western Roman Provinces", in B. Borg (ed.), *A Companion to Roman Art.* Hoboken: Wiley Blackwell, 496–530.

Wrede, H. (1975). "Lunulae im Halsschmuck", in Institut für Klassische Archäologie München (ed.), *Wandlungen: Studien zur antiken und neueren Kunst. Festschrift Ernst Homann-Wedeking.* Waldsassen: Stiftland, 243–54.

Zadoks-Josephus Jitta, A.N. and Witteveen, A.M. (1977). "Roman Bronze Lunulae from the Netherlands", *Oudheidkundige Mededelingen*, 58: 167–95.

6   Female status and gender on the Roman frontier in Britain

Between representation and reality

Robyn Crook

Introduction

As one of the last provinces to be conquered and joined to the Roman Empire, Britannia offers an interesting opportunity to explore the relationship between Roman and non-Roman gendered status, including sexuality, as well as the interplay between these and other facets of identity. From the initial conquest of A.D. 43 until the early fifth century, Britannia was the northernmost province of the empire, with a substantial military population and frontier zone. Over the course of centuries, boundaries changed and people from across the empire inhabited Britain and interacted with indigenous groups. As a result, identities were constantly being created, negotiated, and maintained by those living there. The evidence of these encounters and associated processes are of particular interest for contextualising the evolving contemporary understanding of gender and sexuality in Roman Britain. Accepting that Roman Mediterranean ideals of gender and status are well defined, adoption of or deviations from these norms should be apparent in a provincial context, though identifying cultural aspects that are distinctly local or indigenous can be difficult in the broader mosaic of multicultural provincial societies.

Gender and sexuality must be situated in relation to each other and different elements of identity, at the individual and group levels. Identity is a complex, multi-faceted social construct which is embodied, maintained, and changed through interaction between people and groups (Meskell 2002; Gardner 2004; Diaz-Andreu and Lucy 2005: 5–6; Jenkins 2008: 16–17). While it is not possible within the scope of this chapter to explore identity in full, variations and limitations in the archaeological evidence mean that it is not always possible to situate information about gender and sexuality in relation to or against other identity categories such as social status, ethnicity, age, health, occupation, and religion.

Within the study of overlapping and interrelated identities, considerations of gender and its importance as a structuring element of past (and present) societies have come to the forefront of research in the last few decades. Gender is the identification by self and others of a specific gender category or the interpretation of culturally understood sexual difference (Gilchrist 1999: 1; Diaz-Andreu 2005: 14). This complex relationship encompasses cultural definitions and knowledge of concepts like masculinity and femininity, organisation of reproduction, and sexual divisions of labour (Bradley 1996: 205, also see Gilchrist 1991; Johnson 1999; Diaz-Andreu 2005; Voss 2006; Brumfiel 2007; Balme and Bulbeck 2008; Joyce 2008; Casella and Voss 2012). This chapter focuses on both gender and sexuality in the textual and material record of the Roman frontier zone in Roman Britain relative to the social status of the women evidenced. Sexuality in this context is 'a broad assemblage of socialities and affects – a constellation of embodied and expressive human intimacies – that range from the seductive, pleasurable, and erotic, through the familial, parental, normative and homosocial, and into the involuntary, strategic, and exploitative', which varies through time and between cultures (Casella and Voss 2012: 1–2; also see Baker 2000: 59; Nelson 2004: 3; Diaz-Andreu 2005: 14; Voss 2008; Geller 2009: 508). Sexuality is rarely explicit in the archaeological or textual evidence, and often it must be inferred from its situation to representations of gender or other identity categories.

Gender, sexuality, and sex can be explored in terms of how they are all mutually constituted, how they are acted upon and reproduced in daily life, often mimicking or repeating a precedent or existing norms, and how their construction and maintenance in the past can be problematised (Voss 2008: 328). This performance or repetition of behaviours and ideas can be seen through patterns in material culture, leading us to look not only at these patterns, but for 'otherness' or deviance from the norm. Many earlier discussions of sex and sexuality have been based on heteronormative and monogamous assumptions projected onto the past (Voss 2008: 329; see Chapter 8). Yet our search for the 'other' can be problematic and confusing in that definitions or understandings of normative and deviant within past cultures may not have been the same as our own, calling for an examination of previous research and biases.

To see this in the dynamic context of the frontier zone, textual and archaeological sources are assessed for information about gender and sexuality relative to the context in which the information was provided. Priority is given to evidence pertaining to women, but it is also useful to contrast the representation of women with men. The evidence, both textual and archaeological, can be separated relative to the status of the woman represented: indigenous queens at the top of a native British social scale during the Roman conquest of Britain; elite women of the Roman frontier; and non-elite women of the frontier. First, Roman writers have provided 'historical' accounts of British queens, and while the evidence must be viewed through the lens of the Roman historiographic tradition, there are revealing points of agreement between the sources. Second, the writing tablets recovered at Vindolanda, including letters written between peers, provide a less politically biased insight into female relationships with both men and other women. Lastly, funerary monuments provide a publicly focused record of individuals through text and (sometimes) imagery. While this is not a comprehensive account of all lines of evidence available for this type of study, it will serve as a jumping off point from which to compare and contrast additional datasets and expand upon such studies moving forward.

Combined, these data provide a glimpse into gender and sexuality in frontier areas of Roman Britain in the first to the third centuries A.D. Furthermore, the predominance of the Roman army and its multicultural constituency provides a greater opportunity to identify practices different to metropolitan Roman ideals.

Metropolitan Roman ideals of gender and sexual relations

Classical sources such as Celsus (*De Medicina*) demonstrate that the differences between the physical male and female forms were acknowledged and explained in medical texts and similar documents (Holmes 2012: 37). The terms *sexus* and *genus* referred generally to male and female in Latin, though social constructs of gender do not necessarily correspond with physiological attributes. This has the potential to complicate investigations based on physical characteristics such as gendering burials through analysis of human remains (see Chapter 7). Thus, regardless of anatomy, ideas about the body and how it relates to gender or sexual habits were culturally and historically constructed, using material culture to structure and communicate socially understood differences and encouraging discussions that include possibilities outside of the two-sex system (Butler 1993, 2004: 212; Geller 2009; Holmes 2012: 70; also see Chapter 8). In the context of their lives as elite men, Roman writers replicated 'accepted' models of gender for the Roman man and woman in their texts, which were generated for an audience of other elite men and women within the framework of a particular genre, such as history or poetry. Thus, Roman texts are not themselves representative of gender constructs across the entirety of the social spectrum. Rather, they provide the opportunity to identify the ideal characteristics of Roman masculinity and femininity as well as to highlight deviation from those ideals. This is particularly important when assessing the accounts of the British queens below.

Masculinity, like sexuality, has been contextualised in terms of power and action in the past (Holmes 2012). In fact, the idea of action, of doing, has long been gendered as masculine in itself with passive roles being gendered feminine (Richlin 1993: 525; Butrica 2005: 232; Williams 2010; Holmes 2012: 79; Olson 2014: 184). The Roman man was often shown wearing either the toga or military attire, illustrating a focus on civic duty and Roman strength and right to rule, with examples of this ranging from statues of the emperor in Rome to funerary monuments of soldiers and businessmen from across the empire (Rothe 2009: 9; Olson 2014: 186–7; Nathan 2015: 1; see also Chapter 8). As we see in many contemporary contexts, an individual's appearance affected their presentation of masculinity or femininity. For Roman men, the removal of body hair, adoption of an elaborate hairstyle, donning of exotic clothing or excessive perfumes, and how they carried themselves could affect perceptions of an individual's masculinity (Clarke 2005: 279–80; Holmes 2012: 114–15; Olson 2014: 182–5). The earlier focus on representations of a man's political and military service changed to a broader ethical concept when the aristocracy no longer generally participated in battle. It came to include the denial of excessive pleasures (sexual – with males or females – and otherwise) through self-control and applied to the man himself and those within his household (Nathan 2015: 11). These elements of masculinity were separate from other actions, including sexual acts, which are the primary defining feature of sexuality in Western cultures (Holmes 2012: 114–15).

With masculinity being defined in terms of action in deeds and relationships, femininity was defined as passivity in relationships of power, sexual and otherwise. The 'ideal' Roman woman, or *matrona*, was often represented in monuments in modest dress, at times including the *stola* or clothing associated with religious roles (D'Ambra 2007: 3–4, 46; Hughes 2007, 2010; Rothe 2009: 44), and could be shown with weaving implements (Rothe 2009: 26; Carroll 2012: 300–1). This emphasised a woman's modesty or respectability, her civic contribution through religion, and her role in providing for her family through the production of textiles (D'Ambra 2007: 46; Rothe 2009: 9). These themes were reiterated in textual materials in which a *matrona* was described as a chaste or modest woman, responsible for maintaining their husband's household, raising their children to be good Roman citizens, and supporting the state through religious participation (Boswell 1995: 28–9; Watts 2005: 87; D'Ambra 2007: 46; Hope 2009: 141–2).

However, these ideas of masculinity and femininity exist as representations of cultural ideals at a specific time and, undoubtedly, would not have represented the day-to-day lives of men or women. 'Norms' for dress, representation, behaviour would have varied temporally, socially, and regionally across the empire (D'Ambra 2007: 5–6; Hughes 2007; Rothe 2009; Carroll 2012: 282, 300–1). In being aware of the conditions under which these representations were constructed, recognising these ideals can help in understanding why certain elements were emphasised in depictions of women and men throughout the empire.

Roman sexual practice was inextricably linked with the status and gender of those involved in any activities. Sexuality in the past was not necessarily understood in terms of modern categories of heterosexuality, homosexuality, or as a separate identity category (Olson 2014: 184–5; see Chapters 8 and 11), requiring a sensitivity to power dynamics and the relationship of sex acts to other parts of identity. The ideal sexual relationship which accompanied the ideals of masculinity and femininity discussed above was that which took place between a (married) man and woman of the same social status (Boswell 1995: 32–3, 104; Cherici 1995: 18). That said, the primary sources indicate the complex reality and sheer variety of sexual relationships in the Roman world. The practice of Roman men having sexual relationships with other men (including younger/male children) has been explored for some time (Boswell 1995; Butrica 2005: 223–36; Williams 2010; for more on Roman sexual protocol, see Chapter 8). Looking at older males, the *cinaedus* was a man who not only enjoyed being penetrated by other men, but one who went against the norms of masculinity as outlined above. They were said to dress elaborately, wear makeup, or have long hair (Richlin 1993: 541–2; Butrica 2005: 221–2; Clarke 2005: 272; Williams 2010; Holmes 2012: 94; Olson 2014: 187–93). The interpretation, then, is that the *cinaedii* were classified as deviant or of a distinct social or gender identity rather than as a separate sexuality entirely (Holmes 2012: 94; Voss 2008: 323–4). Boswell (1995: 65–72) discusses the many types of same-gender (most often male–male) relationships that were documented in the primary sources, including those which were considered to be permanent and were 'characterized by general equality'. There were also examples in which marriage ceremonies took place, mirroring those for heterosexual couples. The objections Boswell (1995: 65–72, 107) describes from the primary sources were in regard to the idealised and socially accepted gender roles, and when these ideals were not adhered to. Interestingly, sex between women is rarely mentioned in Roman sources, except in jest (Butrica 2005: 238). This indicates that a combination of factors, including sexual acts, played into the construction and maintenance of gender.

In contrast to Roman practice, Caesar (*Gallic War* v.14) and Cassius Dio (*Roman History* 77.12.1–5) wrote that it was common for the Caledonians and Britons to share wives among groups of men and raise their offspring in common (Cherici 1995: 17). Caesar (*Gallic War* v.14) specifies that this sharing took place between 'groups of ten or twelve men, especially [...] brothers and fathers and sons' and that children belonged to the first man with whom a woman lived. While otherwise similar, Cassius Dio simply states that children were raised in common. There are multiple ways these accounts can be interpreted, bearing in mind that Cassius Dio was writing at least 250 years after Caesar and that both were writing for elite Roman metropolitan audiences. It could be an example of a form of polyandry, or the misunderstanding of a woman's affiliation from the protection of her father's family to that of her husband, or the practice of a tribe claiming or caring for children on equal or greater terms than the biological parents (Condren 1989: 27; Ellis 1992: 21; Cherici 1995: 17; Watts 2005: 14; Allason-Jones 2008: 15). It is also interesting to consider if this arrangement was seen to have sexual connotations, if it was an element of family or cultural structure, or both. In this regard, it is the contrast with Roman cultural expectations, with legal implications, that may have resonated most with Roman elite audiences. For example, if children were raised communally, or wives were shared by groups of men, how could adultery be identified, and how did one identify their legal heir?

In addition to sexual relationships between men and women in Roman Britain, what about the relationships that potentially fall outside this particular Roman ideal? Strabo (*Geography* 4.4.6) and Aristotle (*Politics* 2.6.5–6/1269b) all note that the Celts did not consider homosexuality (as we would define it now) as an oddity, deviant behaviour, or shameful practice (Watts 2005: 14–15). Athenaeus (*Deipnosophists* 13.79) wrote in the early third century A.D. that the Celts had the most attractive of the barbarian women, yet they made 'great favourites of boys: so that some of them often [went] to rest with two lovers on their beds of hide', a similar account to one made by Diodorous Siculus

(5.32.7) in the first century B.C. As none of the sources were writing detailed ethnographies, it is possible that these descriptions were serving a socio-political agenda to emphasise the differences between Roman society and that of the 'barbarian other', including perceived immorality or inferiority based on their view of homosexual relationships, or women having sexual relations with more than one man, or unknown paternity of children. Representations of the 'barbarian other' could thus underscore a just cause for war, conquest and enslavement of the people, and their need to be 'civilised'.

Politics and British queens

Britain is described as being ruled by kings and chieftains chosen from the boldest men in the period pre-dating and during the Roman conquest by Diodorus Siculus (v.21.3–6), Tacitus (*Agricola* 12), Strabo (4.5.2), and Cassius Dio (*Roman History* 77.12.1–5; 60.20). While speaking in general terms the sources referred to the leaders of the province as men, but they also record examples of women leading both tribes and armies. Boudicca of the Iceni, Cartimandua of the Brigantes, and a Caledonian queen were described by Tacitus and Cassius Dio as rulers of their respective tribes; but this is where the portrayals diverge. These queens are considered not in chronological order, but relative to the Roman perception of the queens as positive (Boudicca), negative (Cartimandua), and ambivalent (Argentocoxus' wife).

Boudicca was married to Prasutagus, king of the Iceni and a ruler who had come to terms with Rome years before his death in A.D. 60 (Tacitus *Annals* 14.31–7). Upon his death, Prasutagus left his kingdom to the Emperor Nero and his two daughters in order to keep them from harm. When they were raped and his wife was flogged, Boudicca responded by taking up arms against Rome and led the Iceni and Trinovantes into battle in A.D. 60–1 (Tacitus *Annals* 14.31–7; Hingley and Unwin 2005: 41, 47; Watts 2005: 8; Ireland 2008: 60). Boudicca was the wife of the Iceni king rather than the direct inheritor of the title, and Cassius Dio (*Roman History* 62.1–2) praised her capacity to govern by saying that not only was she the one person worthy of leadership, but was 'a woman of the British royal family who possessed more spirit than is usual among women'. He did not detract from this capability when he stated that early in Boudicca's revolt, Roman losses were 'sustained at the hands of a woman, something that in fact caused them the greatest of shame' (*Roman History* 62.1). Instead this was a comment upon his negative portrayal of the army and of Rome itself based in part on Roman ideals of masculinity and the male role in conflict.

Cassius Dio (*Roman History* 62.3–6) and Tacitus (*Agricola* 16; *Annals* 14.35) attribute a speech to Boudicca that was given just before her final battle against the Romans. The speech highlights Boudicca's noble birth and the legitimacy of her rule, as well as the custom of Britons to follow female leaders into war. Elsewhere in the speech, Boudicca asked for victory against unmanly Romans, those who would 'bathe in warm water, eat fancy foods, drink unmixed wine, smear themselves with myrrh, sleep on soft beds with boys – boys past their prime at that – and are slaves' to Nero, whom she called a woman (Cassius Dio *Roman History* 62.3–6). Here Boudicca becomes the voice of Tacitus and Dio as judges of Roman masculinity. In making the distinction 'boys past their prime', Tacitus hints at a recognised age distinction regarding appropriate relationships that are in line with Roman practices, or possibly a variation on how 'appropriate' masculinity could be constructed (Holmes 2012: 78). The speech presents an immoral Rome, underscoring Boudicca's rebellion as just and the legitimacy of her leadership (Hingley and Unwin 2005: 60–1).

While the speech is fictional, the example of Boudicca may give some insight into Iceni rules of inheritance and gender roles in that it suggests women could inherit both positions and wealth, though whether this is tribe or status-specific is unknown (Allason-Jones 2005: 9; Hingley and Unwin 2005: 42–3; Ireland 2008: 64). Tacitus (*Agricola* 16), however, noted that the existence of queens in Britain was not indicative of overall equality with men. Similarly, Rankin (2002: 251) asserts that recognition of queens in Celtic-language-based groups does not presuppose the existence of a matriarchy. Tacitus (*Annals* 14.36) elaborated on the presence of women at battles when he recorded the Roman general Suetonius as saying that there were more women than fighting men visible in the Iceni and Trinovantes ranks, with the possibility that they could have been participants or part of a large group of people accompanying the army.

The sources describe Boudicca's appearance as being tall with fair hair that reached all the way to her hips, having a harsh voice and piercing gaze. She wore a multi-coloured tunic, a cloak fastened with a brooch, a gold torc, held a spear, and rode in a chariot (Cassius Dio *Roman History* 62.2; Hingley and Unwin 2005: 4, 8, 50–1). While they may not have been completely accurate, representative of most women, or examples of everyday clothing, these types of descriptions are useful to compare against representations of women from funerary monuments later in this chapter. The gold torc seems to be an indicator of high social status, while the spear and chariot seem to indicate her role as a war leader, while her long fair hair and harsh voice were probably intended to signal her barbarism and femininity. Though the sources differ on the manner of her death (by self-administered poison or succumbing to illness), Dio indicates that she was given a costly burial and her people mourned her greatly as their leader (*Roman History* 62.12.1–6; Hingley and Unwin 2005: 56–7).

Queen Cartimandua of the Brigantes is similar to Boudicca as a female tribal leader of the mid-first century A.D. of noble birth, though she directly inherited her position of authority (Tacitus *Annals* 12.35–7; Hingley and Unwin 2005: 8). In contrast, Cartimandua is not presented as noble as Boudicca. Cartimandua gained Roman favour *c.*A.D. 51, when she captured Caratacus, leader of the British resistance, in defiance of her role as his host and then turned him over to the Romans, virtually paving 'the way for Claudius' triumph' (Tacitus *Histories* 3.45).

Tacitus described the success and wealth that followed her decision to detain Caratacus and credited it as the incentive for what Tacitus equated with adultery, portraying the queen as immoral:

> She rejected her husband Venutius and took his armour-bearer Vellocatus as her husband and consort. The royal house was straightaway scandalised by this shameful event: the people sided with the husband, the adulterer was bolstered by the lust and savagery of the queen.
>
> (*Histories* 3.45)

Venutius was angered by this rejection, and opposed both Cartimandua and her cooperation with Rome (Tacitus *Histories* 3.45). When Cartimandua waylaid some of Venutius' travelling family members it exacerbated this animosity, and Venutius and a band of his men invaded her kingdom (Tacitus *Annals* 12.40). Roman intervention allowed Cartimandua to retain her throne, though it was the very relationship with Rome which Venutius opposed (Tacitus *Histories* 3.45; Watts 2005: 8).

In contrast to Boudicca, the portrayal of Cartimandua in Roman sources is largely negative. Howarth (2008) suggests that this anger toward and negative portrayal of the queen may have been in response to her choice of partner – both her ability to choose who her partner was, and her potentially politically motivated choice of Vellocatus, even if her separation from Venutius occurred several years before her choice to marry Vellocatus. In establishing Cartimandua as an ally of Rome, the authors are establishing *jus bellus*, or just cause for war. While also demonstrating her personal immorality in terms of adultery and the weakness of her rule in her request for Roman support, they justify in this way the subsequent incorporation of her kingdom directly into the empire.

The portrayals of these women differ greatly considering they were both individuals of noble birth who had inherited (through marriage or birth) the right to rule. Boudicca was shown as a noble adversary of Rome, her motivation to fight a response to a violation of her husband's wishes and good will, and the assault of her daughters. Boudicca's leadership, in Roman eyes, is upheld as righteous as it co-exists with the Roman ideal of women as dedicated mothers and which only emerged because of her lack of husband or son. In rather stark contrast to this, Cartimandua was portrayed as a hedonistic woman whose self-gratification led her to spurn her husband and take another lover in defiance of Roman ideals for female behaviour (Tacitus *Histories* 3.45). The accounts of both of these powerful women, while likely outrageous and exciting to the authors, may have served to emphasise the perceived barbarity of the Britons through the involvement of women in politics and warfare, again contrasting Roman ideals for women's behaviour (Hingley and Unwin 2005: 8, 42).

Along the same line as the account of Queen Cartimandua, representations of the relative freedom of sexual choice enjoyed by native British women are further corroborated in the account of yet another queen and her interaction with a Roman woman with exceptional political power. Cassius Dio (*Roman History*

77.16.5; Allason-Jones 2008: 15) described an encounter in Scotland, during which the Empress Julia Domna asked the wife of the Caledonian chieftain Argentocoxus about 'the free intercourse of her sex with men in Britannia'. Her reported response was that local women openly consorted with the best men, as opposed to Roman women who 'let themselves be debauched in secret by the vilest' (Cassius Dio *Roman History* 77.16.5; Howarth 2008: 123). This could once again be political commentary relating to the less-than-ideal reputation of Julia Domna in terms of the Roman ideals or expectations discussed above. It could also be an example of the more open sexuality of the inhabitants of Britain, or an emphasis in the differences between the people of Rome and those of the province. Whatever the context was for this account, its existence and focus on women's choices and actions makes it an interesting point to consider when moving forward.

Looking in depth at three British queens does not provide information on ordinary individuals as they and other aristocratic women in Roman Britain likely had more latitude in what were considered acceptable roles or behaviours than those for the majority of people (Rankin 2002: 248). This does not make them irrelevant for discussing gendered roles in Romano-British society. These differing portrayals of powerful women from the province are consistent with the roles possible for women in Iron Age and later societies with Celtic-based languages, which were more varied than what was permitted in Greece or Rome (Rees and Rees 1961: 74–5, 255, 261; Kinsella 2002; Rankin 2002: 253; Watts 2005: 13). They give information on possible rules of inheritance, as mentioned earlier, and Roman perspectives on British sexuality. They also bring to light the possibility that women may have had a say in who they married and divorced, or took as lovers, or that there was a type of balance between the functions of men and women, if not outright equality (Rees and Rees 1961: 74–5, 255, 261; Kinsella 2002; Rankin 2002: 253; Watts 2005: 16). These examples also show how Roman ideals of masculinity, femininity, and behaviours associated with these categories were projected onto the people they were describing, and how conflict with these women or those associated with them could be justified by ancient authors through weaponisation of their gender or sexuality relative to Roman ideals.

Elite and non-elite women of the Northern Frontier

Tacitus, Cassius Dio, and other primary sources were writing in the Roman historiographic tradition, focusing on key political events, interpreted by and for elite audiences. However, other sources provide insight into provincial societies. Elite and non-elite women are attested in a range of sources, such as the Vindolanda tablets, military diplomas, and funerary monuments. Details from each of these sources can be limited, or even fragmentary, but when combined they contribute significant information for the exploration of gender identity in Romano-British society.

Vindolanda tablets

The Vindolanda tablets offer a rare glimpse into the lives of elite and non-elite women in a late-first-century frontier (Bowman 2003: 71; Allason-Jones 2005: 46–7; Greene 2013a: 376). These tablets are both examples of the material culture of daily life and a primary source material dealing with specific individuals living within Britain during the Roman period. These thin wooden tablets made of birch, alder, and oak, with ink writing on them, come from periods 2–5 at Vindolanda and date from approximately A.D. 92 to 130. They have been found in the areas of the fort along the *via principalis* including the *praetorium*, barrack blocks, and bonfire events in the fort (Bowman 1983: 18–28, 2003: 6–9; Greene 2013a: 372). While many of the Vindolanda tablets give information on political and military figures (e.g. Emperor Hadrian's visit: Birley 2005: 122; *Tab. Vindol. II* 344), military divisions and troop numbers (e.g. First Cohort of Tungrians: Birley 2005: 98; *Tab. Vindol. II* 154), official events and holidays (e.g. preparations for the Saturnalia: *Tab. Vindol. II* 301), and other bureaucratic information, they also shed light on some aspects of everyday life for people on the frontier.

The letters to and from Sulpicia Lepidina, the wife of Vindolanda's commander, and their children, are a perfect example of this. These individuals would have been the 'first family' of Vindolanda and were of higher status than most people living on the frontier (Bowman 2003: 51, 71; Allason-Jones 2005: 46; Greene 2013a: 373). The tablets give evidence of close familial relationships or a close-knit community within the larger military structure that included wives, children, sisters, and parents (Greene 2013a: 374, *Tab. Vindol. II* 310; *Tab. Vindol. III* 643), and that women had close social relationships with others at different forts (Bowman 2003: 71; Allason-Jones 2005: 37; *Tab. Vindol. II* 291–4).

One example is a birthday invitation from Claudia Severa, wife of Aelius Brocchus, sent to Sulpicia Lepidina (Figure 6.1), the wife of Flavius

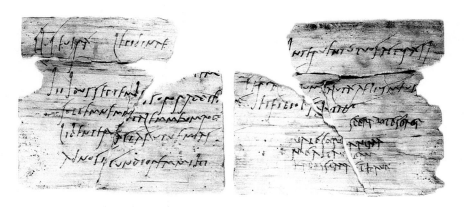

Figure 6.1 Vindolanda tablet no. 291: birthday party invitation

Cerialis, commanding officer of Vindolanda *c*.A.D. 100–5 (Bowman 2003: 19; *Tab. Vindol. II* 291). It reads:

Cl(audia) Seuerá Lepidinae [suae [sa]l[u]tem	Claudia Severa to her Lepidina greetings.
Idus Septembr[e]s soror ad diem sollemnem natalem meum rogó libenter faciás ut uenias ad nos iucundiorem mihi [diem] interuentú tuo facturá si Cerial[em t]uum salutá Aelius meus [te]. et filiolus salutant	On 11 September, sister, for the day of the celebration of my birthday, I give you a warm invitation to make sure that you come to us, to make the day more enjoyable for me by your arrival, if you are present [?]. Give my greetings to your Cerialis. My Aelius and my little son send him [?] their
[*In a second hand*] sperabo te soror uale soror anima mea ita ualeam karissima et haue	greetings. [*In a second hand*] I shall expect you, sister. Farewell, sister, my dearest soul, as I hope to prosper, and hail.
[*Back of the letter, first hand*] Sulpiciae Lepidinae Cerialis a S[e]uera	[*Back to the first hand*] To Sulpicia Lepidina, wife of Cerialis, from Severa

This invitation shows that even on the frontier elite women maintained close relationships and attended social gatherings, though not to the same extent as those in urban contexts may have (Bowman 2003: 71, 135, 169; Allason-Jones 2005: 46–7; Greene 2013a: 376–7). In this letter, Claudia Severa refers to Lepidina as 'sister' and conveys her happiness at the prospect of enjoying the presence of her friend. Another letter from Claudia Severa to Sulpicia Lepidina indicates that she had asked her husband if she could visit (*Tab Vindol II* 292). It reads:

Salutem	Greetings. Just as I had spoken with
ego soror sicut tecum locuta fueram et promiseram ut peterem a Brocchó et uenirem at te peti et res[po]ndit mihi ta corde[1] semp[er li] citum uná quomodocumque possim at te peruenire sunt enim necessariá quaedam qua[e] rem meum epistulas meas accipies quibus scies quid sim actura haec nobis .ra eram et Brigae mansura Cerialem tuum a me salutem	you, sister, and promised that I would ask Brocchus and would come to you, I asked him and he gave me the following reply, that it was always readily [?] permitted to me, together with … to come to you in whatever way I can. For there are certain essential things which … you will receive my letters by which you will know what I am going to do … I was … and will remain at Briga. Greet your Cerialis from me.
[*Back of the letter, in a second hand*] [ual]e m. soror karissima et anima ma desideratissima	[*Back in a second hand*] Farewell my sister dearest and most longed-for soul.
[*First hand*] Sulpiciae Lepidi- nae Ceria[li]s a Seuera B[rocchi	[*First hand*] To Sulpicia Lepidina, wife of Cerialis, from Severa, wife of Brocchus [?]

While it appears that Claudia Severa was to remain at Briga, this was not her home or where she and Brocchus lived, rather a place she had stopped at while travelling or visiting (*Tab. Vindol. II* 292). The permission she sought from her husband was probably related to safety and security at a potentially hazardous frontier rather than matrimonial control; importantly, the letter indicates regular communication and a very close relationship between the two women (Bowman 2003: 71–2; Allason-Jones 2005: 47; Greene 2013a: 376–7; *Tab. Vindol. II* 292).

In another letter to Sulpicia Lepidina, a woman named Paterna greets her most warmly and promises to bring her two remedies, a remedy for fever and one for an unidentified ailment (Figure 6.2; *Tab. Vindol. II* 294; Greene 2013a: 377). It is uncertain whether Paterna was making the remedies herself or obtaining them elsewhere (Allason-Jones 2005: 37). Either way, this suggests that women were responsible to some extent for medical treatments within the home, broadening our understanding of potentially gendered roles and the responsibilities of women at the Roman frontier (Bowman 2003: 51, 72–3; Allason-Jones 2005: 37; Jackson 2011; *Tab. Vindol. II* 294).

Letters like those between Claudia Severa and Sulpicia Lepidina show that these women played an important role within a larger military context. These relationships would have been a structuring element of everyday life, playing into constructions of gender and identity for these women (Greene 2012, 2013a: 372–4, 377, 379). Relationships between women, whether related or not, would

Figure 6.2 Vindolanda tablet no. 294: Lepidina and cures
(With kind permission and © of The Vindolanda Trust)

have been integral to how they understood and expressed themselves both as women and as individuals. The Vindolanda tablets show that elite women at the frontier travelled for social events, were involved in medical treatments within their homes, and maintained longstanding relationships with one another (Bowman 2003: 71; Allason-Jones 2005: 46–7; Greene 2013a: 376).

Further tablets indicate the place of women within broader social networks, through their relationships with men, whether friends, family members, or husbands. Many tablets request greetings to be sent to the wives or family members of the soldiers being written to, showing the presence of wives (legally recognised or de facto), extended families, and potentially longstanding friendships at frontier locations. An argument for the recognition of de facto marriages (to be discussed further below) seen in the Vindolanda tablets can be seen in Tablet 181. Robin Birley (1990: 30) suggests that the term *contuberni* refers to a wife or partner of a flag bearer at Vindolanda named Tagomas/Tagamatis, rather than a friend or mess mate as was previously suggested (Figure 6.3; *Tab. Vindol. II* 181). Another tablet sends greetings to a woman named Verecunda as well as the writer's 'fellow countrymen and friends' (*Tab. Vindol. III* 650). It has been suggested that this tablet is proof that, in many cases, wives of soldiers would either be of the same tribe as the men themselves or from another military family, again indicating a close community of family and friends within the military at the frontier (Greene 2013a: 374–5, 2015). A letter from Chrauttius to Veldeius is very reminiscent of numerous other letters written over the centuries: Chrauttius chastises his 'brother' for not writing sooner and enquires about the status of a pair of shears he had purchased (Bowman 2003: 141; *Tab. Vindol. II* 310). This letter also asks that Veldeius pass along greetings to their (?) sister, Thuttena, and write back with word of how another woman, Velbutena, was (Bowman 2003: 141; *Tab. Vindol. II* 310).

We also encounter well wishes and greetings in the correspondence of Aelius Brocchus and Flavius Cerialis, as they had a close relationship much the same as that of their wives (*Tab. Vindol. II* 244, 247, 274). There are over 65 letters and partial letters that are tentatively attributed to Cerialis (either to or from), with eight probable examples of correspondence between Cerialis and Brocchus (*Tab. Vindol. II* 233, 243–8, 274). In these letters, they address each other very warmly, as 'brother', and ask after each other's families (discussed above) in addition to their discussions of military matters. These close friendships or examples of extended family along the frontier were an important part of the everyday lives of these men. Lower status soldiers also had similar correspondence (*Tab. Vindol. II* 210; Bowman 1983, 2003; Bowman et al. 1994; Birley 2002; Bowman and Thomas 2003; Mattingly 2006: 190; Allason-Jones 2008: 43, 112; Birley 2009; Greene 2011, 2013a, 2013b). While these have traditionally been glossed over in discussions of military life, they would have been integral to the construction and expression of gender and identity on a daily basis. Once again, the Vindolanda tablets highlight the importance of the interplay and importance of family, friendships, and sexual relationships in constructions of gender, sexuality, and overall identity.

Figure 6.3 Vindolanda tablet no. 181: Tagomas/Tagamatis' girlfriend
(With kind permission and © of The Vindolanda Trust)

Military diplomas

Roman military diplomas, like the Vindolanda tablets, are fascinating documents
that combine military records with a source of information about family structure across the empire. These tablets included copies of the *constitutio* (copied
from Rome), the names of the soldier and family members (when included),
and the names of the seven witnesses authenticating the document. Though
most diplomas that are found are fragmentary, the formulaic nature of the document and inclusion of the names of the soldier and sometimes family members
are valuable sources of information for frontier contexts such as northern
Roman Britain. Roman military diplomas were issued after 25 years of service
by auxiliary soldiers, and were a portable copy of the rights they were given
after their service. This included his own *civitas Romana*, the right of *conubium*
with a peregrine wife that he had either lived with or chose to live with in the
future, and citizenship for all of their existing children (Greene 2015: 131).
This allowed these men to enter into legal marriage with someone who was not

a citizen themselves: it allowed their children Roman citizenship and the right for future children to be citizens as well.

Although marriage for soldiers was legally banned until the late second century, there are many clear examples of men having settled family lives in which they considered their partners to fill the role of their wife (Phang 2001, 2002a; Allason-Jones 2005: 12, 50–1; Watts 2005: 26; Briscoe 2010: 42, 47; Greene 2015: 125). Indications of this are seen in the recording of wives and children in military retirement diplomas dating to the first to the early third centuries, after which time they ceased to be issued (Greene 2015: 125). These diplomas give information about the military service of an individual, their origins within the empire, that of their wives, and the status of their heirs/children (Greene 2015). Other legal documents of the time allowed for men to name foreign women as heirs in their wills (Gaius *Institutes* 2.110) which would have potentially allowed for some legal legitimation of these de facto marriages (Greene 2015: 134). I will follow the example of Greene (2015) in using the terms 'wife' and 'marriage' to refer to these de facto relationships, though these individuals were not allowed to marry, and I am therefore not referring to *iustum matrimonium*, or the legal form of marriage for Roman citizens unless otherwise indicated.

The diplomas seem to indicate that men often brought their wives with them and therefore came from the same tribe as they did, or that they married within the larger military community which would have included the sister or daughters of other members of the military (Greene 2013b: 17, 2015: 125–7, 137–43). It was long understood that men married or had relationships with local women or that those who accompanied the military were 'a straggling group of camp-followers in which the women are typically identified as locals-turned-concubines or unsavoury hangers-on', but these diplomas call this assumption into question (Greene 2013b: 30, 2015: 126–7). Documentary evidence also mentions mothers, mothers-in-law, and sisters of the soldiers in some instances (as discussed above), confirming that some men brought much of their household and family with them in their military service (Greene 2013b: 27, 30, 2015). This further supports the existing (and rapidly expanding) body of evidence supporting the presence of women and children at even the early military sites such as Vindolanda and other parts of the Roman frontier (Speidel 1997; Wells 1997; van Driel-murray 1999; Allison 2006, 2008; Greene 2013b: 17, 2015). The trend in the information seen in the military diplomas further corroborates that these individuals are in many cases the families (whether recognised legally or not) of the soldiers accompanying men on their assignments, with an increase in the mention of families over time (Greene 2015: 132–3).

Unfortunately, there are only three published military diplomas from the frontier zone of Roman Britain at present (RIB 2401.4; 2401.9; 2401.10), but all of these examples make it clear that upon retirement they received the rights outlined above. Specifically, they had 'the right of legal marriage with the wives they had when citizenship was granted to them, or, if any were unmarried, with

those they later marry, but [they could have] only a single one each' (RIB
2401.4). The diploma from York dating from January to May A.D. 108 dictates
that citizenship is also granted to the children and descendants of the men,
where the examples from Vindolanda (RIB 2401.9) and Chesters (RIB
2401.10 – more fragmented), that date to January–March A.D. 146 and either
10 December A.D. 145 or 9 December A.D. 146 respectively, do not mention
children, reflecting the change in the formula of the grants in the A.D. 140s.
RIB 2401.9 not only provides information about the military history of the individual receiving the diploma, but that his name was Amandius. It is likely that
he or his father was from Gaul or Germania, and he was part of the First
Cohort of Tungrians (Bowman 2003: 23; Birley 2005: 144). While these
examples do not survive in full and therefore can only give us partial information about the exact nature of military families in this part of the Roman world,
they do show the existence of recognised (if not strictly legal) families and relationships, supporting the assertion that family life was a large part of everyday
experiences within the military landscape (Phang 2002b; Greene 2015).

Communicating gender in death

As public-facing monuments, tombstones provide a contemporary testament to
how an individual was commemorated, with inscriptions and figural carvings
presenting a range of aspects of identity, including gender. There are examples
of standing stones as memorials to the dead or as declarations of identity from
the pre-Roman Iron Age of Central and Western Europe including Brittany and
Ireland. While these examples are not anthropomorphic figural art or inscription,
and were rare in comparison to the proliferation of the practice in the Roman
period, they are still important to note as this practice was not completely foreign and may have affected how local populations understood this practice
moving forward (Harding 2004: 246; Mattingly 2006: 224). This type of monument is associated with Roman influence and is closely tied to the presence of
the military in our frontier region. The funerary monuments from Roman Britain are simpler in comparison to those from other parts of the empire in terms
of size and decoration, and are fewer in number than from other provinces in
the empire (Mann 1985; Hope 1997: 246–7). Numerous examples of funerary
monuments and inscriptions mentioning men and military involvement across
northern Britain, along with other inscriptions, clearly show the degree and
nature of Roman military influence in the area. Funerary monuments mentioning
women in Roman Britain only make up 10 per cent of inscriptions, but there
are a number of interesting examples that give us information about these
women, their identities, and associated ideals in the province at this time
(Allason-Jones 2005: xi).

In addition to evidence provided via inscription, figural representation in
Roman funerary monuments also means it is essential to consider the role that
dress and adornment play in representation and identity. In life, the act of dressing oneself was a complex process closely tied to expressing individual and

group identities (real or idealised), as well as symbolic meaning. Adoption of new elements of dress had much to do with the history of the relationship between groups such as the native Britons and Romans, and negotiation of status and roles within society at a given time. In the context of the Roman provinces, the length of time exposed to Roman populations and influence, the nature of the relationships between groups (allies or resistance/confrontation), the expectations of different classes or communities upon individuals, the traditional practices of a group, the climate, and availability of materials would have all factored into how individuals dressed in everyday contexts as well as how they were represented in death (Rothe 2009: 2–7; see also Chapter 7). In death, these complex cultural processes incorporated in dress are often simplified or idealised.

One example is the tombstone of Regina, a freedwoman of the Catuvellaunian tribe of southern Britain who married Barates from Palmyra (RIB 1065). The inscription was provided in Latin and Palmyrene (Aramaic), while the figural sculpture shows her in the 'Gallic coat' (common in the north-western provinces of the empire), wearing a torc, in addition to bracelets and earrings (Wild 2002; Allason-Jones 2005: 104–5, 116; Rothe 2009: 3–37; Carroll 2012: 284–97, 2013; McCarthy 2013: 112). She is depicted with a spindle and distaff as well as balls of wool, and her right hand is on a small chest, implying idealised qualities of a wife and an impression of wealth (Allason-Jones 2005: 104; Carroll 2012: 299–305). Regina and/or her husband chose to represent her British heritage on the monument by mentioning her tribe, in the type of dress she was shown wearing, and some of her accessories. In this context, representation of these more traditional elements of native dress may reflect the importance of British identity and customs, the expectations of Regina's class or status, or an idealised construction of her identity as understood and portrayed by her husband in his commemoration of her. Also worth considering is that the genders emphasised different elements of their identities depending on the time and situation – with death being a prime example. The stone was found at the fort at South Shields at the eastern end of Hadrian's Wall supports other material culture in showing that women lived in and around forts as military wives and family, and in and around *colonia* and urban settings as the wives or daughters of craftsmen or merchants alongside other individuals from across the empire (Allason-Jones 2005: 58; Gardner 2007: 48–50; Chenery et al. 2010; Carroll 2012: 285; Greene 2013a).

The adoption of Roman tradition in local monuments can be seen on the tombstone of Pervica, which was found near Great Chesters fort (Figure 6.4; RIB 1747). This example has little text and a very simple image of a woman in a mid-calf-length dress with long sleeves and hair tied back. This monument for a woman with a unique name reflects a style of dress that was native to the north-western provinces of the empire, if simple in its representation. Another example is the monument of Flavia Augustina from York which was set up by her husband (RIB 685). It shows Flavia Augustina, her husband (a veteran), her son, and her daughter who both died before the age of two. She is dressed in a tunic and shawl, he in a tunic and long cloak, with their children dressed and posed in the same manner as their parents, giving us an idea of both fashion and the composition of a family living in Roman Britain (Allason-Jones 2005: 56, 105; Watts 2005: 93). One final piece of information that may shed some light on the self-perception of Romano-British women is the fact that they often listed themselves as the heirs and/or wives of military men whose tombstones they erected, though they were not legally considered wives until the late second century (Allason-Jones 2005: 12, 50–1; Briscoe 2010: 42, 47). In this regard, local identity was not subject to official marital status on funerary monuments.

Monuments for men and women of British origins who died in northern Britain show some marked differences. A woman of the Cornovii tribe (RIB 639) buried at Ilkley, whose name was not preserved in full, was shown wearing a tunic and cloak, with her hair parted and in long braids, potentially representing a local hairstyle and style of clothing similar to that of Regina. This styling of the hair and representation of clothing is also shown on the funerary monument of Decimina from York (RIB 692; Allason-Jones 2005: 132, 2008: 100). A similarly simple hairstyle, with a centre parting, is seen in the monument of Aelia Sentica, set up by her husband, Aurelius Verulus, at Low Burrow Bridge. Sentica is a name with Celtic-language roots, further indicating a possible tie to the native populations of Britain (Frere et al. 1992: 312, no 8; Allason-Jones 2005: 130). The monument of Julia Velva, found at York, contains imagery that is common across the western empire from the Flavian period onwards in the form of the dining scene (Figure 6.5; Hope 1997: 254, 2009: 161; Rothe 2009: 25). The deceased is shown reclining on a couch, surrounded by wine, food, a boy servant holding a jug, and a girl holding a pet bird (RIB 688; Watts 2005: 114). The inscription indicates that 'she lived most dutifully', conforming to the ideals for Roman women that were discussed above (Watts 2005: 87). These elements are common on Roman tombstones elsewhere in the north-western provinces and imply ideals for lifestyle and behaviour to those who view the monument (Rothe 2009: 25). In addition to her name which contains Celtic-language elements, Julia Velva is also shown with her hair parted in the middle like the women of the Cornovii tribe, Decimina and Aelia Sentica. This not only supports the claim that this was a hairstyle commonly worn by women in Roman Britain, but that this monument is an example of the incorporation of more provincial images or styles and those associated with contact with the Roman empire.

Other women who have local or Celtic-language-based names include Tancorix (RIB 908; Allason-Jones 2005: 10), whose monument was found at Carlisle in the territory of the Carvetii, and Verecunda Rufilia, daughter of Rufus (RIB 621; Allason-Jones 2005: 10). Verecunda Rufilia was a member of the Dobunni who moved north during her life and was memorialised at Templebrough by her husband, Excingus, who also had a local name (Watts 2005: 40). The simpler execution of these monuments illustrates that men and women of

Figure 6.4 Funerary inscription for Pervica, RIB 1747

(With kind permission and © Great North Museum: Hancock)

Figure 6.5 Tombstone of Julia Velva, RIB 688
(Courtesy of York Museums Trust)

different social classes or levels of wealth within the local populations of Roman Britain were taking part in the erection of funerary monuments for the deceased. They also indicate that women of British origins were commemorated through these monuments as individuals as well as with their spouses. In other instances, women are named as heirs, as in the case of Martiola, daughter and heir of Flavius Martius (RIB 933). While this practice appears to have been quite widespread in the Roman provinces (Pölönen 2002), it is worth noting here as it is reminiscent of the rights of inheritance implied in the above discussion of British queens and potential pre-Roman traditions regarding women.

In contrast to female monuments, funerary inscriptions and images of males emphasise or more starkly incorporate Roman metropolitan gender ideals. For example, the monument commemorating six-year-old Marcus Cocceius Nonnus (RIB 932) from Old Penrith depicts the boy holding a palm branch in his right hand and a whip in his left, possibly tied to victory in a boy's game of chariot racing. Nectovelius, age 29, son of Vindex and a member of the Brigantian tribe, was commemorated at Mumrills, the largest fort on the Antonine Wall (Figure 6.6; RIB 2142). The inscription also records his nine years of service in the Second Cohort of Thracians, emphasising both his tribal and military associations while north of his home territory. Similarly, Flavius Martius' quaestorian rank and positions as a councillor and ex-quaestor of the Carvetii were documented on his funerary monument which was erected in his tribal territory (RIB 933). In recording both their tribal identity as well as their political and military service and achievements, the monuments of these men serve to communicate idealised Roman elements of masculine identity discussed above (see also Chapter 8). While this is important to acknowledge, it is not out of the question that these types of service were similarly tied to local ideals of masculine behaviour and identity at the frontier as well.

Conclusions

Textual information remaining on the very late Iron Age and Roman periods of Britain were not written as ethnographic accounts of a group (or groups) of people. These texts were influenced by the time in which they were written along with the biases of the authors, often including political commentary and

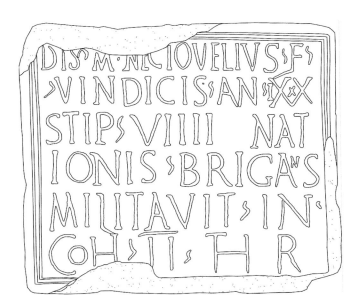

Figure 6.6 Drawing of a funerary inscription for Nectovelius, RIB 2142. Located at the National Museums of Scotland

(With kind permission and © Matthew Munro)

an emphasis on the 'otherness' of the group being described. These caveats taken into consideration, these documents still provide valuable information about elements of gender, sexuality, and identity during this time. British queens were shown as powerful women in their own right, though the exact details of the circumstances surrounding and motivations for their actions remain somewhat blurred by the agendas of the Roman authors that provided the accounts. The accounts of Boudicca and Cartimandua indicate that royal women could inherit resources, titles, and positions of power in the same way men could. These accounts are also indicative that high status women in some of the British tribes had a degree of sexual freedom and choice of their partner or spouse, including the power to divorce them. However, at present it is diffi-cult to determine the degree of choice or sexual sovereignty available to women regardless of their social status.

The Vindolanda tablets highlight the importance of friendship and family ties for both men and women in northern Britain. Friendships between women would have played an integral part in the daily experience of being a woman in this part of the province, as illustrated in the letters between Claudia Severa and Sulpicia Lepidina. These and other letters show that women were undertaking some medical care within the home, that they planned social events, travelled, and had close relationships with their husbands as well as other family members in more distant parts of the empire. These letters show us much of the same for men at Vindolanda. These men maintained close relationships with friends and family across the empire in addition to their involvement in the military world of which they were a part. These texts and the few surviving military diplomas from the study area show that family and children were very important to the men on the frontier, and that their spouses did not have to be legally considered their wives for them to take on that role. For those men who did not have wives (de facto or legal), the friends that they made in the military or the family members that resided nearby took on the roles and responsibilities of the heir, again emphasising the importance of friendships between men and their impact in gender expression and lived experiences.

The funerary monuments discussed above highlight differences in gender expression and ideal gender roles, but were created for wealthier individuals and therefore obscure much of this information for those of lower social status. Monu-ments for both men and women show the importance of naming traditions, though women are more often shown with British elements of dress and adornment, such as hairstyles. Though the majority of the monuments erected for males in the fron-tier zone of Britain were military in nature, the examples discussed above indicate that more factors than a rank or position contributed to social status. Women's monuments showed the importance of tribal identity and family in terms of names, including tribal affiliation, and British representations of clothing and hair-styles. Some examples corroborate women's rights to inherit that were recorded in the sources, and though this is not uncommon or extraordinary when looking at the Roman Empire as a whole, it is essential to consider how local and provincial traditions may have influenced these practices over time. The monuments also show that these identities were just as relevant, or perhaps more so upon moving away from their home territory. Women were also associated with weaving, motherhood, and loyalty, elements that parallel Roman ideals for women.

Men's monuments emphasise citizenship, military service, and social status: actions and accomplishments of these men who in some cases include their tribal identity alongside other information. While this type of monumentality was not common in Britain before the Roman presence, it was a practice that was used increasingly by members of society at a number of levels over time. This does not suggest that it was adopted as a perceived 'improvement', but a conscious decision made by individuals and groups for many possible reasons. This could have been a method of self-expression, to show 'ideals' or a particular representation of an individual in death that may have differed from the reality of their everyday life, or to continue an existing tradition of remembrance or memorialisation of the dead in a way that would be longstanding and was understood by members of a changing population.

Two threads that run through the sources are the lack of a separate category based on sexual relationships alone, and the lack of any indication of gender categories separate from the male/female binary as outlined in the Roman sources. The sources and funerary monuments from northern Britain that have been discussed here provide an interesting, if incomplete, picture of what gender and sexuality were for the various inhabitants of the province, both indigenous and those coming from abroad, during the Roman period. Sex, sexuality, and gender cannot be separated out from one another for study, as has been highlighted by the data discussed above. For women, the choice in who they had sexual relationships with, who they married, the family that resulted from these choices, their friendships with other women, and their right to inherit would have shaped their lives in terms of the roles and responsibilities (often in line with the Roman 'ideals' discussed above) that they were then faced with on a daily basis. The same can be said for men, as their involvement in military or political service ('ideal' activities for constructing Roman masculinity as discussed above, see also Chapter 8), their friendships, and the importance of their children or heirs would have shaped their daily lived experiences. These choices and actions would continue to be reflected in death as it was often family members or friends who were responsible for commemorating the deceased (men or women) in their funerary monuments.

Note

1 Bowman (2003: 137) suggests 'cori' for this, potentially referring to the place name of Coria (Corbridge).

Bibliography

Allason-Jones, L. (2005). *Women in Roman Britain*. York: Council for British Archaeology.
Allason-Jones, L. (2008). *Daily Life in Roman Britain*. Westport, CT: Greenwood World, Oxford.

Allison, P.M. (2006). "Mapping for Gender. Interpreting Artefact Distribution inside 1st-and 2nd-Century A.D. Forts in Roman Germany", *Archaeological Dialogues*, 13(1): 1–20.

Allison, P.M. (2008). "The Women and Children inside 1st-and 2nd-Century Forts: Comparing the Archaeological Evidence", in U. Brandl (ed.), *Frauen Und Römisches Militär; Beiträge Eines Runden Tisches in Xanten Vom 7. Bis 9. Juli 2005*. BAR International Series, 1759. Oxford: Archaeopress, 120–139.

Baker, M. (2000). "Gender: Enabling Perspective or Politically Correct Term? An Analysis of how Gender and Material Culture are Viewed by 1990's Academia", in M. Donald and L. Hurcombe (eds), *Gender and Material Culture in Archaeological Perspective*. London: Macmillan, 56–68.

Balme, J. and Bulbeck, C. (2008). "Engendering Origins: Theories of Gender in Sociology and Archaeology", *Australian Archaeology*, 67(December): 3–12.

Birley, A. (2002). *Garrison Life at Vindolanda: A Band of Brothers*. Stroud: The History.

Birley, A. (2005). *The Roman Government of Britain*. Oxford: Oxford University Press.

Birley, R. (1990). *The Roman Documents from Vindolanda*. Greenhead: Roman Army Museum.

Birley, R. (2009). *Vindolanda: A Roman Frontier Fort on Hadrian's Wall*. Stroud: Amberley.

Boswell, J. (1995). *Same-Sex Unions in Premodern Europe*. New York: Vintage.

Bowman, A.K. (1983). *Roman Writing Tablets from Vindolanda*. London: British Museum.

Bowman, A.K. (2003). *Life and Letters on the Roman Frontier: Vindolanda and Its People*. London: British Museum.

Bowman, A.K. and Thomas, J.D. (2003). *The Vindolanda Writing Tablets: Tabulae Vindolandenses*. vol. III. London: British Museum.

Bowman, A.K., Thomas, J.D. and Adams, J.N. (1994). *The Vindolanda Writing-Tablets: (Tabulae Vindolandenses II)*. London: British Museum.

Bradley, H. (1996). *Fractured Identities: Changing Patterns of Inequality*. Cambridge: Polity.

Briscoe, K.T. (2010). *A Comparative Study of Indigenous Female Identity in the Roman Provinces of Britain and Egypt*. Unpubl. M.A. dissertation, Southern Methodist University.

Brumfiel, E.M. (2007). "Methods in Feminist and Gender Archaeology: A Feeling for Difference and Likeness", in S.M. Nelson (ed.), *Women in Antiquity: Theoretical Approaches to Gender and Archaeology*. New York: Altamira, 1–28.

Butler, J. (1993). "Critically Queer", *GLQ: A Journal of Lesbian and Gay Studies*, 1(1): 17–32.

Butler, J. (2004). *Undoing Gender*. London: Routledge.

Butrica, J.L. (2005). "Some Myths and Anomalies in the Study of Roman Sexuality", *Journal of Homosexuality*, 49(3/4): 209–269.

Carroll, M. (2012). "'The Insignia of Women': Dress, Gender and Identity on the Roman Funerary Monument of Regina from Arbeia", *Archaeological Journal*, 169(1): 281–311.

Carroll, M. (2013). "Ethnicity and Gender in Roman Funerary Commemoration: Case Studies from the Empire's Frontiers", in L. Nilsson Stutz and S. Tarlow (eds), *The Oxford Handbook of the Archaeology of Death and Burial*. Oxford: Oxford University Press, 559–580.

Casella, E.C. and Voss, B. (2012). "Intimate Encounters: An Archaeology of Sexualities within Colonial Worlds", in B. Voss and E.C. Casella (eds), *The Archaeology of*

Colonialism: Intimate Encounters and Sexual Effects. Cambridge: Cambridge University Press, 1–10.

Chenery, C., Eckardt, H., Leach, S., Lewis, M. and Muldner, G. (2010). "A Lady of York: Migration, Ethnicity and Identity in Roman Britain", *Antiquity*, 84: 131–145.

Cherici, P. (1995). *Celtic Sexuality: Power, Paradigms and Passion*. London: Duckworth.

Clarke, J.R. (2005). "Representations of the Cinaedus in Roman Art", *Journal of Homosexuality*, 49(3–4): 271–298.

Condren, M. (1989). *The Serpent and the Goddess: Women, Religion, and Power in Celtic Ireland*. San Francisco, CA: Harper and Row.

D'Ambra, E. (2007). *Roman Women*. Cambridge: Cambridge University Press.

Diaz-Andreu, M. (2005). "Gender identity", in Diaz-Andreu et al, 13–42.

Diaz-Andreu, M. and Lucy, S. (2005). "Introduction", in Diaz-Andreu et al, 1–12.

Diaz-Andreu, M., Lucy, S., Babić, S. and Edwards, D. eds, (2005). *The Archaeology of Identity: Approaches to Gender, Age, Status, Ethnicity, and Religion*. London: Routledge.

Ellis, P.B. (1992). *Celtic Inheritance*. London: Constable.

Frere, S., Hassall, M.W.C. and Tomlin, R.S.O. (1992). "Roman Britain in 1991", *Britannia*, 23: 255–323.

Gardner, A. (2004). "Agency and Community in 4th Century Britain: Developing the Structuralist Project", in A. Gardner (ed.), *Agency Uncovered*. London: University College of London, 33–49.

Gardner, A. (2007). "Fluid Frontiers: Cultural Interaction on the Edge of Empire", *Stanford Journal of Archaeology*, 5: 43–60.

Geller, P.L. (2009). "Bodyscapes, Biology, and Heteronormativity", *American Anthropologist*, 111(4): 504–516.

Gilchrist, R. (1991). "Women's Archaeology? Political Feminism, Gender Theory, and Historical Revision", *Antiquity*, 65: 495–501.

Gilchrist, R. (1999). *Gender and Archaeology: Contesting the Past*. London: Routledge.

Greene, E.M. (2011). *Women and Families in the Auxiliary Military Communities of the Roman West in the First and Second Centuries AD*. Unpubl. Ph.D. thesis, The University of North Carolina at Chapel Hill.

Greene, E.M. (2012). "Sulpicia Lepidina and Elizabeth Custer: A Cross-Cultural Analogy for the Social Role of Women on a Military Frontier", in F. McIntosh, D.J. Rohl and M. Duggan (eds), *TRAC 2011: Proceedings of the Twenty-First Annual Theoretical Roman Archaeology Conference*. Oxford: Oxbow Books, 105–114.

Greene, E.M. (2013a). "Female Networks in Military Communities in the Roman West: A View from the Vindolanda Tablets", in E. Hemelrijk and G. Woolf (eds), *Women and the Roman City in the Latin West*. Leiden: Brill, 369–390.

Greene, E.M. (2013b). "Before Hadrian's Wall: Early Communities at Vindolanda and on the Northern Frontier", in R. Collins and M.F.A. Symonds (eds), *Breaking Down Boundaries: Hadrian's Wall in the 21st Century*. Journal of Roman Archaeology Supplementary Series 93. Portsmouth, RI: Journal of Roman Archaeology, 17–32.

Greene, E.M. (2015). "Conubium Cum Uxoribus: Wives and Children in the Roman Military Diplomas", *Journal of Roman Archaeology*, 28: 125–159.

Harding, D.W. (2004). *The Iron Age in Northern Britain: Celts and Romans, Natives and Invaders*. London: Routledge.

Hingley, R. and Unwin, C. (2005). *Boudica: Iron Age Warrior Queen*. London: Hambledon Continuum.

Holmes, B. (2012). *Gender: Antiquity and Its Legacy*. Oxford: Oxford University Press.

Hope, V. (2009). *Roman Death: Dying and the Dead in Ancient Rome*. London: Continuum.

Hope, V.M. (1997). "Words and Pictures: The Interpretation of Romano-British Tombstones", *Britannia*, 28: 245–258.

Howarth, N. (2008). *Cartimandua: Queen of the Brigantes*. Stroud: History Press.

Hughes, L.A. (2007). "Unveiling the Veil: Cultic, Status, and Ethnic Representations of Early Imperial Freedwomen", *Material Religion: The Journal of Objects, Art and Belief*, 3(2): 218–241.

Hughes, L.A. (2010). "Morals, Piety, and Representations of Veiled Women in Augustan Rome", *Material Religion*, 6(3): 377–378.

Ireland, S. (2008). *Roman Britain: A Sourcebook*. London: Routledge.

Jackson, R. (2011). "Medicine and Hygiene", in L. Allason-Jones (ed.), *Artefacts in Roman Britain: Their Purpose and Use*. Cambridge: Cambridge University Press, 243–268.

Jenkins, R. (2008). *Social Identity*. London: Routledge.

Johnson, M. (1999). *Archaeological Theory: An Introduction*. Oxford: Blackwell Publishing.

Joyce, R.A. (2008). *Ancient Bodies, Ancient Lives: Sex, Gender, and Archaeology*. New York: Thames and Hudson.

Kinsella, T. (2002). *The Tain: From the Irish Epic Tain Bo Cuailnge*. Oxford: Oxford Paperbacks.

Mann, J.C. (1985). "Epigraphic Consciousness", *Journal of Roman Studies*, 75: 204–206.

Mattingly, D. (2006). *An Imperial Possession: Britain in the Roman Empire, 54 BC–AD 409*. London: Penguin.

McCarthy, M.R. (2013). *The Romano-British Peasant: Towards A Study of People, Landscapes, and Work During the Roman Occupation of Britain*. Oxford: Windgather Press.

Meskell, L. (2002). "The Intersection of Identity and Politics in Archaeology", *Annual Review of Anthropology*, 31: 279–301.

Nathan, G. (2015). "The Ideal Male in Late Antiquity: Claudian's Example of Flavius Stilicho", *Gender and History*, 27(1): 10–27.

Nelson, S.M. (2004). *Gender in Archaeology: Analyzing Power and Prestige*. New York: Altamira Press.

Olson, K. (2014). "Masculinity, Appearance, and Sexuality: Dandies in Roman Antiquity", *Journal of the History of Sexuality*, 23(2): 182–205.

Phang, S.E. (2001). *The Marriage of Roman Soldiers (13 B.C.–A.D. 235): Law and Family in the Imperial Army*. Leiden: Brill.

Phang, S.E. (2002a). "The Families of Roman Soldiers (First and Second Centuries A.D.): Culture, Law, and Practice", *Journal of Family History*, 27(4): 352–373.

Phang, S.E. (2002b). "The Timing of Marriage in the Roman Army", in P. Freeman (ed.), *Limes XVIII: Proceedings of the XVIIIth International Congress of Roman Frontier Studies held in Amman 2000*. BAR International Series 1084. Oxford: Archaeopress, 873–878.

Pölönen, J. (2002). "The Division of Wealth Between Men and Women in Roman Succession (c.a. 50 BC – AD 250)", in P. Setälä, R. Berg, R. Hälikkaä, M. Keltanen, J. Pölönen and V. Vuolanto (eds), *Women, Wealth and Power in the Roman Empire*. Rome: Institutum Romanum Finlandiae, 147–179.

Rankin, D. (2002). *Celts and the Classical World*. London: Routledge.

Rees, A.D. and Rees, B. (1961). *Celtic Heritage: Ancient Tradition in Ireland and Wales*. London: Thames and Hudson.

Richlin, A. (1993). "Not Before Homosexuality: The Materiality of the Cinaedus and the Roman Law against Love between Men", *Journal of the History of Sexuality*, 3(4): 523–573.

Rothe, U. (2009). *Dress and Cultural Identity in the Rhine-Moselle Region of the Roman Empire*. BAR International Series 2038. Oxford: Archaeopress.

Speidel, M. (1997). "Frauen und Kinder Beim Römischen Heer", *Jahresbericht der Gesellschaft Pro Vindonissa*, 53–54.

van Driel-murray, C. (1999). "Dead Men's Shoes", in W. Schlüter and R. Wiegels (eds), *Rom, Germanien und die Ausgrabungen von Kalkriese*. Osnabrück: Osnabrücker Forschungen zu Altertum und Antike-Rezeption, 169–189.

Voss, B. (2006). "Engendered Archaeology: Men, Women, and Others", in M. Hall and S. W. Silliman (eds), *Historical Archaeology*. Malden, MA: Blackwell, 107–127.

Voss, B. (2008). "Sexuality Studies in Archaeology", *Annual Review of Anthropology*, 37 (1): 317–336.

Watts, D.J. (2005). *Boudicca's Heirs: Women in Early Britain*. London: Routledge.

Wells, C.M. (1997). "'The Daughters of the Regiment': Sisters and Wives in the Roman Army", in W. Groenman-Van Waateringe, B.L. van Beek, W.J.H. Willems and S. L. Wynia (eds), *Roman Frontier Studies 1995: Proceedings of the XVIth International Congress of Roman Frontier Studies*. Oxford: Oxbow, 571–574.

Wild, J.P. (2002). "The Textile Industries of Roman Britain", *Britannia*, 33: 1–42.

Williams, C.A. (2010). *Roman Homosexuality*. Oxford: Oxford University Press.

7 Dressed for death?

A study of female-associated burials from Roman-period Slovenia

Kaja Stemberger

Introduction

The present chapter analyses the burial record of two of the most well-known Roman towns in Slovenia. In this study I selected the cemeteries from Colonia Iulia Emona (modern Ljubljana) and Colonia Ulpia Traiana Poetovio (modern Ptuj), as they are among the best published in the region and offer a substantial amount of material for analysis (Figure 7.1). Moreover, Emona and Poetovio are the largest Roman-period settlements within the borders of present-day Slovenia, where one could expect to find large cemeteries. This offers us the opportunity to analyse numerous burials that reflect diverse urban populations that were composed of a multitude of different groups.

This chapter focuses more narrowly on the intersection of female gender, ethnicity, and expressions thereof through dress in the burial record of Emona and Poetovio. This is done for two main reasons. The first is practical, since elements of women's attire (clothing and jewellery) are much more distinctive than those of men in cemeteries from the Roman period in Slovenia. The second reason is the notion that the items placed into the graves were put there intentionally. This makes the information deriving from them more explicit in the discussion of what was intentionally or unintentionally expressed through the dress items at death. There is a particularly strong connection between identity and elements of attire. What we wear and how we wear it can express multiple different elements of identity, such as age, gender, marital status, wealth, occupation, or ethnic affiliation (Rothe 2009; Hoss 2016, 2017; Chapter 6). The individual parts of one's clothing are worn directly on the body and, in a sense, can function as its extension. The arrangement of fabrics, colours, and additional adornment, usually in the form of jewellery, adds to the visual language of clothes. This is the reason why in this chapter I concentrate on elements of attire rather than other categories of objects: they are worn directly on the body and can function as its extension.

The first section of this chapter provides a brief overview of the two sites, including their geographical and chronological context. The next section presents a general discussion of various aspects of identity and how they are traditionally studied in Slovenian archaeology. This is done in order to address

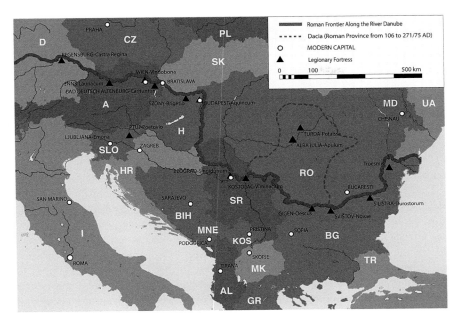

Figure 7.1 Locations of Emona and Poetovio in relation to modern and Roman borders (Map by FRE-Projekt, Danube Limes – UNESCO World Heritage Project/Institut für Österreichische Geschichtsforschung, under CC-BY-NC)

several outdated or ill-defined concepts currently used in Slovenian archaeology to interpret identity in the Roman period. The following section analyses the funerary material from Emona and Poetovio and what it can tells us about the similarities and differences in the burial record of these two colonies. The chapter concludes by assessing what these analyses can add to our understanding of how female gender and ethnic affiliation may or may not be expressed through objects of personal adornment and their combinations placed into graves.

Two colonies: an overview of Emona and Poetovio

The nature of the colonies and their respective histories played important roles in how and which identities were expressed through funerary rituals. Colonia Iulia Emona, subsequently "Emona", was established during the late Augustan or early Trajanic period. This date comes from a building inscription (CIL III 10768, p. 2328,26), which is most likely related to the construction of the colony's defensive wall. Emona is situated under the modern Slovenian city of Ljubljana and belonged to Regio X of Augustus' division of peninsular Italy, as confirmed by the discovery of a boundary stone between the *ager* of Aquileia and Emona (Šašel Kos 2002, 2003). Unlike Emona, the provincial affiliation of

Poetovio is complex. It is unclear whether it initially belonged to Noricum or Illyricum. However, we know that between A.D. 69 and 79 it became a part of the province of Pannonia, and later, under Diocletian's reign, it was included in Noricum Mediterraneum.

The settlement of Emona was built *ex novo* in A.D. 14 along an orthogonal plan, positioned on the western bank of the Ljubljanica River between what is now the Grajski grič ("Castle Hill") and Rožnik hill (Gaspari 2010, 2014: 146–7). Emona served as a control point and outpost for the conquest of the Balkan Peninsula mainly in the first century A.D., but was predated by a military camp on the eastern bank of the Ljubljanica River (Gaspari 2014: 127–41). In the vicinity of this camp, traces of prehistoric dwellings have also been unearthed.

Large areas of the Roman colony and its surroundings were unearthed during several building projects in the modern-day Slovenian capital. Amongst the most prominent features unearthed are: the forum with its temple of the Capitoline triad (Plesničar Gec and Kos 2006), the south-eastern insulae (Gaspari 2010), the early Christian centre (Plesničar Gec 1973), the cloaca and fortification (Šašel 1968), the area to the north of the northern city wall (Gaspari et al. 2015), and the military camp across the Ljubljanica River towards the east of Emona. Material remains of various activities that would indicate the occupation of the inhabitants of Emona are relatively scarce. Excavations have identified a handful of pottery and glass kilns as well as traces of (gold)smithing. Although not discovered at present, the colony should have a river port, especially after the destruction of Nauportus in A.D. 14 (Tacitus *Annales* 1.20), after which Emona likely took over as the main port on the Ljubljanica River. From here, goods were shipped eastwards (Horvat 1990; Mušič and Horvat 2007).

The majority of Emona's known cemeteries lay towards the north of the colony, although smaller ones have been excavated towards the east and west. The area to the south of the colony was most likely too swampy to be used for burials (Stemberger 2018: 54). Along these main roads, Emona's cemeteries have produced more than 3000 burials at present. Their excavations and those at the settlement itself have occurred from the eighteenth century onwards. Reports up to 1909 consisted mainly of daily press articles and short notes in various journals. The first substantial research work was undertaken in 1912 by Walter Schmid, who excavated the northern cemetery, known as Titova cesta. Sonja Petru (1972) gathered together the data from most of the numerous small-scale excavations and part of the northern cemetery (including Titova cesta). This publication included a catalogue of finds and all of the material coming from Emona's cemeteries between 1635 and 1960. In addition to Petru's catalogue, Ljudmila Plesničar Gec (1972) produced another major publication of more than 800 graves. Several smaller cemeteries excavated after 1960 were published in individual articles, for example by Petru (1962), Slabe (1968), and Plesničar Gec (1980). Modern excavations in Emona after the year 2000 have been significant in their scope (Mulh 2008, 2012; Hofman 2009; Klasinac 2011; Tomažinčič 2011; Gaspari et al. 2015), yet these publications present either preliminary results or partial studies of a few cases. It is important to emphasise that excavations are still ongoing in the city centre of Ljubljana.

The character of Emona's population in the first century A.D. was strongly influenced by settlers from the area of northern and central Italy, including some notable merchant families such as the Barbii and Caesernii (Šašel 1960, 1966; see also Istenič et al. 2003: 83). Epigraphic (Šašel Kos 2003) and funerary records (Stemberger 2018) indicate the presence of soldiers and veterans (for the former see Šašel Kos 1997; for the latter see Šašel Kos 2003), as well as members of other professions such as doctors, priests, and civil servants. The epigraphic evidence also attests to the presence of slaves as well as freed and freeborn men and women.

Similar to Emona, the area of Poetovio was already inhabited prior to the Roman occupation in the first decades of the first century A.D. Horvat et al. (2003: 158) consider the tribes living on the territory of Poetovio to have belonged to the Taurisci. Pliny the Elder mentions the Serretes, Sirapilli, Iasi, and Andizetes as living along the Drava River (*Nat. His.* III. 147–8). As a colony, Poetovio was established slightly less than a hundred years later than Emona, during the reign of the Emperor Trajan. Poetovio is generally estimated to have been much larger than Emona for much of its existence, and reached its peak during the third century when it was larger than contemporary London. It was not laid out geometrically, but stretched along the main eastward road. Several distinct districts of the town are known, including the residential and industrial areas, and the religious quarters with the remains of five mithraea. Based on the size of Poetovio compared to Emona's, the colony's cemeteries should presumably contain more individual burials than Emona's, but they have not been studied to the same degree. In typical Roman fashion, they stretched alongside the main roads entering and exiting the city. Poetovio offers more evidence of the military's presence in the region, with the Legio VIII Augusta and XIII Gemina and the Pannonian fleet (Classis Flavia Pannonica) stationed at the colony on several occasions (Sanader 2003: 463). Just as at Emona, the population of Poetovio consisted of members of the military, traders, priests, civil servants, freedmen/freedwomen, and slaves. The preserved kilns and other workshops indicate that the colony produced significant amounts of pottery (Istenič et al. 2003) and glass objects (Lazar 2003: 221). There is also evidence of stone-working activities since marble was transported to Poetovio from the nearby Pohorje mountains (Jarc et al. 2010).

The cemetery included in this research extended to the west of the colony along the road leading to Celeia, modern Celje (Istenič 1999, 2000). It was excavated relatively early, between 1889 and 1908, but the documentation is nonetheless fairly detailed and reliable. The most comprehensive publications are the catalogues by Janka Istenič (1999, 2000), based on the finds from the remains of 784 graves. Of later excavations, only the eastern cemeteries of Poetovio have received a comprehensive and substantial publication, with the catalogue by Zilka Kujundžić (1976). Several other twentieth-century excavations were smaller in scope; these include the cemeteries published by Tušek (1993, 1997) and Vomer Gojkovič (1997).

State of research

Before proceeding with the analysis of the funerary evidence from Emona and Poetovio, it is necessary to make a few observations regarding the state of research. Both colonies had large cemeteries that were excavated mainly before the full adoption of modern excavation techniques: the first excavations were conducted in the eighteenth century, but the majority occurred in the 1960s and 1970s. This means that grave units are largely reconstructed on the basis of the excavators' heterogeneous notes and diaries. The main sources for Emona are two catalogues by Petru (1972) and Plesničar Gec (1972), and for Poetovio two volumes by Istenič (1999, 2000) and one by Kujundžić (1976). These five works comprise the majority of the material excavated at their time of publication, including the earliest eighteenth-century excavations. The greatest drawback of this large dataset lies in the lack of chronological and osteological data at a modern level of detail. While a handful of summaries of osteological analyses have been published, the information they provide cannot be connected with any specific graves or grave goods. Furthermore, artefact descriptions in these interim reports are prohibitively generic and the illustrations not sufficiently detailed for anything but the most rudimentary typological classification. Typically, three types of information can be retrieved from the catalogues: grave location, burial manner, and the artefacts buried with the deceased.

Excavation reports from the eighteenth and nineteenth centuries typically indicate locations using toponyms that are now difficult or impossible to trace, or in relation to buildings that once stood in the vicinity. However, precise or at least approximate locations can be reconstructed for a great majority of the graves at Emona and Poetovio. The style of burial is often recorded to varying extents, ranging from generic labels to elaborate descriptions. In the case of the western cemetery of Poetovio, Istenič (2000: 48–9) could only classify most graves as either cremations or inhumations, unlike the much more detailed typology available for most of Emona's burials (Petru 1972: 11–12; Plesničar Gec 1972: 10–12). Often only outstanding arrays of grave furnishings were documented in detail in the eighteenth and nineteenth-century excavations. In some cases, like the earliest excavations at Poetovio, not even these were recorded, and "plain" or broken objects were simply omitted. Although documentation standards improved significantly at the beginning of the twentieth century, it was not until the second half of that century that damaged artefacts came to be systematically documented, as demonstrated by the case of pottery sherds from Emona (Stemberger 2018, ch. 4). Particularly disturbing is the absence of information regarding burial manner and grave location for many of Poetovio's graves (Istenič 1999: 48).

In this research, the discussion of identities of the deceased individuals at Emona and Poetovio is based on the analysis of grave goods. Of the available publications, the catalogue produced by Istenič (2000) is the best source for a typo-chronological analysis of grave artefacts. While primarily focusing on Poetovio's ceramic objects, it also comments on other large ensembles, and is grouped by the material of the object. Grave goods from burials not included in Istenič's catalogue, be they from Poetovio or Emona, were primarily discussed in general studies of material culture of Roman-period Slovenia. The last major study effort of this kind was undertaken in 1979, where different authors addressed various groups of artefacts in the Slovenian archaeological journal *Arheološki Vestnik*. The following objects from the entire territory of present Slovenia were included: amber artefacts (Bertoncelj-Kučar 1979), bone pins (Dular 1979), belt buckles (Sagadin 1979), metal bracelets (Budja 1979), and earrings (Mihovilić 1979). I have also consulted a number of more specific studies published before 1979, which concentrated on thin walled cups and beakers from Emona (Plesničar Gec 1987), oil lamps (Šubic 1975, 1976b), and different glass forms (Šubic 1976a). The general study of glass objects from across Slovenia by Irena Lazar (2003) includes the material from Poetovio, but not that from Emona.

Questions and problems of identity in Slovenian Roman archaeology

There are relatively few Slovenian studies that focus primarily on interpreting various forms of identities existing in the Roman period in the study region. Even though the topic is frequently invoked, this is usually done in passing, as part of general introductory or concluding remarks, most commonly in the context of burial manner or material culture studies (Knez 1968; Plesničar Gec 1972: 10–14; Petru 1972). There are a number of reasons for this, but the most important ones are the problems of imprecise terminology and the limited adoption of modern theoretical notions. There are a number of terms in Slovenian that are commonly used in Slovenian archaeology, but have not been properly defined or subjected to much theoretical scrutiny. One clear example is that the term for ethnic affiliation (*etnična pripadnost*) can be used synonymously with cultural affiliation (*kulturna pripadnost*); researchers also may use them idiosyncratically without stating the intended meaning. Similarly, gender and sex are rarely distinguished. The common term that may mean either or both, *spol*, can be qualified by adjectives to denote biological sex (*biološki spol*) or gender (*družbeni spol*); this is typically not done and *spol* is used to discuss both concepts, leading to a conflation even in contexts where the two should be kept separate. When discussing identity in settings with limited information about the deceased, this is particularly problematic, since the interpreter's conception of gendered objects is often used to assign "sex" to the deceased. As mentioned above, the majority of recovered human bones from Emona and Poetovio have been lost or disconnected from their original graves, rendering it impossible to determine the sex of the deceased for a significant number of burials.

Furthermore, the majority of Slovenian writings on the topic of Roman-period cultural affiliation still rely on the concept of "Romanisation" and maintain a binary opposition between the pre-Roman/native and Italic traditions. This is in comparison with the extensive and ongoing Romanisation debate in Anglo-Saxon (amongst others Gardner 2013, 2016; Versluys 2014) and, to some extent, German archaeology (Schörner 2005) where the notion has been debated for more than two decades.

A typical interpretation ascribes grave pits to the indigenous population (Petru 1972: 10–13), while *tegula* constructions and amphorae graves (or stone cist and walled graves) are considered purely Italic (Knez 1968; Plesničar Gec 1972). However, these interpretations cannot be so straightforward, despite their potential validity in specific cases: the intentions behind certain aspects of a burial might vary for a number of reasons as will be discussed below.

These problems are augmented in discussions on regional dress, usually referred to as Norico-Pannonian, and its relation to the expression of cultural, ethnic, and gender identities. Surviving elements of the dress are known mostly from first and second centuries A.D. Noricum and Pannonia, although why it is confined to this area is still the subject of a number of discussions (Rothe 2013a, 2013b). The dress typically included undergarments, a long-sleeved bodice, a skirt, a tunic held together by a belt and a pair of brooches, a cloak, and some sort of hat (Figures 7.2 and 7.3; Rothe 2012: 178). Of this array, only brooches and belts are actually preserved in the graves of Poetovio and Emona.

The handful of Slovenian studies focusing specifically on cultural identity and its expression through dress interpret the Norico-Pannonian attire within the framework of Romanisation (Mikl-Curk 1996; Istenič and Štekar 2002 for Poetovio; Plesničar Gec 1985; DeMaine et al. 1999 for Emona). For example, the women buried in Poetovio's graves with elements of the distinct Norico-Pannonian dress are interpreted as local wives married to Roman soldiers (Istenič and Štekar 2002). Another example of this kind of interpretation suggests that Poetovio's tombstones bearing depictions of women clad in the Norico-Pannonian fashion alongside men in typical Roman costume demonstrate that "the women of Poetovio were Romanised to a lesser degree than its men"; this is based on the assumption that "women were more conservative" culturally and that "Roman veterans who settled in Poetovio married local women" (Šajn 2012: 372).

The reason for such readings lies in how the research on Norico-Pannonian dress developed in Slovenian archaeology. The term *norisch-pannonische Tracht*, deriving from the seminal publication by Joachim Garbsch (1965), is translated as *noriško-panonska noša*. Although *noša* literally means "wear", it is most frequently used in relation to the post-Romantic national costume, as in the phrase *narodna noša*, with which it is strongly associated. Consequently, the Norico-Pannonian dress is usually understood in Slovenian archaeology more as a costume worn on exceptional occasions than as an everyday combination of clothes. To my knowledge, this implication has not yet been critically addressed. It is worth noting that, at present, Slovenians have no single national

Figure 7.2 Schematic drawing of the main components of the Norico-Pannonian dress: 1 – a high-necked, long-sleeved bodice; 2 – skirt; 3 – loose, sleeveless overtunic worn with belt and pair of brooches; 4 – a cloak; 5 – hat or hair cover

(With kind permission and © Ursula Rothe 2012: 178, fig. 26)

costume, but rather use several regional dresses for folkloristic events. Nevertheless, when the goal is to express the common Slovenian identity, the regional costume of Gorenjska region in north-west Slovenia is typically selected and therefore oftentimes doubles as the "national" dress. It developed from the garments worn by nineteenth-century peasants from Gorenjska on special occasions and was later adapted by the bourgeoisie in order to support the notion of a common national identity. The contemporary and standardised form of the dress is thus based on a festive outfit that was donned for masses, weddings, funerals, and other important events. The Gorenjska costume would not have been worn on a daily basis by everybody in its full splendour, not least because it would have been too impractical, but certainly when status or local identity had to be expressed. The everyday dress was similar, but simpler, without expensive jewellery and probably from more affordable and durable materials.

Aspects of the modern conception of a single national costume are completely in line with the work of Garbsch (1965) and are regularly projected back onto the interpretation of the Norico-Pannonian dress by Slovenian researchers.

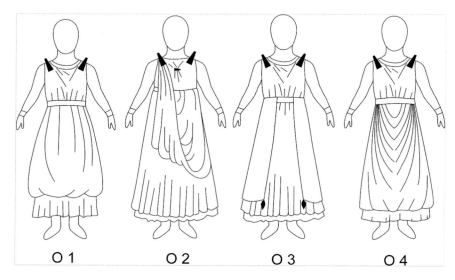

Figure 7.3 Different types of overtunics worn in the middle Danube region. (O1) is present in the area of Poetovio

(With kind permission and © Rothe 2012: 184, fig. 31)

Garbsch's work is the most comprehensive attempt at establishing the core composition of the Norico-Pannonian dress and remains essentially undisputed in Slovenian archaeology. It does have few major drawbacks, however. First of all, it received immediate criticism upon its publication from scholars such as Jenő Fitz (1966a, 1966b) and later by Ortolf Harl (1991) and Erwin Pochmarski (1996, 2004a, 2004b, 2006), all of whom highlighted the chronological inconsistency of Garbsch and the theoretical issue of projecting the modern notions of national costume onto the Norico-Pannonian dress. Second, the supposed Norico-Pannonian dress had been a topic of international debate long before Garbsch's (1965) publication. Political purposes likely motivated some of these arguments, depending on which modern country in the territory of ancient Noricum and Pannonia the authors came from. Initially, researchers focused predominantly on recording and studying portraits of the deceased dressed in this attire on tombstones from the area of Noricum and Pannonia (Hampel 1880; Láng 1919; Schober 1923; von Geramb 1933), while later attention shifted to specific elements of the dress. As noted by Rothe (2012: 140), the debate centred on material culture, whose elements were studied in isolation (brooches only: Kovrig 1937; Jobst 1975; Sedlmayer 1995, 2009; Gugl 1995; Demetz 1999; other types of jewellery: Facsády 2001a, 2001b, 2008; Kuzmová 2008). Third, Garbsch's conclusions were not sufficiently substantiated by analyses of actual combinations of Norico-Pannonian dress elements in graves. This is an interpretational problem: the presence of Norico-Pannonian dress elements in graves does not justify the direct conclusion that the deceased were culturally or ethnically "Norican" or "Pannonian". Moreover, if any aspect of the conception of ethnic costumes should be used to supply an analogy for the Norico-Pannonian dress, it should be the quotidian clothing of the nineteenth-century peasants. That is to say, the Norico-Pannonian dress did not undergo any deliberate standardisation during the Roman period, just as the pre-Gorenjska dresses were organic phenomena. This means that the Norico-Pannonian dress probably did not have one universal composition, but that it must have been characterised by regional, temporal, personal, and other variations (Rothe 2012, 2013a).

In what follows, I use the funerary data from the cemeteries of Emona and Poetovio to argue that the archaeological evidence presents a far more complex picture of how objects may have been used to manipulate the expression of various forms of identities. These identities are not necessarily limited to the projection of bounded "Norico-Pannonian" affiliation or the female gender.

Dressed for death: a comparison of Emona's and Poetovio's burial artefacts

At the outset, it must be stated that the number of material remains associated with dress is somewhat low, as organic materials such as textiles, leather, and wood are not commonly preserved in the graves at Emona and Poetovio. Only in a handful of cases were items of luxurious clothing indicated by the presence of gold threads (Figure 7.4). Therefore, what little can be reconstructed of

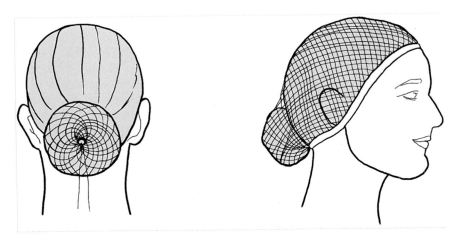

Figure 7.4 Reconstructions of hairnets, one of the rare examples of preserved textiles at Emona. The reconstruction is based on a photo published by Petru (1972: 120, Sl. 26–7). The specimens come from exceptionally rich graves, which in some cases contained remnants of golden threads around the head of the deceased

(Drawing and © Kaja Stemberger)

clothes in funerary contexts at both cemeteries largely relies on the less perishable parts of clothes such as belt fittings, buttons, and brooches, as well as the aforementioned enhancements made of precious metals (Stemberger 2014).

As the majority of the material included in this research originates from graves with scientifically undetermined sex or age, it is essential to specify the criteria used for considering a grave to be female. For determining likely gender association, I applied principles similar to the methodology used by Martin-Kilcher (1998) in a study of the cemeteries of Lago Maggiore. First of all, I considered graves with spinning and weaving equipment to be female (Aurisicchio et al. 2002; Gostenčnik 2010), since wool-working equipment, especially distaffs, was a clear marker of female status in Roman culture (Larsson Lovén 2003, 2007, 2013). Other items I considered statistically reliable indicators of female graves were items of jewellery and mirrors (Wyke 1994: 138; Shumka 2008: 177; Berg 2010: 290–1; Allison 2015: 119–20). Numerous studies have shown that simple glass bead necklaces as well as amber items were more commonly placed in female or children's graves (Allason-Jones 1995). Determining the gender of the deceased by the presence of pins in grave assemblage is rather tricky as pins were used for hair decoration as well as fastening clothes (McGregor 1976: 13; Bíró 2003). Hair pins may indeed be used to indicate the presence of females, while pins for fastening the clothes could have been used by both men and women. However, I counted graves with ornamented hairpins as female because of the general scholarly consensus to regard them as such (Crummy 1983: 19; Riha 1990: 95; Philpott 1991: 132; Böhme-Schönberger 1997: 83–5; Deschler-Erb 1998: 31–6).

Less clear-cut are the gender associations of simple bracelets, brooches, rings, and belt parts (Allason-Jones 1995). Some information about brooch use was gleaned from monuments depicting women wearing brooches across the Roman Empire (Böhme 1972; Ettlinger 1973; Riha 1979, 1994; Böhme-Schönberger 2002, 2008; Carroll 2013; Allison 2015: 116–19). For certain provinces, the manner of wearing two or more brooches is considered to be a female custom, while the male style was to wear one brooch only (Ivleva 2017: 78; also see Croom 2002; Hoss 2016). This does not, however, assist our interpretation of these objects in Emona or Poetovio, since burials at both sites are mostly cremations, where artefact positioning is irrelevant. Only rarely are brooches at Emona or Poetovio associated with skeletons, and even more rarely are other female artefacts clearly found with brooches still in their original position. Therefore, I only counted graves with more than one accompanying, reliably "female" item as female.

The analysis of the dress accessories from cemeteries at Emona and Poetovio has revealed the following results that are of particular importance to the discussion of the expressions of female gender and other possible identities in the burial records of these two colonies. In Emona, the graves contained an outstanding number of bone distaffs dated to the Flavian period. In contrast, Poetovio only had a handful. Jewellery is relatively rare in Emona, but it is present in a small group of graves which span the second to the fourth centuries A.D.

These contain an abundance of gold and silver jewellery, sometimes paired with remains of gold or silver dust, flakes, or threads. At Poetovio, jewellery was likewise rare. Mirrors were often part of female grave goods at both Emona and Poetovio; jewellery boxes are generally rare in both colonies, and are difficult to trace due to their wooden materials (Graves 75 and 652 from the western cemetery of Poetovio: Istenič 2000: 65; Graves 405 and 700 from Emona's northern cemetery: Plesničar Gec 1972: 81, 117; and Grave 803 from Titova cesta at Emona: Petru 1972: 72). Mirrors and jewellery boxes in female graves have parallels in Italy, such as at Porta Nocera in Pompeii (Brives 2013). Tombstones from across the Norican Kingdom also depicted both of these items (Garbsch 1965: 116–17, T1–2).

The most prominent difference in burial assemblage between Emona and Poetovio is the occurrence of certain elements of Norico-Pannonian dress (Figure 7.5). At Emona, Norico-Pannonian belt fittings are known only from two graves, while at Poetovio these are found in much greater quantities and varieties. The graves of Poetovio contain belt buckles of Garbsch's types C2b and C2c, but judging by the material from the western cemeteries of Poetovio alone, strap ends are much more diverse, comprising nine of Garbsch's types (B1a, B2, B3, B4b, B4c, E2, E3, Ka, and Kb: Istenič 2000: 62–3). Brooches are the most prominent part of the Norico-Pannonian ensemble (Figure 7.2), and the Almgren 236/237 types are somewhat more numerous at Poetovio. The most common brooches in the graves of Emona are Almgren 236 varieties and

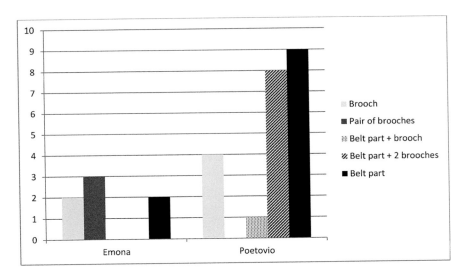

Figure 7.5 Comparison between female graves with brooches and belt parts in Emona and Poetovio. Data from Plesničar Gec (1972), Petru (1972) and Istenič (1999, 2000). Norico-Pannonian brooches and *Kräftig profilierte Fibeln* are combined for clarity

the Italic-influenced Norico-Pannonian derivatives, known as *kräftig profilierte Fibeln* (Almgren IV; Type 6 in Štukl 2002). At Poetovio, the most common type of brooches are Almgren 236/237, 238, and the derivative *kräftig profilierte Fibeln*. However, the most striking contrast is the presence of a combination of belt fittings and brooches in the burial record of Poetovio: this combination is missing completely from Emona (Figure 7.6). It is worth noting that portraits of women in Norico-Pannonian attire depicted on the stelae found at Poetovio and across its *ager* include the same types of brooches found in the graves, while the belts are generally concealed by clothes in the depictions (Figure 7.7; Šajn 2012). Another noticeable feature is the absence of "female-associated" artefacts in the graves of Poetovio that had belt parts (with or without brooches). This stands in contrast to the graves with brooches, but without belt parts, which also contained mirrors, curiously all of Isteničʼs Type X. Mirrors of this type lack handles and are supposed to have been mounted in a special box. Only in one example out of the more than 750 Poetovio graves

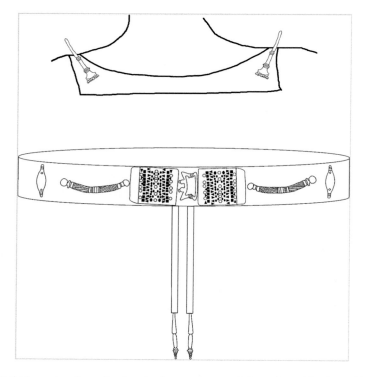

Figure 7.6 Reconstruction of a female dress attire consisting of combination of belt and brooches based on finds from Poetovio

(Drawing and © Kaja Stemberger)

Figure 7.7 Left: drawing of a funerary medallion depicting woman in a typical Norico-Pannonian attire showing brooches with concealed belt, from Vurberk (see also lupa.at/4276). Right: drawing of a part of a lid of a stone chest depicting four women, from Poetovio (Ptuj Ormož Regional Museum, inv. no. PMPO:RL-0000748)

(Drawings and © Kaja Stemberger)

published by Istenič (1999, 2000), in Grave 652, was a large assemblage of grave goods that included some clearly female-associated items found together with Norico-Pannonian dress elements (a single brooch). Thus, graves at Poetovio with "female items" such as mirrors and distaffs do not contain Norico-Pannonian belt parts (Graves 80, 139, 167, 177, 443). Consequently, burials that contain only Norico-Pannonian brooches and no other gender-defining object remain difficult to interpret in terms of the gender identity of the deceased.

Another notable difference between the two colonies is the occurrence of artefacts made of amber. Amber objects are significantly more numerous at Poetovio and are found in cemeteries, settlement areas, and as unstratified finds (Jevremov 1985; Vomer Gojkovič and Kolar 1993; Vomer Gojkovič 1996). This result is unexpected, since Emona is located between Poetovio and Aquileia, which is believed to have been the regional centre of amber production (Calvi 2005). The larger size of Poetovio and its greater population may account for the larger number of amber artefacts in its graves. Amber objects are typically associated with female adornment and generally are found in the graves of women and children (Montagna Pasquinucci 1975: 264–71; Allason-Jones 1996; Migotti 2007). The cemeteries of both cities follow this trend, with the exception of one (incompletely published) grave at Emona. This is a grave of an osteologically sexed male that contained shards of amber (Mulh 2008). The most outstanding grave goods made of amber from Emona are a knife handle and a shell figurine found in Grave 1489 (Petru 1972: 129). Other amber-made artefacts include distaffs, rings, miniatures in the form of a fish, an amphora, a figurine of a woman, and even a spoon (Istenič 2000: 80; Stemberger 2018: 178).

Discussion

Emona and Poetovio were colonies with diverse populations and are associated with large numbers of excavated graves. Based on the analysis of the material evidence from the cemeteries of both colonies, it is clear that they have several characteristics in common. First of all, gender can be studied only in a small number of the burials. In the case of Emona, approximately 200 out of the *c.*3000 known burials could be interpreted as belonging to women based on the kind of artefacts present and, to a lesser extent, limited osteological analyses. Within this group, the complexity of the burials as well as the amount and quality of information they provide varies. At Poetovio, of the 1201 graves (from the combined publications of Kujundžić 1976; Istenič 1999, 2000), approximately 4 per cent could be classified as female. At both sites, cremation was the prevalent treatment of the body in the first and second centuries A.D., accompanied by simpler treatments such as simple pit burials. Jewellery, especially made from precious materials such as amber, gold, or gemstones, is generally rare at both sites, as are toiletry items except for mirrors. Items with clear religious association are nearly absent from both towns' cemeteries. Certain female graves at both sites stand out in terms of burial manner, richness of the artefacts, and uniformity. Based on Martin-Kilcher's criteria (2000), I have recognised such rich graves of females in Emona (Stemberger 2014); these are predominantly presumed to be teenagers or women in their early 20s. Poetovio contains at least one such grave (Grave 139: Istenič 1999). As in Emona's cases, the deceased wore no locally specific attire. The sole exception in this regard is Emona's grave 1489, where a cultural affiliation with North Africa might be assumed based on the presence of an amber knife handle. This object is similar in design to a bone specimen found in London (Figure 7.8; Ridgeway et al. 2013). These lavish female burials are not from the same period at either site. The relative rarity of extremely rich graves could be explained perhaps in terms of unfinished rites of passage (van Gennep 1960), or more precisely as *mors immatura* (Martin-Kilcher 2000). Therefore, I usually describe such graves as belonging to "women around the time of marriage", as the unexpectedly rich sets of grave goods are suggestive of a symbolic conclusion of an unfinished rite of passage (Stemberger 2014, 2018).

The difference between the cemeteries of Emona and Poetovio is nevertheless quite stark in several respects. Emona's burial record is characterised by a material culture closer to northern Italy (Mikl-Curk 1979; Plesničar Gec 1987). For instance, items such as thin walled pottery (Plesničar Gec 1987) or *terra sigillata* ware (Mikl-Curk 1979) were documented at Emona in much larger numbers than at Poetovio. On the other hand, the Norican influence was much stronger in Poetovio as discussed above (see also Istenič and Štekar 2002). The nature of such stark differences is unclear. The traditional explanation of this phenomenon views local customs and traditions of a "native", pre-Roman identity surviving into the Roman period at Poetovio. It is certainly true that the political and cultural background of Poetovio was different from that of

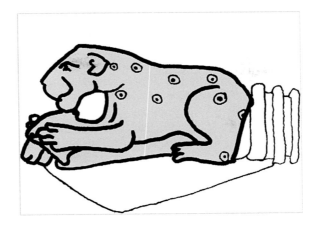

Figure 7.8 Reconstruction of a knife handle from grave 1489 in Emona. The reconstruction is based on an illustration by Petru (1972, T. XCV, 39), and the specimen from the Southwark excavation (Millard 2013: 46)

(Drawing and © Kaja Stemberger)

Emona, and the argument could be made that one colony should contain more "Roman" elements than the other. Poetovio was the larger and more influential colony and had a greater military presence. It also had a clear presence of different cults affiliated with Roman religion, with its five mithraea. Emona was established approximately 100 years earlier, was never part of the provinces, and had better connections with Aquileia, a known and influential emporium.

A more nuanced approach would discard the idea derived from Romanisation debates that pre-Roman identities existed in opposition to or apart from a Roman identity. It is possible that the Norico-Pannonian dress in the Roman period, at least in the funerary sphere, was used to emphasise a unique, but not separate, cultural identity. While these garments were likely based on a previous tradition, its significance and function in terms of signalling various forms of identities would have been greatly changed. Its utility for expressing identity in the funerary sphere could be a result of the nature of burial, which is intended not only for the deceased, but more importantly for the survivors, as observed by Aarts and Heeren (2017: 123). Following their argument, based partly on the works of van Gennep (1960) and Hertz (1960), burial is a process with two parallel aims: the rite of passage for the deceased and to reshape the social order of the survivors. In terms of the material from the graves, this produces two separate questions, of which only one can be answered to a certain extent. The first, unanswerable question, is how the deceased perceived themselves. There is evidence that some people in the Roman period laid out funeral plans in their wills or even made arrangements while still alive (with the epigraphic formula *ex testamento iussit*). However, this is likely to reflect how they wished to be perceived and need not have coincided with their actual self-perception. The second is how they would have been perceived by others (Hodos 2010: 3). This question can be answered partially, since the dead do not bury themselves (Parker Pearson 2003: 3); the study of Roman culture allows us to interpret at least some of the meanings behind the symbols associated with burials. Therefore, the treatment of the body is primarily a projection created by the family and friends of the deceased. They could have various motives to create such arrays, such as representing personal relationships or to express groups that the deceased belonged to in his or her life. The latter could play an important role in the reinforcement of the family or group tradition, beliefs, or social status. The invention of (mythical) ancestry was not unusual even in the leading houses of Rome (Bickermann 1952; Wiseman 1974, 1983; Jones 1999) and could feature prominently in small communities as well.

Individual elements of the so-called Norico-Pannonian attire from the graves of Poetovio can be understood as a reinforcement of identity based on a cultural tradition, without relying on the notion that there ever was a uniform costume. Before the Roman occupation, Poetovio was part of the Regnum Noricum, which enjoyed autonomy possibly until the reign of Claudius. Moreover, unlike the *ex novo* Emona, Poetovio's settlement likely had continued since prehistory (Horvat et al. 2003: 153–5). If the Norico-Pannonian dress is to be understood as the reinforcement of a local identity through the repurposing of a tradition in the funerary setting, it would not be without parallels from other parts of the Roman Empire, nor indeed from other Roman-period sites within the area of modern-day Slovenia. A renaissance of prehistoric ceramic forms is known at Emona during the Flavian period (Plesničar Gec 1977: 63), with similar behaviours also identified in, for instance, Roman Spain (Jiménez 2008). These material anachronisms can be interpreted as a desire to reinforce or revive a potentially idealised ancestral culture. This shift does not originate with the first or second generation to have lived within the Roman Empire, but with later ones that were integrated better into society and could afford to evoke the ancestral ties that their parents and grandparents had had to tone down. A modern parallel for this phenomenon is found in Hanif Kureishi's short story, *My Son the Fanatic* (1999), which portrays the integration of two different generations of modern immigrants. Similarly, it has been argued that under Roman occupation people could feel themselves to be immigrants due to the changes in culture and landscape imposed by the Roman Empire (Purcell 1990).

The self-identification in everyday life as well as the representation in death is therefore conditioned by the situation of the individual who desires to express a certain identity; it is also influenced by the flexibility allowed by the culture in expressing diverse identities. In the study area, it is clear that differences had existed in how men and women chose to portray themselves in death, as suggested by depictions of couples on funerary monuments in which the man wears "Roman" dress (i.e. the toga), while the woman is clad in "Norico-Pannonian" dress. It must be emphasised that this duality in male and female funerary expression does not directly mirror the actual identities: male family members would probably not have perceived themselves purely in "Roman" terms and female ones as "native". As soon as one abandons Binford's (1972: 229) idea that grave goods directly mirror the entity that the deceased represented in life, one of the possible interpretative tools is to look for parallels. Therefore, one can ask the question: does the variety of grave goods necessarily relate to gender, or can it be correlated with the expression of the social standing of the deceased? Parker Pearson's (1982, 2003) studies of contemporary funerary rituals in modern Britain have shown that actual wealth is not always translated into grave furnishings; similarly in the Roman period, this practice often could have acted as a reinforcement of wealth (Hope 1994) or higher status (advancing from being a slave to being free). In a similar vein, one could argue that the variability in funerary displays at Emona and Poetovio was related more to the social status of the deceased and their families, who used clothing to convey influence and power in terms of more than one cultural tradition. Similar customs have been observed elsewhere in the Empire, such as in Rothe's (2013a) study of the funerary record at Arlon (Belgium) and Flavia Solva (Austria). Flavia Solva is significant to the present study, since it lay in Noricum, like Poetovio, meaning that similar interpretations may apply. Rothe (2013a: 262) suggests that within familial unions different members asserted status and wealth differently through a variety of means. To me, this interpretation seems more plausible than the view that Poetovio's burials represent unions of Roman soldiers and "native" women, as has been advanced by Istenič and Štekar (2002).

Thus, the Norico-Pannonian dress cannot be understood simply as a "native" relict embedded into Roman culture. The distinct composition of clothes in this dress was established only in the twentieth century, and only through analyses of depictions found on tombstones from the provinces of Noricum and Pannonia (Garbsch 1965). This dress likely developed through complex interactions with Roman culture. For instance, Pásztókai-Szeőke (2011) demonstrated that distaffs were present in female graves in Pannonia, but only after the Roman occupation. Similarly, I have observed that mirrors often appear on Norico-Pannonian stelae together with the depiction of the Norico-Pannonian dress (lupa.at/897, 912, 914–16, 923). Yet, these mirrors are almost entirely absent from the La Tène graves of Slovenia (with a few exceptions such as La Tène Grave 201 from Beletov vrt in Novo mesto: Guštin 1984: 7). Such mirrors only began appearing in the graves of Emona in the Roman period. The absence of distaffs and mirrors in pre-Roman graves does not necessarily indicate that such objects were unknown at the time, but rather that they were not incorporated into funerary rituals. Distaffs and mirrors played an important role in asserting Roman family values and acted as a visual and artistic counterpart to *lanam fecit* epitaphs (Larsson Lovén 1998, 2007), especially taking into consideration that not everyone was fully literate. It is believed that the majority of the population were able to read at least some commonplace words or sentences, so objects and their artistic representations would act as a visual aid (Bowman 1991; Raybould 1999; Hope 2001).

Moreover, the conclusion that the full Norico-Pannonian dress was absent in the funerary record of Emona cemeteries is based primarily on the absence of metal artefacts, but this could be misleading. The presence of brooches and belts in graves not as sets, but as single objects, may be an example of *pars pro toto*; other elements of the dress could have been made of organic materials and thus not be preserved. A major problem with interpreting the Norico-Pannonian dress is also defining what exactly should be considered an element of the dress (Rothe 2013b). In the process of determining its composition, we may inadvertently whittle the dress down to a standardised uniform that resembles contemporary national costumes, devoid of the variation and individualisation that must have occurred. Similar problems are faced by modern folklorist groups in trying to recreate traditional costumes (Knific 2009): there is a fine balance between variable, individualising elements and the core features that define a type of dress and render it recognisable.

A possible explanation for the difference in Norico-Pannonian artefact distributions between the graves at Emona and Poetovio could be explained by the metal parts of the dress being primarily an expression of fashions, migrations, and trade networks (Rothe 2013a, 2013b). In this sense, Emona's grave goods can be interpreted as a combination of various stylistic influences. The influence of Italic fashions was strong at Emona due to its vicinity to urban centres such as Aquileia, to which Emona was well connected by trade routes. Furthermore, a significant number of Emona's deceased are known to have moved there from northern Italy (Šašel 1960, 1966; Istenič et al. 2003: 83). In contrast, Poetovio was farther removed from northern Italy, which is reflected in the much smaller numbers of Italic imports here than at Emona, especially in terms of the *terra sigillata* and thin-walled pottery.

Conclusion

There is a definite difference between the attire of women buried at Emona and those from Poetovio. However, while it is reasonable to assume that these material differences express different identities, there is nothing to support the notion that it exclusively reflects Norican or Pannonian ethnicity or female gender. Both sites have high status burials characterised by a relatively uniform manner of burial, a substantial amount of body ornaments frequently made of precious metals, and some with items made of amber. These graves could belong to pan-Mediterranean elites, are potentially related to rites of passage, and may belong to the same group as discussed by Martin-Kilcher (2000). The female gender of a deceased person could be determined only for burials with enough preserved grave goods that were associated with female attire. Yet, this usually refers to expensive dresses or lavishly furnished graves, which in itself suggests that elements of the Norico-Pannonian attire at both Emona and Poetovio were also a display of wealth and status (Stemberger 2018).

The difference between the attire of women buried at Emona and those from Poetovio could also be explained by the difference in the ways in which ancestry, either actual or fictional, was conveyed. It is also worth noting that ethnicity and ancestry are not necessarily the only criteria by which the items buried with the individuals were chosen. Besides completely personal factors, which are in most cases not recognisable, the grave arrays could express the deceased's status. Thus, a contextual reading of the grave goods at these two cities may represent new ways in which status is negotiated, including using old artefacts and forms in new manners and roles.

Acknowledgements

This chapter is based on the initial observations made during my PhD at King's College London, which was funded for two years by Ad Futura, the Public Scholarship, Development, Disability and Maintenance Fund of the Republic of Slovenia.

Bibliography

Aarts, J. and Heeren, S. (2017). "Buried Batavians: Mortuary Rituals of a Rural Frontier Community", in J. Pearce and J. Weekes (eds), *Death as a Process. Studies in Funerary Archaeology.* Oxford: Oxbow Books, 123–54.

Allason-Jones, L. (1995). "'Sexing' Small Finds", in P. Rush (ed.), *Theoretical Roman Archaeology: Second Conference Proceedings.* Avebury: Aldershot, 22–32.

Allason-Jones, L. (1996). *Roman Jet in the Yorkshire Museum.* New York: The York Museum.

Allison, P.M. (2015). "Characterizing Roman Artifacts to Investigate Gendered Practices in Contexts Without Sexed Bodies", *American Journal of Archaeology*, 119(1): 103–23.

Aurisicchio, C., Ferro, D. and Martinell, G. (2002). "A Study of a Distaff of the Second Century A.D. from a Necropolis of Boccone D'Aste (Rome, Italy) – Tomb 75", *Journal of Cultural Heritage*, 3: 107–16.

Berg, R. (2010). "Lo specchio di Venere: Riflessioni sul mundus muliebris nella pittura pompeiana", in I. Bragantini (ed.), *Atti del X Congresso Internazionale dell'AIPMA, Association Internationale Pour la Peinture Murale Antique, Napoli 17–21 Settembre 2007.* Naples: Università degli studi di Napoli "L'Orientale", 289–300.

Bertoncelj-Kučar, V. (1979). "Nakit iz stekla in jantarja/Glas- und Bernsteinschmuck", *Arheološki Vestnik*, 30: 254–78.

Bickermann, E. (1952). "Origines gentium", *Classical Philology*, 47: 65–81.

Binford, L.R. (1972). "Mortuary Practices: Their Study and Potential", in L.R. Binford (ed.), *An Archaeological Perspective.* New York: Academic, 208–43.

Bíró, M. (2003). "Ein neuerer Beitrag zur pannonischen einheimischen Frauentracht", in Á. Szabó and E. Tóth (eds), *Pannonica Provincialia et Archaeologia. Studia Sollemnia E. Fitz Octogenario Dedicate.* Budapest: Magyar Nemzeti Múzeum, 89–103.

Böhme, A. (1972). "Die Fibeln der Kastelle Saalburg und Zugmantel", *Saalburg Jahrbuch*, 29.

Böhme-Schönberger, A. (1997). *Kleidung und Schmuck in Rom und den Provinzen.* Stuttgart: Württembergisches Landesmuseum.

Böhme-Schönberger, A. (2002). "Die Distelfibel und die Germanen", in K. Kuzmová, K. Pieta and J. Rajtár (eds), *Zwichen Rom und dem Barbaricum. Festschrift für Titus*

Kolnik zum 70. Geburtstag. Nitra: Archäologisches Institut der Slowakischen Akademie der Wissenchaften, 215–24.

Böhme-Schönberger, A. (2008). "Die Distelfibeln – Sind sie Männer- oder Frauenfibeln?", in U. Brandl (ed.), *Frauen und Römisches Militär: Beträge eines runden Tisches in Xanten vom 7. bis 8. Juli 2005.* Oxford: Archaeopress, 140–45.

Bowman, A. (1991). "Literacy in the Roman Empire: Mass and Mode", in J. Humphrey (ed.), *Literacy in the Roman World.* Journal of Roman Archaeology Supplementary Series III. Ann Arbour: Journal of Roman Archaeology, 119–31.

Brives, A.L. (2013). "Métal et Petit Mobilier en Contexte Funéraire", in W. van Andringa, H. Duday and S. Lepetz (eds), *Mourir à Pompéi. Fouilles d'un Quartier Funéraire de la Nécropole 318 Omaine de Porta Nocera (2003-2007).* Volume 2. Collection de l'Ecole Française de Rome 468. Rome: Collection de l'École française de Rome, 1247–64.

Budja, M. (1979). "Kovinske Zapestnice V Rimskih Grobovih Slovenije/Metallarmreifen in den Romergräbern Sloweniens", *Arheološki Vestnik*, 30: 243–53.

Calvi, M.C. (2005). *Le Ambre Romane di Aquileia.* Aquileia: Associazione Nazionale per Aquileia.

Carroll, M. (2013). "Ethnicity and Gender in Roman Funerary Commemoration: Case studies from the Empire's Frontiers", in S. Tarlow and L. Nilsson Stultz (eds), *The Oxford Handbook of the Archaeology of Death and Burial.* Oxford: Oxford University Press, 559–79.

Croom, A. (2002). *Roman Clothing and Fashion.* Stroud: Amberley.

Crummy, N. (1983). *Colchester Archaeological Report 2: The Roman Small Finds from Excavations in Colchester 1971–1979.* London: Colchester Archaeological Trust and the Council for British Archaeology.

DeMaine, M.R., Lazar, I. and Vidrih Perko, V. (1999). "Middle-class Burials in Three Provincial Roman Cemeteries: Emona, Celeia, Šempeter", in M. Taylor and M.R. DeMaine (eds), *Life of the Average Roman.* White Bear Lake (Minnesota): PZA Pub, 35–49.

Demetz, S. (1999). *Fibeln der Spätlatène- und frühen römischen Kaiserzeit in den Alpenländern, Frühgeschichtliche und Provinzialrömische Archäologie.* Materialien und Forschungen 4. Rahden: Leidorf.

Deschler-Erb, S. (1998). *Römische Beinartefakte aus Augusta Raurica: Rohmaterial, Technologie, Typologie und Chronologie.* Forschungen in Augst Band 27/1. Augst: Römermuseum.

Dular, A. (1979). "Rimske Koščene Igle iz Slovenije/Römische Knochennadeln aus Slowenien", *Arheološki Vestnik*, 30: 278–93.

Ettlinger, E. (1973). *Die römischen Fibeln in der Schweiz. Handbuch der Schweiz zur Römer-und Merowingerzeit.* Bern: Francke.

Facsády, A. (2001a). "Trésors de Bijouterie Trouvés en Pannonie", *Belgian Archaeology in a European Setting*, 1: 57–69.

Facsády, A. (2001b). "La Parure et le Costume Traditionnels", in A. Facsády and P. Zsidi (eds), *Romains de Hongrie.* Lyon: Réunion des musées nationaux, 42–48.

Facsády, A. (2008). "Earrings on Stone Monuments from Pannonia", in Franek et al (2008), 229–42.

Fitz, J. (1966a). "Rez. Garbsch: Die norisch-pannonische Frauentracht im 1. und 2. Jahrhundert", *Gnomon*, 38: 619–25.

Fitz, J. (1966b). "Rez. Garbsch: Die norisch-pannonische Frauentracht im 1. und 2. Jahrhundert", *Antik Tanulmányok*, 13: 148.

Franek, C., Lamm, S., Neuhauser, T., Porod, B. and Zöhrer, K. eds, (2008). *Thiasos. Festschrift Erwin Pochmarski*. Veröffentlichungen des Instituts für klassische Archäologie der Karl-Franzens Universität Graz, Band 10. Vienna: Phoibos.

Garbsch, J. (1965). *Die Norisch-Pannonische Frauentracht im 1. und 2. Jahrhundert*. München: Beck.

Gardner, A. (2013). "Thinking about Roman Imperialism: Postcolonialism, Globalisation and Beyond?", *Britannia*, 44: 1–25.

Gardner, A. (2016). "Debating Roman Imperialism: Critique, Construct, Repeat?", in M. J. Mandich, T.J. Derrick, S. Gonzalez Sanchez, G. Savani and E. Zampieri (eds), *TRAC 2015: Proceedings of the 25th annual Theoretical Roman Archaeology Conference*. Oxford: Oxbow Books, 1–14.

Gaspari, A. (2010). *Apud Horridas Gentis: Začetki Rimskega Mesta Colonia Iulia Emona/ Beginnings of the Roman Town of Colonia Iulia Emona*. Ljubljana: Muzej in Galerije Mesta Ljubljane.

Gaspari, A. (2014). *Prazgodovinska in Rimska Emona: Vodnik Skozi Arheološko Preteklost Predhodnice Ljubljane/Prehistoric and Roman Emona. A Guide through the Archaeological Past of the Ljubljana's Predecessor*. Ljubljana: Muzej in Galerije Mesta Ljubljane.

Gaspari, A., Bekljanov Zidanšek, I., Masaryk, R. and Novšak, M. (2015). "Augustan Military Graves from the Area of Kongresni trg in Ljubljana", in J. Istenič, B. Laharnar and J. Horvat (eds), *Evidence of the Roman Army in Slovenija*. Katalogi in monografije/Catalogi et monographiae 41. Ljubljana: Narodni Muzej Slovenije, 125–69.

Geramb, V., von (1933). *Steirisches Trachtenbuch II: Die Norisch-Pannonische Tracht*. Graz: Leuschner and Lubensky.

Gostenčnik, K. (2010). "The Magdalensberg Textile Tools: a Preliminary Assessment", in E. Andersson Strand, M. Gleba, U. Mannering, C. Munkholt and M. Ringgaard (eds), *North European Symposium for Archaeological Textiles X, Copenhagen 2008. Ancient Textiles Series 5*. Oxford: Oxbow Books, 73–90.

Gugl, C. (1995). *Die römischen Fibeln aus Virunum*. Klagenfurt: Landesmuseum Kärnten.

Guštin, M. (1984). "Die Kelten in Jugoslawien", *Jahrbuch des Römisch-Germanischen Zentralmuseums Mainz*, 31: 305–63.

Hampel, J. (1880). "An Múzeum Érem És Régiségosztályának Gyarapodása", *Archaeologiai Értesítő*, 14: 340–58.

Harl, O. (1991). "Historische Selektion und Datierung römischer Steinskulpturen im Ostalpenraum", in *2. Internationales Kolloquium über Probleme des Provinzialrömischen Kunstschaffens. Vorträge der Tagung in Veszprém*. Veszprém: 15–51.

Hertz, R. (1960). "The Collective Representation of Death", in R. Needham and C. Needham (eds), *Death and the Right Hand*. Aberdeen: Cohen and West, 27–86.

Hodos, T. (2010). "Local and Global Perspectives in the Study of Social and Cultural Identities", in S. Hales and T. Hodos (eds), *Material Culture and Social Identities in the Ancient World*. Cambridge: Cambridge University Press, 3–31.

Hofman, B. (2009). *Poročilo o Zaščitnih Arheoloških Izkopavanjih na Lokaciji Ljubljana-Tobačna, parc. št. 188/1, 188/2, 188/8 in 18894 k.o. Gradišče II EŠD 18810 Ljubljana – Arheološko najdišče ob Tržaški cesti*. Unpubl. Excavation Report.

Hope, V.M. (1994). *Reflections of Status: A Contextual Study of the Roman Tombstones of Aquileia, Mainz and Nimes*. Unpubl. Ph.D. dissertation. University of Reading.

Hope, V.M. (2001). *Constructing Identity: The Roman Funerary Monuments from Aquileia, Mainz and Nîmes*. British Archaeological Reports, International Series 960. Oxford: Archaeopress.

Horvat, J. (1990). *Nauportus (Vrhnika)*. Dela 1. razreda SAZU 33. Ljubljana: SAZU.

Horvat, J., Lovenjak, M., Dolenc Vičič, A., Lubšina Tušek, M., Tomanič, M., Jevremov, B. and Šubic, Z. (2003). "Poetovio, Development and Topography", in M. Šašel Kos and P. Scherrer (eds), *The Autonomous Towns of Noricum and Pannonia/Die autonomen Städte in Noricum und Pannonien*. Situla 41. Ljubljana: Narodni Muzej Slovenije, 153–89.

Hoss, S. (2016). "Of Brooches and Man", in A. Whitmore and S. Hoss (eds), *Small Finds and Ancient Social Practices in the North-West Provinces of the Roman Empire*. Oxford: Oxbow Books, 35–75.

Hoss, S. (2017). "The Roman Military Belt – A Status Symbol and Object of Fashion", in Martin and Weech (2017), 94–114.

Istenič, J. (1999). *Poetovio, Zahodna Grobišča I. Grobne Celote iz Deželnega Muzeja Joanneuma v Gradcu/Poetovio, the Western Cemeteries I: Grave-groups in the Landesmuseum Joanneum, Graz*. Katalogi in monografije/Catalogi et monographiae 32. Ljubljana: Narodni Muzej.

Istenič, J. (2000). *Poetovio, Zahodna Grobišča II. Grobne Celote iz Deželnega Muzeja Joanneuma v Gradcu: Katalog/ Poetovio,the Western Cemeteries I: Grave-groups in the Landesmuseum Joanneum, Graz: Catalogue*. Katalogi in monografije/Catalogi et monographiae 33. Ljubljana: Narodni Muzej.

Istenič, J., Daszkiewtcz, M. and Schnider, G. (2003). "Local Production of Pottery and Clay Lamps at Emona (Italia, regio X)", *Rei Cretariae Romanae Fautorum Acta*, 38: 83–91.

Istenič, J. and Štekar, I. (2002). "The Western Cemetery of Poetovio: Burial Evidence and Cultural Identity", *Histria Antiqua*, 8: 165–73.

Ivleva, T. (2017). "'Active Brooches': Theorising Brooches of the Roman North-West (First to Third centuries AD)", in Martin and Weech (2007), 69–93.

Jarc, S., Maniatis, Y., Dotsika, E., Tambakopoulos, D. and Zupancic, N. (2010). "Scientific Characterization of the Pohorje marbles, Slovenia", *Archaeometry*, 52(2): 177–90.

Jevremov, B. (1985). "Novosti O Obrtniških Dejavnostih in Nekaj Drobcev iz Arheoloških Izkopavanj v Letih 1970–1980", *Ptujski Zbornik*, 5: 419–30.

Jiménez, A. (2008). "A Critical Approach to the Concept of Resistance: New 'Traditional' Rituals and Objects in Funerary Contexts of Roman Baetica", in C. Fenwick, M. Wiggins and D. Wythe (eds), *TRAC 2007: Proceedings of the Seventeenth Annual Theoretical Roman Archaeology Conference*. Oxford: Oxbow Books, 15–30.

Jobst, W. (1975). *Die römischen Fibeln aus Lauriacum*. Linz: Landesmuseum.

Jones, C.P. (1999). *Kinship Diplomacy in the Ancient World*. Cambridge, MA: Harvard University Press.

Klasinac, R. (2011). *Fazno Poročilo o Arheoloških Izkopavanjih na Lokaciji PGH Kozolec (II.faza) 2011*. Unpubl. Excavation Report for Site Kozolec.

Knez, T. (1968). "Oblike Antičnih Grobov na Dolenjskem/Antike Grabformen in Dolenjsko Unterkrain", *Arheološki Vestnik*, 19: 221–38.

Knific, B. (2009). "Costuming of Folk-Dance Groups: Demonstrating Identity under the Pretence of Historical Witness", *Etnološka Istraživanja*, 14: 115–31.

Kovrig, I. (1937). *Die Haupttypen der kaiserzeitlichen Fibeln in Pannonien*. Dissertationes Pannonicae ex Instituto Numismatico et Archaeologico Universitatis de Petro Pázmány nominatae Budapestinensis provenientes.

Kujundžić, Z. (1976). *Poetovijske nekropole/Die Nekropolen von Poetovio.* Katalogi in Monografije 20. Ljubljana: Narodni muzej.

Kureishi, H. (1999). "My Son the Fanatic", in H. Kureishi, *Love in a Blue Time: Short Stories.* New York: Simon and Schuster, 119–32.

Kuzmová, K. (2008). "Torques-Darstellungen auf den römischen Grabsteinen Nordpannoniens", in Franek et al. (2008), 545–52.

Láng, M. (1919). "Die pannonische Frauentracht", *Österreichische Jahreshefte,* 19/20: 207–60.

Larsson Lovén, L. (1998). "Lanam Fecit – Woolworking and Female Virtue", in L. Lovén Larsson and A. Strömberg (eds), *Aspects of Women in Antiquity: Proceedings of the First Nordic Symposium on Women's Lives in Antiquity,* Göteborg 2-15 June 1997. Mediterranean Archaeology monograph series 153. Partille: Paul Aströms Förlag, 85–101.

Larsson Lovén, L. (2003). "Funerary Art, Gender and Social Status: Some Aspects from Roman Gaul", in A. Strömberg and L. Larsson Lovén (eds), *Gender, Cult and Culture in the Ancient World from Mycenae to Byzantium.* Partille: Paul Åströms Förlag, 54–70.

Larsson Lovén, L. (2007). "Wool Work as a Gender Symbol in Ancient Rome. Roman Textiles and Ancient Sources", in C. Gillis and M. Nosch (eds), *Ancient Textiles: Production, Crafts and Society.* Oxford: Oxbow Books, 229–36.

Larsson Lovén, L. (2013). "Female Work and Identity in Roman Textile Production", in J. Pásztókai-Szeöke and M. Gleba (eds), *Making Textiles in Pre-Roman and Roman Times. People, Places, Identities.* Oxford: Oxford University Press, 109–25.

Lazar, I. (2003). *Rimsko steklo Slovenije/The Roman Glass of Slovenia.* Opera Instituti Archaeologici Sloveniae 7. Ljubljana: Založba ZRC.

Martin, T.F. and Weech, R. eds, (2017). *Dress and Society: Contributions from Archaeology.* Oxford: Oxbow Books.

Martin-Kilcher, S. (1998). "Gräber der späten Republik und der frühen Kaiserzeit am Lago Maggiore: Tradition und Romanisierung", in H.V. Hesberg, P. Fasold, T. Fischer and M. Witteyer (eds), *Bestattungssitte und kulturelle Identität.* Xantener Berichte 15. Köln: Rheinland-Verlag, 198–252.

Martin-Kilcher, S. (2000). "Mors Immatura in the Roman World – a Mirror of Society and Tradition", in J. Pearce, M. Millett and M. Struck (eds), *Burial, Society and Context in the Roman World.* Oxford: Oxbow Books, 63–76.

McGregor, A. (1976). *Finds from a Roman Sewer System and an Adjacent Building in Church Street, York.* York: York Archaeological Trust.

Migotti, B. (2007). "Rimska Bulla u Panoniji", *Vjesnik Arheološkog Muzeja u Zagrebu,* 40(1): 187–219.

Migotti, B., Manson, P., Nadbath, B. and Mulh, T. eds, (2012). *Scripta in Honorem Bojan Djurić.* Monografije CPA1. Ljubljana: Zavod za varstvo kulturne dediščine Slovenije.

Mihovilić, K. (1979). "Prstenje i Naušnice v Rimskih Grobovih Slovenije/Anelli ed Orecchini di Epoca Romana in Slovenia", *Arheološki Vestnik,* 30: 223–43.

Mikl-Curk, I. (1979). "Terra Sigillata iz Emonskih Grobišč/Terra sigillata aus den Gräberfeldern von Emona", *Arheološki Vestnik,* 30: 339–71.

Mikl-Curk, I. (1996). "Arheološki Vir k Vlogi Ženske v Rimskem Ptuju/Archäologische Quellen zur Rolle der Frau", *Ptujski Zbornik,* 6(1): 158–87.

Millard, A.R. (2013). "Metal and Bone Objects", in Ridgeway et al. (2013), 43–48.

Montagna Pasquinucci, M. (1975). "Le Ambre 'Romane' di Età Imperiale: Problematica e Area di Diffusione", in *Atti della Cooperazione Interdisciplinare Italo-Polacca: Studi*

234   Kaja Stemberger

e Ricerche sulla Problematica Dell'Ambra 1. Roma: Consiglio Nazionale delle Ricerche, 259–77.

Mulh, T. (2008). *Poročilo o Zaščitnih Arheoloških Izkopavanjih na Lokaciji Potniški center Ljubljana 2007/2008 (poročilo št. 1/2003 –BV TM)*. Ljubljana: Zavod za varstvo kulturne dediščine Slovenije, območna enota Ljubljana.

Mulh, T. (2012). "Pasna Garnitura VTERE FELIX iz Severne Emonske Nekropole/The VTERE FELIX Belt Accoutrements from the Northern Cemetery of Emona", in Migotti et al. (2012), 377–45.

Mušič, B.J. and Horvat, J. (2007). "Nauportus – An Early Roman Trading Post at Dolge njive in Vrhnika", *Arheološki Vestnik*, 58: 219–83.

Parker Pearson, M. (1982). "Mortuary Practices, Society and Ideology: An Ethnoarchaeological Study", in I. Hodder (ed.), *Symbolic and Structural Archaeology*. Cambridge: Cambridge University Press, 99–114.

Parker Pearson, M. (2003). *The Archaeology of Death and Burial*. Stroud: The History Press.

Pásztókai-Szeőke, J. (2011). "The Mother Shrinks, the Child Grows. What Is It? The Evidence of Spinning Implements in Funerary Context from the Roman Province of Pannonia", in C. Alfaro Giner, M.J. Martinez Garcia and J. Ortiz Garcia (eds), *Mujer y Vestimenta. Aspectos de la Identidad femenina en la Antigüedad*. Valencia: SEMA, Universitat de Valencia, 125–40.

Petru, S. (1962). "Križišče Titove in Prešernove Ceste", *Varstvo Spomenikov*, 8: 298.

Petru, S. (1972). *Emonske Nekropole. Odkrite med Leti 1635–1960*. Katalogi in monografije 7. Ljubljana: Narodni Muzej.

Philpott, R. (1991). *Burial Practices in Roman Britain: A Survey of Grave Treatment and Furnishing, A.D. 43–410*. British Archaeological Reports, British Series 219. Oxford: Tempus Reparatum.

Plesničar Gec, L. (1972). *Severno Emonsko Grobišče/The Northern Necropolis of Emona*. Katalogi in monografije 8. Ljubljana: Narodni Muzej.

Plesničar Gec, L. (1973). *Starokrščanski Center v Emoni/Old Christian Center in Emona*. Katalogi in monografije 21. Ljubljana: Narodni Muzej.

Plesničar Gec, L. (1977). *Keramika Emonskih Nekropol*. Ljubljana: Mestni Muzej.

Plesničar Gec, L. (1980). "Rimski Grob z Dolenjske Ceste", *Situla, Razprave Narodnega Muzeja v Ljubljani/ Situla,Dissertationes Musei Nationalis Labacensis*, 20–21: 459–65.

Plesničar Gec, L. (1985). "Emonske Nekropole, Etnični in Družbeno Ekonomski Aspekti na Podlagi Pokopa in Pridatkov/Necropolises of Emona, Ethnic and Social-Economical Aspects on a Base of Burial and Grave-Goods", in N. Tasić (ed.), *Enterrement des Défunts de L'Aspect des Mouvements Sociaux et Économiques dans la Préhistorie et L'Antiquité*. Rapports présentés au congres de Mostar 1980. Materiali XX/Actes XX. Beograd: SavezArheoloških društava Jugoslavije, 151–68.

Plesničar Gec, L. (1987). "Thin-Walled Pottery from Slovenia", *Rei Cretariae Romanae Fautorum Acta*, 25/26: 451–64.

Plesničar Gec, L. and Kos, P. (2006). *Emonski Forum/Emona Forum*. Koper: Annales.

Pochmarski, E. (1996). "Severische Reliefs aus dem Stadtterritorium von Virunum", in G. Bauchhenss (ed.), *Akten des 3. Internationalen Kolloquiums über Probleme des Provinzialrömischen Kunstschaffens*. Cologne: Rheinland-Verlag, 127–39.

Pochmarski, E. (2004a). "Das Sagum. Urtrachtlicher keltischer Umhang und/oder römischer Uniformmantel", in H. Heftner and K. Tomaschitz (eds), *Festschrift für Gerhard Dobesch zum 65. Geburtstag*. Vienna: Wiener Humanistischen Gesellschaft, 571–78.

Pochmarski, E. (2004b). "Das sogenannte norische Mädchen. Ein Beispiel für den Ausdruck lokaler Identität in der provinzialrömischen Plastik", in A. Schmidt-Colinet (ed.), *Lokale Identitäten in Randgebieten des Römischen Reiches. Akten des Internationalen Symposiums in Wiener Neustadt, 4.–26. April 2003.* Vienna: Phoibos Verlag, 161–73.

Pochmarski, E. (2006). "Zu Fragen der Typologie und der Chronologie der römischen Porträtstelen in Noricum", *Römisches Österreich*, 29: 89–114.

Purcell, N. (1990). "The Creation of Provincial Landscape: The Roman Impact on Cisalpine Gaul", in T.M. Blagg and M. Millett (eds), *The Early Roman Empire in the West.* Oxford: Oxbow Books, 7–29.

Raybould, M.E. (1999). *A Study of Inscribed Material from Roman Britain: An Inquiry Into Some Aspects of Literacy in Romano-British Society.* Oxford: Archaeopress.

Ridgeway, V., Leary, K. and Sudds, B. (2013). *Roman Burials in Southwark. Excavations at 52-56 Lant Street and 56 Southwark Bridge Road, London SE1.* Pre-Construct Archaeology Limited Monograph No 17. London: Museum of London.

Riha, E. (1979). *Die römischen Fibeln aus Augst und Kaiseraugst.* Forschungen in Augst 3. Augst: Römermuseum Augst.

Riha, E. (1990). *Der römische Schmuck aus Augst und Kaiseraugst.* Augst: Römermuseum Augst.

Riha, E. (1994). *Die römischen Fibeln aus Augst und Kaiseraugst Die Neufunde seit 1975.* Wien: Römermuseum.

Rothe, U. (2009). *Dress in the Rhine–Moselle Region of the Roman Empire.* Oxford: Archaeopress.

Rothe, U. (2012). "Clothing in the Middle Danube Provinces: The Garments, Their Origins and Their Distribution", *Jahreshefte des Österreichischen Archäologischen Instituts*, 81: 137–231.

Rothe, U. (2013a). "Whose Fashion? Men, Women and Roman Culture as Reflected in Dress in the Cities of the Roman North-West", in E. Hemelrijk and G. Woolf (eds), *Women and the Roman City in the Latin West.* Mnemosyne Supplements, History and Archaeology of Classical Antiquity 360. Leiden: Brill, 243–68.

Rothe, U. (2013b). "Die norisch-pannonische Tracht: Gab es sie wirklich?", in G. Grabherr and B. Kainrath (eds), *Verwandte in der Fremde: Fibeln und Bestandteile der Bekleidung als Mittel zur Rekonstruktion von interregionalem Austausch und zur Abgrenzung von Gruppen vom Ausgreifen Roms während des 1. Punischen Krieges bis zum Ende des Weströmischen Reiches: Akten des Internationalen Kolloquiums Innsbruck 27. bis 29. April 2011.* Innsbruck: Innsbruck University Press, 33–48.

Sagadin, M. (1979). "Antične Pasne Spone in Garniture v Sloveniji/Antike Gürtelschnallen und Garnituren in Slowenien", *Arheološki Vestnik*, 30: 294–338.

Šajn, M. (2012). "Upodobljena Oblačila na Rimskih Nagrobnih Spomenikih iz Območja Mest Petovione in Celeje ter Njunih Agrov/Depictions of Costume on Roman Funerary Monuments from the Area of the Towns and Territories of Poetovio and Celeia", in Migotti et al. (2012), 361–85.

Sanader, M. (2003). "Rimske Legije i Njihovi Logori u Hrvatskom Dijelu Panonskog Limesa", *Opuscula Archaeological*, 27: 463–8.

Šašel, J. (1960). "Caesernii", *Živa Antika*, 10: 210–21.

Šašel, J. (1966). "Barbii", *Eirene*, 5: 117–37.

Šašel, J. (1968). "Emona", *Paulys Realencyclopädie der classischen Altertumswissenschaft*, Supplement 11: 540–78.

Šašel Kos, M. (1997). "The Roman Inscriptions in the National Museum of Slovenia", *Situla, Razprave Narodnega Muzeja v Ljubljani/ Situla,Dissertationes Musei Nationalis Labacensis*, 35.

Šašel Kos, M. (2002). "The Boundary Stone between Aquileia and Emona", *Situla, Razprave Narodnega Muzeja v Ljubljani/ Situla,Dissertationes Musei Nationalis Labacensis*, 41: 11–19.

Šašel Kos, M. (2003). "Emona Was in Italy, Not in Pannonia", in M. Šašel Kos and P. Scherrer (eds), *The Autonomous Towns of Noricum and Pannonia I/Die autonomen Städte in Noricum und Pannonien: Pannonia I*. Situla 41. Ljubljana: Narodni Muzej Slovenije, 11–19.

Schober, A. (1923). *Die römischen Grabsteine von Noricum und Pannonien*. Vienna: E. Hölzel and Co.

Schörner, G. ed., (2005). *Romanisierung – Romanisation. Theoretische Modelle und praktische Fallbeispiele*. British Archaeological Reports International Series 1427. Oxford: Archaeopress.

Sedlmayer, H. (1995). *Die römischen Fibeln von Wels*. Volume 4: Quellen und Darstellungen zur Geschichte von Wels. Sonderreihe zum Jahrbuch des Musealvereines Wels. Wels: Musealverein.

Sedlmayer, H. (2009). *Die Fibeln vom Magdalensberg. Funde der Grabungsjahre 1948 – 2002*. Klagenfurt am Wörthersee: Verlag des Landesmuseums Kärnten.

Shumka, L. (2008). "Designing Women: The Representation of Women's Toiletries on Funerary Monuments in Roman Italy", in J. Edmondson and A. Keith (eds), *Roman Dress and the Fabrics of Roman Culture*. Phoenix Supplementary Volumes 46, Studies in Greek and Roman Social History 1. Toronto: University of Toronto Press, 172–91.

Slabe, M. (1968). "Antični Grobovi v Komenskega Ulici/Les Tombes Antiques dans la Komenskega Ulica a Ljubljana", *Arheološki Vestnik*, 19: 419–25.

Stemberger, K. (2014). "Identity of Females Buried at Colonia Iulia Emona/Rekonstruiranje Identitet Žensk z Emonskih Nekropol", *Arheo*, 31: 69–81.

Stemberger, K. (2018). *An Analysis of Funerary Evidence and Identity at Colonia Iulia Emona*. Unpubl. PhD thesis. King's College London.

Štukl, J. (2002). *Rimske Fibule v Sloveniji*. Unpubl. essay. University of Ljubljana.

Šubic, Z. (1975). "Rimske Oljenke v Sloveniji/Römische Lampen in Slowenien", *Arheološki Vestnik*, 26: 82–99.

Šubic, Z. (1976a). "Tipološki in Kronološki Pregled Rimskega Stekla v Poetovioni/Revue Typologique et Chronologique de Verre Romain de Poetovio", *Arheološki Vestnik*, 25: 39–62.

Šubic, Z. (1976b). "Rimske Oljenke v Sloveniji", *Rei Cretariae Romanae Fautorum Acta*, 16: 82–99.

Tomažinčič, Š. (2011). *Poročilo o Zaščitnih Arheoloških Izkopavanjih na Območju Izgradnje Podzemnih Zbiralnic na Štefanovi 4 v Ljubljani*. Unpubl. excavation report.

Tušek, I. (1993). "Rimsko Grobišče na Novi Obvoznici ob Potrčevi Cesti v Ptuju", *Ptujski Arheološki Zbornik*: 385–448.

Tušek, I. (1997). "Skupina Poznorimskih Grobov iz Območja Izkopa za Stanovanjski Blok B-2 v Rabelčji Vasi – Zahod na Ptuju", *Arheološki vestnik*, 48: 289–300.

van Gennep, A. (1960). *The Rites of Passage*. London: Routledge.

Versluys, M.J. (2014). "Understanding Objects in Motion. An Archaeological Dialogue on Romanisation", *Archaeological Dialogues*, 21(1): 1–20.

Vomer Gojkovič, M. (1996). "Rimski Jantarni Predmeti s Ptuja", *Arheološki Vestnik*, 47: 307–22.

Vomer Gojkovič, M. (1997). "Poznorimski Grobovi z Grobišča pri Dijaškem Domu v Rabelčji Vasi na Ptuju", *Arheološki Vestnik*, 48: 301–24.

Vomer Gojkovič, M. and Kolar, N. (1993). *Archaeologia Poetovionensis: Stara in Nova Arheološka Spoznanja*. Ptuj: Pokrajinski Muzej Ptuj.

Wiseman, T.P. (1974). "Legendary Genealogies in Late Republican Rome", *Greece and Rome*, 2nd Ser., 21(2): 153–64.

Wiseman, T.P. (1983). "Domi Nobiles and The Roman Cultural Élite", in M. Cébeillac Gervasoni (ed.), *Les Bourgeoisies Municipales Italiennes aux II et I Siècles av. J.C.: Centre Jean-Bérard, Institut français de Naples, 7–10 décembre 1981 (Paris)*. Neaples: Bibliothèque de l'Institut français de Naples, 299–307.

Wyke, M. (1994). "Woman in the Mirror: The Rhetoric of Adornment in the Roman World", in L.J. Archer, S. Fischler and M. Wyke (eds), *Women in Ancient Societies: An Illusion of then Night*. London: Routledge, 134–51.

Part III

The stuff of "man"

8 Coming out of the provincial closet

Masculinity, sexuality, and same-sex
sexual relations amongst Roman
soldiers in the European north-west,
first–third centuries A.D.

Tatiana Ivleva

Introduction

In the latest volume on the archaeology and history of Roman Britain, *The Oxford Handbook of Roman Britain* (Millett et al. 2016), the part titled 'Society and the Individual' focuses on topics related to various forms of identity and its expression in literacy, dress, and language, amongst other things, in Romano-British society. Although the collection omits the topic of ancient sexuality, it does address gender, but only as an informed discussion of recent theoretical and historical advances in interpreting and identifying gendered behaviour in the archaeological record (Sherratt and Moore 2016). Such an approach has been typical of archaeological scholarship on gender and sexuality in the Roman provinces, which has noticeably lacked a critical discussion about dimensions of gender and variability in sexual relations in provincial and frontier settings. At the same time, another scholarly tendency has been to gender and sexualise provinces by formal analogy, such that the nature of provincial sexual relations, including marriages and other relationships, has been studied almost exclusively from a heteronormative perspective (Brandl 2008; Allison 2011; Greene 2011, 2015, 2016; Juntunen 2018). Indeed, only a handful of discussions have addressed other forms of genders and other, out-of-the-heterosexual-box, provincial sexual relations such as same-sex and polygamous ones (Matthews 1994, 1999; Friedl 1996; Phang 2001: 262–96; Allason-Jones 2004: 277–8; Pinto and Pinto 2013; Collins and Ivleva 2018; Ivleva 2018a).

In response, this chapter focuses on the topic of same-sex sexual relations in the provincial and frontier settings amongst Roman soldiers stationed at various locations in the European north-west in the period dating from the late first to the third centuries A.D. Although investigating such relations could take several routes, I have consciously avoided discussing figures typically associated with such relations—for example, the *cinaedus*, a figure that looms large in discussions on the topic (Richlin 1992[1983]; Gleason 1995; Parker 1997; Halperin 1998; Clarke 2005)—but also examples of provincial gender transgression and the growing number of cases in the archaeological record that scholars have labelled 'third-gender' individuals (cf. Pinto and Pinto 2013 for a suspected *gallus* from *Cataractonium*/Catterick; for critiques of third gender in archaeology, see Matić 2012; Moral 2016). In particular, this chapter examines Roman soldiers involved in same-sex sexual behaviour, because this group has often been marginalised in scholarship and treated as special case or exception to the heteronormative rule, possibly due to attitudes amongst some in modern society that gay people do not make good soldiers (e.g. 'Homosexuality is incompatible with military service', in 'Homosexuals in the Armed Forces: United States General Accounting Office Report', issued 12 June 1992; for a critique, see Boswell 1994: 63; also Zeeland 1993, 1995, 1997 for the accounts on gay networks within the U.S. Army and Air Force). My goal is not to answer definitely certain questions about same-sex sexual relations in Roman military settings but to introduce new ways of thinking about the study of gender and sexuality in Roman provinces. Therefore, the chapter not only maps same-sex sexual behaviours in military frontier environments but also contextualises them within current theoretical frameworks employed to examine sexualities and genders from the past. A secondary goal is to highlight sources available for investigating the topic as well as to chart what sort of information is unavailable, due to either the nature of the evidence and the elusiveness of artefacts mentioning or depicting same-sex sexual relations, or the inability or unwillingness of scholars to search for the right evidence in the right places.

In this chapter, I strive to reach an understanding of male sexual identities expressed in performances of masculinity in Roman military settings. I begin by describing what constituted soldierly identities and how the masculinity and sexual behaviour of soldiers factor into those identities. Next, I delve into Roman masculine and sexual protocols gleaned from documentary evidence, after which I present evidence that, interpreted within the framework of those protocols, indicate practices of same-sex sexual relations in the Roman army. The digression into the protocols may seem unnecessary to scholars of sexuality in the Mediterranean Roman core, for they feature in every volume addressing Greek and Roman sexualities (Holmes 2012; Hubbard 2014; Skinner 2014; Blondel and Ormand 2015; Orrells 2015). Likewise, scholars of Roman provincial society may find the discussion on soldierly identity redundant given the extensiveness of the debates on the topic to date (Haynes 1999, 2016; James 1999, 2001; Gardner 2007; Collins 2008). Nevertheless, the topics are not mutually exclusive, and the need to address both underscores the persistent disconnect between the disciplines of Classical and Roman provincial archaeology.

Compulsory masculine and heterosexual soldierly identity in studies on the Roman provinces and frontiers

In the few scholarly discussions addressing what constituted Roman soldiers' identities (James 1999, 2001; Haynes 2016), epigraphic evidence (e.g. funerary and votive stone monuments) has served as the primary source of information. However, artefacts of material culture can also illuminate soldiers' identities, for the use of often uniform dress and military equipment amongst soldiers in different corners of the Roman world suggests 'the shared articulation of military identity' (Haynes 2016: 452; also James 2001: 82–3). Because identity operates on individual and communal levels (Eckardt 2014: 4, citing Meskell 2001: 189), a division between official dimensions of military identity and the identity of an individual soldier has also been acknowledged (Haynes 1991, 1999; James 2001). On the one hand, being part of an institution with its own forms of ranking, dress, rituals, and even living arrangements clearly contributed to a shared sense of being a Roman soldier, or *miles*. That shared sense of belonging to the military community set soldiers apart from other groups and communities that formed the Roman Empire—traders or craftspeople of various professions, amongst others—with their own ways of expressing identity (James 1999: 2, 2001: 79; Haynes 1999, 2016). The collective military identity was expressed and performed within military communities on a daily basis, for instance, while on the move, during drills, and at religious festivals (James 1999: 18–21; Collins 2008: 49). On the other hand, what appears to have been a monolithic, homogeneous group at a glance varied widely at the level of individuals, who were bound by local and regional affiliations, and preferences to various communities outside the military milieu (Haynes 1999: 7; James 2001: 79–80). Therefore, what constituted the 'personal identity of a man as a soldier' (Coulston 1988: x) was seldom predictable.

Collins's (2008: 47) list of 18 roles or layers of identity of legionary legates demonstrates the internal complexity and diversity of the soldierly identity at the individual level. Moreover, the many facets of identity on the list elucidate the social roles both internal and external to a soldier as a member of the Roman army (James 1999: 18; Collins 2008: 47; Haynes 2016: 453):

- Being a man;
- Being of a particular social background;
- Being of a particular financial background;
- Being a freeborn or Roman citizen;
- Being a son;
- Having kin;
- Being head of a close-knit family;
- Being head of an extended family including servants and slaves;
- Belonging to a specific age group;
- Belonging to a specific ethnic group by birth;
- Belonging to a specific military unit;
- Belonging to a particular century, *turma* or cohort within a military unit;
- Belonging to a *contubernium* ('a barrack block');
- Belonging to a specific ranked group within the military unit (e.g. ordinary soldier, soldier receiving pay and a half, and soldier receiving double pay);
- Being a member in particular (local) cults;
- Being a member of a particular local (ethnic) group due to professional or personal relations;

- Having specific physiological characteristics;
- Having specific physical characteristics.

All of those aspects can be summarised as contributing to gender, age-based, status-based, ethnic, and religious identities that form a composite of the self, and which are contextually dependent, situationally dynamic, and mutually inclusive (Eckardt 2014: 5–7). Yet, the sexual identity of a man as a soldier does not feature in the discussions on soldierly identity. The image that emerges in most scholarship on that topic is of a soldier as a husband, married with children. For instance, James (2001: 80, my emphasis) has portrayed soldiers 'acting as heads of families, *husbands and fathers*, as owners of slaves, as clients and as patrons of freedmen and women'; however, he has also acknowledged that 'soldierly identity as a particular [form of] masculinity' merits far more scrutiny from scholars. In that sense, we are presented with an image of a Roman soldier as a man having a heterosexual relationship with one or more women, if not also being a father, whose sexuality was grounded within the presumed notion of masculinity. In James's (1999: 16) words, being *miles* meant being part of 'an overtly masculine environment, governed by a distinctive warrior value system'. As a result, the sexuality of Roman soldiers is 'compulsory heterosexual' (the term is borrowed from the title of Rich's 1980 paper). Furthermore, that soldierly heterosexuality is measured in terms of masculinity, and vice versa, where masculinity is conceived as relating to preferences in sexual partners. In other words, being heterosexual is normative for masculine men, and being homosexual is deviant, un-masculine, even feminine, and suitable only for third-gendered persons. However, such views do not accurately reflect accounts of sexual values and practices documented in Latin literature. According to Ormand and Blondell (2015: 6), 'Romans were (not) thinking with our modern sexual categories, but rather that they were thinking with their own'. Moreover, that understanding of soldierly sexuality as 'compulsory heterosexual' grounded in soldiers' masculinity very much derives from the stereotypical modern Western reading of what makes a man 'a man' (Connell 2005[1995]). Yet, in many past and contemporary societies, being 'a man' has run parallel to engaging in homosexual practices (Díaz-Andreu 2005: 15; also Herdt 1981). All these views already ask scholars interested in life in the Roman provinces to re-evaluate their preconceived notions about soldierly masculinity and sexuality.

In what follows, I set out, albeit in a cursory fashion (see also Chapters 6 and 11), the sexual norms, roles, and practices depicted in Latin texts and the image of (soldierly) masculinity that can be extracted from them. As a result, I propose a new framework for conceptualising and studying masculinity in the Roman army and Roman provinces that emphasises how Roman soldierly masculinity and sexuality were not two sides of the same coin.

Roman masculinity and sexual protocols

In the Roman view, a man's manliness, or what made him 'a man', was not equated with that man's sexual preferences (McDonnell 2006: 167–8). In Latin, the word used to denote 'manliness' was *virtus*, which derives from *vir*, meaning, unsurprisingly, 'man' (McDonnell 2006: 2; Skinner 2014: 270). *Virtus* was used to characterise the ideal behaviour of a man, determined by public-facing qualities essential for the conduct of war, success in politics, and religious piety (McDonnell 2006: 2–3, 169, 172; Holmes 2012: 112; Masterson 2014a: 22–3). Accordingly, *virtus* was not innate but something to be achieved; a concept loaded with wide-ranging moral, social, and political meanings amid temporal shifts in the meaning of the word itself (McDonnell 2006: 6–9; Williams 2010: 4, 11; Holmes 2012: 112; Skinner 2014: 271). In that sense, sexuality neither factored into *virtus* nor specifically referred or related to its expression (McDonnell 2006: 167 but see Williams 2010: 118–22). On the contrary, sexuality, or actual sexual activity, existed on the periphery of the concept of *virtus*, and the word *virilitas*, semantically related to *vir* and *virtus*, implied 'the sexual and procreative aspects of masculinity' and referred to 'male sexual characteristics' and 'sexual maturity' (McDonnell 2006: 167).

For most metropolitan Roman males, the choice of whom to have sexual intercourse with did not depend on the biological sex of the person, nor did any discretion based on sexual orientation exist. After all, the divisions of hetero-, homo-, bi-, and pansexuality are relatively modern constructs (Foucault 1985 [1984]; 1986[1984]; Parker 1997; see Richlin 1993 for an opposing view). At the same time, whereas modern Western society is preoccupied with sexual practices such as monogamy, adultery, prostitution, homosexuality, paedophilia, sexual harassment, rape, and pornography (Langlands 2006: 14), metropolitan Romans expressed anxieties about adultery amongst females, same-sex sexual relations between women, women playing assertive masculine roles, the sexual integrity of Roman citizens, the social status of sexually penetrated individuals, and becoming effeminate (Halperin 1998: 100–1; Langlands 2006: 21; Williams 2010: 3). Nevertheless, because the basis for divisions of sexuality within Roman society continues to be debated by classicists, my treatment of the topic here necessarily remains cursory (see Chapter 11; Ormand and Blondell 2015).

Amy Richlin (1992[1983]; cf. Parker 1997) was the first scholar to advance the priapic or phallocentric model of Roman sexuality, also known as the 'penetration model', which views 'sex as a hierarchical relationship' (Skinner 2014: 274). The choice of partner was based upon the social articulation of power (i.e. superordinate versus subordinate social identity) and the sexual act was based on roles that partners played during the intercourse (i.e. active versus passive). In general, Roman sexual protocol consisted of three rules (Williams 2010: 18–19). First, it was centred on 'a self-respecting Roman freeborn citizen who must always give the appearance of playing the insertive role in penetrative acts, and not the receptive role' (Williams 2010: 18)—in other words, on '*vir* as an impenetrable and enthusiastic penetrator of others' (Masterson 2014a: 24; also Parker 1997: 54–5; Skinner 2014: 280). Neither blame nor shame was attributed to a man who engaged in extramarital sexual activities, for example, with his male or female slaves or with male or female prostitutes, as long as he played the penetrative role in sexual intercourse (Williams 2010: 20–9; Skinner

2014: 258, 260). The second rule addressed the status of sexual partners whom men penetrated; women, boys, and slaves of any sex were viewed as eligible objects of male desire, whereas freeborn male Roman citizens were off limits (Williams 2010: 19). The third rule concerned the age of sexual partners; because smooth, adolescent bodies were preferred, the ideal male partner, for example, was between 12 and 20 years of age—that is, between the onset of puberty and maturity (Eger 2007: 133; Williams 2010: 19; Laes 2011: 247–52, 262–8). Once older, a person generally ceased to be attractive to older males (cf. *exoleti*, Williams 2010: 90–3). The model thus suggests the image of a dominant, penetrating, adult Roman male (*vir*) who engages in sexual activity with—that is, sexually penetrates—subordinate persons of any sex. The choice of sexual partners for metropolitan Roman males has therefore never been equated with their biological sex but depended on a variety of variables, including the partners' social and political status, and age (Parker 1997: 47; Walters 1997; Flemming 2010; Skinner 2014: 256).

As Roman sexual protocol suggested, *virtus* did not encompass a man's desire for any bodies. At the same time, what might have compromised his masculinity and violated the protocol was effeminacy, which could be expressed by performing specific behaviours, by dressing and presenting himself in certain ways and by taking the receptive or penetrated role during sexual intercourse (Gleason 1990, 1995: 55–130; Halperin 1998: 101–2; Williams 2010: 141; Holmes 2012: 114; Skinner 2014: 280). In short, whereas domination and the expression of power were means to communicate and safeguard the manliness of the *vir*, receptivity and effeminacy were traits of roles assigned to his sexual partners.

The priapic model favours the binary division of sexuality by differentiating penetration from being penetrated, and masculinity as active from femininity as passive. However, recent scholarship on phallocentrism and priapic sexuality has also acknowledged the complexity of sexual behaviours possible beyond the penetrative paradigm and brought the power of individual sexual agency to the fore (Langlands 2006: 7; Holmes 2012: 104–6; Levin-Richardson 2013; Kamen and Levin-Richardson 2015a, 2015b). Likewise, the current understanding of available evidence emphasises the variability of Roman sexuality and sexual relations under the umbrella of phallocentrism (Matthews 1994: 123; Eger 2007: 150–1; Holmes 2012: 92–110; Masterson 2014a: 28). For instance, Masterson's (2014a: 27–8) analysis of selections from two literary texts—one from the ancient heroic epic *Punica* by Silius Italicus, the other from Statius' set of poems titled *Silvae*—has revealed how priapic sexuality also shared 'the stage with imperfectly acknowledged counterdiscourses of indulgence in passivities of all kinds'.

The same type of ambiguity characterised the same-sex sexual practices of Roman soldiers within the mainstream of Roman society in Mediterranean regions. The few discussions or surveys addressing that practice in Roman military contexts have primarily referred to evidence from the ancient texts and discussions of the armies of the Roman Republic and early Roman Empire (Phang 2001: 262–95; Williams 2010: 109, 120; Leitao 2014). Even then, they have all emphasised the ubiquity of soldiers' same-sex sexual relations with their male slaves and prostitutes. In particular, Phang's (2001: 268–78) collection of literary evidence showcases how Roman army officers of various ranks engaged in same-sex sexual relations with their male slaves and prostitutes (also Ivleva 2018a). Such relations were unproblematic, tolerated, and accepted, for no evidence indicates that pursuing intercourse with male slaves or prostitutes would have compromised a soldier's masculinity or warranted severe punishment. For instance, Polybius (6.37.9) wrote (my emphasis) that 'the bastinado is [...] inflicted [...] *on young men who have abused their persons*', meaning that the punishment would be administered on soldiers who made themselves available as *passive* partners in sex acts with other soldiers (Phang 2001: 282–3). Such passivity was cause for prosecution, because making oneself vulnerable to other men suggested a similar tendency to be vulnerable to enemies on the battlefield (Walters 1997; Leitao 2014: 235). By contrast, the passage does not refer to the punishment of soldiers who performed penetrative acts on other male bodies. Thus, in line with the priapic paradigm, only soldiers who played the penetrated or receptive role and showed traces of effeminacy would have been ridiculed and scorned. At the same time, the boundaries of the paradigm were sometimes debatable and fluid in certain respects, and in some cases, albeit rarely, soldiers described as masculine did play receptive roles. An oft-cited example is that of a soldier in Pompey's army who, though clearly exhibiting all the signs of effeminacy and sexual receptivity, was honoured by Pompey himself for his bravery on a battlefield (Phang 2001: 285–6; Williams 2010: 213, 216; Leitao 2014: 236). Even though his receptive role in sexual intercourse was apparently well known, it did not diminish his status or prevent the acknowledgement of his military deeds (but see Leitao 2014: 236, who urges scholars to interpret that and similar tales cautiously, for they defy Roman phallocentric norms).

Although a diversity of gender and sexual patterns existed under the umbrella of phallocentrism, more important to the purpose of this chapter is the disconnect between Roman ideas about masculinity and men's sexual behaviour. Because studies on the Roman provinces have lagged behind in applying that perception of sexuality and gender roles, I now turn to discuss the range of masculinities within the Roman army. In a subsequent section, I furnish evidence of sexual diversity by presenting evidence of same-sex sexual relations. To that end, I aim to emphasise that the outward projection of being a Roman soldier or being masculine does not undermine evidence of sexual diversity in the Roman military milieu. In other words, in both sections together, I seek to dispel the myth of heterosexual masculinity in the Roman army by dissociating masculinity from sexual behaviours.

Soldierly masculinity in Roman provinces revisited

In answering the question as to what sorts of masculinities can be traced specifically to the Roman military milieu I follow Knapp (1998: 368) who states that it is simply impossible to pinpoint what might have constituted masculinity, which was not only divergent but also culturally specific and in constant flux (cf. Connell 2005[1995]: 37). Although the full spectrum of masculinities in any culture cannot be mapped, scholars can nevertheless attempt to identify some 'protocols that governed the discourses that pervade them' (Halperin 2015: 317). For the Roman Empire specifically, scholars acknowledged that Roman masculinity—be it normalised, protocolled, or agency-bounded—is 'a structure containing contradictions of various kinds' (Masterson 2014a: 18; also see Langlands 2006: 35–6 on the multiplicity of Roman sexual morality).

With regard to Roman soldierly masculinity, one of the most recognisable form is the one exercised, internalised, and reproduced as a cultural norm in the Roman army: 'hegemonic masculinity' powered by the distinct ways in which soldiers indicated their manliness at different levels, whether conceptually, visually, or performatively. In that case, the notion of hegemony implies that such masculinity occupied a predominant position in society or the community and, at the same time, acted as an embodiment of power and domination (Connell 2005[1995]: 76–8).

This kind of masculinity was 'expressed through general lifestyle rather than specific sexual behaviour' (Phang 2001: 292). Whereas *virtus* in Rome depended on public-facing qualities essential for the conduct of war, success in politics, and religious piety, in the Roman army manliness was especially associated with martiality. Upon joining the army, recruits underwent indoctrination in martiality and were taught the importance of martial achievements, reinforced with material or status-oriented rewards for displays of martial bravery (Maxfield 1981; McDonnell 2006: 184; also James 1999, 2001; Haynes 1999, 2016). Such martial masculinity was also exalted in a specific dress code. Classical scholars have repeatedly described how Roman clothing reflected, articulated, and strengthened 'a man's sense of his masculine self' (Olson 2017: 135). How one dressed, walked, gestured, groomed, and even spoke determined the general category or mixture of categories to which a person could be assigned: masculine or feminine and aristocratic or servile (Olson 2014, 2017: 137). Just as masculinity in Rome was projected and communicated visually (Gleason 1995: 68), soldierly masculinity in the provinces and frontiers was enacted and performed by way of appearance and adherence to a vestimentary code. Apuleius (Met. IX, 39) wrote that a soldier could be easily recognised according to his 'dress and manner', or *habitus atque habitude*. That male sartorial code of hegemonic masculinity included bearing weapons, for soldiers were the only individuals in the Roman Empire allowed to carry arms on the streets. Another piece of dress that distinguished a soldier from a civilian was the military belt, which acted as a visual and symbolic manifestation of 'being a soldier' and thus represented authority, martiality, and, in turn, manliness (Hoss 2012: 30, 44, 2014). Funerary and votive monuments of soldiers in the provinces also indicate the exhibition of heroic martial *virtus*, for images of a mounted warrior riding down a barbarian and a soldier in full armour were common topoi by which to showcase a soldierly quality (Figure 8.1; McDonnell 2006: 387,

Figure 8.1 Gravestone of rider Marcus Aurelius Victor, Chesters, UK; RIB 1481
(© and reproduced by kind permission of NU Digital Heritage, Newcastle University)

149–54; also see Coulston 2014 for additional examples from the Romano-British frontier zone).

However, because 'the model is one thing and reality another' (Masterson 2014a: 26), such formalised masculinity did not necessarily represent a rigid behavioural code imposed upon every soldier as a matter of state policy. At the individual level, the ideology could have been affirmed or violated, for one could choose behavioural patterns as one wished as long as it did not compromise military morality. It might have been that only a few men rigorously practised and enacted the hegemonic form of masculinity because it allowed them to validate socially their own masculinity, given that manliness is an 'achieved state identified by culturally specific signs' (Holmes 2012: 115, 124). In that light, such hegemonic masculinity could be interpreted as a form of rhetoric, as a normative standard, and as an ideology to which some might have wished to adhere while others resisted or followed their own codes of conduct (Williams 2010: 170; Masterson 2014a: 18; Halperin 2015: 321; cf. Holmes 2012: 110). After all, rhetoric aside, practising hegemonic masculinity might have become a burden.

James (2001: 85) has encouraged scholars to acknowledge that within the structures of the Roman army, 'many routine domestic aspects of life may have been "below the horizon" of both institutional military, and collective soldierly culture' and thus expressed 'other dimensions of identity entirely' (also Haynes 1999: 8). Numerous cases of such structures have been found in which cultural roles, codes, formalised behaviours, and laws have been tacitly acknowledged within society and guided ethical, moral, and other societal developments; however, such evidence does not mean that all members of the society subscribed to or identified with those structures (Parker 1997: 61–2; also see Langlands 2006: 24 for the Roman period and Eckardt 2014: 6, who cites Beaudry et al. 1991, on alcohol consumption policies, policing, and 'below the horizon' behaviours in nineteenth-century Massachusetts). By extension, the shadow of military service did not necessarily follow every soldier, as evident, for instance, in the fact that not all tombstones made for and by soldiers depicted the deceased in full martial attire (Figure 8.2). Indeed, some were depicted as family men embracing their wives and children (Figure 8.3; for other examples, see lupa.at/694; 2850; 3062; 3269; 3549; 4305; 4250), and on such gravestones, military heroism and an abundance of medals are replaced by imagery expressing sentiment for the ordinary. The existence of those stones debunks the myth of a dominant military focus sometimes assigned to the Roman army, for some soldiers might have prioritised being a family man instead of a protector of the Roman Empire.

Along those lines, the concept of soldierly hegemonic masculinity could have been acknowledged, endorsed, and propagated at the level of collective military

Figure 8.2 Gravestone of Aurelius Secundianus, duplicarius of Legio II Italica, Sankt Thomas am Zeiselberg, Magdalensberg, Austria, lupa.at/862

(© and photo O. Harl)

Figure 8.3 Funerary monuments depicting soldiers with their families. Left: tomb relief depicting Flavius Ursus, a *biarcus* in a cavalry unit, his wife Aurelia Munnia, and their daughter Aurelia Ursina, Budapest, Hungary. Kept in Aquincum Museum, inv. nr. 2000.14.5; lupa.at/10559. Right: tomb relief depicting Claudius Secundus, legionary soldier in *Legio II Adiutrix*, his wife Aelia Catta, and their son Secundinus, Budapest, Hungary. Kept in Aquincum Museum, inv. nr. 81.7.6; lupa.at/5042

(Both photographs by O. Harl, courtesy and © BHM–Aquincum Museum)

identity but been fractured at the level of the individual soldier. At that level, multiple non-hegemonic (i.e. subaltern) masculinities could have been based, albeit not exclusively, on the origins of soldiers. Because the Roman army was culturally and ethnically diverse (Haynes 2013), the transcultural redefinition of masculine Roman virtue and hegemonic military masculinity within one legionary or auxiliary unit could have been the order of the day. Socio-economic status within a unit might have been yet another impetus for variable masculinities; a centurion might have enacted hegemonic masculinity in a way unlike that of an ordinary soldier. Because such topics also warrant a discussion in their own right, in this brief section I can do little more than hint at variable masculinities and suggest the need to breach the limits of current assumptions regarding masculinities in Roman society by demonstrating their salient contradictions and complexities.

None of the possible masculinities are heterosexual by default, however. In the following section, I probe the sexual behaviours and same-sex sexual practices of Roman soldiers, whether they exhibited hegemonic or non-hegemonic masculine traits. In doing so, I consider evidence of same-sex sexual relations and what it reveals about same-sex conventions in the Roman army. After reviewing the evidence, I analyse whether any such evidence suggests that Roman sexual protocol changed or differed from one province to the next.

Soldierly sexuality in Roman north-west provinces revisited: same-sex sexual relations in the Roman army

Of the available evidence in which same-sex sexual relations in provincial Roman garrisons might be detected, literary and sub-literary (e.g. epigraphic) evidence is crucial, albeit rarely supplemented by ancient iconography or corroborated by artefactual discoveries. Although images of sexual acts circulated widely on everyday objects such as ceramics, lamps, and knives (Vucetic 2014; Chapter 2), depictions of same-sex sexual acts have rarely been found (Johns 1982: 102). For instance, as Vucetic's (2014) analysis of sexual imagery on lamps has revealed, portrayals of such acts are wholly absent on artefacts of that mass-produced medium. Though a few Arretine and South Gaulish samian wares depict intercourse between two males (Figure 8.4; Johns 1982: 102; Clarke 1993; Williams 2010, plate 11; Skinner 2014: 367), they are the only examples of such imagery in a provincial and frontier context known to the author. Seeking an explanation for its absence within the iconographic repertoire of everyday objects, Johns (1982: 102) has suggested that same-sex sexual imagery was not popular on pottery possibly in response to the consumers' preference for male–female couplings. However, a more credible explanation comes from Williams (2010: 351, n. 150), who has suggested that nineteenth-century archaeologists might have never published or even destroyed imagery of same-sex sexual relations given the taboo of homosexual relations in

Figure 8.4 Fragmentary bowl with Cupid on a column between two couples making love; the scene shown displays a male–male couple; Arretine pottery, early Imperial period, Museum of Fine Arts, Boston, inv. nr. 053

(Photograph © Museum of Fine Arts, Boston)

their day (Voss 2008: 318; Skinner 2014: 369–70; see also Chapters 2, 4, and 5). Another possibility is that the priorities of researchers since then have marginalised the study of provincial sexuality and that its depictions have not therefore been investigated in much detail (Johns 1982; Vucetic 2014). For those reasons, more Roman-period images of same-sex sexual intercourse might have existed or even still exist to this day but remain hidden from view.

In rare studies on the material culture of same-sex sexual relations in Roman provinces, the pressing task has been identifying objects that might have represented same-sex sexual behaviour or indicated that a particular male practised alternative modes of masculinity. Matthews (1994: 126–9) has suggested that pieces of jewellery associated with females found in a grave of a biologically sexed male might signify that the deceased was a receptive sexual partner who used the jewellery to effeminise himself. Quite often, such burials are classified as deviant or as burials of third-gender individuals. For instance, the inhumation burial of a male from Catterick has been classified as that of a *gallus*, a castrated priest of the goddess Cybele, partly because various pieces of female-associated jewellery were found on the body of the deceased (Cool 2002: 29–30; Pinto and Pinto 2013: 170). The person was buried with a complete 100-mm shale bangle on his left arm and a twisted, 95-mm, copper-alloy bracelet, possibly an anklet, located near his right leg. Bracelets and bangles are usually regarded as ornaments for females, although some worn and unworn bracelets made with a range of materials, from copper alloy to jet, have been found in the graves of osteologically sexed males across Roman Britain (Allason-Jones 1995: 27; Cool 2004: 391; Ivleva 2018b). The use of specific dress accessories to determine the sex or gender, and sexual preferences for that matter, of a particular individual is therefore debatable (Allason-Jones 1995; cf. Chapter 7).

Phang (2001: 266) has argued that whereas evidence of same-sex sexual relations amongst soldiers and provincials has primarily come from literary sources, the contribution of other forms of evidence has been underappreciated. In the southern and eastern provinces of the Roman Empire, personal correspondence found on papyri might attest to same-sex sexual relations there (Montserrat 1996), whereas evidence of such relations in western provinces is more likely to rely on writing tablets (on the potential of Vindolanda writing tablets, see Chapter 6). Nevertheless, the question remains as to how scholars might detect expressions of same-sex desire in correspondence of official character and written by scribes (Ivleva 2018a, following Allason-Jones unpubl.; cf. Masterson 2014b).

Another type of evidence that can be used to locate same-sex sexual relationships, or any type of sexual relations, is graffiti (Levin-Richardson 2013). However, in the frontier regions, as far as I am aware, only one such graffito has emerged from a site on the Roman frontier. Found in *Rigomagus*/Remagen, Germany, the verse in Latin rather bluntly states that anyone who frequently visits both male and female prostitutes will be punished with poverty: *quisquis am{m}at pueros s<i=E>ne finem puellas rationem sacc(u)li no(n) refert* (AE 1908, 0189=CLE 2153; Williams 2010: 29, 315, n. 73). Albeit a sole example, it nevertheless indicates that prostitutes of both sexes worked on the fringes of the Roman Empire and that visiting them was commonplace. More importantly, however, it reveals that same-sex sexual relations in frontier regions were not novel.

Epigraphy is another source of information to explore the evidence for same-sex sexual relations. The most explicit one is a funerary monument from Obernburg am Main, Germany, which attests to a certain 16-year-old Diadumenus who was a 'home-born slave' (AE 1929, 106 = AE 1932, 50 = EDCS-11202229 and lupa.at/6973, including image). The dedication was erected by a centurion, Marcus Ulpius Vannius, in the Eighth Augustan legion, who was a patron to the boy but also most likely his lover. After all, the monument refers to Diadumenus as *delicatus*, a term used in specific cases to designate a male object of desire (Phang 2001: 274; Skinner 2014: 359).

Apart from that example, explicit evidence of same-sex sexual relations is absent in the epigraphic record, largely due to the absence of a Latin phrase denoting a long-term sexual partner (Skinner 2014: 359). It is not that those relationships went unrecorded; on the contrary, they might have been recorded without the use of specific words or terms. Bearing that possibility in mind, I propose that funerary monuments for male slaves and freedmen, paid for by their (former) masters, act as testimonies to their same-sex sexual relationships. Contextualising those monuments within a wider pool of inscriptions evincing patron–female slave/*liberta* relations support that argument.

My premise derives from Skinner's (2014: 359) point that 'slaves who had been boyfriends [were] warmly remembered'. Funerary monuments erected by masters for their male slaves or freedmen indicate this clearly. For instance, Numerianus, a trooper in the First Cavalry Regiment of Asturians, stationed at South Shields on Hadrian's Wall, commissioned a tombstone for his 20-year-old freedman, Victor (Figure 8.5; Ivleva 2018a: 1051–3). The tombstone must have been costly to produce, for it was clearly a special commission; the simple text of an inscription is accompanied by a full portrait of the deceased Victor, dressed in tunic and long robe, and reclining on a mattress atop a couch. The rendering of details in the portrait further suggest that care was taken in its production. For one, concerning the choice of accessories for eternal commemoration, Victor is depicted holding a branch of leaves in his right hand and a cup in his left. Furthermore, the carving itself, with naturalistic frills on the pillow and creases in the mattress, suggests exceptional and, in turn, expensive artisanship. Along with that tombstone in the corpus of funerary monuments from South Shields, a few other tombstones stand out as 'the most notable sculptures of Roman Britain', and all thought to have been carved by a skilled sculptor from Palmyra (Smith 1959: 207). Whereas the other tombstones were made to commemorate the wives and female partners of soldiers, Victor's is the exception: it was erected for a former 20-year-old male slave by his master. Furthermore, the wording on the inscription that Numerianus 'most devotedly conducted him [Victor] to the tomb' and that Victor was freed at a young age of 20 suggest a relationship that has clearly advanced beyond that of a master

Figure 8.5 Gravestone of Victor, the Moor, RIB 1064. South Shields held by Tyne and Wear Archives and Museums, UK

and slave. All things considered, Victor's funerary monument was most likely a lover's gift.

Further epigraphic evidence similar to Victor's funerary monument comes from a late first-century tombstone found in Gardun, Croatia. It honours a 60-year-old auxiliary soldier, Marcus Pytha, son of Segnus, who erected a tombstone for himself as well as his freedman, Felix (Figure 8.6; CIL III 14934 = lupa.at/24915 = EDCS-30200432). The monument depicts two men dressed in tunics, whose portraits suggest a slight difference in age; the man on the right side is older than the figure on the left. Albeit large at 1.35 metres in height and 0.76 metres in breadth, it is relatively a standard monument with portraits of the deceased and a simple inscription recording their names, ages, and status.

The absence of the names of any wives, children, or other heirs (e.g. fellow soldiers or barrack-block mates) and the decision to depict the deceased together with the freedman suggest that the monument depicts a same-sex couple involved in a romantic relationship. Furthermore, the wording is typical of funerary monuments erected by patrons for their freedwomen, which are usually interpreted as recording a romantic relationship between an opposite-sex couple. For instance, a tombstone from Solin, Croatia, was paid for by legionary veteran Caius Vatinius Capito for himself and his freedwoman, Vatinia Felicula, who was undoubtedly his sexual companion (CIL III 08764). Another example is a tombstone from Mainz-Weisenau, Germany, that attests to the death of a 27-year-old freedwoman, Smertuca, by her patron and the father of her child, a trooper in a cavalry unit named Tiberius Iulius Diviciacus (CSIR Deutschland II 6, no. 28). All three cases show the use of dry, epigraphic language recording only necessary information: the name, age, status of the deceased freedman/freedwoman, or slave, and the name of the (former) patron.

If we are to take Victor's and Felix's inscriptions and, more specifically, their epigraphic formula as records of same-sex sexual relations in the same way that inscriptions for freedwomen and female slaves paid for by their patrons record their opposite-sex sexual relations (Perry 2014), then four additional monuments can also be regarded as representing same-sex sexual bonds:

- A mid-to-late-first-century tombstone of a 27-year-old slave, Romanus, erected by Titus Avidus Cordus, a legionary centurion (Mainz, CIL XIII 6954);
- A second-century monument recording the death of a 25-year-old slave, Epigonus, by Aelius Maximus, a legionary centurion (Mainz, CIL XIII 11836 = lupa.at/16608 = EDCS-12700345);
- A gravestone commemorating the 17-year-old Priscus, a slave of a legionary eagle-bearer (i.e. *aquilifer*), Publius Cassius (Mainz, CIL XIII 6888 = lupa.at/16601);
- A third-century sarcophagus, now lost, recording the death of a freedman, Pompulenius Adauctus, by his patron, Pompulenius Iunius, a legionary centurion (Budapest, CIL III 03561 = lupa.at/2718 = EDCS-28600022).

Figure 8.6 Gravestone of Pytha, son of Segnus, soldier in *cohors II Chyrrhesticorum*, and Felix, his freedman. Gardun near Sinj held by Archaeological Museum in Split, Croatia, inv. nr. AMS A-2777; lupa.at/24915

(Photo O. Harl, courtesy and © Archaeological Museum in Split)

Those monuments record a type of same-sex relationship that fell within the normative Roman sexual protocol. Despite the impossibility of confirming that the patrons played a penetrative role and the slaves and freedmen a receptive one—that is, the first rule of the protocol—the second and third rules can be confirmed.

The second rule, addressing the status of the penetrating and penetrated partners, stipulated that the latter must not be freeborn Roman males. In all cases mentioned, the monuments were erected by soldiers for their slaves or freedmen. Moreover, Phang (2001: 270) has posited that officers 'were more likely [than ordinary soldiers] to afford pretty boy slaves', because their salaries allowed the purchase of sexual partners. Likewise, legionary centurions paid for the funerary monuments of their freedmen and male slaves. As a mere trooper in an auxiliary unit, Numerianus is an exception, which is further indicative of a strong bond between him and Victor.

The third rule of the protocol is the differentiation of sexual partners by age (Leitao 2014: 233). Boys were considered to be attractive prior to the arrival of a full-grown beard, usually at the time of their 20th birthday (Williams 2010: 19, 24; Laes 2011: 264–5). The sample above contains a case of a 17-year-old, Priscus, a slave of legionary standard-bearer, or *aquilifer*, Publius Cassius (Ivleva 2018a: 1053). Cassius's position as an *aquilifer*, a senior legionary officer, held enormous prestige as a rank that legionary soldiers did not attain before their 30s. Although Cassius's age at the time of Priscus's death remains unknown, his rank doubtlessly indicates that he was far older than his slave. A second example might be Victor, who, at 20 years of age, was too young to be a freedman. Numerianus could have freed Victor once he had lost his youthful beauty and could no longer serve his master's purpose (Sarah Levin-Richardson, personal communication; also see Butrica 2005: 210–21 on the end of a male slave's sexual duty once freed).

I am not suggesting that every funerary monument with which a patron commemorated a male slave who died at a tender age has to be regarded as recording same-sex sexual relations. Each monument and each inscription should be studied case by case, with close attention to different criteria in order to elucidate the nature of the relationships. At the same time, I do not mean to suggest that every soldier was involved in sexual acts with his male slaves and that same-sex sexual relations were practised universally throughout the Roman army.

Another aspect of hegemonic masculinity during the Roman period was procreation and the establishment of a family (McDonnell 2006: 168; Flemming 2010: 812; Mattingly 2011: 98). A Roman auxiliary soldier received citizenship and associated privileges after completing 25 years of service, upon which his children were also granted citizenship and those privileges (Greene 2015; Chapter 6). To some extent, raising a new generation of citizen-soldiers was of paramount concern to the Roman state. Arguably, it was also a societal concern of communities living on the peripheries of the Roman Empire to have Roman citizens amongst their ranks, for they would have enjoyed access to certain privileges by virtue of their citizenship. Because procreation as necessity and marriage 'as a vehicle for property transmission' were common sentiments amongst the elite in Rome (Skinner 2014: 319, 336; Flemming 2010: 812), a soldier could have been (unofficially) married to a woman for the purpose of procreation, though there was nothing to stop him having extramarital intercourse with slaves and prostitutes of any sex (see Williams 2010: 50–9 for that practice in Rome). Of course, the latter practice was somewhat tempered by concerns about excessive sexual behaviour and how it compromised a soldier's effectiveness during war and undermined a unit's fighting quality (Phang 2001: 278; Leitao 2014: 235–7).

Overall, some soldiers may have had a preference for female bodies, some for male bodies, and some for both. Such preferences are more frequently documented for individuals of high status. The Emperor Claudius preferred female bodies only, while Galba had a preference for male ones (Parker 1997: 55–6; see also p. 60 on men and women who were attracted exclusively to the same sex in Roman society; Williams 2010: 249). By extension, scenarios that could have played out in similar fashion in a military environment can include:

- A soldier married to a woman for the purpose of procreation and producing heirs but also having a sexual relationship with a male slave;
- A soldier unmarried but having a sexual relationship with one or more male/female slaves;
- A soldier in a sexual relationship with a male slave whom he had chosen to free for one reason or another;
- A soldier in a sexual relationship with a female slave whom he had chosen to free for one reason or another;
- A soldier in a sexual relationship with a freeborn woman whom he officially married upon his discharge from the army.

Naturally, the list is not exhaustive and many other scenarios can be added to it.

One thing to keep in mind is the danger of romanticising or idealising the relationship between a patron and a (former) slave in a slave-owning society. Some relationships outlined above can be interpreted through the prism of reciprocal sexual relationships, but can also be characterised by sexual abuse and exploitation. In Rome as in the provinces, slaves of both sexes were expected to attend every sexual desire of their masters (Williams 2010: 31–6, 107; Laes 2011: 259–62; Mattingly 2011: 117; Skinner 2014: 357; Baird 2015). Taking those norms into consideration, can scholars gauge the emotional depth of the discussed same-sex sexual relationships whatsoever? Ormand and Blondell (2015: 7) have warned that any notion of 'sexuality as dependent on the depth and authenticity [of] emotion, as an expression of love' is 'a product of the same modern discourse of romance that produces hetero- and homosexuality, but [...] tells us little about the sexual categories of the ancient Greeks and Romans'. What constituted love may have operated on different levels of perception; just as Romans had their own discourses about sex, sexual, and gender relations (Ormand and Blondell 2015: 15), they also had their own discourses and ideals about love and reciprocity (Skinner 2014: 319 and 332). Parker (1997: 57) has suggested that the rigid boundaries of Roman sexual protocol did not permit any mutuality or reciprocity and, in turn, love was an oxymoron within Roman sexual arrangements (also Flemming 2010: 806 on the 'foundational failure of reciprocity'). Following that line of argument, scholars may imagine that, for Romans, love was substituted by preference and sexual desire substituted by a physical act, the need to procreate or the urge to relieve sexual tension. In any case, because the model for Roman sexual intercourse prioritised sexual acts based on the exhibition of power underneath the umbrella of phallocentrism, scholars may never be able to recover the emotions in the hearts and minds of the people involved in sexual relationships (Parker 1997: 60; Eger 2007: 137).

In that light, two monuments for a freedman and a freedwoman, respectively, are worth revisiting: the one for Victor and his patron, Numerianus, and the one for Regina and Barates (Figures 8.5 and 8.7). Of the Catuvelaunian tribe in

Figure 8.7 Gravestone of Regina, RIB 1065, at South Shields and held by Tyne and Wear Archives and Museums, UK

southern Britain, Regina was a freedwoman and a wife of a Palmyran trader, Barates, from what is now Syria. Regina passed away when she was 30 years old and was commemorated by Barates with a lavish funerary monument most likely made by the same sculptor who carved Victor's tombstone (Smith 1959). Although their marriage may have involved reciprocity, Regina, similar to Victor, was a former slave, which suggests that Barates as well as Numerianus purchased their partners at a slave market, no matter how discomforting that likelihood may be.

Of course, not every soldier purchased a slave boy or girl because he wanted him or her as a sexual partner, and the mere fact of slave ownership does not signify that sexual relations existed, only that they were possible. As for Victor, Regina, and many others mentioned, it is difficult to remain objective about their relationships with their (former) masters, and given the impossibility of determining whether they were reciprocal, readers have to decide for themselves the extent to which they are willing to interpret that quality in those relationships. On the one hand, it is intriguing that both Victor and Regina were portrayed on their monuments in a fashion typically reserved for respectable men and women of their class. Regardless of reciprocity, that portrayal at least suggests a desire by the former master of each to portray their relationships as 'respectable' and 'proper' (Rob Collins, personal communication). On the other hand, although both Numerianus and Barates indeed 'most devotedly conducted' their sexual partners to the tomb, neither Victor's nor Regina's consent enters into the equation given the dry language of the funerary inscriptions, nor perhaps should it enter into readings of their relationships. Despite their immortalised faces, their voices and agency, both integral in every presumed love story, are missing.

A topic not yet addressed is the case of same-sex sexual relations between soldiers themselves. The passage in Polybius (6.37.9) quoted above refers to soldiers who take a receptive role in sexual relations with other soldiers and, for that, should be severely prosecuted (Phang 2001: 282); however, no evidence directly indicates that sexual relations between soldiers were illicit. What can be gleaned from literary evidence is that as long as the relations were within the boundaries of Roman sexual protocol, they would have been condoned (Phang 2001: 278–82; Williams 2010: 19, 130–6; Leitao 2014: 232–3, 235, 237; Skinner 2014: 257–8). However, even within Roman texts, there is mention that, in some cases, the protocol was violated: they refer to illicit sexual relations by Roman men with freeborn males (Williams 2010: 110, 135, 137 and especially Appendix 2 addressing marriages between freeborn males). Again, such instances underscore the variability of sexual relations beneath the umbrella of phallocentrism, where it was always possible to choose how to behave and which roles to take within structures of sexuality, even if certain behaviours and roles could provoke social judgement and ridicule (Eger 2007; Flemming 2010: 807).

If the same method is applied in searching for such relations—for example, on an expensive monument commemorating a fellow soldier without any mention of female heirs, wives, or children—then monuments depicting two men side by side can be considered to represent cases of same-sex sexual relations between soldiers. For instance, a tombstone from Celje, Slovenia, commemorating Aurelius Gaianus, a decurion, who died at the age of 50, depicts two men dressed in similar fashion (ILJug-01, 00389 = Illpron 01601 = lupa.at/ 674). The epitaph commemorates another man, Aurelius Maximus, who died at the age of 35 and is recorded as *nepos* ('nephew'). Two other people mentioned on the inscription are men as well, although the nature of their relationship with either Gaianus or Maximus is not established. It is possible that *nepos* was used figuratively to conceal or politely refer to a same-sex sexual relationship in order to uphold the official code of conduct. This would suggest that such relationships were allowed to be recorded but only in a way that suited public opinion. Another similar all-male tombstone is that of 25-year-old Aurelius Maximus, of no relation to the previously mentioned Aurelius Maximus, by his brother, Aurelius Bassus, and a certain Aurelius Sabinus, the nature of whose relationship to either Maximus or Bassus remains unknown, though he is recorded as coming from the same village as them (CIL III 11701 = lupa.at/ 3614).

Apart from the epitaphs, there are portraits without any accompanying text, such as a funerary stone medallion of two unnamed soldiers from Graz, Austria (lupa.at/1208), that uncannily resemble many such medallions depicting a man and a woman (e.g. lupa.at/304; 306; 831; 833; 834; 837; 839; 5744). The use of such stone medallions has been confined to the Roman province of Noricum, and out of approximately 130 monuments of that type recorded in the lupa.at database, only three show couples other than a male–female pair. One depicts the couple of the abovementioned soldiers, whereas another bears the image of two women (lupa.at/835, Friesach, Austria). In both cases, one person has placed a hand on the shoulder of the other, in a stance commonly employed in funerary art to signify either marriage or a familial relationship (e.g., mother–son, mother–daughter, and father–son). By contrast, the third stone medallion depicts two men dressed in military cloaks (Figure 8.8). Although each medallion might depict a parent and his or her child, what suggests otherwise is the way in which the figures are positioned on the tombstones. In all cases in which medallions depict male–female couples, the figures are positioned on the same level. Conversely, in portraits of fathers and sons (Figure 8.9; see also lupa.at/4141 from Crnci, Slovenia, and 26274 from Bjelovar, Croatia) or family portraits, the artistic convention seems to have been to depict children as smaller than, and positioned in front of and below, their parent(s) in order to emphasise their status and age (see also Figure 8.3). By comparison, the three medallions discussed above all show figures positioned on the same level, as does Pytha and Felix's monument.

How might those monuments be interpreted? Undoubtedly, they are complicated cases, and viewing them as an open record of same-sex sexual relations may constitute overt sexualisation for which no explicit evidence exists. However, because their outward appearance coincides in stylistic and artistic

Figure 8.8 Gravestone depicting two soldiers, Seggauberg, Austria, lupa.at/1329
(© and photo O. Harl)

conventions with funerary portraits depicting male–female couples and families, I argue that the monuments record the same-sex sexual relations of men and women of equal status that operated outside Roman sexual protocol.

Overall, some monuments discussed in this chapter exhibit behaviour typically associated with Roman sexual protocol. A few, however, contain somewhat ambiguous evidence of changes to or adaptations of the said protocol across the Roman Empire: the preference for somewhat older males, records of relations using visual conventions instead of epigraphic formulae, and the practice of manumitting sexual partners. To clarify whether such adaptations resulted from different attitudes towards sexuality and different gender systems in operation across the multicultural societies that populated the Roman provinces and frontiers, scholars need data from other chronological periods with which to make comparisons. Unfortunately, such data have not been generated (Aldhouse-Green 2004: 77–82). The topics of sexuality and gender behaviour remain under-developed in studies of Iron Age and pre-Roman societies (Moore and Armada 2011b: 55–6; also Pope 2007, 2018; Pope and Ralston 2011). Whether same-sex sexual relations existed in Iron Age societies and whether same-sex

Figure 8.9 Tomb relief depicting Aurelius Bitus, musician from *Legio II Adiutrix*, and his son Vitalis, Budapest, Hungary. Kept in Aquincum Museum, inv. nr. 64.10.7; lupa.at/ 2846

(Photo O. Harl, courtesy and © BHM–Aquincum Museum)

sexual intercourse was practised should not be questioned, for they surely were, and scholars need to 'stop taking heterosexuality for granted' (Joyce 2008: 90). Instead, the question is how those relations were perceived. Although Roman authors attested to broadly positive 'Celtic' attitudes towards same-sex sexual relations (Strabo *Geography* 4.4.6; Aristotle *Politics* 2.6.5-6/1269b; Chapter 6), variability across time and space is not acknowledged in such over-generalising statements (McCoskey 2005).

The coming of Rome into the provinces and the appropriation of Roman attitudes on sexual relations might have created new boundaries to understanding one's sexuality and catalysed the reorganisation of gender and sexual behaviours. The advent of Roman imperial rule would have thus resulted in the emergence of new forms of masculinity, in which sexual practices were reshaped under the umbrella of phallocentrism, and priapic sexuality was formalised in the provinces to such an extent that it pushed the boundaries for the transformation of cultural norms related to sexual practices (Mattingly 2011: 96–8). Indeed, such regulations are discernible in imperial encounters in other periods (Conkey and Spector 1998: 29). For instance, Voss (2010: 272) has written about the architecture of sexual control and sexual politics in colonial institutions in eighteenth-century Spanish military settlements in the Americas and, in doing so, provided cases of the regulation and restructuring of indigenous female sexuality (see Chapter 6 on similar threads in the Romano-British context; Voss 2000).

In the context of Roman imperialism, new forms of same-sex sexual behaviour and new attitudes towards such relations might have emerged alongside heightened attention to soldierly hegemonic masculinity as projected by the Roman state. Meanwhile, same-sex sexual relations based on structural dominance might have started to surface as a cultural norm. The increased surveillance of the fulfilment of the priapic protocol might have also spurred new ways of commemoration, such that individuals recorded as slaves or freedmen might not have had such status, which was used only figuratively as 'a subtle code for same-sex relations' (Sarah Levin-Richardson, personal communication). Such a code might have been applied to indicate existing relationships that suited priapic norms and, in that way, skirt social judgement. It could also have been part of a cultural vocabulary clearly understood by the parties involved. Although that hypothesis may seem far-fetched, striking similarities in the way that unofficial female spouses of soldiers were commemorated indicate a specific practice in Roman culture. As long as affairs were kept private, illicit activities were tolerated by society, because public acknowledgement of such activities would only end in social disruption (Williams 2010: 212). Although soldiers were banned from marrying by law, unofficial, informal unions were widely formed, socially recognised, and tolerated (Phang 2001; Greene 2015). Leitao (2014: 232, citing Saller and Shaw 1984) has indicated that due to the marriage ban, soldiers were infrequently commemorated by their unofficial spouses or commemorated them in return. The preference not to record openly relations on everlasting tombstones may have been a direct outcome of fear of punishment and legal sanctions for the surviving members of the family. It might have been that similar unofficial rules applied to persons involved in same-sex sexual relations; communities knew and tolerated them, but they were not officially promoted. Neither having unofficial wives amid the marriage ban nor same-sex sexual relationships was likely to be regularly recorded, because 'the power protocols that structured normative Roman sexuality' did not allow their open functioning (Leitao 2014: 237). Accordingly, strong wishes to record 'below-the-horizon' relationships, whether with women or men, for posterity were fulfilled in ways that did not violate official codes of conduct or formalised norms and that suited public opinion. For that reason, it is possible that scholars today cannot see those relationships, even with their eyes wide open, and that recognising privacy and a fear of disturbing the public order can be keys to understanding the absence of explicit testimonies of same-sex sexual relations amongst Roman soldiers (Phang 2001: 295).

Conclusion: beyond a compulsory heterosexual masculinity framework

I began this chapter with an exploration of Roman soldierly identity, particularly in relation to sexual and masculine categories that can be reconstructed from Latin texts and epigraphic sources, and I end this contribution on a similarly exploratory note. The chapter's discussions of hegemonic and non-hegemonic masculinities, same-sex sexual relations between soldiers/patrons and slaves, and a few possible cases of such relations between freeborn persons have only touched upon some of the complex sexual dynamics likely in operation in the Roman military environment in Roman provinces and frontiers.

First, divergent multiple masculinities were culturally and temporally specific in the Roman Mediterranean and in the provinces (Halperin 1996, 2015; Skinner 2014: 270–1; Masterson 2014a; Chapter 6). Although the accumulated data from various regions indicate widespread hegemonic masculinity in the Roman military milieu, a few signs of non-hegemonic masculinities or other 'below-the-horizon' masculinities are nevertheless evident. Ethnic differences in constructions of masculinity must be taken into account as each individual unit consisted of an astounding array of soldiers from various corners of the Roman world. Although complex gender spectra that went beyond the simple binary male–female system, and the coexistence of variable gender roles with roots in societies predating the expansion of the Roman Empire, may have been in operation in each unit (Pope and Ralston 2011; Chapter 6), the shortage of data makes forming any meaningful conclusion difficult.

Second, cross-cultural variability in sexual practices existed in societies that formed the Roman world. The described image of a dominant penetrating male—the priapic *vir*—derived from a system discernible in Latin texts written by elite males to be read by an elite male audience (Matthews 1994: 122; Flemming 2010: 811; Williams 2010: 9; Holmes 2012: 99–100; Skinner 2014: 321). The Roman sexual protocol described here might not have been taken for granted beyond Rome and the Mediterranean, however, and, in some situations, it might have even been transcended. Scholars of Roman sexuality often tend to imagine the universal adoption of Roman sexual conventions in the provinces; however, because individual identity is complex and multifaceted (Eckardt 2014: 4), the sexual facet of identity should also be conceived as such (see Halperin 1998: 109 on the term *sexual identity*). Even if the complexity of sexual identities within the Roman Empire at the provincial level is a given (Phang 2001: 265; Flemming 2010: 798; Williams 2010: 250; Mattingly 2011: 95; Vucetic 2014: 141; Chapter 6), it remains necessary to establish methods by which models of same-sex sexual behaviour can be constructed. The textually and visually based evidence analysed in this chapter has confirmed the basic premise that same-sex sexual relations were common in Roman military communities (Ivleva 2018a). By extension, archaeological evidence has the potential to reveal additional clues and expand current understanding of same-sex sexual practices, although only if the right research questions are asked (Voss 2000: 54). Specifically, to chart changes and continuities in the expression of sexual behaviours and practices, it might prove fruitful to integrate actively prehistoric data, including information about double-gender figurines or burials with assemblages atypical for the biological sex of the deceased (Aldhouse-Green 2004; Pope 2007, 2018; Pope and Ralston 2011; but see Allason-Jones 1995).

At a bare minimum, this chapter suggests that, for most north-western regions and especially the frontiers of the Roman Empire, in situating same-sex sexual relations in the Roman military scholars need to abandon androcentric readings of masculinity. It is not singular and as unstable as gender itself, given the multiple genders, masculinities, and femininities in existence (Knapp 1998: 369; Masterson 2014a: 18; Chapter 6). Moreover, I have argued that same-sex relations existed in the Roman army alongside the predominance of the hegemonic masculinity paradigm imposed on soldiers. That such relations were relatively common in a wider provincial context has been met with some resistance in academic circles. Many times, the relationships discussed have been suggested to represent nothing more than friendships. However, such readings take a distorted perspective, and the examples offered here contribute to mounting evidence of the variability in relations under the umbrella of phallocentrism. This contribution has extended the evidence of variability to soldiers on the edges of the Roman world.

Acknowledgements

I would like to express my gratitude to Sarah Levin-Richardson, Rob Collins, and Uroš Matić, as each offered valuable comments upon an early draft of the chapter, which helped me to sharpen the development of its arguments. The responsibility for the interpretations offered here and all errors made are my own.

Bibliography

Aldhouse-Green, M. (2004). *An Archaeology of Images. Iconology and Cosmology in Iron Age and Roman Europe*. London: Routledge.

Allason-Jones, L. (1995). "Sexing' Small Finds", in P. Rush (ed.), *Theoretical Roman Archaeology: Second Conference Proceedings*. Avebury: Aldershot, 22–32.

Allason-Jones, L. (1999). "Women and the Roman Army in Britain", in Goldsworthy and Haynes (1999), 41–51.

Allason-Jones, L. (2004). "The Family in Roman Britain", in M. Todd (ed.), *A Companion to Roman Britain*. Oxford: Wiley, 273–88.

Allason-Jones, L. unpubl. **"Attitudes to Sex and Marriage in Roman Britain",** [Unpublished typescript presented at a seminar at St. Hilda's College, Oxford as part of a series 'Sex in the Ancient World'].

Allison, P. (2011). "Soldiers' Families in the Early Roman Empire", in B. Rawson (ed.), *A Companion to Families in the Greek and Roman Worlds*. Malden, MA: Wiley, 161–83.

Baird, J.A. (2015) "On Reading the Material Culture of Ancient Sexual Labor", *Helios*, 42 (1): 163–75.

Beaudry, M.C., Cook, L.J. and Mrozowski, S.A. (1991). "Artifacts and Active Voices: Material Culture as Social Discourse", in R.H. McGuire and R. Paynter (eds), *The Archaeology of Inequality*. Oxford: Blackwell, 150–91.

Blondell, R. and Ormand, K. eds, (2015). *Ancient Sex. New Essays*. Columbus: The Ohio State University Press.

Boswell, J. (1994). *Same-Sex Unions in Pre-Modern Europe*. Oxford and New York: Vintage.

Brandl, U. (2008) "'Soldatenbräute' – Ausgewählte epigraphische Zeugnisse zum Verhältnis zwischen römischen Soldaten und Frauen", in U. Brandl (ed.), *Frauen und römisches Militar. Beitrage eines Runden Tisches in Xanten vom 7. bis 9. Juli 2005*. British Archaeological Reports International Series, Band 1759. Oxford: Archaeopress, 62–65.

Butrica, J.L. (2005). "Some Myths and Anomalies in the Study of Roman Sexuality", *Journal of Homosexuality*, 49 (3/4): 209–69.

Clarke, J. (1993). "The Warren Cup and the Contexts for Representations of Male-to-Male Lovemaking in Augustan and Early Julio-Claudian Art", *The Art Bulletin*, 75: 275–94.

Clarke, J. (2005). "Representations of the *Cinaedus* in Roman Art: Evidence of 'Gay' Subculture", *Journal of Homosexuality*, 49 (3/4): 271–98.

Collins, R. (2008). "Identity in the Frontier: Theory and Multiple Community Interfacing", in C. Fenwick, M. Wiggins and D. Wythe (eds), *TRAC 2007: Proceedings of the Seventeenth Annual Theoretical Roman Archaeology Conference, London 2007*. Oxford: Oxbow Books, 45–52.

Collins, R. and Ivleva, T. (2018). "Introduction: Sex on the Frontiers. Textual and Material Representations of Human Sexuality at the Edge of Empire", in Sommer and Matešić (2018), 1035–38.

Conkey, M.W. and Spector, J.D. (1998). "Archaeology and the Study of Gender", in Hayes-Gilpin and Whitley (1998), 11–47.

Connell, R.W. (2005[1995]). *Masculinities*. Cambridge: Polity Press.

Cool, H.E.M. (2002). "An Overview of the Small Finds from Catterick", in P.R. Wilson (ed.), *Cataractonium: Roman Catterick and Its Hinterland. Excavations and Research, 1958–1997. Vol 2*. York: Council for British Archaeology, 24–43.

Cool, H.E.M. (2004). *The Roman Cemetery at Brougham: Excavations 1966–67.* Britannia Monograph Series no. 21. London: Society for the Promotion of Roman Studies.

Coulston, J. (2014). "Monumentalising Military Service: Soldiers in Romano-British Sculpture", in R. Collins and F. McIntosh (eds), *Life in the Limes. Studies of the People and Objects of the Roman Frontiers.* Oxford: Oxbow Books, 65–79.

Coulston, J.C.N. ed., (1988). *Military Equipment and the Identity of Roman Soldiers. Proceedings of the Fourth Roman Military Equipment Conference.* British Archaeological Reports International Series 394. Oxford: Archaeopress.

Díaz-Andreu, M. (2005). "Gender Identity", in M. Díaz-Andreu, S. Lucy, S. Babić and D. N. Edwards (eds), *The Archaeology of Identity: Approaches to Gender, Age, Status, Ethnicity and Religion.* London: Routledge, 13–43.

Eckardt, H. (2014). *Objects and Identities: Roman Britain and the North-Western Provinces.* Oxford: Oxford University Press.

Eger, A.A. (2007). "Age and Male Sexuality: 'Queer Space' in the Roman Bath-house", in M. Harlow and R. Laurence (eds), *Age and Ageing in the Roman Empire.* Journal of Roman Archaeology Supplementary Series 65. Portsmouth, RI: Journal of Roman Archaeology, 131–52.

Flemming, R. (2010). "Sexuality", in A. Barchiesi and W. Scheidel (eds), *The Oxford Handbook of Roman Studies.* Oxford: Oxford University Press, 797–815.

Foucault, M. (1985 [1984]). *The History of Sexuality. Vol. 2. The Use of Pleasure.* Trans. By R. Hurley. New York: Penguin Books.

Foucault, M. (1986 [1984]). *The History of Sexuality. Vol. 3. The Care of the Self. Trans. By R. Hurley.* New York: Penguin Books.

Friedl, R. (1996). *Der Konkubinat im kaiserzeitlichen Rom: Von Augustus bis Septimius Severus.* Historia-Einzelschriften, Band 98. Stuttgart: Franz Steiner Verlag.

Gardner, A. (2007). *An Archaeology of Identity. Soldiers and Society in Late Roman Britain.* Walnut Creek, CA: Left Coast Press.

Gleason, M.W. (1990). "The Semiotics of Gender: Physiognomy and Self-Fashioning in the Second Century C.E.", in D.M. Halperin, J.J. Winkler and F.I. Zeitlin (eds), *Before Sexuality: The Construction of Erotic Experience in the Ancient Greek World.* Princeton, NJ: Princeton University Press, 389–415.

Gleason, M.W. (1995). *Making Men: Sophists and Self-Presentation in Ancient Rome.* Princeton, NJ: Princeton University Press.

Goldsworthy, A. and Haynes, I.P. eds, (1999). *The Roman Army as a Community, Including Papers of a Conference Held at Birkbeck College, University of London on 11–12 January, 1997.* Journal of Roman Archaeology Supplementary Series no 34. Portsmouth, RI: Journal of Roman Archaeology.

Greene, E.M. (2011). *Women and Families in the Auxiliary Military Communities of the Roman West in the First and Second Centuries AD.* Unpubl. PhD dissertation, Univ. of North Carolina at Chapel Hill.

Greene, E.M. (2015). "*Conubium Cum Uxoribus*: Wives and Children in the Roman Military Diplomas", *Journal of Roman Archaeology*, 28: 125–59.

Greene, E.M. (2016). "Identities and Social Roles of Women in Military Settlements in the Roman West", in S. Budin and J. Turfa (eds), *Women in Antiquity: Real Women across the Ancient World.* London: Routledge, 942–53.

Halperin, D. (1996). *Saint Foucault: Towards a Gay Hagiography.* Oxford: Oxford University Press.

Halperin, D. (1998). "Forgetting Foucault: Acts, Identities, and the History of Sexuality", *Representations*, 63: 93–120.

Halperin, D. (2015). "Not Fade Away", in Blondell and Ormand (2015), 308–29.

Hayes-Gilpin, K. and Whitley, D.S. eds, (1998). *Reader in Gender Archaeology*. London: Routledge.

Haynes, I. (2013). *Blood of the Provinces. The Roman Auxilia and the Making of Provincial Society from Augustus to the Severans*. Oxford: Oxford University Press.

Haynes, I. (2016). "Identity and the Military Community in Roman Britain", in Millett et al. (2016), 448–64.

Haynes, I. (1999). "Introduction: The Roman Army as a Community", in Goldsworthy and Haynes (1999), 7–13.

Herdt, G.H. (1981). *Guardians of the Flutes: Idioms of Masculinity*. New York: McGraw Hill.

Holmes, B. (2012). *Gender. Antiquity and Its Legacy*. Oxford: Oxford University Press.

Hoss, S. (2012). "The Roman Military Belt", in M.-L. Nosch (ed.), *Wearing the Cloak. Dressing the Soldier in Roman Times*. Oxford: Oxbow Books, 29–45.

Hoss, S. (2014). *CINGULUM MILITARIS. Studien zum römischen Soldatengürtel vom 1. bis zum 3. Jh. n. Chr.* Unpubl. PhD thesis, Leiden University.

Hubbard, T.K. ed., (2014). *A Companion to Greek and Roman Sexualities*. Malden, MA: Blackwell Publishing.

Ivleva, T. (2018a). "Same-Sex and Polygamous/Polygynous Unions in the Northwest Roman Provinces and Frontiers", in Sommer and Matešić (2018), 1051–57.

Ivleva, T. (2018b). "Multifunctionality of a Romano-British Glass Bangle: Between Theory and Practice", in T. Ivleva, J. de Bruin and M. Driessen (eds), *Embracing the Provinces: Society and Material Culture of the Roman Frontier Regions*. Oxford: Oxbow Books, 71–87.

James, S. (1999). "The Community of the Soldiers: A Major Identity and Centre of Power in the Roman Empire", in P. Baker, C. Forcey, S. Jundi and R. Witcher (eds), *TRAC 98: Proceedings of the Eighth Annual Theoretical Roman Archaeology Conference*. Oxford: Oxbow Books, 14–25.

James, S.T. (2001). "Soldiers and Civilians: Identity and Interaction in Roman Britain", in S. James and M. Millett (eds), *Britons and Romans: Advancing and Archaeological Agenda*. CBA Research Report 125. York: Council for British Archaeology, 77–89.

Johns, C. (1982). *Sex or Symbol. Erotic Images of Greece and Rome*. London: British Museum Publications.

Joyce, R.A. (2008). *Ancient Bodies, Ancient Lives: Sex, Gender, and Archaeology*. London: Thames and Hudson.

Juntunen, K. (2018). "'Married with Children'–The Marital Patterns of Roman Auxiliary Soldiers in the *Diplomata Militaria*", in Sommer and Matešić (2018), 1039–45.

Kamen, D. and Levin-Richardson, S. (2015a). "Revisiting Roman Sexuality. Agency and the Conceptualization of Penetrated Males", in M. Masterson, N. Sorkin Rabinowitz and J. Robson (eds), *Sex in Antiquity. Exploring Gender and Sexuality in the Ancient World*. London: Routledge, 449–60.

Kamen, D. and Levin-Richardson, S. (2015b). "Lusty Ladies in the Roman Imaginary", in Blondell and Ormand (2015), 231–52.

Knapp, A.B. (1998). "Boys Will Be Boys. Masculinist Approaches to a Gendered Archaeology", in Hayes-Gilpin and Whitley (1998), 365–74.

Laes, C. (2011). *Children in the Roman Empire. Outsiders Within*. Cambridge: Cambridge University Press.

Langlands, R. (2006). *Sexual Morality in Ancient Rome*. Cambridge: Cambridge University Press.

Leitao, D.D. (2014). "Sexuality in Greek and Roman Military Context", in Hubbard (2014), 230–44.

Levin-Richardson, S. (2013). "*Fututa Sum Hic*: Female Subjectivity and Agency in Pompeian Sexual Graffiti", *Classical Journal*, 108: 319–45.

Masterson, M. (2014a). "Studies of Ancient Masculinity", in Hubbard (2014), 19–32.

Masterson, M. (2014b). *Man to Man. Desire, Homosociality, and Authority in Late-Roman Manhood*. Columbus: Ohio State University Press.

Matić, U. (2012). "To Queer or Not to Queer? That Is the Question: Sex/ Gender, Prestige and Burial No. 10 on the Mokrin Necropolis", *Dacia*, LVI: 169–85.

Matthews, K. (1999). "The Material Culture of the Homosexual Male: A Case for Archaeological Exploration", in M. Donald and L. Hurcombe (eds), *Gender and Material Culture in Archaeological Perspective*. London: Macmillan, 3–19.

Matthews, K. (1994). "An Archaeology of Homosexuality? Perspectives from the Classical World", in S. Cottam, D. Dungworth, S. Scott and J. Taylor (eds), *TRAC 94: Proceedings of the Fourth Annual Theoretical Roman Archaeology Conference*. Oxford: Oxbow Books, 118–32.

Mattingly, D. (2011). *Imperialism, Power and Identity Experiencing the Roman Empire*. Princeton, NJ: Princeton University Press.

Maxfield, V.A. (1981). *The Military Decorations of the Roman Army*. London: Batsford.

McCoskey, D.E. (2005). "Gender at the Crossroads of Empire: Locating Women in Strabo's Geography", in D. Dueck, H. Lindsay and S. Pothecay (eds), *Strabo's Cultural Geography: The Making of a Kolossourgia*. Cambridge: Cambridge University Press, 56–72.

McDonnell, M. (2006). *Roman Manliness. Virtus and the Roman Republic*. Cambridge: Cambridge University Press.

Meskell, L. (2001). "Archaeologies of Identity", in I. Hodder (ed.), *Archaeological Theory*. Cambridge: Polity, 187–213.

Millett, M., Revell, L. and Moore, A. eds, (2016). *The Oxford Handbook of Roman Britain*. Oxford: Oxford University Press.

Montserrat, D. (1996). *Sex and Society in Graeco-Roman Egypt*. London: Routledge.

Moore, T. and Armada, X.-L. eds, (2011a). *Atlantic Europe in the First Millennium BC: Crossing the Divide*. Oxford: Oxford University Press.

Moore, T. and Armada, X.-L. (2011b). "Crossing the Divide: Opening a Dialogue on Approaches to Western European First Millennium BC Studies", in Moore and Armada (2011a), 3–81.

Moral, E. (2016). "Qu(e)erying Sex and Gender in Archaeology: A Critique of the 'Third' and Other Sexual Categories", *Journal of Archaeological Method and Theory*, 23: 788–809.

Olson, K. (2014). "Masculinity, Appearance, and Sexuality: Dandies in Roman Antiquity", *Journal of the History of Sexuality*, 23 (2): 182–205.

Olson, K. (2017). *Masculinity and Dress in Roman Antiquity*. London and New York: Routledge.

Ormand, K. and Blondell, R. (2015). "One Hundred and Twenty-Five Years of Homosexuality", in Blondell and Ormand (2015), 1–22.

Orrells, D. (2015). *Sex. Antiquity and Its Legacy.* Oxford: Oxford University Press.

Parker, H. (1997). "The Teratogenic Grid", in J. Hallett and M. Skinner (eds), *Roman Sexualities*. Princeton, NJ: Princeton University Press, 47–65.

Perry, M.P. (2014). *Gender, Manumission, and the Roman Freedwoman.* Cambridge: Cambridge University Press.

Phang, S.E. (2001). *The Marriage of Roman Soldiers (13 BC–AD 235): Law and Family in the Imperial Army.* Leiden: Brill.

Pinto, R. and Pinto, L.C.G. (2013). "Transgendered Archaeology: The Galli and the Catterick Transvestite", in A. Bokern, M. Bolder-Boos, S. Krmnicek, D. Maschek and S. Page (eds), *TRAC 2012: Proceedings of the Twenty-Second Annual Theoretical Roman Archaeology Conference, Frankfurt 2012.* Oxford: Oxbow Books, 169–81.

Pope, R. and Ralston, I. (2011). "Approaching Sex and Status in Iron Age Britain with Reference to the Nearer Continent", in Moore and Armada (2011a), 375–417.

Pope, R.E. (2007). "Ritual and Roundhouse: A Critique of Recent Ideas on Domestic Space in Later British Prehistory", in C. Haselgrove and R. Pope (eds), *The Earlier Iron Age in Britain and the near Continent.* Oxford: Oxbow Books, 204–28.

Pope, R.E. (2018). "Gender and Society", in C. Haselgrove, K. Rebay-Salisbury and P.S. Wells (eds), *The Oxford Handbook of the European Iron Age.* Oxford: Oxford University Press. doi:10.1093/oxfordhb/9780199696826.013.4

Preucel, R.W. and Mrozowski, S.A. eds, (2010). *Contemporary Archaeology in Theory: The New Pragmatism.* Second Edition. Chichester: Wiley-Blackwell.

Rich, A. (1980). "Compulsory Heterosexuality and Lesbian Existence", *Signs: A Journal of Women in Culture and Society,* 5/4: 631–60.

Richlin, A. (1992[1983]). *The Garden of Priapus: Sexuality and Aggression in Roman Humor.* Revised edition. New York: Oxford University Press.

Richlin, A. (1993). "Not before Homosexuality: The Materiality of the *Cinaedus* and the Roman Law against Love between Men", *Journal of the History of Sexuality,* 3/4: 523–73.

Saller, R. and Shaw, B. (1984). "Tombstones and Roman Family Relations in the Principate: Civilians, Soldiers, and Slaves", *Journal of Roman Studies,* 74: 124–55.

Sherratt, M. and Moore, A. (2016). "Gender in Roman Britain", in Millett et al. (2016), 363–81.

Skinner, M.B. (2014). *Sexuality in Greek and Roman Culture.* Second edition. Malden, MA: Wiley.

Smith, D. (1959). "A Palmyrene Sculptor at South Shields?", *Archaeologia Aeliana,* Ser. 4, 37: 203–10.

Sommer, C.S. and Matešić, S. eds, (2018). *Limes XXIII – Proceedings of the 23rd International Congress of Roman Frontier Studies Ingolstadt 2015. Akten Des 23. Internationalen Limeskongresses in Ingolstadt 2015.* Beiträge zum Welterbe Limes Sonderband 4. Mainz: Nünnerich-Asmus Verlag.

Voss, B. (2000). "Colonial Sex: Archaeology, Structured Space, and Sexuality in Alta California's Spanish-Colonial Missions", in R.A.S. Schmidt and B.L. Voss (eds), *Archaeologies of Sexuality.* London: Routledge, 35–62.

Voss, B. (2008). "Sexuality Studies in Archaeology", *Annual Review of Anthropology,* 37: 317–36.

Voss, B. (2010). "Domesticating Imperialism: Sexual Politics and the Archaeology of Empire", in Preucel and Mrozowski (2010), 265–81.

Vucetic, S. (2014). "Roman Sexuality or Roman Sexualities? Looking at Sexual Imagery on Roman Terracotta Mould-made Lamps", in H. Platts, J. Pearce, C. Barron, J. Lundock and J. Yoo (eds), *TRAC 2013: Proceedings of the Twenty-Third Annual Theoretical Roman Archaeology Conference, King's College, London 2013*. Oxford: Oxbow Books, 140–58.

Walters, J. (1997). "Invading the Roman Body: Manliness and Impenetrability in Roman Thought", in J.P. Hallett and M.B. Skinner (eds), *Roman Sexualities*. Princeton, NJ: Princeton University Press, 29–47.

Williams, C.A. (2010). *Roman Homosexuality: Ideologies of Masculinity in Classical Antiquity*. Oxford: Oxford University Press.

Zeeland, S. (1993). *Barrack Buddies and Soldier Lovers*. New York: Harrington Park Press.

Zeeland, S. (1995). *Sailors and Sexual Identity: Crossing the Line between 'Straight' and 'Gay' in the U.S. Navy*. New York: Harrington Park Press.

Zeeland, S. (1997). *The Masculine Marine: Homoeroticism in the U.S. Marine Corps*. New York: Harrington Park Press.

9 The phallus and the frontier

The form and function of phallic imagery along Hadrian's Wall

Rob Collins

Introduction

The phallus is a ubiquitous symbol across the ancient world, visualised across the spectrum in exquisite (or excruciating) naturalistic detail to abstracted iconographic representations (Chapters 4, 5, and 10). These representations are not limited to a single medium, but are found in sculpture, portable objects, mosaics, frescoes, and more generic carvings. As has been eloquently argued and appreciated for some time now (Johns 1982), the phallus can be symptomatic of eroticism in the Roman world, but it often invoked and performed a magical, apotropaic function (see Chapters 4 and 10). While undeniably true, the apotropaic function covers a broad range of use and intention. Archaeology offers the potential to explore and refine our understanding of the magic and/or erotic phallus, particularly in those instances where a phallus is found *in situ* and with an associated context. Given that Pompeii is commonly held up as an example of the frequency and commonality of phalli in the Roman world, it is essential to explore the frequency and occurrence of phalli in other locations and cultural situations.

The Hadrian's Wall corridor boasts a number of phalli in stone and fashioned as objects, many of which were discovered *in situ*, and some of these remain *in situ*. In this regard, it is important to understand that Hadrian's Wall is not a simple monument consisting solely of an extensive wall built in one episode. Rather, it is a monumental complex built *c.*A.D. 120 and occupied by the Roman army until at least the early fifth century A.D. There are multiple phases of building just in the Hadrianic period, with further changes made subsequently; there is also a long and rich research history with an established specialist lexicon (Breeze 2014; Hodgson 2017). The Wall is best understood as a system of layered components, the most fundamental of which is a monumental wall—known as the curtain to specialists—that connects a series of installations together in a linear fashion. The largest installations are forts, typically the base of a 500-strong army unit, with an extramural settlement. Located approximately every mile (or 1.6 km) is a small fortlet known as a milecastle, and spaced evenly between each milecastle are two towers known as turrets. Bridges were built across major rivers, carrying the curtain in an uninterrupted fashion. The curtain is also complex, having been built in varying widths at different points in its construction, with the western third of the Wall originally executed in turf and timber and subsequently replaced with a stone construction. Furthermore, Hadrian's Wall is not *the* frontier, but a monumental focus of the Roman army in a much larger frontier region that broadly corresponds to the area north of the Humber estuary and south of the Firth of Forth. In this chapter, "Wall" refers to the monumental complex, and "curtain", "bridge", or another specific term will be used when appropriate.

Phalli have been encountered along the Wall throughout its long history of investigation. Excavations undertaken at the behest of John Clayton in the later nineteenth century revealed a large phallus in relief on a raised circular base on a flagstone found in the courtyard of the *principia* at Chesters fort (Figure 9.1),

Figure 9.1 The phallus carved in relief in the centre-front of the image, located on a paving stone in the *principia* courtyard of Chesters fort

(© Rob Collins)

and Clayton's stone collection also boasts a number of further phalli (CSIR I.1, nos 405–7). It is notable that phalli were not hidden in a "secret cabinet" or destroyed due to their base or vulgar imagery. During the course of research, only one example of destruction was encountered, found at Maryport in the seventeenth or early eighteenth century (Gordon 1726: 100): "Mr Sen-house … told me, there was a *Penis* cut in *Relievo*, which was so offensive to chaste Eyes, that they caus'd it to be broke and destroy'd." Yet, it should also be noted that no synthetic treatment of those phalli discovered along the Wall has previously been undertaken. No doubt, these discoveries alongside those made in the other *limites* of the Roman Empire created and sustained the association between phallic imagery and the Roman army (Parker 2017), but the topic has yet to be explored in great detail or consistently across all the former provinces of the Roman Empire. This chapter takes a focused approach in compiling a catalogue for the Hadrian's Wall World Heritage Site, adding to Parker's (2017) initial study of phallic stones from the northern frontier zone of Britain.

The frequency with which phalli can be found along Hadrian's Wall begs questions about the significance of phalli in the frontiers. A common assumption, often overheard from visitors' comments at sites along Hadrian's Wall, sees phalli as graffiti, with bored Roman soldiers scratching the proverbial "cock and balls" onto stone in much the same fashion as a bored student scrawls one into his school textbook. While it is impossible to dismiss the possibility of graffiti entirely, there are enough examples of phalli carved in relief, requiring a higher investment of time and skill, that the blanket assumption can be challenged.

A study of phalli along the Wall carved into or out of stone has produced a catalogue of 59 confirmed examples (see Appendix 9.1), with 37 of these (63 per cent) associated with a primary or secondary archaeological context. These figures do not include portable objects that bear phallic imagery (see Chapters 4, 5, and 10), nor are ithyphallic figures or stone monuments that could be described as phalloform included. Not only are ithyphallic figures like Priapus and phalloform monuments like the Serpent Stone from Maryport (Coulston 1997: 121–3) relatively rare along Hadrian's Wall, but they are likely to have other functions and associations than a phallus on its own. Therefore, the catalogue includes specimens that are only a phallus (including testicles) carved into or out of stone, with one exception on a ceramic tile. The number of stone phalli and high incidence of associated contexts provides two opportunities. First, the phalli can be considered as a cohesive assemblage, executed by the people of the Wall communities. This provides an opportunity to look at the diversity of execution and distribution across space and time. Second, contextual associations provide the opportunity to explore more nuanced readings of phallic imagery, looking beyond the basic question of graffiti or apotropaic intentions. Contextual associations provide site-specific intentions to be inferred, and this highlights occurrences of consistent placement. Arguably, it also points toward a better understanding of Hadrian's Wall itself, challenging our understanding beyond that of a purely physical barrier. Therefore, the approach undertaken here can be classed as materialist, in contrast to more theoretical or conceptual approaches to phallic symbolism (see Chapter 4).

A wall of willies?

The catalogue presented in Appendix 9.1 consists of 59 individual phalli recorded from 22 different sites across the Wall corridor and the Cumbrian coast, from South Shields at the mouth of the River Tyne to Maryport on the Irish Sea. These 59 phalli have been carved on 50 different stones. Two larger stones were carved with multiple phalli. A substantial block from the burial monument at Shorden Brae outside Corbridge had four phalli on one face and two further phalli on an adjacent face (cat. nos 27–32; Gillam and Daniels 1961: 51–2). A second stone at Vindolanda had phalli on three faces, with a pair of phalli side by side on one face (cat. nos 47 and 48), a "double" phallus on an adjacent end face (cat. no. 50), and a single phallus on a broad face (cat. no. 49). These two stones are the exception, however, and all other stone carved with phalli have only borne a single example, with two notable exceptions. The quarry face at Gelt has two phalli carved into it, but the size of the face and different location of the phalli means that the face should not be considered a single stone. The second exception is a stone bearing a phallus from the fort at South Shields (cat. no. 34) on one flat face; it also has an ithyphallic figure carved into the face of the opposite side (Croom 1998). These are considered in more detail below.

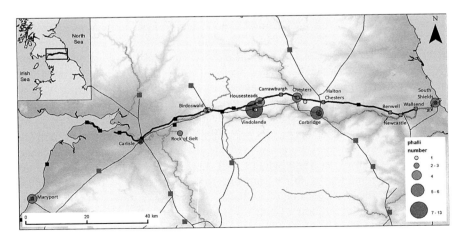

Figure 9.2 The distribution of phalli along Hadrian's Wall, by site

(© Rob Collins, created by Nicky Garland)

The phalli are not distributed evenly along the Wall corridor (Figure 9.2). Initially, it is clear that sites which have benefited from a more extensive and longer history of exploration and collection have more occurrences of phalli, but the number of phalli does not correlate consistently or directly with the area of excavation. While Vindolanda boasts the most phalli ($T = 13$) and has benefitted from extensive excavation across the fort and extramural settlement, the forts at South Shields and Wallsend and the Roman town at Corbridge (including Shorden Brae) have all hosted extensive excavations but yielded far fewer phalli ($T = 4$, 1, and 8, respectively). As a site type, forts and extramural settlements have the most frequent occurrence, with no examples confirmed from milecastles or turrets. While the incidence of phalli at other site types is low, the fact that they have been found at quarry sites, and in the fabric of the Wall's curtain and bridges, demonstrates that phalli are not restricted to settlements with larger populations.

There is no inherent reason why one fort or settlement should have more phalli than any other. The uneven distribution, both in terms of geography and by site type, thus suggests that the assemblage from the Wall is incomplete. New phalli were identified at Vindolanda on stones bearing other carvings or inscriptions during the course of research while examining stones in the store, and another previously unknown phallus was found on a stone from Housesteads in the store. Fieldwork at Gelt completed just prior to publication revealed two new phalli *in situ*, previously unrecorded. It seems likely, therefore, that other large stone collections in the Wall corridor may contain previously unrecognised or forgotten phalli. Furthermore, many sites along Hadrian's Wall have been robbed of stone over the centuries, a process which will have actively removed, reused, and possibly destroyed stones bearing phalli. This observation of robbing is borne out by the discrepancy between the eastern and central sectors of the Wall compared to the western sector. The western end has generally poor survival of curtain, and the forts have been built over by settlements, making archaeological investigation difficult and infrequent. Carlisle and Maryport, the only settlements with any phalli in the west, have benefitted from a longer history of collection that was not shared by Bowness, for example. In contrast, encountering at least a single phallus is typical in the eastern and central sector forts. It remains impossible to quantify how many phalli have been lost, though it is not unreasonable to expect more to pop up with further excavation and re-examination of museum holdings. Of the 13 catalogued from Vindolanda, only 5 were known in 1988 when CSIR I.6 was published. Still, if Vindolanda was accepted as a fairly standard fort in the Wall corridor, then that would allow for a projection of at least 10 phalli per fort (with an accompanying extramural settlement) and town along the Wall corridor, approximating 200 phalli between South Shields and Bowness, in addition to those from the Wall curtain and bridges and the forts along the Cumbrian coast. This provides a conservative maximum estimation that approximately 25 per cent of all stone-carved phalli have survived, been discovered, and/or recorded.

The possibility that phalli were carved into or from wood and may have been painted must also be borne in mind. No wooden phalli comparable to those executed in stone are known, but given that wood functioned in a similar fashion to stone as a building medium means that the possibility cannot be dismissed completely. If this is the case, then there will have been an even higher number of carved phalli. No confirmed examples of painted phalli have been found in the study area, though a painted surface would have provided further visual enhancement and advertisement of the presence of a phallus. Furthermore, phalli may have been painted onto a surface without an accompanying carving.

A new typology

The cataloguing of phalli from the Wall highlighted morphological variation and lent itself to a comparison of phalli from other parts of the Roman Empire. However, while phalli have been photographed or illustrated and included in analyses of phallic representation and symbolism, it is striking that no one had constructed a typology for stone phalli. Given the utility of typologies to analyse data and facilitate comparison, the corpus from the Wall provided an excellent opportunity to establish a base typology for future research.

The phalli in the catalogue were visually examined, photographed and illustrated, and clustered based on their style of execution, and shared metric and morphological traits. Each of these is summarised in brief below, though the typology is offered in more detail elsewhere (Collins 2019). Measurements enabled the identification of a proportionality of the phallus shaft to establish if a phallus could be assigned to one of three forms. Morphological traits were used to establish a type. Form and type combined enables a shorthand typological description of a given phallus, such as a "mean Rocket" or a "slim Pointer". The typology is intended to be easily memorable and uncomplicated, and makes use of flippant and colloquial terminology for both form and type to reinforce the visual impression of each. Admittedly, any typology using descriptive terms favours the language in which it originates. It is hoped that the use of humour in the typology will add to the appeal of having to learn yet another typology for the non-native reader.

Execution

All 59 phalli could be attributed a style of execution, either incised, relief, or sculpture. The clear majority were incised ($T = 39$, 66 per cent), with approximately half that number in relief ($T = 19$, 32 per cent). Only one example can be classified as sculpture, and this will be discussed below relative to its context and presumed function. It is unsurprising that incised phalli are nearly twice as common as those in relief; incision is both faster and requires less skill than carving in relief. Experimentation by the author indicates that, with modern tools, a phallus of comparable size to those from the Wall can be incised on a stone face in approximately 15 minutes, in contrast to a period of 120 minutes to carve a similarly sized phallus in relief (Figure 9.3). But it is the fact that there are so many that is important. The

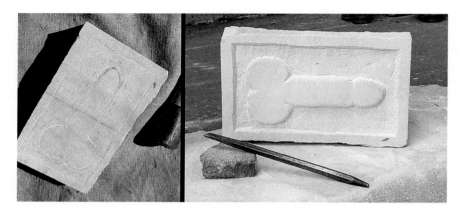

Figure 9.3 Experimental carving by the author using modern hand tools to incise a phallus on a flat sandstone face (left), and carve the same phallus in relief on the same stone (right)

(© Rob Collins)

greater time and skill required to carve in relief supports the assumption that phalli were not only graffiti but had a specific purpose. This is reinforced by distribution (Table 9.1). Of eleven sites bearing more than one phallus, eight sites had at least one phallus in relief, and five had two phalli in relief. No sites had more than two phalli in relief, and it is notable that Corbridge town had two phalli in relief while the six incised examples were from the burial monument at Shorden Brae outside the town. Chesters has an equal number of phalli in relief as incised, and Carlisle actually has more phalli in relief than incised. Only Vindolanda bears a highly disproportionate ratio of incised phalli to those in relief. The 11:1 ratio at Vindolanda may be the most accurate, given the extent of excavation and the number of phalli discovered through excavation over the past 30 years, though it should be

Table 9.1 The number of phalli incised and carved in relief at key fort and town sites in the Wall corridor

Site	No. incised	No. in relief	Ratio (incised:relief)
South Shields	4	0	4:0
Corbridge	6	2	3:1
Chesters	2	2	1:1
Housestead	4	0	4:0
Vindolanda	11	1	11:1
Birdoswald	2	1	2:1
Carlisle	1	2	1:2
Maryport	2	2	1:1

remembered that these phalli were not necessarily all visible or even known to the occupants of Vindolanda at any given point in time. There was an accumulation of carvings through the decades and centuries that the site was occupied, and some of these phalli were actively removed from "circulation" during the repeated processes of dismantling and rebuilding structures. For example, cat. no. 39 was built into the wall of an early third-century structure that was left *in situ* when the structure was demolished and subsequently covered and built over.

Size and form

The phalli vary considerably in size, determined largely by the face of the stone where each was carved. It was not possible to measure each phallus directly, as some stones were missing/unlocated or not practically accessible, resulting in only 41 of the 59 phalli yielding information about their size. Even so, there was considerable variation in size. The largest phallus was incised onto a quarry face below the peak of Barcombe Hill, just east of Vindolanda, which was 490 mm in total length and 205 mm at maximum width. The smallest phallus was carved in relief on a stone set into the wall of the extramural bathhouse at Chesters, measuring 76.7 mm in total length and 44.1 mm at maximum width. In this regard, each phallus can be understood to have been carved relative to the area of the stone face that is being worked, in which case the phallus is tailored to its location and/or context.

Measurement of phalli was completed as consistently as possible, with dimensions restrained to length and width. For specimens carved in relief, measurements were taken from the base of the relief; for incised specimens, measurements were taken from the outside edge of the incision. Two sets of measurements were taken, the maximum length and width which includes the testicles along with the shaft of the phallus, while the second set measured the length and width of the phallus without the testes. For the first set of measurements, width was always measured across the testicles, while for the second set width was measured at the broadest position of the shaft, often but not always the base (Collins 2019, fig. 1). This was done to determine if there was a consistent proportion of the shaft of the phallus distinct from the often varied positions, sizes, and shapes of the accompanying testes. For example, testicles fairly consistently accounted for 20–25 per cent of the total length of the depiction, but were far more variable in accounting for 20–80 per cent of the width of any depiction, masking any attempt to determine a preferred proportionality. These measurements were then used to establish an accurate proportionality (e.g. 2.4:1), which was then rounded to the nearest 0.5 (e.g. 2.4:1 becomes 2.5:1, which equals 5:2). Focusing on shaft measurements, the shaft length:width proportionality falls between the extremes of 13:2 and 3:2, but the majority cluster between 2:1 and 4:1. The frequency of each proportion is indicated in Table 9.2, and each proportion is assigned to one of three forms: chunky (any proportion of 2:1 or lower); mean (any proportion greater than 2:1 up to and including 4:1); and slim (any proportion greater than 4:1).

Table 9.2 Proportional form of phalli determined by the proportion of length:width of each phallus shaft

Form	Proportion	Total
Chunky	3:2	1
	2:1	5
Mean	5:2	12
	3:1	5
	7:2	7
	4:1	4
Slim	9:2	1
	5:1	1
	11:2	2
	13:2	1

Type

The phalli from the Wall were clustered based on shared morphological traits. The key traits that supported the clustering were: shape of the shaft (including curvature); position of the testicles relative to the shaft; depiction of the glans (head); the presence of more than one shaft per pair of testicles; the occurrence of ejaculate; and the addition of any other features to the phallus (e.g. feet, wings). Initial sorting of types was then compared to stone-carved phalli from other parts of the Roman Empire, specifically identifying any types that were not present along the Wall. This resulted in nine types, as listed in Table 9.3 and depicted in Figure 9.4. Based on frequency of occurrence and significance of representation, it was decided that depiction of the glans and occurrence of ejaculate were not distinctive features in and of themselves to establish a distinct type; rather, these features were of more importance to indicate sub-types. It was felt the corpus was not sufficiently large enough at present to establish any meaningful sub-types, though the terminology and mechanisms for their definition is under consideration.

The typology can be graphically distinguished by execution, form, and type (Figure 9.4), though due to constraints in the Wall corpus, not every phallus can be included. For example, incomplete phalli or those that were not viewed could not contribute measurements, and thus could not be attributed a form. For example, cat. no. 20, the sole example of a Running Hard type from Housesteads, is only attested from an early archaeological notebook (Blair 1894); while it can be confidently assumed that the phallus was incised and had bird legs, the accuracy of the drawing for measurements and other details cannot be relied on, as Blair's illustration of cat. no. 12 from Chesters is fairly representative but not accurate. The six phalli carved on a stone from the Shorden Brae

Table 9.3 Phalli from the Wall were identified as belonging to one of nine types, established through clustering of morphological traits

Type no.	Type name	Key features	Total no.
1	The Rocket	Straight shaft of oblong or (sub)triangular form; testicles at shaft base	35
2	The Hammer	Straight shaft of incised line or narrow relief; glans wider than shaft; testicles at shaft base horizontally aligned	2
3	The Kinky-Winky	Bent, curving, or kinked shaft	5
4	The Splitcock	Inverted V-shaped shaft, each side terminating in scrolling or circular testicles	6
5	The Pointer	Oblong shaft; testicles "hang" side-by-side beneath base of shaft	1
6	The Double-Dong	Two (or more) shafts emerging from a single pair of testicles	1
7	Running Hard	Phallus bearing bird legs beneath the shaft or replacing the testicles	1
8	The Beast	Phallus with testicles replaced by hind legs of animal (often feline) with a tail (possibly also phallic); may have erect phallus between legs; may also have wings	0
9	Lucky Dip	Ambiguous carving that may depict male and/or female genitalia	0

mausoleum, cat. nos 27–32, are not illustrated and the stone does not seem to have been retained, so form and type could not be ascertained.

In terms of form, a mean proportionality is most common, with 28 examples from a total of 39 (72 per cent), while the Rocket is the most common type at 34 examples from a total of 49 (69 per cent). The Rocket is also the only type to occur in the Wall corpus in all three forms. Along the Wall, the mean Rocket is the form-type most likely to be encountered.

It is clear that incision is the dominant form of execution, with only one example of sculptural execution, confined to the Kinky-Winky type. Relief is only attested in two types, the Rocket and Pointer. As there is only one example of a Pointer, it is difficult to determine any significance of its execution in relief. The majority of Rockets were incised, but when broken down by form, mean Rockets are almost equally found in relief ($T = 12$) as incised ($T = 11$).

With the typology established, it is feasible to provide more contextual analyses to determine if there are any further patterns discernible.

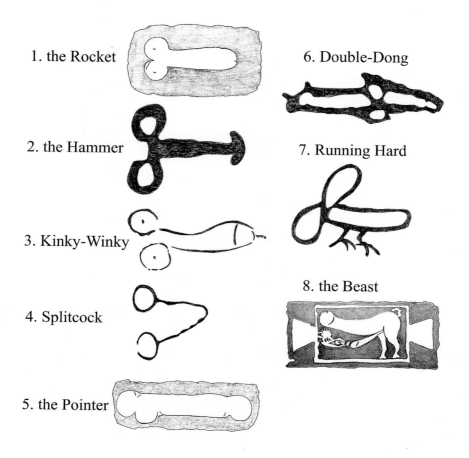

1. the Rocket

2. the Hammer

3. Kinky-Winky

4. Splitcock

5. the Pointer

6. Double-Dong

7. Running Hard

8. the Beast

Figure 9.4 The types of phalli in simple schematic form, illustrated with one example each. Grey shading indicates the removal of stone to more readily identify incision from relief

(© Rob Collins, drawings by Rebecca Lee)

Contextual analyses

There are a range of contextual analyses that can be completed with the Wall corpus, and these offer important insight into the use of the phallus as a symbol. The relatively high occurrence of phalli in known archaeological contexts significantly enhances interpretation, providing useful evidence for dating, and the association of phalli with other symbols. Most important, however, is the locational context of these phalli, which can be explored relative, though not limited, to their visibility, private or public usage, associations with water, and as markers of boundaries.

Dating

Dating the stone-carved phalli is feasible, though problematic. Out of the total 59 phalli listed in the catalogue, 24 (41 per cent) lack sufficient context to date with certainty (though some can be given a probable date) and 35 (59 per cent) can be attributed a context dated to a century (some even more accurately). However, dating typically provides a *terminus ante quem* (TAQ) for carving, and many of the contexts are suggestive of the reuse of stone bearing phalli that may have been carved in earlier decades or centuries. Furthermore, the low numbers of well-dated forms and some types means that at present neither form nor type can be conclusively demonstrated as time specific. However, some preliminary patterns can be observed in the corpus that may point to chronological trends, though the domination of phalli attributed to the third century cuts across all other observations.

Three specific horizons or periods warrant mention: the "first phase" occurrence; the Severan period and early third century; and the mid–late fourth century. First-phase or primary contexts cannot be dated to a specific time, but indicate the earliest phase of activity at any given site. For most locations in the Wall corridor, the first phase can be attributed to the Hadrianic period of c.A.D. 120–138, but there are sites that have pre-Hadrianic or post-Hadrianic origins. There are a number of examples of phalli, that survive *in situ*, of primary use, or whose reuse suggests occurrence in primary or first-phase contexts. In the latter case, cat. no. 8 consists of a Splitcock drawn into pila tile that was reused in a road surface dated to A.D. 125–150 in the fort at Carlisle. This Hadrianic–Antonine paving probably made use of rubble from an earlier-phase building of later Flavian or Trajanic date, and this surviving tile fragment is the best example of a probable first-century occurrence of phallic imagery in stone or stone-like media in the Wall corridor, best associated with the pre-Hadrianic (and thus pre-Wall, before c.A.D. 120) system of military installations located on the Stanegate road that connected Corbridge to Carlisle. Cat. no. 51, a chunky Rocket inscribed onto a quarry face in Wall-mile 25 relates to Hadrianic quarrying of material to build the Wall that probably dates to c.A.D. 120–130. Cat. nos 11 and 13 were built into the subfloor of the Hadrianic extramural bathhouse. Cat. nos 52–4 consist of Rockets in relief on facing stones built into the stone curtain in the Birdoswald sector; these are part of the original stone-built Wall, but in this sector, the stone curtain replaced the primary Turf Wall, and the exact dating is uncertain, though probably late Hadrianic, c.A.D. 135–138. These three phalli are particularly interesting in regards to the contextualised interpretation of the symbol (discussed below).

The best-dated horizon of use of phalli can be attributed to the Severan period and early third century, c.A.D. 193–230, with a total of 14 certain and probable contexts (cat. nos 1, 6, 10, 14, 26, 33, 34, 35, 39, 41, 44, 46, 58, and 59). The sites of South Shields, Chesters, and Vindolanda are conspicuous here, due to the amount of building activity associated with this period at each site.

At Newcastle, cat. no. 26, a Splitcock incised onto a stone that was part of the primary wall of the *principia* is an example of both "first-phase" occurrence and is possibly Severan in date (late second to early third century A.D.). The location of the phalli on the quarry face at Gelt (cat. nos 58 and 59) are in the same area as an inscription dated to the Severan period, and by association are probably of the same date. This horizon should not be surprising, as there is good evidence across a range of data, including inscriptions, of high levels of activities relating to the Wall and Severan campaigns north of the Wall (Hodgson 2017: 109–11), but it is significant in demonstrating apparent primary use, and by extension carving, of phallic symbols in the early third century. This alone warns against assumptions that undated phallic imagery should be attributed to the first or second centuries.

A number of phalli date to contexts from the mid–later fourth century, though these almost certainly attest to the reuse of phalli carved earlier. The most closely dated examples are from a stone incorporated into the walls of a structure immediately north of the west gate at Vindolanda, in which the collapse of the wall can be dated to the late fourth/early fifth century, but which is thought to have been constructed in the mid-fourth century (Andrew Birley, personal communication). In addition to cat. nos 47–9 that are carved into other faces of the stone, this stone also provides the only example of a Double-Dong (cat. no. 50) from the Wall corridor. Unfortunately, a mid-fourth-century TAQ is the best date that can be provided. A similar late-fourth-century TAQ is also the best that can be provided for cat. nos 27–32, the unlocated phalli carved on a stone from the Shorden Brae funerary monument, providing a date for when the stone was buried rather than carved (Gillam and Daniels 1961). Cat. no. 19 is a mean Hammer carved into a quoin stone that was used in the construction of a small bathsuite at the east end of Building XV at Housesteads in A.D. 340 or 360, probably reused. Though the carving of the phallus cannot be proven to date to the fourth century in any of these examples, it does suggest that the symbol still had currency.

Associated symbols

There are eight stones in the Wall corpus in which there are other representations or symbols carved on or from stone adjacent to phalli. The most common association is a pointed oval or closely similar shape that depicts the Evil Eye and/or a vulva, found with Rockets from Maryport (Figure 9.5, no. 22), Vindolanda (Figure 9.5, no. 42), and Chesters (Figure 9.5, no. 12). Another Rocket from Vindolanda appears to have palm trees to the left of the phallus (Figure 9.5, no. 33), and a worn Rocket from Chesters bathhouse has the phallus centred and pointing up on the stone, flanked by now unidentified carvings in relief to either side (Figure 9.5, no. 11), though the symbol to the left is drawn as a person with uncertain detail in Holmes (1887, plate 5). A Kinky-Winky from South Shields has a horse and rider bearing a sword and shield overlying the incision of the phallus (Figure 9.5, no. 35). The large Rocket from Chesters Bridge may have an

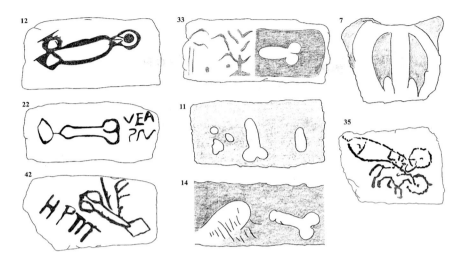

Figure 9.5 Schematic drawings of phalli on stones with associated symbols. The numbers
refer to the catalogue entry for each phallus

(© Rob Collins, drawings by Rebecca Lee)

unfinished symbol to the left of the shaft, surviving in high relief, but of uncertain
identification (Figure 9.5, no. 14). Finally, a Rocket from Carlisle is framed by
a wreath, also in relief (Figure 9.5, no. 7). While the Rocket is the clearly dominant type with any associated symbols, it is so numerically frequent that no firm
conclusions can be drawn from this association. What is more certain is that the
phallus is always pointing in the direction of the other symbols, or framed/flanked
by them. The exception is the horse and rider from South Shields, which seems to
have superseded the phallus, presumably immediately after carving and before
the stone was set into the wall of the barrack.

The other symbols presumably enhanced the efficacy of the phallus, as with the
combination of phallic-vulvate symbolism with a horse harness (see Chapter 5).
The phallus is often given primacy due to its iconic representation, familiarity, and
apotropaic interpretation, but this needs to be considered carefully in the context of
the carving itself: Is the phallus more prominent in size or position than other symbols, and how might the other symbols mitigate the potency of the phallus? Unfortunately, only three of these stones (cat. nos 11, 14, and 35) have survived *in situ*.
The horse and rider of cat. no. 35 may be invoking a protector deity in conjunction
with the protective magic of the phallus, but the possible associated symbol in front
of the Rocket (cat. no. 14) at Chesters Bridge is unidentified and probably unfinished in execution. A more complex invocation may be the intention of the stone in
the baths at Chesters (cat. no. 11), but it is difficult to interpret without being able
to identify all three symbols on the stone.

Visibility and public or private phalli

A key question is whether the presence of a phallus is enough to evoke its apotropaic properties, or whether the phallus must also be visible to be deemed effective. The Wall corpus provides examples of phalli that were probably carved and placed by personal initiative for both private and personal benefit, while there is no doubt that some phalli were intended to be visible. The large mean Rocket in relief on a paving slab in the *principia* courtyard at Chesters (cat. no. 10) is prominent to visitors now, despite weathering and wear; its sharper detail and high, stepped relief must have made it even more visible for its Roman contemporaries (Figure 9.1). Similarly, the Rockets on facing stones set into the curtain of the Wall in the Birdoswald sector (cat. nos 52–4) were also probably intended to be visible, being carved in high relief and set at shoulder-head height relative to the Roman ground level. The sculpted Kinky-Winky from Vindolanda (cat. no. 44) was found in collapsed rubble south of the west gate of the fort dated to the third century, but examination of the stone indicates that its base was carved so that the hyper-erect phallus would fit into a socket, presumably to project out from the stone wall of the gate toward the road. At 282 mm in length, it is likely to have been intended as a clearly visible phallus, perhaps even imitating or functioning as a herm. The visibility of these phalli can be determined simply on the basis of their *in situ* survival, but they could also have been enhanced through application of paint(s) or some other rendering to their surfaces. Whether carved and placed on the initiative of the builders/masons or demanded by the officers responsible for new building work, all of these phalli were public-facing and underscore the phallus as a socially acceptable, perhaps even common, symbol for frontier communities.

In contrast, there are some phalli which are unlikely to have been intended for public display, by dint of the impractical position for the general viewer or being completely obscured from viewing. The phalli pecked into stone faces incorporated into a barrack building at South Shields (cat. nos 33–5) would not have been visible to anyone, and only the builders of the barrack would have known of their presence. This raises the question of whether the builders were also the occupiers. Furthermore, the phalli are pecked in a fashion that suggests relatively rapid execution of someone completing something quickly. Regardless, the stones bearing phalli were incorporated into the structure despite their invisibility to the barrack's inhabitants. This underscores the belief in the efficacy of a phallic carving, as the presence of these stones would not have been known to all the barrack's inhabitants across subsequent years and decades.

There are also phalli that were not necessarily highly visible or intended as such. For example, the phalli from quarries (cat. nos 1 and 51) were presumably carved through personal initiative, but were not necessarily intended for or seen by an audience larger than the workforce of the quarry itself. In other cases, the phallus was related to a "public" resource, as in the bridge at Chesters (cat. no. 14) or drains at Vindolanda (cat. nos 42 and 46), but these would not normally have been visible.

Only a few types of identifiable buildings have phalli associated with them: baths, barracks, and headquarters. This association may be a result of recovery bias, as all three types of buildings are readily recognised and are more likely to have been explored or excavated by antiquarians and early archaeologists; baths and headquarters are also large, monumental buildings that required more substantial investment in both labour and materials. Of these buildings, the most phalli are associated with *principia*, or headquarters buildings. The large mean Rocket in relief on a paving slab in the *principia* courtyard at Chesters (cat. no. 10) has already been noted, but to this can be added a mean Rocket in the southeast corner of the early third-century *principia* at Carlisle (cat. no. 6) and the Splitcock in the primary wall of the late second/early third-century *principia* at Newcastle (cat. no. 26). Though unconfirmed, the Kinky-Winky from South Shields (cat. no. 36) is thought to have been part of the mid-second-century *principia*, and the mean Rocket carved into a square column base from Housesteads may also be most likely to have come from the *principia* (cat. no. 21), though other locations are possible. Two distinct headquarters buildings at Vindolanda have associated phalli: the slim Hammer found in the rubble of the Severan *principia* (cat. no. 39) and the early third and early fourth century phalli associated with drains leading out of the *principia* of the latest stone fort (cat. nos 46 and 42, respectively). The phalli are visible in some cases, and less visible or even hidden from view in other cases, reinforcing the interpretation that visibility is not essential to the efficacy of the phallus. If the associations of South Shields and Housesteads are accepted, then 8 out of the 59 phalli in the corpus (14 per cent) are linked to a *principia*. The consistency of occurrence across the Wall corridor, at South Shields (probably), Newcastle, Housesteads (possibly), Vindolanda, and Carlisle, in a range of positions/locations relative to the building, establishes a strong association of the phallus with the headquarters building, indicating a Roman desire to lend the apotropaic strength of the symbol to the spaces of the *principia*. The *principia* is a "public" building for a unit of the Roman army, containing offices and presumably important records, the shrine of the standards, the strong room with pay chests, and the basilica hall and courtyard (usually) for assembly, which included dispensing justice. This is the building where civilians are also likely to be found to conduct business with the army. Given the significance of the *principia* and the activities important to the unit as a whole, it is perhaps not surprising that such a building was imbued with protection by its builders. However, the frequency of phalli associated with *principia* highlights the absence with other buildings in a Roman fort where the apotropaic power is missing, such as granaries (*horrea*) and commanding officers' houses (*praetoria*), with the exception of cat. no. 39.

The burial monument at Shorden Brae, incorporating a stone with six phalli (cat. nos 27–32), would also have been highly visible, assuming the two faces of the stone bearing the carvings faced outward. The stone was recovered from a pit with other sculpture dated to the fourth century, indicating its earlier second or third-century usage. This provides an association of the phallus with mortuary practice and beliefs, but it is feasible that the stone was reused from another position or context prior to its use as a burial monument. In a slightly different ideological context, the unprovenanced altar bearing a Rocket in relief would have been highly visible. The stone bearing the four phalli (cat. nos 47–50) seems to have been used as a facing stone for a wall at Vindolanda, with only one of the three faces bearing phalli visible. At present, it cannot be said which face that would have been, but it is notable that, in this instance, the multiple phalli on the stone could not be seen by all and sundry. Given the date of the context it was found in, from the late fourth or early fifth century, reuse of a stone from an earlier structure seems likely, and it is intriguing to speculate what sort of structure might need the apotropaic magic invoked by a Double-Dong, a single Rocket, and a pair of Rockets on three faces.

Across the corpus, then, there are examples of highly visible phalli that were indisputably intended to be seen by a broader audience of the military community. Yet there are also examples of phalli that would be rarely visible or completely invisible to the community. These phalli are more instructive, for they suggest that it was the presence of a phallus and inclusion in a structure that provided benefit, distinct from its visibility. In that regard, the phallus can be understood as a symbol imbued with genuine belief and faith at both the personal level and by military authorities. This assumes the phallus functioned as an apotropaic symbol by its very presence. It is possible, however, that a visible phallus may have instigated some other behaviour, such as a gesture or offering of a prayer that might "recharge" the phallus or channel its power to the individual (Adam Parker, personal communication).

Watery associations

Phalli have been associated with bathhouses and homes at Pompeii, either on their own or as essential components of a scene to invoke humour or shock, interfering with the malevolence of the Evil Eye (Clarke 2003; Chapters 4 and 5). There are phalli from two bathhouses along the Wall, but it is notable that they are unlikely to be visible, or to invoke humour or shock. At the extramural bathhouse at Chesters, a mean Rocket flanked by now unrecognisable symbols on one stone sits adjacent to another stone bearing a chunky Kinky-Winky (cat. nos 11 and 13). These stones were probably placed in the primary Hadrianic construction of the bathhouse (Snape and Stobbs 2016: 80, fig. 18 makes this clear), but they would not have been visible, sitting beneath the surface of the raised floor. It should also be noted that the Kinky-Winky was interpreted at the time of its discovery as a bird, and while this interpretation remains a possibility, I would argue that a phallus is a more likely carving to encounter than a bird (Holmes 1887). The mean Hammer carved into a quoin stone at Housesteads (cat. no. 19) was located at shoulder-head height on the wall of the hot-plunge-bath alcove and may have been visible to bathers in the mid–late fourth century, but it may also have been covered with plaster or some other rendering.

Other phalli have been found associated with drains and wells. The highly visible mean Rocket at Chesters in the *principia* courtyard (cat. no. 10) was also proximal to the well there. At Vindolanda, a mean Rocket incised into a block of stone (cat. no. 46) was used to build the side of a drain in the early third century, carrying water and waste out of the *principia* to the west. Another drain, emerging out of the north-east wall of the *principia* and probably built in the early fourth century, had a slab across the top, on the underside of which was incised another mean Rocket, possibly with wings (cat. no. 46). All three of these phalli can be associated with a *principia* and water, perhaps as a means of protecting or purifying the sacrosanct headquarters at the heart of the fort.

Phalli were also incorporated into at least two significant bridges included in the curtain of Hadrian's Wall. The Severan-phase bridge at Chesters, crossing the North Tyne, was the most substantial of the sequence of river crossings there, incorporating a bridge built integral to the south face of the Wall curtain. The eastern abutment of this bridge contained substantial header stones, and the fifth course contained a large, mean Rocket in high relief (cat. no. 14) (Bidwell and Holbrook 1989: 19). This seems to have been a newly carved stone for the bridge abutment, and the position of the phallus faced upstream. The third-century phase of the Wall at Willowford, carrying the Wall and a bridge across the River Irthing, also incorporated an incomplete Rocket in its fabric (Bidwell and Holbrook 1989: 93). In contrast to Chesters Bridge, however, the Willowford phallus seems to have been reused from an earlier phase, as well as being broken into at least two different building stones.

The association of phalli with water can be distinguished by the function of the spaces they occur in, as well as prospective dangers they guarded against. In nearly all the instances above, the visibility of the phallus can be called into question. In the baths and drains, there is a question as to whether each phallus was to protect or purify the water, or to protect the building from water. The bridges, on the other hand, were exposed to regular and presumably fierce flooding episodes, and the incorporation of a protective phallus can be understood in these contexts as warding against the power of a violent body of water, or perhaps the spirits (nymphs) of the water body. This raises questions about the efficacy of a broken or incomplete phallus reused at Willowford. Did it still retain "power"? The stone at Chesters Bridge, though, seems to have been added not only to protect the structure of the bridge, but was also located in a position facing the greatest danger from invaders or floodwaters.

Physical boundaries

There are nine phalli that can be distinctly attributed to a context that should be understood as a physical threshold or boundary, with three at the scale of personal space, three at the scale of the settlement, and three at the scale of the monument. The occurrence at these three scales underscores the apotropaic function of the phallus for both personal and public benefit.

The three phalli incorporated into the early third-century barrack at South Shields have been noted above relative to their date and invisibility to any occupants or visitors to the barracks (cat. nos 33–5). However, a closer examination of their exact findspots also provides a contextual understanding of the intended function of the phalli. All three stones were found in the north wall of the barrack, specifically relating to rooms 4 and 5 (Figure 9.6). The door to room 4 was flanked by phalli, a mean Splitcock (cat. no. 34) to the east and a mean Kinky-Winky (cat. no. 35) to the west. The position of these stones meant than anyone entering or exiting the barrack room passed between both stones. The third stone, a mean Rocket (cat. no. 33), was found built into the north wall of room 5, not adjacent to the door, but approximately 1 metre distant. These stones seemed to have been specifically in the only walls that allowed access into the barrack rooms, the permeable boundary of the building.

A similar logic applies to the occurrence of phalli with fort gates, positioning the apotropaic symbol where access into and out of the fort was certain. The sculpted Kinky-Winky projecting out of a gate wall at Vindolanda (cat. no. 44) was a highly visible example, though its exact position and height relative to the single portal of the gate is unknown. At Birdoswald, a window voussoir was inscribed with a mean Rocket (cat. no. 4) that was found in the medieval collapse of the gate, but which was probably part of the second-century gate construction (Wilmott 1997), though it is uncertain when the phallus was

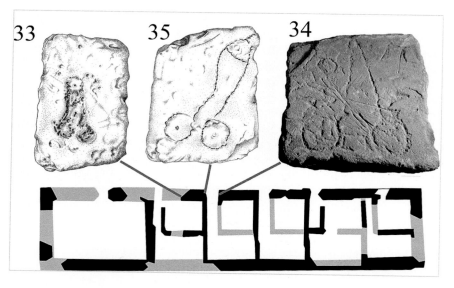

Figure 9.6 The location of individual phalli found in the early third-century barrack at South Shields

(© Rob Collins, drawings by Rebecca Lee)

carved into the stone. Blair (1894) provides the only record of the incised Running Hard visible in a guard room of a gate at Housesteads (cat. no. 20), though he does not unfortunately indicate which gate. Repeated attempts by the author to relocate the phallus have been unsuccessful.

Perhaps the most intriguing of all the phalli are the three mean Rockets found in the Birdoswald sector, carved in relief on facing stones positioned on the south face of the stone curtain at chest-head height. Cat. nos 52 and 53 were located east of the fort of Birdoswald, both pointing west toward the fort. Cat. no. 54 was located west of Birdoswald fort, pointing east toward the fort (Figure 9.7). These are the only phalli in the corpus in which the direction of the erection may have significance, signposting the way to the fort. Directionality, though, does not preclude concurrent apotropaic function.

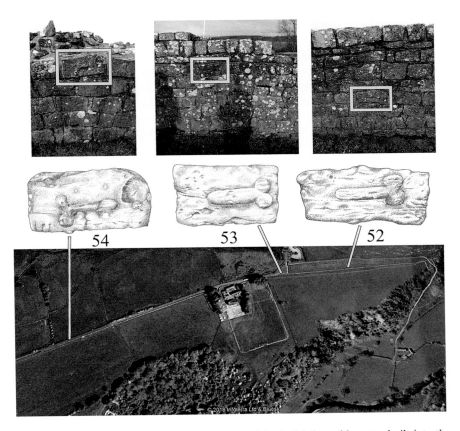

Figure 9.7 The location of individual phalli found in the Birdoswald sector, built into the southern face of the stone curtain of Hadrian's Wall

(© Rob Collins, drawings by Rebecca Lee with satellite image from Google Earth)

The inclusion of phalli in the curtain fabric of the Wall here is intriguing, and prompts a fundamental question: Why are they found in the Birdoswald sector but not in the curtain elsewhere? There are a number of possible explanations for this occurrence, though it is difficult to determine which explanation is most likely. The survival of these three phalli can be explained in some measure by the excavation history, with the two east and one west of Birdoswald only revealed by excavation undertaken by the Ministry of Works in the 1950s (Whitworth 2009: 61–3). The south face of the curtain was protected up to a height of approximately 2 metres due to the build-up of soil over the centuries, allowing the facing stones to survive *in situ*, in direct contrast to the north face of the curtain, which was thoroughly robbed prior to the 1950s. In addition to the phallic stones, a number of centurial stones were also found *in situ*. Centurial stones, recording the name of a legionary century responsible for building a portion of curtain, are known from the length of Hadrian's Wall, but were almost never left *in situ*. Thus, survival is a key factor. It is notable that of the exposed lengths of the curtain of Hadrian's Wall, very little of it survives to a height of more than 1.5 metres. So if stones bearing phalli were placed in positions ranging from 1.5–2 metres in height, most of these will have been lost in antiquity. It is striking, however, that there are more than 200 centurial stones that have been recognised and collected over the past 400 years and far fewer phalli.

An alternative explanation may be found in the history of the Birdoswald sector. West of the River Irthing, the Wall curtain was originally constructed in turf in the 120s. The curtain was replaced in stone over time, from *c*.A.D. 130 (Hodgson 2017: 69), and the stones with the phalli would have been carved and placed at this time. So these three phalli cannot be understood as primary to the Wall's construction, and there are no other phalli that can be dated to it. The phalli may have been a new secondary element for a different reason—one related to their apotropaic function. There are indications that the Birdoswald sector may have been more dangerous, either requiring more observation or perhaps even being prone to more violence. In the pre-Wall frontier, there are a number of installations along the pre-Hadrianic Stanegate road: the fort at Carvoran, Throp fortlet, Mains Rigger tower, Nether Denton fort, and Old Church Brampton fort in addition to the numerous temporary camps that are largely undated (English Heritage 2014). Second, west of the Irthing, building the Wall in turf seems to be a decision related to the need for priority and speed for the barrier (Hodgson 2017: 67). Third, the erection of milecastles and turrets probably also followed a priority programme (Symonds 2005, 2019), which included the Birdoswald sector. It may be that when the opportunity arose to replace the turf wall with a stone curtain, it was deemed useful to add some supernatural strength to the physical barrier.

Conclusion

At present, the Wall corpus of stone-carved phalli consists of 59 examples of an individual phallus, which has been conservatively estimated to be no more than

25 per cent of the total assemblage in the Roman era. It is fully anticipated that new phalli will be discovered in future excavations, as well as rediscovered in museum stores. The Wall corpus, in conjunction with phalli from other parts of the Roman Empire, was used to established a typology based on how the carving of a phallus was executed, the form determined by the length:width ratio of the phallus shaft, and the type determined by morphological characteristics. The typology has the potential to characterise phalli across the former Roman Empire and provide some standardisation of terminology and practice (e.g. Museo Nacional 2015). Of the nine types and three forms, the mean Rocket is the most commonly occurring in the typology. Incised phalli are more frequent across the whole corpus, but there is a very high proportion of Rockets in relief. Sculptural execution was limited to a single example.

Though occurring at a number of discrete sites, the phalli from the Wall present a significant corpus of material that is valuable for comparison with other large assemblages, for example at Pompeii, which forms the basis for an intriguing comparative study. The typology has elucidated the variability of phallic carving, with slight suggestions of some chronological preference or variation. Significantly, phalli were carved and seemingly positioned with intention through the second and early third centuries at least, and there is a case to be made that the apotropaic function of phallic symbolism was still recognised and acknowledged in the fourth century.

The most important aspect of the Wall corpus, however, is the number of phalli with known archaeological contexts, allowing a more contextualised interpretation of the symbolism of the phallus. There were no clear examples of graffiti on stone. Rather, there are a number of situations in which the apotropaic phallus was employed. Examples found in barrack walls, fort gates, and the curtain of the Wall itself suggest that a phallus could reinforce the physical properties of structure by stopping or excluding metaphysical problems. Phalli are also found in bathhouses, with a significant association to be made with the *principia*, the headquarters building in the centre of every fort. Significantly, some carvings indicate that the phallus did not need to be publicly visible to have efficacy. The protective aspects of the phallus were also employed with bridges, perhaps to combat local spirits associated with violent seasonal flooding.

In these examples, publicly visible or not, we can understand the phallus as a symbol imbued with genuine belief and faith. But how did it function, or at least, how did the Romans perceive the "lucky" or "holy" phallus to function? There may also be a distinction to be made in terms of the effect or efficacy of phalli made in other materials or media, though the portable nature of small objects can make like-for-like contextual comparisons difficult. However, a distinction can perhaps be made between small objects as focusing at the level of the individual, while those static phalli carved in stone can be perceived as benefitting a wider community. As stated above, the very presence of the phallus seems to have been enough. As such, it may have been expected to generate a spatial effect, like a literal sphere of influence or protective bubble. The modern reader may benefit from thinking of this in terms of a force-field, "cock-blocking" bad luck or evil intent from those that invoked the protection of the phallus. In this regard, it may be tentatively suggested that multiple or larger phalli are intended to provide a greater area or volume of protection, as with the substantial Rockets in relief in the *principia* courtyard at Chesters (cat. no. 10) or built into the bridge at Chesters (cat. no. 14).

Fortunately, the typology and a former empire full of phalli allows for further identification of associations and testing of the conclusions offered here.

Acknowledgements

Thanks are gratefully extended to the curators of various Wall collections for providing assistance, information, and access to their fine phalli, particularly: Andrew and Barbara Birley (Vindolanda Trust); Alex Croom (TWAM); Jane Laskey (Senhouse Trust); Frances McIntosh and David Hanks (English Heritage); Tim Padley (Tullie House Trust); and Andrew Parkin and Joanne Anderson (GNM). Jon Allison kindly provided information on newly discovered carvings from the quarry face at Gelt just prior to publication. Graeme Stobbs and Pete Savin provided photos that contributed to illustration. My wife and children provided assistance, patience, and good cheer on family phallus-hunting trips along the Wall in both sun and snow. Adam Parker, Tatiana Ivleva, and the peer reviewer kindly provided further comments and observations that improved this chapter, though all errors remain my own. Funding from the research committee of the School of History, Classics and Archaeology at Newcastle University supported commission of the illustrations of phalli.

Appendix 9.1: Catalogue of phalli from Hadrian's Wall corridor

The catalogue provides details of the 59 phalli that contributed to this study. The collection distinguishes if the phallus is *in situ* or held in a museum store, or if unlocated. Where no published reference is available, the accession number is provided, for example HO at Housesteads, MAYSM for the Senhouse Collection at Maryport, and SF for Vindolanda. Full bibliographic details for the published reference can be found in the Bibliography. Cat. nos 53 and 54 use standard notation among Wall scholars to designate location, with MC being short for milecastle in no. 53, and T49b SW indicating turret 49b (the second turret in Wall-mile 49) of the stone wall (in contrast to the turf wall).

1. Site: Barcombe Quarry
   Execution: incised
   Form: mean
   Type: Rocket (1)
   Context: inscribed into rock in a Roman quarry
   Context date: third century

Collection: *in situ*
Reference: CSIR I.6, no. 442; R Birley 1973: 117

2. Site: Benwell
   Execution: incised
   Form: N/A
   Type: Rocket (1)
   Context: used in building facing in the fort
   Context date: second–fourth century
   Collection: SANT
   Reference: Ian Farmer Associates 1998

3. Site: Birdoswald
   Execution: incised
   Form: slim
   Type: Rocket (1)
   Context: unstratified
   Context date: N/A
   Collection: English Heritage
   Reference: Wilmott 1997: 317–18, no. 285

4. Site: Birdoswald
   Execution: incised
   Form: mean
   Type: Rocket (1)
   Context: window voussoir of *porta principalis sinistra* found collapsed in rubble
   Context date: Medieval collapse
   Collection: English Heritage
   Reference: Wilmott 1997: 64–5

5. Site: Birdoswald
   Execution: relief
   Form: mean
   Type: Rocket (1)
   Context: unknown, but found on site; received in 1901 from Birdoswald [site] sculpture gallery
   Context date: N/A
   Collection: Tullie House
   Reference: CSIR I.6, no. 461

6. Site: Carlisle
   Execution: relief
   Form: mean
   Type: Rocket (1)
   Context: fourth course over foundation near corner of south wall of period 6A *principia*
   Context date: early third century
   Collection: Tullie House
   Reference: Henig 2009: 871

7. Site: Carlisle
   Execution: relief
   Form: N/A
   Type: Rocket (1)
   Context: unknown; found on the Castle site (Roman fort) in 1981
   Context date: N/A
   Collection: Tullie House
   Reference: CSIR I.6, no. 529

8. Site: Carlisle
   Execution: incised
   Form: N/A
   Type: Splitcock (4)
   Context: pila tile reused in road surface
   Context date: A.D. 125–150
   Collection: Tullie House
   Reference: Pringle 2009, no. 14

9. Site: Carrawburgh
   Execution: relief
   Form: chunky
   Type: Rocket (1)
   Context: formerly inside fort
   Context date: N/A
   Collection: SANT
   Reference: CSIR I.6, no. 411

10. Site: Chesters
    Execution: relief
    Form: mean
    Type: Rocket (1)
    Context: paving slab in courtyard of *principia*
    Context date: third century
    Collection: *in situ*
    Reference: CSIR I.6, no. 406

11. Site: Chesters
    Execution: relief
    Form: mean
    Type: Rocket (1)
    Context: subfloor of extramural bathhouse
    Context date: Hadrianic
    Collection: *in situ*
    Reference: CSIR I.6, no. 405

12. Site: Chesters
    Execution: incised
    Form: mean
    Type: Rocket (1)
    Context: unknown

Context date: second or third century
Collection: Chesters Museum
Reference: CSIR I.6, no. 407

13. Site: Chesters
Execution: incised
Form: chunky
Type: Kinky Winky (3)
Context: subfloor of E wall of warm room in extramural bathhouse
Context date: Hadrianic
Collection: *in situ*
Reference: Holmes 1887, plate V

14. Site: Chesters Bridge
Execution: relief
Form: mean
Type: Rocket (1)
Context: fifth course of north wing of bridge 2 east abutment
Context date: Severan
Collection: *in situ*
Reference: CSIR I.6, no. 404; Coulston 1989, no. 1

15. Site: Corbridge
Execution: relief
Form: N/A
Type: Rocket (1)
Context: N/A
Context date: N/A
Collection: English Heritage
Reference: CSIR I.1, no. 175

16. Site: Corbridge
Execution: relief
Form: mean
Type: Pointer (5)
Context: N/A
Context date: N/A
Collection: English Heritage
Reference: CSIR I.1, no. 176

17. Site: Halton Chesters
Execution: relief
Form: N/A
Type: N/A
Context: found 1960
Context date: N/A
Collection: unlocated
Reference: CSIR I.1, no. 334

18. Site: Housesteads
Execution: incised

      Form: N/A
      Type: Splitcock (4)
      Context: N/A
      Context date: N/A
      Collection: English Heritage
      Reference: CSIR I.6, no. 434; HO349

19. Site: Housesteads
      Execution: incised
      Form: mean
      Type: Hammer (2)
      Context: right side of quoin stone used in hot plunge alcove wall (facing N, internally) in late baths of building 15
      Context date: A.D. 340 or 360
      Collection: *in situ*
      Reference: N/A

20. Site: Housesteads
      Execution: incised
      Form: N/A
      Type: Running Hard (7)
      Context: on stone in guardhouse of uncertain gate
      Context date: probably second century
      Collection: unlocated [*in situ* late nineteenth century]
      Reference: Blair 1894

21. Site: Housesteads
      Execution: incised
      Form: mean
      Type: Rocket (1)
      Context: on square column base side-face
      Context date: N/A
      Collection: EH
      Reference: HO324

22. Site: Maryport
      Execution: incised
      Form: mean
      Type: Rocket (1)
      Context: N/A
      Context date: N/A
      Collection: Senhouse
      Reference: RIB 872; Bailey and Haverfield 1915: 158

23. Site: Maryport
      Execution: incised
      Form: mean
      Type: Kinky Winky (3)
      Context: N/A
      Context date: N/A

Collection: Senhouse
Reference: MAYSM.1993.54

24. Site: Maryport
Execution: relief
Form: mean
Type: The Rocket (1)
Context: N/A
Context date: N/A
Collection: Senhouse
Reference: MAYSM.1993.53

25. Site: Maryport
Execution: relief
Form: N/A
Type: N/A
Context: N/A
Context date: N/A
Collection: Senhouse [destroyed]
Reference: Gordon 1726: 100

26. Site: Newcastle
Execution: incised
Form: N/A
Type: The Splitcock
Context: primary wall of *principia*
Context date: late second/early third century
Collection: SANT
Reference: Croom 2002: 129, no. 3

27. Site: Shorden Brae
Execution: incised
Form: N/A
Type: N/A
Context: stone block buried in pit with other sculpture
Context date: fourth century
Collection: unlocated
Reference: Gillam and Daniels 1961: 51–2

28. Site: Shorden Brae
Execution: incised
Form: N/A
Type: N/A
Context: stone block buried in pit with other sculpture
Context date: fourth century
Collection: unlocated
Reference: Gillam and Daniels 1961: 51–2

29. Site: Shorden Brae
Execution: incised
Form: N/A

Type: N/A
Context: stone block buried in pit with other sculpture
Context date: fourth century
Collection: unlocated
Reference: Gillam and Daniels 1961: 51–2

30. Site: Shorden Brae
Execution: incised
Form: N/A
Type: N/A
Context: stone block buried in pit with other sculpture
Context date: fourth century
Collection: unlocated
Reference: Gillam and Daniels 1961: 51–2

31. Site: Shorden Brae
Execution: incised
Form: N/A
Type: N/A
Context: stone block buried in pit with other sculpture
Context date: fourth century
Collection: unlocated
Reference: Gillam and Daniels 1961: 51–2

32. Site: Shorden Brae
Execution: incised
Form: N/A
Type: N/A
Context: stone block buried in pit with other sculpture
Context date: fourth century
Collection: unlocated
Reference: Gillam and Daniels 1961: 51–2

33. Site: South Shields
Execution: incised
Form: mean
Type: Rocket (1)
Context: 23587; N wall of room 5 of Barrack III, period 6B construction, located approximately two-thirds of length of wall from E corner; phallus not visible to viewer
Context date: early third century
Collection: TWAM
Reference: Croom 1998: 68

34. Site: South Shields
Execution: incised
Form: mean
Type: Splitcock (4)
Context: 23588; N wall of room 4 of barrack 3 in period 6B; located along E of doorway into room 4, no phallus visible to external viewers

Context date: early third century
Collection: TWAM
Reference: Croom 1998: 68

35. Site: South Shields
    Execution: incised
    Form: mean
    Type: Kinky Winky (3)
    Context: 23587; N wall of room 5 of Barrack III, at E end of wall so part of the doorway of room 4; phallus facing N against other stone in wall (not visible to viewer); barrack is period 6B construction
    Context date: early third century
    Collection: TWAM
    Reference: Croom 1998: 68

36. Site: South Shields
    Execution: incised
    Form: N/A
    Type: Kinky Winky (3)
    Context: unstratified fill in SE corner of fort; may have originated as pier base for Period 4 *principia* of c.A.D. 163
    Context date: unstratified
    Collection: TWAM
    Reference: 2011.1008

37. Site: Uncertain Wall location
    Execution: relief
    Form: mean
    Type: Rocket (1)
    Context: N/A
    Context date: N/A
    Collection: Chesters Museum
    Reference: CSIR I.6, no. 466

38. Site: Vindolanda
    Execution: relief
    Form: mean
    Type: Rocket (1)
    Context: found reused in core of fort wall near NE corner, 1979
    Context date: third or fourth century
    Collection: Vindolanda
    Reference: CSIR I.6, no, 443; Tomlin 1979: 346

39. Site: Vindolanda
    Execution: incised
    Form: slim
    Type: Hammer (2)
    Context: found in rubble of Severan *praetorium* (site ix), 1969
    Context date: A.D. 208–211

Collection: Vindolanda
Reference: CSIR I.6, no. 446; Birley 1973: 119

40. Site: Vindolanda
    Execution: incised
    Form: slim
    Type: Rocket (1)
    Context: fallen from wall of building in vicus (site xxx), disc 1971
    Context date: third century
    Collection: Vindolanda
    Reference: CSIR I.6, no. 447; Birley 1973: 119

41. Site: Vindolanda
    Execution: incised
    Form: slim
    Type: Rocket (1)
    Context: first course of stone of Severan barrack, set approximately one-fifth of length from SE corner
    Context date: A.D. 208–213
    Collection: Vindolanda
    Reference: Birley 2003: 57

42. Site: Vindolanda
    Execution: incised
    Form: slim
    Type: Rocket (1)
    Context: underside of slab of drain
    Context date: early fourth century
    Collection: Vindolanda
    Reference: Birley et al. 2002, no. 2

43. Site: Vindolanda
    Execution: incised
    Form: mean
    Type: Rocket (1)
    Context: unstratified in field wall
    Context date: post-medieval
    Collection: Vindolanda
    Reference: SF1814

44. Site: Vindolanda
    Execution: sculptural
    Form: mean
    Type: Kinky Winky (3)
    Context: collapsed fort wall immediately S of the W gate
    Context date: third century
    Collection: Vindolanda
    Reference: SF6000

45. Site: Vindolanda
    Execution: incised

Form: chunky
Type: Splitcock (4)
Context: floor of vicus store building (site lxxiv)
Context date: third century
Collection: Vindolanda
Reference: CSIR I.6, no. 445; Birley 1973: 119

46. Site: Vindolanda
Execution: incised
Form: mean
Type: The Rocket (1)
Context: stone forms N side of drain running SW out of *principia*, through W door; presumed reused
Context date: A.D. 213+
Collection: Vindolanda
Reference: CSIR I.6, no. 444

47. Site: Vindolanda
Execution: incised
Form: mean
Type: Rocket (1)
Context: building stone in wall collapse on *intervallum* road from structure built against N face of w gate
Context date: late fourth to early fifth century
Collection: Vindolanda
Reference: SF12801

48. Site: Vindolanda
Execution: incised
Form: mean
Type: Rocket (1)
Context: building stone in wall collapse on intervallum road from structure built against N face of W gate
Context date: late fourth to early fifth century
Collection: Vindolanda
Reference: SF12801

49. Site: Vindolanda
Execution: incised
Form: mean
Type: Rocket (1)
Context: building stone in wall collapse on intervallum road from structure built against N face of W gate
Context date: late fourth to early fifth century
Collection: Vindolanda
Reference: SF12801

50. Site: Vindolanda
Execution: incised
Form: each phallus is mean, though not included in the form quantifications

Type: Double-Dong (6)
Context: building stone in wall collapse on intervallum road from structure built against N face of W gate
Context date: late fourth to early fifth century
Collection: Vindolanda
Reference: SF12801

51. Site: Wall mile 25
    Execution: incised
    Form: chunky
    Type: Rocket (1)
    Context: cut into rock face exposed at Fallowfield Fell, 88 m S of St Oswald's chapel
    Context date: early second century
    Collection: Chesters Museum
    Reference: RIB 1442

52. Site: Wall mile 49 near Birdoswald
    Execution: relief
    Form: mean
    Type: Rocket (1)
    Context: in situ, S face of narrow wall, seventh course of stone, revealed 1956
    Context date: second century
    Collection: *in situ*
    Reference: CSIR I.6, no. 459

53. Site: Wall mile 49 near MC49
    Execution: relief
    Form: mean
    Type: Rocket (1)
    Context: *in situ*, S face of narrow wall, fourth course over foundation
    Context date: second century
    Collection: *in situ*
    Reference: CSIR I.6, no. 458

54. Site: Wall mile 49, near T49b SW
    Execution: relief
    Form: mean
    Type: Rocket (1)
    Context: found in upper course of S face of curtain 12 m W of T49b, revealed 1953–55
    Context date: second century
    Collection: *in situ*
    Reference: Whitworth 2009: 62

55. Site: Wallsend
    Execution: incised
    Form: chunky
    Type: Rocket (1)

Context: reused in road 3 (*via quintana*)
Context date: third century
Collection: Segedunum
Reference: Croom 2016: 3, no. 5

56. Site: Willowford
Execution: relief
Form: N/A
Type: Rocket (1)
Context: S end of bridge 3 abutment, presumed to be reused and originally Hadrianic in date
Context date: third century reuse, probable earlier Hadrianic
Collection: *in situ* [unlocated]
Reference: CSIR I.6, no. 457; Coulston 1989: 142, no. 2

57. Site: unprovenanced altar
Execution: relief
Form: N/A
Type: Rocket (1)
Context: N/A
Context date: second or third century
Collection: SANT [unlocated]
Reference: CSIR I.1, no. 341
NOTE: this altar may be misattributed to the SANT collection by Phillips.

58. Site: Gelt quarry
Execution: incised
Form: mean
Type: Rocket (1)
Context: inscribed into Roman quarry face
Context date: probably early third century
Collection: *in situ*
Reference: Allison Forthcoming

59. Site: Gelt quarry
Execution: incised
Form: chunky
Type: Splitcock (4)
Context: inscribed into a Roman quarry face
Context date: probably early third century
Collection: *in situ*
Reference: Allison Forthcoming

Bibliography

Allison, J.A. (Forthcoming). "Survey of the Roman Quarry Face at the Rock of Gelt".
Bailey, J.B. and Haverfield, F. (1915). "Catalogue of Roman Inscribed and Sculptured Stones, Coins, Earthenware, Etc., Discovered in and near the Roman Fort at Maryport,

and Preserved at Netherhall", *Cumberland and Westmorland Antiquarian and Archaeological Society Transactions*, 15: 135–72.

Bidwell, P.T. and Holbrook, N. (1989). *Hadrian's Wall Bridges*. London: HBMCE.

Birley, A.R. (2003). *The Excavations of 2001–2002: Volume 1*. Bardon Mill: Vindoldanda Trust.

Birley, R. (1973). "Vindolanda – Chesterholm 1969–1972", *Archaeologia Aeliana*, 5th series, 1: 111–22.

Birley, R., Birley, A.R., and Blake, J. (2002). "Vindolanda Excavations 1997", in R. Birley, A.R. Birley, and J. Blake (eds), *All Vindolanda Excavation Reports 1997–2000*. Vindolanda: Vindolanda Trust (cd-rom).

Blair, R. (1894). *Sketchbook*, Vol. 11. Northumberland Record Office, Woodhorn, SANT.

Breeze, D.J. (2014). *Hadrian's Wall: A History of Archaeological Thought*. Kendal: Cumberland and Westmorland Antiquarian and Archaeological Society.

Clarke, J.R. (2003). *Roman Sex, 100 BC-AD 250*. New York: Harry Abrams.

Collins, R. (2019). "Stone-Carved Phalli: A Typology", *Roman Finds Group Datasheet* 10.

Coulston, J.C. (1989). "Sculptures", in P. Bidwell and N. Holbrook (eds), *Hadrian's Wall Bridges*. London: English Heritage, 142.

Coulston, J.C.A. (1997). "The Stone Sculptures", in J.R.A. Wilson (ed.), *Roman Maryport and Its Setting*. Nottingham: Cumberland and Westmorland Antiquarian and Archaeological Society, 112–31.

Croom, A. (1998). "Some Finds from the 1997–1998 Excavations at South Shields Roman Fort", *The Arbeia Journal*, 6–7: 68–73.

Croom, A. (2002). "Sculpture", in M. Snape and P. Bidwell, Excavations at Castle Garth, Newcastle upon Tyne, 1976–92 and 1995–6: The Excavation of the Roman fort. *Archaeologia Aeliana*, 5th series, 31: 129–31.

Croom, A. (2016). "The Building Material", in A. Croom (ed.), *Segedunum: Excavations by Charles Daniels in the Roman Fort at Wallsend (1975–1984), Volume 2: The Finds*. Oxford: Oxbow, 2–15.

English Heritage. (2014). *An Archaeological Map of Hadrian's Wall, 1:25000 Scale*. Revised edition. Swindon: English Heritage.

Gillam, J. and Daniels, C. (1961). "The Roman Mausoleum on Shorden Brae, Beaufront, Corbridge, Northumberland", *Archaeologia Aeliana*, 4th series, 39: 37–61.

Gordon, A. (1726). *Itinerarium Septentrionale: Or, A Journey Thro' Most of the Counties of Scotland, and Those in the North of England*. London.

Henig, M. (2009). "The Roman Sculptural Stone", in C. Howard-Davis (ed.), *The Carlisle Millennium Project: Excavations in Carlisle, 1998–2001, Volume 2: The Finds*. Lancaster: Oxford Archaeology North, 869–72.

Hodgson, N. (2017). *Hadrian's Wall: Archaeology and History at the Limit of Rome's Empire*. Ramsbury: Hale.

Holmes, S. (1887). "On a Building at Cilurnum Supposed to Be Roman Baths", *Archaeologia Aeliana*, 2nd series, 12: 124–29.

Ian Farmer Associates. (1998). *Report for an Archaeological Watching Brief Carried Out at 52 Denhill Park, West Road, Newcastle-upon-Tyne NE15 6QH*. Unpubl. grey literature report.

Johns, C. (1982). *Sex or Symbol: Erotic Images of Greece and Rome*. London: British Museum.

Museo Nacional de Arte Romano. (2015). *Sexo, desnudo y erotismo en Augusta Emerita*. Mérida: Museo Nacional de Arte Romano.

Parker, A. (2017). "Protecting the Troops? Phallic Carvings in the North of Roman Britain", in A. Parker (ed.), *Ad Vallum: Papers on the Roman Army and Frontiers in Celebration of Dr. Brian Dobson*. British Archaeological Reports, British Series 631. Oxford: Archaeopress, 117–30.

Pringle, S. (2009). "Ceramic Building Materials: Catalogue of Illustrated Items", in *The Carlisle Millennium Project: Excavations in Carlisle, 1998–2001, Volume 3: Appendices*. Lancaster: Oxford Archaeology North Carlisle, 1449.

Snape, M. and Stobbs, G. (2016). "The Military Bath House at the Roman Fort of Chesters, Northumberland", *Archaeologia Aeliana*, 5th series, 45: 37–117.

Symonds, M.F.A. (2005). "The Construction Order of the Milecastles on Hadrian's Wall", *Archaeologia Aeliana*, 5th series, 34: 67–81.

Symonds, M.F.A. (2019). "The Purpose of Hadrian's Wall: The Dortohy Charlesworth Lecture Delivered at the Shakespeare Centre, Kendal on 6th November 2017", *Transactions of the Cumberland and Westmorland Antiquarian and Archaeological Society*, 3rd series, 19: 97–122.

Tomlin, R. (1979). "Roman Britain in 1978: Inscriptions", *Britannia*, 10: 339–56.

Whitworth, A. (2009). "Charles Anderson and the Consolidation of Hadrian's Wall", in T. Wilmott (ed.), *Hadrian's Wall: Archaeological Research by English Heritage 1976–2000*. London: English Heritage, 50–71.

Wilmott, T. (1997). *Birdoswald: Excavations of a Roman Fort on Hadrian's Wall and Its Successor Settlements 1987–92*. London: English Heritage.

10 Egyptian faience flaccid phallus pendants in the Mediterranean, Near East, and Black Sea regions

Alissa M. Whitmore

Introduction

Phallic imagery is well known in the Roman period, appearing in a variety of forms and media on rings, pendants, wall carvings, and mosaic floors (Johns 1982: 61–75; Parker 2015, 2017; Faraone 2018: 75–8; Whitmore 2018; see Chapters 4 and 9). While early scholars interpreted these items and iconography as erotica (Fisher and Langlands 2011), scholars today interpret them primarily as apotropaic items offering magical protection (Johns 1982: 42; Clarke 2003: 95–113; Whitmore 2017: 47–50; see Chapter 9).

To explore the connections between phallic iconography, magic, and sexuality, this chapter focuses on pendants in Egyptian faience and similar materials which depict the male pelvis with visibly flaccid genitalia, an interesting and understudied subset of phallic small finds. Primarily from first-century B.C. to third-century A.D. contexts, the iconography of these objects is strongly tied to the Mediterranean, but as I will show, they have also been found in the Near East and Central Asia, sometimes in the burials of adult women and men, and also children. Though these pendants lack the power of apotropaic erections, contextual evidence suggests they offered magical protection to their users through their ties with Phoenician and Egyptian cultures and their association with other amulets.

Glazed composition flaccid phallus pendants

Pendants which depict visibly flaccid male genitalia appear in a variety of materials (Figure 10.1). Bone and metal examples exist and vary greatly in size (H 1.4–6.5 cm), manufacture (i.e. casting, carved antler roundels, embossed gold discs), realism, intended users (humans or animals), and the inclusion of additional motifs, such as a fist and phallus (for examples, see Figure 4.5 and Figure 5.10).[1] This chapter focuses exclusively on pendants in Egyptian faience and visually similar materials, which present a more iconographically cohesive group than bronze and bone examples.

Ranging in colour from very light blue to green, these male genitalia pendants are made of Egyptian faience, frit, glazed ceramic or terracotta, glazed

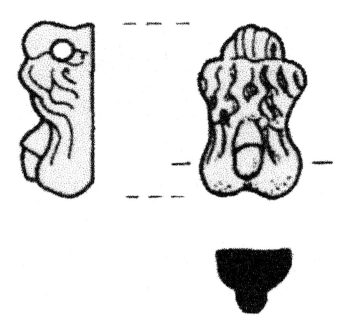

Figure 10.1 Drawing of a green frit male flaccid genitalia pendant, first–second century A. D., ed-Dur (United Arab Emirates). H 2.1 cm

(De Waele 2007, fig. 7., © Archaeopress)

stone, and glass or glass paste (*pasta vitrea*), a term used by ancient jewellery scholars for objects made primarily of glass in imitation of precious stones. Distinguishing between these materials can be difficult due to their similar appearance. Egyptian faience is made of sand or powdered quartz, which is fused with limestone and natron or plant ash, and finished with a layer of coloured glaze (Kaczmarczyk and Hedges 1983: 6, 185–95). Frit objects are also composed of powdered quartz, lime, and other additives, but in different quantities than faience, and without glaze (Higgins 1980: 41–2; Kaczmarczyk and Hedges 1983: 214). Frit appears quite similar in appearance to worn faience, so much so that frit and glazed stone objects are often mislabelled as Egyptian faience in museum collections (Vandiver 1983: 4–5, 53).

While it is possible to distinguish between chipped and worn Egyptian faience, frit, and other materials with the use of a microscope and other techniques, including X-ray fluorescence and atomic absorption analysis (Kaczmarczyk and Hedges 1983: 10–19; Vandiver 1983: 51–64), I have no expertise in this area. Furthermore, information on the pendants in this study comes from descriptions and photos in published excavation reports and jewellery catalogues – some of which are quite old – rather than in-person analysis. As a result, I must depend upon the labels and material classifications made by those who have previously excavated, studied, and published these pendants. In acknowledgement of these varied materials and the uncertain classification of some pendants, I will use "glazed composition" to refer to the general corpus of pendants. In the appendices and text describing individual pendants, I will follow the terminology used in their previous publication and will list no material if a label or classification is omitted (as an example, see Appendix 10.1, no. 4). I also note the rare cases in which they mention microscopic or other analyses of a pendant's material.

These glazed composition pendants are 1.4–2.5 cm in height, 0.9–1.5 cm wide, and 0.6–0.8 cm thick, and this small size suggests that they were primarily worn by people (Whitmore 2018: 23–4). A suspension loop is located at the top of the pendants, which are decorated only on the front. The pendants realistically depict the male genitalia, and the portrayal of the penis in context with the lower abdomen and scrotum clearly shows genitalia at rest, rather than sexually aroused.[2] The phalli hang downward and rest upon the testes, rather than projecting up or outward, and are never longer than the depicted scrotum. Some pendants have horizontal lines on the phallus suggesting loose foreskin and vertical lines on the scrotum indicating testicles hanging loosely. In appearance, these pendants differ markedly from those which have a large erect penis, sometimes accompanied by differentiated spherical testicles, as the primary feature.

The geographic and temporal distributions of glazed composition male genitalia pendants

Glazed composition pendants with flaccid male genitalia appear in the Mediterranean, the Near East, and around the Black Sea, with additional examples as far east as Central Asia (Figure 10.2).[3]

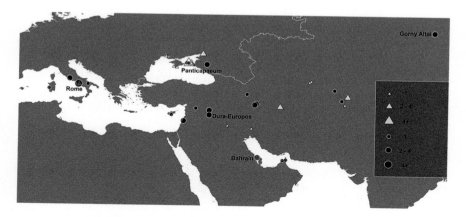

Figure 10.2 Distribution map of glazed composition flaccid phallus pendants; dots indicate sites where the information on the existence of a flaccid phallus pendant has been confirmed; triangles indicate sites with unconfirmed information

The Mediterranean

At least 13 pendants have been recovered in Mediterranean contexts, particularly the Italian sites of Herculaneum (6) and Rome (4), with the majority coming primarily from first-century A.D. contexts (Appendix 10.1).[4] The temporal outliers are from the Mediterranean islands of Tharros (Appendix 10.1, no. 1) and Amathus, Cyprus (Appendix 10.1, no. 2), the latter of which geographically could also be considered a Near Eastern example, and the complexity in the dating of these pendants will be discussed in more detail below. The Vagnari phallus (Appendix 10.1, no. 13; Figure 10.3, left) provides the latest Mediterranean date of the late first–early second century A.D. Six pendants come from mortuary contexts (Tharros, Amathus, Rome, Vagnari; Appendix 10.1, nos 1, 2, 9–11, 13). One pendant was found in a box near Skeleton 3 (a 25–35-year-old man) in Arcade 7 of the Herculaneum Beach (Appendix 10.1, no. 4 and Appendix 10.5, list 1, no. 1).[5] The others were recovered in

Figure 10.3 Examples of flaccid phallic pendants: left – blue glass paste pendant from Vagnari (Italy), late first–early second century A.D. H 1.8 cm, W 0.9 cm; right – blue-green glazed terracotta phallus from Dura-Europos (Syria), first century B.C. to second century A.D.? H 1.9 cm.

(Image on the left: reproduced with kind permission of Professor Alastair Small; image on the right: © Dura-Europos Collection, Yale University Art Gallery, acc. no. 1938.5158.6. Photo: Lisa Brody)

a bathhouse drain and the vestibule of the Palaestra in Herculaneum, and in a household destruction/fill layer in Rome (Appendix 10.1, nos 3, 5–7, and 12).

The materials of these pale blue to green flaccid phallus pendants are glass paste, glass, faience, and glazed composition. Typological variations include the depiction of pubic hair as: curls or waves (four), two stylised rows of lines or curls (three), or no pubic hair (one). Suspension loops have either no decoration or a continuation of the pubic hair, with the exception of the pendant from the Herculaneum bathhouse drain, which has horizontal lines below vertical grooves.

The Near East

At least 22 glazed composition pendants have been found in the Near East, dating primarily from the first century B.C. to the third century A.D. (Appendix 10.2).[6] They are widely dispersed, appearing along the coasts of the Caspian Sea in Iran (seven), the Persian Gulf and Gulf of Oman in Bahrain and the United Arab Emirates (four), and the Mediterranean Sea in Lebanon (two), as well as further inland at the sites of Selenkahiye, Dura-Europos (Figure 10.3, right), and Tell Sheikh Hamad in northern and eastern Syria (nine).[7] The temporal outliers are two Lebanese pendants without archaeological contexts, which the Brussels Royal Museum of Art and History dates to the seventh–fourth century B.C. and considers Phoenician amulets (Appendix 10.2, nos 1–2). The latest Near Eastern pendant was discovered in a Roman-Byzantine period jar burial at Selenkahiye (Syria), and jar burials at this site are generally dated to the mid-third century A.D. (Appendix 10.2, no. 22; van Loon 2001a: 489; Zaqzûq 2001: 516 and 525). All of the pendants with known archaeological contexts come from burials, though this correlation may reflect my preference for pendants with associated human remains.

These male genitalia pendants are made of blue or green faience, frit, glass, and glazed terracotta, ceramic, and earthenware (Figure 10.4). Typologically, the group varies most in the depiction of pubic hair, which is more often stylistically portrayed as two rows of lines or waves (eleven), but sometimes as curls (two) or simple straight or curved lines (three).

The Black Sea

Glazed composition flaccid phallus pendants have been found along the north coast of the Black Sea.[8] While Appendix 10.3 records detailed information for only four of these pendants, Alekseeva's 1975 study records 29 additional pendants that depict male genitalia, which she classifies as Type 90: 17 examples come from Panticapaeum (Kerch, Crimea), four from Tanais (Rostov Oblast, Russia), three from Kepoi (Taman Peninsula, Russia), and single finds from Olbia (Parutyne, Ukraine), Chersonesus (Sevastopol, Crimea), Charax (Gaspra, Crimea), Sennoy (Taman Peninsula, Russia), and Phanagoria (Taman Peninsula, Russia). Alekseeva's (1975: 47, 74–9) study

Figure 10.4 Beaded necklace with three faience flaccid phallus pendants, three amphora pendants, and two grape bunch pendants, first–second century A.D., Amlash? (Iran). Amphora pendant: H 2.5 cm., acc. no. 74.7.8

provides excavation dates, grave numbers, inventory numbers, and use dates for these pendants, but not individual descriptions or images. Therefore, I have not been able to verify whether they depict flaccid genitalia and have omitted them from Appendix 10.3. Alekseeva's illustrations of pendant Type 90, however, suggest that some may indeed feature flaccid phalli. The majority of the Black Sea pendants are from first–second century A.D. burial contexts, and the only strong temporal outliers in Alekseeva's (1975: 77) study were two pendants from a crypt in Panticapaeum, which was dated to the fourth–fifth century A.D.

Male genitalia pendants from around the Black Sea are primarily in blue Egyptian faience, though this term may not be appropriate for all of the pendants in Alekseeva's study (1975: 23–4). Most Black Sea examples have pubic hair stylistically depicted in two rows of vertical or wavy lines, but at least two pendants lack pubic hair and have stylised suspension loops (Alekseeva 1975, pl. 4.3706.02–03 and pl. 12.12).

Central Asia

Four glazed composition flaccid phallus pendants have been found further east in Central Asia, in mortuary contexts dating from the first–third century A.D. (Appendix 10.4; Plate 3). Other pendants in Egyptian faience or visually similar materials have been reported from the Uzbekistan sites of Koi-Krylgan-Kala and Dzhanbas Kala, and burials at Tup-Khona and Tepai-Shah in southern Tajikistan (Rtveladze 1977: 236–7; Bulygina 1986: 249–50; Mairs 2007: 81). As I have not seen them, I have left them off Appendix 10.4, but Rtveladze (1977: 236–7) notes that the examples from Dzhanbas Kala and Koi-Krylgan-Kala are very similar to the Yalangtush Tepe pendant, making it likely that they also depict flaccid genitalia.

These pendants are in blue or blue-green Egyptian faience or glazed stone. The examples from Gorny Altai and Yalangtush Tepe are very similar in appearance, with pubic hair depicted in two rows of diagonal lines, while the Tashravat pendant differs slightly with its shorter, thinner phallus and less styl-ised pubic hair.

The cultural origins and spread of glazed composition male genitalia pendants

While 11 of these glazed composite flaccid phallus pendants are from first cen-tury B.C. to second century A.D. sites in Roman Italy, just as many have been found in similarly dated contexts in the Near East – not only at sites on the edge of the empire like Tell Sheikh Hamad and Dura-Europos, but also loca-tions over 800 km to the east in Iran and over 1700 km south in the United Arab Emirates. This begs the question: where do these glazed composition pen-dants which depict flaccid male genitalia actually come from? As these Near Eastern pendants are most abundant during the first century B.C. to the third century A.D., are they culturally related to the traditions, beliefs, and behaviours of people living in and around Rome during the same period?

While the Mesopotamians, Egyptians, Phoenicians, and Carthaginians also used the phallus as a magical symbol, the Greeks and Romans were the first to depict the phallus with testicles in their magical iconography (Faraone 2018: 75; for the phallus as Hellenistic or Roman symbol, see Toll 1946: 126–7; Crawford and Rice 2000: 186; Zaqzûq 2001: 525). Phalli are carved on Greek walls and kilns, depicted on lamps and loom-weights, and appear on herms (Faraone 2018: 75–6, 132–6). Small phallic amulets that could be worn on the body, however, are rare in Archaic or Classical Greek contexts (Dasen 2015: 196), particularly compared to their regular appearance in the Roman period (Johns 1982: 63–73; Plouviez 2005; Parker 2015; Whitmore 2017).

The glazed composition flaccid phallus pendants from Tharros (Sardinia), Amathus (Cyprus), and Lebanon may be pre-Roman, though it is difficult to assign dates to these objects. The archaeological context of the Lebanese pen-dants is unknown, so museum specialists have dated them to the seventh–fourth century B.C. and identified them as Phoenician symbols of abundance based on the other beads and amulets included on these necklaces (see Musées Royaux d'Art et d'Histoire online database Carmentis, inv. nr. O.04574). The tombs at Tharros are broadly considered to be Phoenician and Punic, though many continued to be reused into the Roman period (Barnett and Mendleson 1987: 33–4). The phallic pendant is reportedly from Tomb 26, which also included Punic, Attic, and Athenian jewellery, pottery, coins, and a lamp which range in date from the seventh–third century B.C. Given the reuse of the Tharros tombs, and the possibility that these grave good assemblages, which were excavated in the 1850s, may have been altered to increase the sale price of these items (Bailey 1962: 38, 43–4), it is impossible to securely date this pendant. Tomb 228 at Amathus similarly appears to have been used multiple times between the Archaic and Roman periods (fifth century B.C. to first century A.D.? Tytgat 1989: 166–8), making a more precise date for its phallic pendant impossible.

Flaccid phallus pendants in different materials have been found at other Punic sites. In Tomb 13, Burial 1, of the fourth–third century B.C. Punic necropolis at Villamar (Sardinia), a bone pendant was found which depicts a flaccid phallus, testes, and pubis decorated with two horizontal lines and no pubic hair (Pompianu 2017: 15–19). A pendant with a flaccid phallus with foreskin, testes, and pubis with two sections of stylised pubic hair was found in a post-third-century B.C. layer at La Alcudia (Spain). Amulets from this site may be Punic imitations of Egyptian originals, either made locally or in Carthage (Ramos Folques 1973: 366–9). At a Punic *tophet* (cinerary cemetery) at Sulcis (Sardinia), at least one undated bone pendant with a flaccid phallus, stylised testes, and pubis has been found. The Sulcis amulets are also suggested to be of local Punic manufacture or imported copies of Egyptian originals (Bartoloni 1973: 183 and 187, pl. LVI).

There is little to suggest that the iconography of flaccid male genitalia on Punic pendants is Egyptian in origin. While faience is certainly associated with Egypt and amulets with clear Egyptian iconography have been found at Punic sites, Barnett and Mendleson (1987: 111) note that phallic amulets are uncommon in Egyptian (and Punic) contexts. While some pendants depicting flaccid male genitalia appear in Petrie's (1972: 11, pl. 1) publication of Egyptian amulets, they date to the Romano-Egyptian period. It is possible that Phoenician and Punic amulets which depict a straight, erect phallus might be inspired by the larger phallic statuettes (called *phalloi*) recovered at New Kingdom (sixteenth–eleventh century B.C.) sanctuaries to the goddess Hathor (Meskell 2004: 140–2; Regev 2013: 105), but this cannot be said for the flaccid examples.

A bronze statue of possible Etruscan date provides a rare example of someone wearing a phallic pendant, and depicts a nude boy wearing on his chest a diagonal strap of amulets (Figure 10.5), including a flaccid phallus with foreskin tapering to a point, testes, and no pubic hair (Bieber 1915: 70, pl. xliv). This statue may depict an amulet string (or *crepundia*), which is sometimes shown in Athenian vase paintings tied around the torsos of children (Faraone

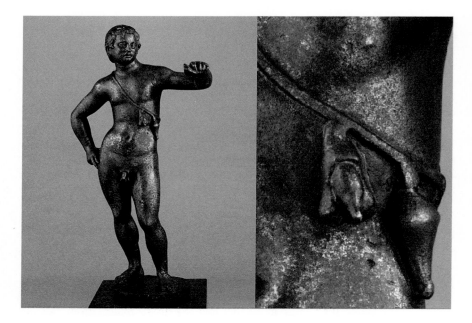

Figure 10.5 Possibly Etruscan bronze statue of a boy wearing a flaccid phallus amulet on his *crepundia*, which also includes amphora and strigil/sickle pendants. Statue: H 34 cm. Inv. nr. Br122

(© Museumslandschaft Hessen Kassel, Antikensammlung)

2018: 28, 32–4), though the *crepundia* on vase paintings rarely include phallic pendants.

The Punic bone flaccid phallus amulets and the pendant on the Etruscan statue differ stylistically from the Phoenician and later glazed composition pendants, particularly in their depiction of foreskin, which on some Punic examples extends past the glans as a small ball or stylised rectangle. However, these early Phoenician, Punic, and potentially Etruscan flaccid phallus pendants, the first-century B.C. to first-century A.D. appearance of glazed composition pendants in both Italy and the Near East, and the history of cultural interactions and trade in this region, all suggest that flaccid male genitalia pendants may be Mediterranean, rather than strictly "Roman", artefacts (Bartoloni 1973: 183; Barnett and Mendleson 1987: 108; Haerinck et al. 1991: 56; Jasim 2006; Mairs 2007; Faraone 2018: 8–10, 78, 132).

Glazed composition male genitalia pendants in first-century B.C. to third-century A.D. contexts in the Near East, the Black Sea, and Central Asia are most often identified as objects imported from or inspired by the Mediterranean,[9] and these items could have easily spread east through trade. Egypt and the Near East had already been trading for thousands of years, and trade routes between Rome and the Parthian empire were likely established by the first century B.C. (Wehry 2013, p. xlviii). Imported glazed composition flaccid phallus pendants appear in the Parthian and Parthian–Roman cemeteries of Gishtagh Ousti, Chojiran, Dura-Europos, Tell Sheikh Hamad, Dibba, and Hassani Mahale by the first century B.C. to the first century A.D., imported from Rome or Roman Egypt. Other Roman objects from first century A.D. burials in the Arabian Peninsula further demonstrate the well-established trade between these areas (Jasim 2006: 234–5; De Waele 2007: 297 and 304).

By at least the first century A.D., flaccid male genitalia pendants appear on the north Black Sea coast. This region has a long history of exchange and interactions with the cultures of the Mediterranean, central Europe, and Asia, and several of the sites (Olbia, Panticapaeum) with glazed composition phallic pendants were founded by Greek colonists in the sixth century B.C. (Petersen 2010: 33–8, 53, 251). Egyptian faience objects may have appeared in the north Black Sea region as early as the seventh–sixth century B.C. (Piotrovski 1958: 20, 23–4), and were widespread by the first century A.D., though figural pendants were rarer and typically recovered near large trading centres, like Panticapaeum (Alekseeva 1970: 166; 1975: 30). The cemeteries with glazed composition flaccid phallus pendants further support cultural interactions in this region: the Novo-Otradnoe cemetery has evidence of Sarmatian as well as Greek burial practices (Arsen'eva 1970), and the Chernyshev phallic pendant burial also contains a Roman Aucissa fibula and a Sarmatian zoomorphic pitcher (Carazzetti and Mazzeo 1990: 32–3).

Glazed composition male genitalia pendants were present in central Asia by the first century A.D., though they are rarer in this region (Bulygina 1986: 247). Trade existed between the eastern Mediterranean and south-central Asia at least by the Greek colonisation of the region in the fourth century B.C. (Mairs 2007: 74–8). Typological similarities may indicate that male genitalia pendants came from the Black Sea to central Asia with Aorsi or Sarmatian traders (Piotrovski 1958: 27; Rtveladze 1977: 237–8), from Iran via the Great Silk Road (Bulygina 1986: 252; cf. Piotrovski 1958: 22), or along both of these routes (Mairs 2007: 81–2). Central Asian nomadic peoples may have brought these pendants further east to Gorny Altai, where they were found in a Hunnu-Sarmatian burial (Bogdanov and Sljusarenko 2007: 77 and 80).

Interpreting flaccid male genitalia pendants

The flaccid genitalia on these glazed composition pendants sets them apart from the larger corpus of Roman phallic pendants, which typically depict an erect, sometimes disembodied, penis. While many of the glazed composition flaccid phallus pendants date to the Roman Republic (cf. Deschler-Erb and Božič 2002: 40), examples persist into the first century A.D. in the Mediterranean and the second–third century A.D. in the Near East, the Black Sea, and Central Asia. In the Mediterranean, erect and flaccid phallus pendants overlap in date and distribution, with both types coming from the same sites, contexts, and assemblages.[10] Therefore, the iconography of Roman period phallic pendants cannot simply be explained as a temporal shift in which depictions of flaccid genitalia were isolated to the Republic and erect phalli to the Empire.

The flaccid state of the phalli on these pendants is significant for their interpretation. Phallic images and objects are primarily interpreted as *apotropaia*, protective objects which ward away evil, illness, and bad luck, but this explanation often hinges upon the power of an *erect* phallus to accomplish this task (cf. Dasen 2015: 186; Chapters 4 and 9).

Many ancient texts suggest that the apotropaic phallus is erect, with several referencing the ithyphallic (erect) fertility gods Priapus or Fascinus (Whitmore 2018: 25–7), who may imbue images of erect phalli with their protective power. The Latin term *fascinum*, which is related to the god Fascinus, translates as bewitchment or charm, and was also slang for penis. Many of these euphemistic uses of *fascinum* reference an erect phallus, and in many cases, erect phallic objects. In Petronius, *fascinum* describes a very large human penis (*Satyricon* 92.3), but also a dildo (*Satyricon* 138.1). In the *Priapea*, Priapus – as the god and statue – has a red (83.8), erect *fascinum* (79.1), which can be used to protect gardens by raping thieves (28.13; Whitmore 2017: 48–50). *Fascinum* linguistically connects erect phalli with protective magic and bewitchments, and in the context of the *Priapea*, this phallic protection carries an aggressive element and threats of sexual violence (Richlin 1992: 121; Dasen 2015: 186–7; Whitmore 2018: 27–8). In Diodorus Siculus' myths of Priapus, his name is said to translate as penis, his statues protect gardens and vineyards, and he punishes those who cast the Evil Eye (4.6.2–4). Statues of satyrs, a rapacious group that is regularly depicted with erections, are also said to protect against the Evil Eye (Plin., *NH* 19.50). Similar links between phallic magical protection and aggression appear on wall carvings and mosaics, where phallic creatures battling the Evil Eye often have erections, and some use ejaculation as a weapon (Johns 1982: 92–4; Clarke 2003: 108–9; Ogden 2002: 225; Parker and Ross 2016; Parker 2017: 117–18; see Chapter 4 and Figure 4.1).

The ancient texts which reference phallic pendants are vague and do not specify whether they depict erect or flaccid genitalia (Plin. *HN* 28.39; Plaut. *Mil.* 1398–9; Varro *Ling.* 7.96–7), but many phallic pendants archaeologically recovered feature erect phalli. In some cases, the pendants are designed in such a way that the pendant's phallus projects from the wearer's body, and this three-dimensionality likely aided in their apotropaic function by making the phallus more visible and thus effective at dispelling the Evil Eye (Whitmore 2017: 55–9). One such ithyphallic pendant has white paint on the glans, suggesting an erect, ejaculating phallus (see Artefacts, AMP-4025). While such phallic pendants are depicted without the rest of the body, they remain quite strongly linked to the biological, sexual processes of erection and ejaculation.

If an erection is what makes a phallus apotropaic, would flaccid phallic pendants confer magical protection? Only in Horace's *Epode* 8 is the magically associated term *fascinum* used for a flaccid penis, and in his commentary on this passage, Porphyrio notes that the word is used since bewitchments were believed to cause impotence (*Commentum in Horati Epodos* 8.18).

An argument can be made that some classical flaccid phalli might be intended as apotropaic. McNiven (1995) suggests that in Athenian vase painting, "proper" citizen males are depicted with small, flaccid genitalia, except during sex. Men who were socially marginalised in Athenian culture, however, such as manual labourers, foreigners, slaves, and dwarves, were regularly depicted with large, flaccid phalli in a variety of non-sexual scenes, which functioned as an artistic shorthand to establish them as the "other". Other vase paintings depict men who expose large, flaccid penises while fighting, vomiting, defecating, and urinating in drunken processions, signifying their loss of control and *hybris*, or arrogance that defies the gods (McNiven 1995: 10–14).

Extending this argument, Clarke (2014: 525) posits that the Romans similarly saw a large, flaccid phallus as an "ugly and comical … physical peculiarity", which represented *atopia* ("unbecomingness"), particularly when it belonged to an individual whose appearance or behaviour did not align with cultural norms. The word *atopia* appears in Plutarch's description of how some amulets could protect against the Evil Eye. While not mentioning phalli, he notes that certain amulets which are unusual in appearance (ἀτοπίαν) draw the evil eye away from the victim, lessening its power (Plut. *Quaest. conv.* 5.7.680c–683b).

In Roman mosaics and wall paintings, African men, slaves, and pygmies often have prominent erections or flaccid "macrophallic" penises that are as wide as a thigh and hang to their knees (Dunbabin 1989, pl. XV, b; Clarke 1996, fig. 80). The hyper-sexualisation of these individuals may function as an apotropaic device, with their unbecoming, over-sized, "un-Roman" phalli eliciting laughter, which – as the opposing force to evil – was effective in disrupting the Evil Eye (Clarke 1996: 193–5; 2003: 111). This explanation of apotropaic phallic power may also extend to ithyphallic depictions of satyrs and the foreign god Priapus, or other iconography which includes an unexpected phallus that might surprise ancient viewers into laughing (Johns 1982: 42; Clarke 2003: 104–12; 2014: 525–6; Whitmore 2017: 56–9; 2018: 25–6).

There are some pendants which feature a large, flaccid phallus. A silver example comes from a first to fourth-century A.D. child's burial in the Necropolis of Julia Apia in France (Figure 10.6; Dumoulin 1958: 218–20). An 1850's excavation in Caerleon (Wales) produced an unstratified antler roundel from the "Castle Baths" which depicts a flaccid penis and elongated scrotum. Secure dates for this artefact and site are lacking, but first-century A.D. Samian ware and coins from the third–fourth century A.D. were recovered.[11] While both objects depict a large flaccid phallus, they diverge from one another (and from the glazed composition flaccid genitalia pendants) in material, suspension method, and the depiction of the phallus and pubic hair. The Julia Apia pendant was found on the chest of a child together with a gold bulla, suggesting that it functioned as an amulet (Dumoulin 1958: 218–20; Dasen 2003: 286). It remains uncertain, however, if Greco-Roman beliefs about "unbecoming" flaccid phalli

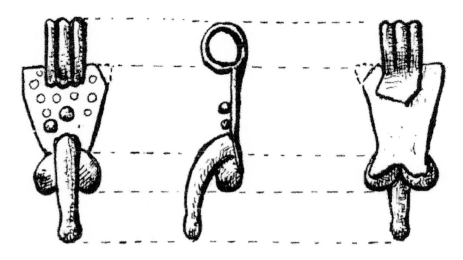

Figure 10.6 Drawing of silver flaccid phallus pendant from the Necropolis of Julia Apia (France). H 1.9 cm, W 0.7 cm.

(After Dumoulin 1958, fig. 25.2)

and apotropaic protection would be applicable outside of the Mediterranean. Furthermore, most pendants depict a small, rather than large, flaccid phallus.

Other Mediterranean flaccid phallus artefacts

Greek terracotta oil flasks, typically dating to the sixth century B.C., offer a visual parallel for pendants depicting flaccid male genitalia (Plate 4). Taking the shape of a phallus, testes, and pubis, these objects range from 8.5 to 11.5 cm tall and have an opening at the top for liquids. Phallic oil flasks vary in their depiction of foreskin, painted or carved patterns on the phallus, pubic hair, and decorative elements on the back. At least two flasks have suspension holes which suggest that they served as votive offerings (British Museum, nos 1861,0425.38 and W.442).

Greek, Etruscan, and Roman phallic ex-voto offerings also resemble flaccid phallus pendants. These objects are known from the fourth century B.C. into the Roman imperial period, and are made of terracotta, bronze, or occasionally marble (Figure 10.7), ranging from 4 to 15 cm in height. They regularly depict a flaccid phallus, testes, and pubis (Johns 1982: 57–9; Grove 2017: 231–2). While many are similar in appearance, variations occur in the depiction of foreskin, pubic hair, and the length of the phallus, though none are macrophallic (for examples see British Museum, nos 1814,0704.1263 and 1974,1107.4; some examples depict partially erect phalli with differentiated testes: British Museum, nos 1814,0704.877, 1814,0704.1256 and 1865,1118.109). Ex-votos may have

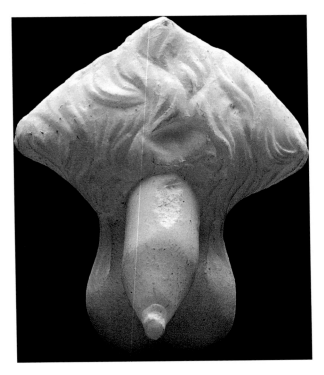

Figure 10.7 Marble votive male genitalia, second century B.C. to fourth century A.D. Est.
    H 15.2 cm, W 12.2 cm. Credit: Wellcome Science Museum, London.
(CC BY 4.0)

been dedicated when asking a deity for help and indicated the part in need of
healing (Adams 2017: 199–207), or were displayed afterwards as thanks (Oberhelman 2014: 47; Schörner 2015: 401–9). Instead of pubic hair, a second to
third-century A.D. bronze example in the Harvard Art Museum has an inscription on the pubis reading "to Hermes, the highest of the gods" and two iron
mounting pins still in place (obj. nr. 2012.1.131). Ex-votos featuring flaccid
male genitalia are often associated with infertility (Schörner 2015: 407), urinary
difficulties, or hernias, and examples from Corinth (Greece) and Ponte di Nona
(Italy) may reference phimosis, a tightening of the foreskin which prevents its
retraction during erection (Johns 1982: 59; Oberhelman 2014: 50, 56–7).
    While pendants, oil flasks, and ex-votos can all take the form of flaccid phalli,
they differ in size, material, date, function, and archaeological context. Oil flasks
were used in bathing, but were also recovered in graves (Johns 1982: 92), functioning as personal possessions or ceremonial objects. The phalli on oil flasks were not
"unbecoming" by Greco-Roman standards, but their (potentially apotropaic) humour
might come from seeing an everyday object shaped like a penis (Johns 1982: 92–3;

cf. Clarke 2003: 116–33). Phalli on votive offerings depict an unwell or healed human penis, rather than an apotropaic god's divine phallus (Grove 2017: 231), and were a way to communicate with healing deities. Given the differences between these objects, flaccid phallus pendants cannot be interpreted as if they are oil flasks or votives, but I will consider potential humorous protective or healing functions for these pendants in more detail below.

Glazed composition flaccid phallus pendants and foreign magic

As objects with ties to multiple Mediterranean cultures, glazed composition male genitalia pendants may have been granted magical power due to their perceived connections with these ancient cultures, particularly during the Roman period, when Egypt and the Near East were characterised as the homelands of magic (Ogden 2002: 33–4).

The Greeks and Romans believed that Egypt was strongly tied to magic, and Egyptian materials, deities, and symbols were often used in Roman amulets (Scatozza Höricht 1989: 80, 92, 95; Ogden 2002: 52–60). Male genitalia pendants from the Black Sea and Central Asia are frequently identified as Egyptian or Egyptianising (Piotrovski 1958; Rtveladze 1977; Bulygina 1986; Clerc 1991: 63; Bogdanov and Sljusarenko 2007; Mairs 2007) and while the symbol of a flaccid phallus is not particularly Egyptian, blue-green faience and visually similar imitation materials[12] were strongly associated with Egypt. Faience symbolised joy, youth, and rebirth (Clerc 1991: 142), and was used for Egyptian statuettes and ritual objects. In ancient Egypt, faience amulets – some of which depicted body parts – were worn in life and used in mummy wrappings to give the deceased supernatural powers, to ensure that bodily functions continued, and to draw away the attacks of evil spirits (Bulygina 1986: 251–2; Taylor 2001: 116, 201–3).

Phoenicia was also a destination to learn magic (Plin. *HN* 30.9), and Lucian (*Alex.* 13) notes that a charlatan mage used Phoenician words in a spell. The glazed composition male genitalia pendants used during the Roman period may well draw upon an earlier Phoenician tradition. Phoenician phallic pendants have been interpreted as symbols of abundance, fertility, and as apotropaic amulets adopted from or inspired by Egypt (Barnett and Mendleson 1987: 42 and 111; Regev 2013: 105). Punic flaccid phallus pendants may also have had an apotropaic function, with their sexual reference offering supernatural protection (Bartoloni 1973: 186).

The protective functions of Egyptian faience and Phoenician and Punic flaccid phallus amulets may have been extended to Roman period glazed composition male genitalia pendants, making them powerful apotropaic devices simply because of their links to these magical cultures.

Archaeological context and the function of glazed composition flaccid phallus pendants

It is difficult to say whether these pendants retained the same meanings over time and across their wide geographic distribution. Particularly in the east, symbolic meanings may not have been imported along with objects (De Waele 2007: 297–8), and we cannot assume that local populations would have associated these pendants with Egyptian or Mediterranean cultures or religions (Bulygina 1986: 251–2; Mairs 2007: 82). Archaeological contexts can, however, provide further insights into how these objects may have been used.

The vast majority of these pendants come from mortuary contexts, with at least four found in child burials (Appendix 10.5).[13] The male genitalia pendants found at the necks of the nine to twelve-month-old Vagnari (Italy) infant, the six to nine-month-old Tell Sheikh Hamad (Syria) infant, and the child from Novo-Otradnoe (Crimea) are reminiscent of the "shameful thing" (*turpicula res*) that is tied at the necks of living children to protect them (Varro *Ling.* 7.96–7; Appendix 10.5, list 1, no. 2; list 2, no. 2; and list 3, no. 1). While a small, flaccid penis would not be shameful in the Roman mindset, this term may have been used in jest and what is shameful and unseemly (and perhaps, surprising and protective) is the sight of a penis out of anatomic position at the neck of a child (Whitmore 2017: 47–50; 2018: 25–6).

At almost every site, these glazed composition flaccid phallus pendants were found in contexts containing other pendants, beads, and amulets. At the Mediterranean sites of Herculaneum's Arcade 7 and Rome's III Casa Circondariale Necropolis, flaccid male genitalia pendants were found in close association and may have been strung with beads and well-known apotropaic amulets, including scarabs, Harpocrates, and a manus fica (Appendix 10.1, nos 4, 9–11). Every Near Eastern phallic pendant in this study was found with other beads and amulets, including grape bunches, amphoras, manus ficas, and a crescent pendant, and five burials included bronze bells, objects which also had an apotropaic function in the Roman world (Parker 2018: 64). In at least five burials – Tell Sheikh Hamad 87/51 and 92/25, ed-Dur, Hassani Mahale, and Selenkahiye – flaccid pendants were reported in close proximity to beads, bronze bells, and manus fica, amphora, grape bunches, and turtle pendants, suggesting that they too were strung as necklaces or bracelets (Appendix 10.2, nos 6, 7, 18, 20–22). A similar pattern exists further east. Around the Black Sea, Egyptian faience amulets were often strung with beads in children's graves (Piotrovski 1958: 24–5), and the child at Novo-Otradnoe was buried wearing a necklace of beads and phallus, amphora, and scarab pendants, with a bronze bell found to the side of the skull (Arsen'eva 1970: 94; Appendix 10.3, no. 1). In Central Asia, the Tup-Khona glazed composition phalli were found with fist, amphora, and frog amulets (Mairs 2007: 81), the Yalangtush Tepe pendant was found with beads, and the Tashravat pendant was worn strung with beads as a necklace (Appendix 10.4, nos 1–2).

While textual and iconographic evidence does not prove that small flaccid phalli were apotropaic, their archaeological association with other amulets may support this interpretation. Just as fist and phallus or ithyphallic lunate pendants combined protective symbols to create a more powerful amulet (Johns 1982: 66–72; Parker 2015; see Chapters 4 and 5), the necklaces or amulet strands with flaccid phallus pendants and other protective symbols might produce a potent composite object. Such amulet strands, or *crepundia*, have a protective or potentially healing function for the children – and in some cases, adult women – who wore them (Faraone 2018: 28–60). While some have suggested a potential Phoenician or eastern origin for *crepundia*, Faraone (2018: 32–5, 304, n. 29) argues that amulet strings worn diagonally on the chest of children or around the arms or thighs of women were a Greek tradition, while the Italic equivalents were amulet cords worn around the neck. While phallic pendants rarely appear in ancient iconographic representations of *crepundia*, Plautus' *Miles Gloriosus* (1398–9) offers one textual allusion, in which a man threatens to castrate another, remarking that his knife "is eager to deprive this adulterer of his genitalia, so that they may now as if on a child's neck hang as *crepundia*".[14]

If apotropaic phallic protection requires distracting, humorous, erect, and oversized penises or ithyphallic deities, small flaccid phallus pendants may offer less protection than their erect counterparts. This perhaps necessitates their association with other amulets on *crepundia*,[15] and only five of the flaccid pendants in this study – one from Vagnari, two from Chernyshev (Black Sea), and two from Gorny Altai (Central Asia) – appear completely in isolation from beads or other types of amulets. It is also possible that the appearance of these flaccid male genitalia pendants in burial contexts reflects the selective interment of the dead with less powerful amulets, with families perhaps saving more powerful erect phallus pendants for those still living.

While glazed composition flaccid phallus pendants and *crepundia* assemblages have been found in Near Eastern, Black Sea, and Central Asian burials, we cannot be certain that these objects retained the apotropaic function that they had in the Mediterranean, even if found in similar archaeological contexts. With the exception of a statuette from Roman Turkey that depicts two phalli sawing an Evil Eye (Johns 1982: 66–8), virtually all of the evidence for the apotropaic phallus comes from the western Mediterranean. The reoccurrence of glazed composition phallus pendants in eastern grave contexts suggests that they were viewed as appropriate – though given their rarity, not necessary – objects for deceased individuals throughout these regions. Apotropaic protection may explain the association between these amulets and the dead, and scholars working with glazed composition pendants and sites in the Near East, northern Black Sea, and Central Asia predominantly suggest an apotropaic use for these objects, in addition to a possible fertility function.[16] If flaccid male genitalia pendants were *apotropaia* in the east, we cannot be certain the magic worked in the same way as in the Mediterranean, and while Near Eastern, Black Sea, and Central Asian burials indicate that these pendants were sometimes worn in death, without additional evidence, it is uncertain if or how they were used in life. However, one significant regional difference does appear in the use of glazed composition flaccid phallus pendants: their association with adult women in the East.

Eastern women and phallic pendants

In the Roman west, phallic pendants were strongly associated with children (Whitmore 2017: 50–4, n. 14; Faraone 2018: 75). While Pliny (*HN* 28.39) notes that generals are also under the protection of Fascinus, this passage likely refers to the use of amulets on military mounts (Whitmore 2018: 22–4). Occasionally, adults are archaeologically associated with phallic pendants in the west. An adult, possibly male, was buried in the third century A.D. with an ithyphallic lunate pendant at Guilden Morden, England (Fox and Lethbridge 1926: 58–60). A 25–35-year-old man with a box of amulets, including a flaccid phallus, was found on the Herculaneum Beach (Appendix 10.1, no. 4), and another adult was found in Pompeii's House of Holconius carrying a box (*pyxis*) of amulets which contained two flaccid phallus pendants of unknown material. This adult has not been anthropologically analysed, but some have suggested it is a woman based on the contents of the box, which include hairpins, a gold ear-ring, bracelets, an ivory comb, and a bronze mirror (Fiorelli 1861: 17–18; Dwyer 2013: 32–3). Besides these examples, however, most individuals found with phallic pendants are children.

Phallic pendants are also associated with children in the east (Piotrovski 1958: 24; Alekseeva 1970: 166; 1975: 30; Wehry 2013: 233), but there are examples of adults buried with them. Appendix 10.5 records the ages and sexes of individuals found with glazed composition flaccid phallus pendants, if the pendants were worn, and a brief summary of associated artefacts. Only nine individuals found with flaccid male genitalia pendants have detailed anthropological information on age and/or sex, and five are adults: the 25–35-year-old man from the Herculaneum Beach, two adults from the Near East, and two women from Central Asia.

The Near Eastern adults with flaccid phallic pendants were not anthropologically analysed, but both were gendered female based on grave goods (Sono and Fukai 1968: 8; Haerinck 2001: 20). The adult from first to third-century A.D. Hassani Mahale was buried with three bracelets, six spindle whorls, and a decorative mirror, objects which were traditionally, though not exclusively, associated with women in the Roman world (Kampen 1996: 22; Allison 2013: 95; Eckardt 2014: 59, 143–4; see Chapter 7). The copper needle (L 9.3 cm, D 0.5 cm) found under the head of the Hassani Mahale adult may be a hair needle, used to create elaborate hairstyles favoured by women during the Roman empire (Stephens 2008). In the first to second-century A.D. ed-Dur burial, the deceased wore a bracelet, ring, and toe-ring, and a stone whorl and bronze needle were also included. Here as well, the bracelet and spindle whorl may suggest a female occupant (Haerinck 2001: 20).

Caution is necessary when using grave goods to gender skeletons, as counter-examples always exist and different practices may have existed in the provinces, particularly in the east (Allison 2013: 81–2). This is especially important here, since many of the flaccid phallus pendants come from graves outside the Roman Empire. As such, while the Hassani Mahale and ed-Dur graves clearly belong to adults, these individuals can only potentially be identified as women.

None of the Black Sea glazed composition phalli in this study were found with adults. Kostsushko-Valjuzinicha (1911: 189) notes that faience phallic pendants are common in Roman period female graves at Chersonesus, though the early publication date calls this gender assignment into question. A blue glass erect genitalia pendant has been found with a 35-year-old woman in a fourth century B.C. grave at Nymphaion, Crimea (Grach 1999: 66). In Central Asia, phallic pendants appear more strongly associated with women than children (Bulygina 1986: 251; Mairs 2007: 81–3). Both of the individuals from Tashravat and Gorny Altai have been anthropologically identified as female. At Gorny Altai, two "faience" flaccid phalli were found at the neck of a 45–55-year-old woman (Bogdanov and Sljusarenko 2007: 77–8), and at Tashravat, a faience phallus and 33 beads were found among the ribs of an adult woman (Bulygina 1986: 248).

Women and children were particularly vulnerable to illness and the Evil Eye in antiquity, and they used amulets for protection in Classical Greece (Faraone 2018: 28), during the Roman Empire (Dasen 2015), in the Near East (Bagherpour Kashani 2011: 272), and in Central Asia (Mairs 2007: 83). Therefore, it is possible that women would have used phallic amulets for protection. While there are no certain examples of western women with phallic pendants, protective phalli appear on objects predominantly used by women, including Greek loom-weights (Faraone 2018: 75 and 246) and on Roman hairpins and earrings (Whitmore 2017: 52).

Four of the five adults in Appendix 10.5, as well as the Pompeian adult from the House of Holconius, wore or carried their flaccid phallic pendants with other beads or amulets, perhaps as a necklace, bracelet, or *crepundia*. While adult men were not strongly associated with these amulet strings, some evidence from the Greek world suggests that adult women may have kept and continued to wear their childhood *crepundia*. A fourth century B.C. Attic jewellery box (*pyxis*) is decorated with a *crepundia*, and women's *crepundia* allow them to be recognised in Roman plays by Terence (*Eun.* 753f) and Plautus (*Cist.* 635f), both of which are based on Greek originals (Faraone 2018: 56–60). Since the plot in these plays centred upon female characters keeping their *crepundia*, it seems probable that this behaviour might have continued into the Roman period. It is tempting to interpret the flaccid phallus pendants carried with Pompeiian and Herculanean adults in this way, with the adult man perhaps carrying the box for a child or female relative.

The unexpected discovery of phallic pendants with women in the east may parallel the recovery of bronze *bullae* in late Roman female graves in the northern provinces of Raetia and Pannonia (Swift 2003: 345; Szilágyi 2005: 21–2; Dasen 2015: 194). While Swift (2003: 345) notes that we cannot assume that these *bullae* functioned in the same way as the *bullae* belonging to Roman children, many do seem to have been amulets, containing medicinal plants and inscribed silver lamella (Dasen 2015: 194). This may be evidence of a provincial custom, where women, who were more vulnerable than men, wore *bullae* for apotropaic protection against illness and harm (Szilágyi 2005: 22). Similarly, phallic pendants in the graves of eastern adults and women could be attributed to the protective abilities of these objects, with the western association of phallic pendants with children either lost along the trade routes or disregarded as irrelevant by local populations (cf. Mairs 2007: 83).

The association between women and flaccid phallus pendants in the Near East and Central Asia may increase the likelihood that these objects had an added fertility function in these regions.[17] While flaccid phallus votive offerings are related to fertility in the Greco-Roman world, and phallic imagery is associated with fertility in a number of cultures (cf. Whitmore 2018: 26–7), pendants depicting erect rather than flaccid phalli seem better suited as amulets for the fertility concerns of adults. Furthermore, it is doubtful that the 45–55-year-old Gorny Altai woman who was buried wearing two flaccid phallus pendants was concerned with her personal fertility.

It is possible, however, that amulets depicting flaccid genitalia provided an indirect fertility benefit for children, particularly male children. Scholars often interpret eastern glazed composition pendants in light of Egyptian body-shaped amulets, which protected the individual by confusing malevolent spirits (Bulygina 1986: 251), perhaps into attacking the amulet, rather than the wearer's body. This same phenomenon exists in Thai culture, where phallic amulets are believed to protect a boy's future virility by drawing spiritual attacks away from the child's genitals (Whitmore 2018: 20). In this way, ancient flaccid phallus pendants might have offered indirect fertility assistance by protecting a child's future virility. This possible function, however, seems unlikely for the adult female wearers of these pendants in the east.

Conclusion

Given that most ancient texts and iconography suggest that apotropaic power centred upon the erect phallus, pendants depicting flaccid genitalia are somewhat anomalous and initially seem more connected to the iconography of humorous phallic vessels or ex-voto offerings, rather than phallic protection. The recovery of flaccid phallus pendants in burials with beads and amulets, however, suggests that they were protective objects, even if this function cannot be readily explained by interpretations of phallic protection rooted in distracting, "un-Roman" phalli or ithyphallic gods. The protective power of glazed composition flaccid phallus pendants in the first century B.C. to the second century A.D. instead is rooted in their perceived connections to the older, foreign, magically inclined Phoenician and Egyptian cultures, and their use in conjunction with other beads and amulets to form a more powerful protective object – a *crepundia*.

With Mediterranean origins dating back to the seventh to fourth century B.C., these pendants may have spread via well-established land and possibly sea trade routes into the mainland Near East by the first century B.C. to the first century A.

D., then up to the north Black Sea Coast and east into Central Asia by the first to second century A.D. In these regions, the recovery of flaccid male genitalia pendants and other amulets in graves suggests that these objects retained an apotropaic function, though different explanations for their power may be necessary. Additional functions might also have been added, including a possible intertwined fertility benefit for boys, with the amulets perhaps acting as decoys to protect their future virility. Women – particularly in Central Asia, but also potentially in the Near East – were occasionally buried with these pendants, suggesting that their use expanded and changed over time as these objects left the Mediterranean.

In the west, glazed composition flaccid phalli are rare after the first century A.D., as other types of amulets become more popular, including fist and phallus amulets, some of which incorporate a flaccid penis between the erect phallus and manus fica that serve as the primary symbols on this type of pendant. Flaccid phallus amulets continued to be used in the Near East, Black Sea, and Central Asia until the third century A.D., which marks the end of this unusual example of phallic apotropaic magic.

Acknowledgements

My thanks to Tatiana Ivleva and Rob Collins for their invitation to contribute to this volume, for their patience during the writing and editing process, and their assistance in securing image reproduction rights for the Museumslandschaft Hessen Kassel bronze statue. Thanks to Lisa Brody (Yale University Art Gallery) and Evgeniy Bogdanov (Russian Academy of Sciences) for providing information and photos of the Dura-Europos and Gorny Altai pendants. I thank Stefanie Hoss, Adam Parker, and the Perry Public Library for helping track down some difficult to find sources, and Tatiana Ivleva for providing the Russian transliterations and the finds distribution map. This chapter was greatly improved by comments from Adam Parker, Stefanie Hoss, Jennifer Baird, the editors, and anonymous reviewers. Any errors are mine alone.

Appendix 10.1: Glazed composition flaccid phallus pendants from the Mediterranean

1. Location: Tharros, Sardinia
    Date: seventh–third c. B.C.?
    Description: green glazed composition phallus. Pubic hair denoted by wavy lines. Heavily worn. H 1.8 cm.
    Context: Tomb 26. Frequently reused and long-lived multi-burial tomb. No information on human remains. Potentially associated grave goods include silver earrings, a beaded necklace, scarabs, an amphora pendant, amulets of Egyptian gods, Punic jewellery, Punic pottery and terracotta, Attic pottery, an Athenian lamp, and a Punic coin.
    Source: Bailey 1962: 43–4; Barnett and Mendleson 1987: 41–2, 109–11, 197–8; British Museum, inv. no 134041.

2. Location: Amathus, Cyprus
    Date: fifth c. B.C.–first c. A.D.?
    Description: turquoise phallus, possibly faience, but exact material unknown since core is not visible (Clerc 1991: 63). Pubic hair denoted by wavy lines. Undecorated suspension loop. H 1.7 cm, W 0.9 cm, T 0.6 cm.
    Context: SW necropolis, Tomb 228. Frequently reused and long-lived multi-burial tomb.
    Human remains and many grave goods, including glass and faience beads, scarabs, bracelets, amulets, strigils, and a mirror, dispersed throughout tomb.
    Source: Tytgat 1989: 166–8; Clerc 1991: 63, 139–43.

3. Location: Herculaneum, Italy
    Date: first c. B.C.–first c. A.D.
    Description: brown (formerly turquoise) glass paste (*pasta vitrea*) phallus. Two horizontal lines indicate foreskin. Pubis has a vertical notch above penis and no pubic hair. Suspension loop decorated with three horizontal lines and two vertical grooves. H 2.0 cm, W 0.9 cm.
    Context: drain of forum baths, under Palaestra. Found with glass paste amphora pendant and amber Harpocrates amulet.
    Source: Scatozza Höricht 1989: 72–3; Whitmore 2013: 174–5, 395.

4. Location: Herculaneum, Italy
    Date: first c. A.D.
    Description: blue-green phallus. Pubic hair denoted by curls which continue up suspension loop. Est. H 2.5 cm.
    Context: Arcade 7, Herculaneum beach, with Skeleton 3 (male, 25–35 years). Found among 45 beads and amulets, including 2 phalli, scarabs, 2 Harpocrates or Zeus, an Egyptian deity, and shells. Likely formed a necklace or bracelet, carried in a wooden box or fabric sack.
    Source: De Carolis 1996: 170–1, 175–6; Torino and Fornaciari 1996: 188; Roberts 2013: 290.

5–7. Location: Herculaneum, Italy
    Date: first c. A.D.
    Description: three turquoise glass paste (*pasta vitrea*) phalli. Heavily worn. H 1.4, 1.5, and 1.9 cm.
    Context: vestibule of the Palaestra, *Ins. Or.* II 4. Found with three glass paste amphora pendants and a scarab.
    Source: Scatozza Höricht 1989: 86–7.

8. Location: Herculaneum, Italy
    Date: first c. A.D.
    Description: green faience phallus. Pubic hair denoted by two horizontal rows of diagonal lines. H. 1.7 cm.
    Context: unknown, but in the Naples Archaeological Museum by 1866.
    Source: Fiorelli 1866: 11; De Caro 2000: 74 and 80.

9–11. Location: Rome, Italy
  Date: first c. A.D.
  Description: three blue glass paste (*pasta vitrea*) phalli (II.335/463477).
  A horizontal line indicates foreskin and two pendants have vertical ten-
  sion lines on scrotum. Pubic hair denoted by curls. H 1.6 cm.
  Context: III Casa Circondariale Necropolis, Via Tiburtina, Rebibbia,
  Tomb 32. Found with a glass paste manus fica pendant and six beads.
  Source: Pantano et al. 2006: 261–2.

12. Location: Rome, Italy
  Date: first c. A.D.
  Description: faience phallus. Two horizontal lines indicate foreskin. Pubic
  hair denoted by two rows of curls. H 1.8 cm, W 1 cm, T 0.8 cm.
  Context: Fassi Gelataria Garden, Corso d'Italia. Found in rich domestic
  destruction/fill layer with wide variety of finds, including a bone phallus,
  faience manus fica, and a bone fist and phallus amulet.
  Source: Scerrato 2006; Piranomonte 2006: 197.

13. Location: Vagnari, Gravina, Italy
  Date: first–second c. A.D.
  Description: pale blue glass phallus. Vertical tension lines on scrotum.
  Pubic hair denoted by curls. Undecorated suspension loop. H 1.8 cm,
  W 0.9 cm, T 0.7 cm. See Figure 10.3, left.
  Context: Trench 9, Burial F38 (9–12 months). Single burial. Found at
  neck. A bent hobnail was also found in the grave.
  Source: Small et al. 2007: 174–6.

Appendix 10.2: Glazed composition flaccid phallus pendants from the Near East

1–2. Location: southern Lebanon
  Date: seventh–fourth c. B.C.?
  Description: one blue and one green flaccid phallus. One has vertical ten-
  sion lines on scrotum. Pubic hair is denoted by wavy grooves. Est.
  H 2.2 cm, W 1 cm.
  Context: archaeological context unknown. Found on beaded necklaces with
  other amulets, including grape bunches, a manus fica, Phoenician and
  Punic masks, and signs of Tanit, Egyptian deities, the oudjat eye, animals,
  and cowrie shells with hieroglyphs.
  Source: Musées Royaux d'Art et d'Histoire online database Carmentis, inv.
  nr. O.04574

3–4. Location: Bahrain, Persian Gulf
  Date: first c. B.C.–first c. A.D.
  Description: two blue-green glazed earthenware phalli. One has two lines
  indicating foreskin. Both have vertical tension lines on scrotum. Pubic hair
  denoted by two rows of wavy grooves. One suspension loop is decorated

by grooves. H 1.9 and 2.2 cm; W 1.2 cm.

Context: Saar Necropolis, Mound 7, Grave 5 and/or Karranah Necropolis, Mound III, Grave C3. No information on human remains. Phalli published with four frit grape bunch pendants. It is unclear which pendants are from which burial.

Source: Crawford and Rice 2000: 186.

5. Location: Gishtagh Ousti (Van), Germi, Iran
   Date: first c. B.C.–first c. A.D.
   Description: frit phallus. Pubic hair denoted by two rows of wavy lines. Suspension loop decorated by vertical grooves. Est. H 2.4 cm.
   Context: Trench A or B, Grave 1 or 2. Single burial in rectangular cist grave. Published with frit grape bunch pendant, glass and frit beads, spotted eye beads, silver bracelets and earrings, and bronze ring and bell. It is unclear in which grave the phallus was found and with what objects.
   Source: Kambakhsh Fard 1998: 17–19; Sarkhosh Curtis et al. 2000: 158–60.

6. Location: Tell Sheikh Hamad (Magdala), Syria
   Date: first c. B.C.–first c. A.D.
   Description: frit? phallus. Heavily worn. H 1.8 cm.
   Context: Tell Sheikh Hamad 1 Cemetery, Grave 87/51. Single pit grave burial (eight years). Found near lower left leg in a raffia basket, which also contained a bronze bell, 14 beads, a bone pin, an iron ring, 3 shells, and an iron nail. Other finds in grave included seven earrings found on the skull, a beaded necklace on the chest, and seven bronze bells by the hands.
   Source: Novák et al. 2000: 278–9, 569.

7. Location: Tell Sheikh Hamad (Magdala), Syria
   Date: first c. B.C.–first c. A.D.
   Description: frit phallus. Pubic hair denoted by curved lines. Suspension loop missing. H 1.5 cm.
   Context: Tell Sheikh Hamad 1 Cemetery, Grave 92/25. Single burial in pit grave. Found below feet of poorly preserved skeleton (no age/sex details), with a frit grape bunch pendant, 25 beads, a bronze bell, 8 pierced shells, and a Roman bronze coin. Other finds in grave included a beaded necklace found on the chest.
   Source: Novák et al. 2000: 290–1, 581; Wehry 2013: 90 and n. 357.

8. Location: Tell Sheikh Hamad (Magdala), Syria
   Date: first c. B.C.–first c. A.D.
   Description: ceramic phallus. Two horizontal lines indicate foreskin. Scrotum has vertical tension lines. Pubic hair denoted by two rows of vertical lines. Undecorated suspension loop. H 2.0 cm, W 1.3 cm.
   Context: Tell Sheikh Hamad 2 Cemetery, Grave 98/09. Single burial (6–9 months) in a ceramic jar. Pendant found between bones of upper body. Frit grape bunch pendant, a bronze bell, and 15 glass and frit beads were found near body.
   Source: Wehry 2013: 90, 189, 477–8.

9.   Location: Dura-Europos, Syria
      Date: first c. B.C.–first c. A.D.?
      Description: blue glazed glass phallus. Pubic hair denoted by wavy grooves. Suspension loop is broken. H 1.5 cm.
      Context: Tomb 23, Loculus XV. Single burial in loculus of communal hypogeum tomb. Found with skeleton (no age/sex details) and items including a bronze mirror and spatula, 3 bronze bells, 6 silver earrings, 3 amphorae, a crescent pendant, and 22 glass and semi-precious beads.
      Source: Toll 1946: 49–50, pl. XLIII. Yale University Art Gallery, online catalogue, inv. nr. 1938.4292.

10–11. Location: Dura-Europos, Syria
       Date: first c. B.C.–first c. A.D.?
       Description: one blue and one green glazed terracotta or glass phalli. Both have vertical tension lines on scrotum. One suspension loop is broken, the other is decorated by vertical grooves. H 1.8 and 1.5 cm.
       Context: Tomb 23, Loculus XXVII. Single burial in loculus of communal hypogeum tomb. Found with skeleton (no age/sex details) and items including a bronze spherical rattle, frit amphora and grape bunch pendants, three melon and glass beads, and a bronze ring.
       Source: Toll 1946: 51, pl. XLIII. Yale University Art Gallery, online catalogue, inv. nr. 1938.4289.

12.   Location: Dura-Europos, Syria
       Date: first c. B.C.–first c. A.D.?
       Description: blue glazed phallus. Pubic hair denoted by wavy grooves.
       Context: Tomb 24, Loculus IV. Single burial in a wooden coffin in loculus of communal hypogeum tomb. Found with skeleton (no age/sex details) and items including four carnelian and melon beads.
       Source: Toll 1946: 54–5, pl. XLIV.

13–15. Location: Amlash, Iran?
       Date: first c. B.C.–second c. A.D.
       Description: three blue-green faience phalli. One phallus is worn. Others have horizontal lines indicating foreskin and vertical and horizontal tension lines on scrotum. Pubic hair denoted by two rows of horizontal lines. Est. H 1.6 cm, W 1 cm. See Figure 10.4.
       Context: archaeological context unknown. Pendants are strung with 3 faience amphora and 2 grape bunch pendants, 14 faience, and 22 carnelian beads.
       Source: Goldstein 1979: 281.

16.   Location: Dura-Europos, Syria
       Date: first c. B.C.–second c. A.D.?
       Description: green glazed terracotta phallus. Pubic hair denoted by two rows of diagonal lines. Broken suspension loop. H 1.9 cm, W 1.1 cm. See Figure 10.3, right.
       Context: Tomb 40, Loculus XIV of communal hypogeum tomb. Found with displaced, disintegrated human remains and items including

a bronze mirror, spatula, two frit amphora pendants, and two melon beads.

Source: Toll 1946: 80, pl. LIV. Yale University Art Gallery, online catalogue, inv. nr. 1938.5158.6.

17. Location: Dibba Al Hisn, Sharjah, United Arab Emirates

Date: first c. A.D.

Description: frit phallus. Scrotum has vertical tension lines. Pubic hair denoted by vertical lines. Suspension loop decorated with vertical lines. Est. H 1.6 cm, W 1.1 cm, T 0.6 cm.

Context: communal burial chamber, Lower Floor. Found with nine disarticulated skeletons (D7–15) of various ages/sexes and grave goods, including other beads, pendants, and an ivory/bone comb.

Source: Jasim 2006: 217–18, 229–30; Jasim, personal communication.

18. Location: ed-Dur, Umm al-Qaiwain, United Arab Emirates

Date: first–second c. A.D.

Description: light green frit phallus. Horizontal groove indicates foreskin. Scrotum has vertical tension lines. Pubic hair denoted by wavy grooves. Suspension loop decorated by vertical lines. H. 2.1 cm. See Figure 10.1.

Context: Area N, Grave 3847. Single burial of unsexed adult. Pendant found near right hand with 39 glass, semi-precious, and frit beads and crystal turtle and bottle-shaped pendants. Other finds include seven beads at neck, bronze bracelet on right arm, bronze ring on left hand, bronze toe-ring on left foot, stone whorl, and bronze needle.

Source: Haerinck et al. 1991: 44; Haerinck 2001: 25–6, pl. 37; De Waele 2007: 304.

19. Location: Chojiran Germi, Iran

Date: first–second c. A.D.

Description: one or two blue green glass or frit phalli. Horizontal lines indicate foreskin. Scrotum has vertical tension lines. Pubic hair denoted by two rows of vertical/diagonal lines. Undecorated suspension loop.

Context: ceramic jar burial. Published as necklace with one or two grape pendants and many beads. It is unclear if necklace represents only beads and pendants found in the Chojiran burial, or if beads and pendants from the Gishtagh Ousti (Van) burial are also included.

Source: Kambakhsh Fard 1998: 17 and 87; Bagherpour Kashani 2011: 202, pl. 46.

20–21. Location: Hassani Mahale, Dailaman, Iran

Date: first–third c. A.D.

Description: at least two blue faience phalli. Horizontal lines indicate foreskin. Vertical tension lines on scrotum. Pubic hair denoted by two rows of vertical lines. Undecorated suspension loops. Est. H 1.6 cm, W 1.1 cm, T 0.7 cm.

Context: shaft-grave, single burial of adult. Found near grave wall with crystal and faience beads, two faience amphora and manus fica pendants, three copper bracelets, earring, signet ring, and five glass and bone spindle-whorls. Other finds include a copper needle behind the head, copper mirror on the chest, copper rings on the first and fourth fingers, and a terracotta spindle whorl.

Source: Sono and Fukai 1968: 8–9, 19, 32. 61–2, pl. LXIV, XXXVIII, Color pl. 3,4.

22. Location: Selenkahiye, Syria
Date: third c. A.D.?
Description: faience phallus. Pubic hair denoted by wavy grooves. Suspension loop decorated by vertical grooves. H 1.8 cm, W 1.5 cm, T 0.8 cm.
Context: jar burial, burial 1. No information on human remains. Found with a faience manus fica pendant, two faience beads, and two cowrie shells.
Source: Zaqzûq 2001: 516, 525–6, 539, pl. 13.17.

Appendix 10.3: Glazed composition flaccid phallus pendants from around the Black Sea

1. Location: Novo-Otradnoe, Crimea
Date: first c. A.D.
Description: blue Egyptian faience phallus. Two horizontal lines indicate foreskin. Pubic hair denoted by two rows of vertical lines. Undecorated suspension loop. Est. H 1.9 cm, W 1.0 cm.
Context: Grave 10, pit grave with stone slab cover. Single burial of a child. Found around skull, with 21 beads, 3 Egyptian paste amphora pendants, a scarab, and traces of bronze suspension wire. Other grave goods include a bronze bell, a bronze wire fibula, and possible earrings.
Source: Alekseeva 1970: 150, pl. 3.4 and 5.4; Arsen'eva 1970: 93–4.

2. Location: Kerch, Crimea
Date: first–second c. A.D.?
Description: Egyptian faience phallus. Scrotum has vertical tension lines. Pubic hair denoted by two rows of curved lines.
Context: found in Roman period burial at Kerch; may have been found with beads in a child's grave?
Source: Piotrovski 1958: 24–5.

3–4. Location: Chernyshev, Republic of Adygea, Russia
Date: first–third c. A.D.?
Description: two blue Egyptian faience phalli. Pubic hair denoted by two rows of vertical or diagonal lines. H 1.8 and 1.9 cm.
Context: Chernyshev I, Kurgan 5, Sepulcher 139. No information on human remains. Found with a Sarmatian clay pitcher with snake handle and an Aucissa fibula.
Source: Carazzetti and Mazzeo 1990: 55, 57–8.

Appendix 10.4: Glazed composition flaccid phallus pendants from Central Asia

1. Location: Tashravat, Ferghana, Uzbekistan
    Date: first–third c. A.D.
    Description: blue phallus, identified as definitively made of Egyptian faience, though the method of examination is not provided (Bulygina 1986: 248, n. 3). Scrotum has vertical tension lines. Pubic hair denoted by vertical and curved lines. H 2 cm, W 1.1 cm, T 0.8 cm.
    Context: Tashravat VIII cemetery, Kurgan 31 (female, adult). Single mound burial. Found on ribs with 31 glass beads and 2 eye beads. Other finds include nine beads, a bronze crossbow brooch, a bronze fibula, and sheep bones.
    Source: Bulygina 1986: 247–8, 252.
2. Location: Yalangtush Tepe, Bandy-khan, Uzbekistan
    Date: first–third c. A.D.?
    Description: blue Egyptian faience phallus. Two horizontal lines indicate foreskin. Scrotum has vertical tension lines. Pubic hair denoted by two rows of diagonal lines. Undecorated suspension loop. Est. H 1.9 cm, W 1 cm, T 0.8 cm.
    Context: Yalangtush Tepe cemetery. Stone chamber burial. No information on human remains; may be multiple burial. Found with pieces of bronze bracelets, seven cowrie shells, six beads, and a coin of Soter Megas.
    Source: Rtveladze 1977: 236–7.
3–4. Location: Gorny Altai, Altai Republic, Russia
    Date: second–third c. A.D.
    Description: two blue-green glazed steatite phalli. Vertical tension lines on scrotum. Pubic hair denoted by two rows of diagonal lines. Undecorated suspension loop. Very worn. H 1.9 cm, W 1 cm. See Plate 3.
    Context: Kuraika Cemetery, Burial 39 (female, 45–55 years). Single mound burial. Found near cervical vertebra and clavicles.
    Source: Bogdanov and Sljusarenko 2007.

Appendix 10.5: Glazed composition flaccid phallus pendants found with aged and anthropologically sexed individuals

List 1: Mediterranean region

1. Site: Herculaneum, Italy (Arcade 7)
    Date: first c. A.D.
    Age: 25–35 years.
    Sex: Male.
    Worn: No.
    Context: bead and amulet necklace carried in box or sack during Vesuvius eruption.

2. Site: Vagnari, Italy
    Date: first–second c. A.D.
    Age: 9–12 months.
    Sex: undetermined
    Worn: Yes.
    Context: single pendant found at neck.

List 2: Near East

1. Site: Tell Sheikh Hamad, Syria (Grave 87/51)
    Date: first c. B.C.–first c. A.D.
    Age: 8 years.
    Sex: undetermined
    Worn: No.
    Context: beaded necklace found in basket with bell, bone pin, iron ring, shells, iron nail, coin, and glass vase.
2. Site: Tell Sheikh Hamad, Syria (Grave 98/09).
    Date: first c. B.C.–first c. A.D.
    Age: 6–9 months.
    Sex: undetermined
    Worn: Yes.
    Context: single pendant between bones of upper body.
3. Site: ed-Dur, United Arab Emirates
    Date: first–second c. A.D.
    Age: Adult.
    Sex: undetermined
    Worn: Yes.
    Context: bead and amulet bracelet found near right hand.
4. Site: Hassani Mahale, Iran
    Date: first–third c. A.D.
    Age: Adult.
    Sex: undetermined
    Worn: No.
    Context: bead and amulet necklace found near grave wall with copper bracelets, ring, earring, five bone and glass spindle whorls, and copper deer figurine.

List 3: Black Sea

1. Site: Novo-Otradnoe, Crimea
    Date: first c. A.D.
    Age: Child.
    Sex: undetermined
    Worn: Yes.
    Context: bead and amulet necklace strung on bronze wire found around skull.

List 4: Central Asia

1. Site: Tashravat, Uzbekistan
    Date: first–third c. A.D.
    Age: Adult.
    Sex: Female.
    Worn: Yes.
    Context: beaded necklace found among ribs.
2. Site: Gorny Altai, Russia
    Date: second–third c. A.D.
    Age: 45–55 years.
    Sex: Female.
    Worn: Yes.
    Context: two phallic pendants found near cervical vertebrae and clavicles.

Notes

1   Bone: Deschler-Erb and Božič (2002); Lassányi and Bechtold (2006: 75–6); Holland (2017: 154). Metal: Johns 1982, pl. 10; Spasich-Churech 2008: 140–2; British Museum (BM) Collection, nr. M.537. Bronze horse pendants: Nicolay 2007, pl. 92 (209.62); BM, nos 1814,0704.1240–1; 1814,0704.1260–1; PAS: BH-F31E4C; SF-2D10C4. Metal fist and phallus pendants with central flaccid phallus: BM, nos 1814,0704.1248; 1814,0704.1269; 1814,0704.1278; 1976,0818.20.
2   There are pendants that depict a pubis, scrotum, and erect penis. Glass: Nymphaion (Crimea), Grave A125, fourth century B.C. (Grach 1999: 66, 231); Antikythera (Greece), first century B.C. (Gadolou 2012: 54). Bone: Viminacium (Serbia), Grave G-189, second century A.D. (Spasich-Churech 2008: 128–30, 141). Bronze horse pendants: PAS: KENT-E3D152; GLO-221C74. BM, nr. 1814,0704.1264.
3   Two frit or glass flaccid phallus pendants appear on an amulet necklace in the Indiana University Art Museum (no. 66.37.8). While it lacks contextual details, it resembles similar amulet necklaces from known archaeological contexts, and may date to the Phoenician or Roman Imperial period (Rudolph and Rudolph 1973: 30; Musche 1988: 172–3).
4   Other flaccid phallus pendants of uncertain material were found in Pompeii: two on an amulet necklace that an adult carried in a box at the House of Holconius (Faraone 2018: 59–60), and another on a necklace of beads and amulets from House V, 3, 11 (Ziviello 1989: 228). Fiorelli (1866: 11) records three additional faience or green paste phallic pendants with a pubis (*falli pantici*) from the Naples Archaeological Museum, but it is uncertain if they depict flaccid genitalia (cf. De Caro 2000: 74).
5   There is a discrepancy with this pendant's context. In De Carolis' (1996: 168) plan of Arcade 7, the box appears closest to Skeleton 3, which is anthropologically identified as an adult man (Torino and Fornaciari 1996: 188). Roberts (2013: 291), however, identifies Skeleton 3 as a female child.
6   Five additional frit, glass, or faience pendants depict a phallus, scrotum, and pubis from Babylon (Iraq), Bastam (Iran), and Masjide-e Suleiman (Iran; Bagherpour Kashani 2011: 202–3). While I have not examined these pendants, the Babylon example appears to depict flaccid genitalia (Musche 1988: 171, pl. LVII, 22.3).
7   Several Dura-Europos pendants are in the Yale University Art Gallery's online collection: Tomb 23, Loculus XV, acc. no. 1938.4292; Tomb 23, Loculus XXVII, acc. no. 1938.4289; Tomb 40, Loculus XIV, acc. no. 1938.5158. The Amlash (Iran) pendant is also in the Corning Museum of Glass's online collection, acc. no. 74.7.8.

8   Three Egyptian faience or glass pendants with flaccid male genitalia dating to the first–second century A.D. are in Moscow's State Historical Museum (inv. no. 78607), but their find spots are unknown (Zuravlev 2006: 90–1).

9   Near East: Roman imports (Jasim 2006: 234–5; De Waele 2007: 304; Wehry 2013: 189) or Roman–Egyptian imports (Sarkhosh Curtis et al. 2000: 159). Black Sea: Mediterranean imports (Petersen 2010: 223). Central Asia: Roman Mediterranean imports (Bogdanov and Sljusarenko 2007: 80), Roman–Egyptian imports (Rtveladze 1977: 237–8; Bulygina 1986: 251–2), or possible local production (Mairs 2007: 81).

10 At Herculaneum, an erect bone phallus was found in a different section of the Forum Bath drains (Pagano 1999: 181–3) and amber and lead erect phallus pendants were among the other amulets carried by the man from Arcade 7 on the beach (Roberts 2013: 290). An erect bone phallus and a bone fist and phallus pendant were also found in the same destruction layer as the faience flaccid phallus in Rome's Fassi Gelataria Garden (Scerrato 2006).

11 Caerleon Roman Legionary Museum, acc. no. 31.78. Published references are few (Lee 1862: 61 n. 1), but a description of this roundel is included in a note under 'Bone Object no. 20' in Boon's unpublished *Caerleon Vicus Catalogue*. Dated finds from the Castle Baths: Lee 1862: 100; Zienkiewicz 1986: 35–6.

12 Kaczmarczyk and Hedges (1983: 214) suggest that frit functioned as a substitute for Egyptian faience.

13 Most pendants in this study were found in burials with no published information on human remains (13), in communal tombs with mixed age/sex occupants (2), or with skeletal remains too poorly preserved for analysis (1).

14 Plaut. *Mil.* (1398–9): "*Quin iamdudum gestit moecho hoc abdomen adimere, u tea iam quasi puero in collo pendeant crepundia.*" Thanks to Craig Gibson for this translation.

15 The bone flaccid phallus buried with a one-and-a-half-year-old from Budapest was found with amulets depicting an erect phallus, manus fica, comb, axe head, dagger, money bag, and a human figure, and this group is explicitly identified as a *crepundia* (Lassányi and Bechtold 2006: 75–6).

16 Near East: apotropaic function: Sarkhosh Curtis et al. 2000: 159; Wehry 2013: 233; apotropaic and fertility functions: Sono and Fukai 1968: 19; Crawford and Rice 2000: 186; De Waele 2007: 304. Northern Black Sea: Piotrovski 1958: 24; Alekseeva 1975: 30; Carazzetti and Mazzeo 1990: 33–4. Central Asia: Bogdanov and Sljusarenko 2007: 80; on fertility in Central Asia: Bulygina 1986: 251–2; Mairs 2007: 82–3.

17 Some scholars have also suggested a potential secondary function of virility or fertility enhancement for phallic pendants in the west: Turnbull 1978: 199; Nicolay 2007: 229; Crummy 2010: 51; Parker 2015: 141–3; Whitmore 2018: 26–7.

Bibliography

Adams, E. (2017). "Fragmentation and the Body's Boundaries: Reassessing the Body In Parts", in Draycott and Graham (2017), 193–213.

Alekseeva, E.M. (1970). "Klassifikatsja bus nekropolja y derevni Novo-Otradnoe/Classification of Necklaces from the Burial Near the Village of Novo-Otradnoe", in Melykova (1970), 150–69.

Alekseeva, E.M. (1975). *Antichnje Busi Severnogo Prichernomorja/Antique Necklaces from the North Sea region*. Moscow: Nauka.

Allison, P.M. (2013). *People and Spaces in Roman Military Bases*. Cambridge: Cambridge University Press.

Arsen'eva, T.M. (1970). "Mogilnik y Derevni Novo-Otradnoe/Burial Near the Village of Novo-Otradnoe", in Melykova (1970), 82–149.

Bagherpour Kashani, N. (2011). *Studies of Ancient Depositional Practices and Related Jewellery Finds, Based on the Discoveries at Veshnaveh: A Source for the History of Religion in Iran*. Unpub. PhD Thesis, Ruhr-University Bochum.

Bailey, D.M. (1962). "Lamps from Tharros in the British Museum", *Annual of the British School at Athens*, 57: 35–45.

Barnett, R.D. and Mendleson, C. (1987). *Tharros: A Catalogue of Material in the British Museum from Phoenician and Other Tombs at Tharros, Sardinia*. London: British Museum Publications.

Bartoloni, P. (1973). "Gli Amuleti Punici del *Tofet* di Sulcis", *Rivista di Studi Fenici*, 1(2): 181–203.

Bieber, M. (1915). *Die Antiken Skulpturen und Bronzen des Königl. Museum Fridericianum in Cassel*. Marburg: N.G. Elwertsche Verlagsbuchhandlung.

Bogdanov, E.S. and Sljusarenko, I.Y. (2007). "Egyptian Faience Amulets from Gorny Altai", *Archaeology, Ethnology, and Anthropology of Eurasia*, 4(32): 77–80.

Boon, G.C. (Unpubl.) *Caerleon Vicus Catalogue*. Caerleon: National Roman Legionary Museum.

Bulygina, T.N. (1986). "Novii Nachodki Egipetskich Izdelij v Fergane/New Finds of Artefacts of Egyptian Manufacture in Fergana", *Sovetskaj Archeologia/Soviet Archaeology*, 2: 247–54.

Carazzetti, R. and Mazzeo, D. eds, (1990). *I Tesori dei Kurgani del Caucaso Settentrionale*. Roma: Leonardo-De Luca Editori.

Clarke, J.R. (1996). "Hypersexual Black Men in Augustan Baths: Ideal Somatotypes and Apotropaic Magic", in N.B. Kampen (ed.) *Sexuality in Ancient Art*. Cambridge: Cambridge University Press, 184–98.

Clarke, J.R. (2003). *Roman Sex. 100 BC – AD 250*. New York: Harry N. Abrams.

Clarke, J.R. (2014). "Sexuality and Visual Representation", in T.K. Hubbard (ed.), *A Companion to Greek and Roman Sexualities*. Malden: Wiley Blackwell, 509–33.

Clerc, G. (1991). "Aegyptiaca", in V. Karageorghis, O. Picard and C. Tytgat (eds), *La Nécropole d'Amathonte, Tombes 110 – 385*. Nicosie: Imprimerie Nicolaou et fils Ltd, 1–158.

Crawford, H. and Rice, M. ed., (2000). *Traces of Paradise: The Archaeology of Bahrain, 2500 BC – 300 AD*. London: The Dilmun Committee.

Crummy, N. (2010). "Bears and Coins: The Iconography of Protection in Late Roman Infant Burials", *Britannia*, 41: 37–93.

Dasen, V. (2003). "Les Amulettes D'Enfants dans le Monde Gréco-Romain", *Latomus*, 62(2): 275–89.

Dasen, V. (2015). "*Probaskania*: Amulets and Magic in Antiquity", in D. Boschung and J. N. Bremmer (eds), *The Materiality of Magic*. Paderborn: Wilhelm Fink, 177–204.

De Caro, S. (2000). *The Secret Cabinet in the National Archaeological Museum of Naples*. Naples: Soprintendenza Archaeologica di Napoli e Caserta.

De Carolis, E. (1996). "Lo Scavo dei Fornici 7 e 8 Sulla Marina di Ercolano", *Rivista di Studi Pompeiani*, 6: 167–86.

De Waele, A. (2007). "The Beads of ed-Dur (Umm al-Qaiwain, UAE)", *Proceedings of the Seminar for Arabian Studies*, 37: 297–308.

Deschler-Erb, E. and Božič, D. (2002). "A Late Republican Bone Pendant from the Münsterhügel in Basel (CH)", *Instrumentum*, 15: 39–41.

Draycott, J. and Graham, E.-J. eds, (2017). *Bodies of Evidence. Ancient Anatomical Votives: Past, Present and Future*. London: Routledge.

Dumoulin, A. (1958). "Recherches Archéologiques dans la Région d'Apt (Vaucluse)", *Gallia*, 16(1): 197–241.

Dunbabin, K.M.D. (1989). "*Baiarum Grata Voluptas*: Pleasures and Dangers of the Baths", *Papers of the British School at Rome*, 57: 6–46.

Dwyer, E.J. (2013). *Pompeii's Living Statues: Ancient Roman Lives Stolen from Death*. Ann Arbor: University of Michigan Press.

Eckardt, H. (2014). *Objects and Identities: Roman Britain and the North-Western Provinces*. Oxford: Oxford University Press.

Faraone, C.A. (2018). *The Transformation of Greek Amulets in Roman Imperial Times*. Philadelphia: University of Pennsylvania Press.

Fiorelli, G. (1861). *Giornale degli Scavi di Pompei, Anno 1861*. Naples.

Fiorelli, G. (1866). *Catalogo del Museum Nazionale di Napoli, Raccolta Pornografica*. Naples.

Fisher, K. and Langlands, R. (2011). "The Censorship Myth and the Secret Museum", in S. Hales and J. Paul (eds), *Pompeii in the Public Imagination from its Rediscovery to Today*. Oxford: Oxford University Press, 301–15.

Fox, C. and Lethbridge, T.C. (1926). "The La Tène and Romano-British Cemetery, Guilden Morden, Cambs", *Proceedings of the Cambridge Antiquarian Society*, 27: 49–63.

Gadolou, A. (2012). "Life on Board", in N. Kaltsas, E. Vlachogianni and P. Bouyia (eds), *The Antikythera Shipwreck: The Ship, the Treasures, the Mechanism*. Athens: National Archaeological Museum, 50–56.

Goldstein, S.M. (1979). *Pre-Roman and Early Roman Glass in the Corning Museum of Glass*. Corning: Corning Museum of Glass.

Grach, N.L. (1999). *Nekropol Nimpheja/Cemetery of Nimphej*. St. Petersburg: Nauka.

Grove, J. (2017). "Votive Genitalia in the Wellcome Collection: Modern Receptions of Ancient Sexual Anatomy", in Draycott and Graham (2017), 214–36.

Haerinck, E. (2001). *The University of Ghent South-East Arabian Archaeological Project. Excavations at ed-Dur (Umm al-Qaiwain, United Arab Emirates). The Tombs, vol. II*. Leuven: Peeters.

Haerinck, E., Metdepenninghen, C. and Stevens, K.G. (1991). "Excavations at ed-Dur (Umm al-Qaiwain, U.A.E.) – Preliminary Report on the Second Belgian Season (1988)", *Arabian Archaeology and Epigraphy*, 2: 31–60.

Higgins, R. (1980). *Greek and Roman Jewellery*. 2nd edition. Berkeley, CA: University of California Press.

Holland, L. (2017). "Phallic Amulet/Pendant Made of Bone or Horn", in N. de Grummond (ed.), *Wells of Wonder: New Discoveries at Cetamura del Chianti*. Florence: Edifir edizioni Firenze, 154.

Jasim, S.A. (2006). "Trade Centres and Commercial Routes in the Arabian Gulf: Post-Hellenistic Discoveries at Dibba, Sharjah, United Arab Emirates", *Arabian Archaeology and Epigraphy*, 17: 214–37.

Johns, C. (1982). *Sex or Symbol? Erotic Images of Greece and Rome*. London: British Museum Press.

Kaczmarczyk, A. and Hedges, R.E.M. (1983). *Ancient Egyptian Faience: An Analytical Survey of Egyptian Faience from Predynastic to Roman Times*. Warminster: Aris and Phillips.

Kambakhsh Fard, S.O. (1998). *Parthian Pithos-Burials at Germi (Azarbaijan)*. Iranian Journal of Archaeology and History, Supplement No. 1. Tehran: Iran University Press.

Kampen, N. (1996). "Gender Theory in Roman Art", in D.E.E. Kleiner and S.B. Mateson (eds), *I Claudia: Women in Ancient Rome*. Austin: University of Texas Press, 14–25.

Kostsushko-Valjuzinicha, D.N. (1911). "Raskopki v Xersonese/Excavations in Chersonesos", *Izvestija Imperatorskoj Archeologicheskoj Komissii/News from Emperor's Archaeological Committee*, 39: 184–95.

Lassányi, G. and Bechtold, E. (2006). "Recent Excavations in the Cemetery along the Aranyhegyi Stream", *Aquincumi Füzetek*, 12: 73–78.

Lee, J.E. (1862). Isca Silurum; *or An Illustrated Catalogue of the Museum of Antiquities at Caerleon*. London: Longman, Green, Longmans and Roberts.

Mairs, R.R. (2007). "Egyptian Artefacts from Central and South Asia", in R.R. Mairs and A. Stevenson (eds), *Current Research in Egyptology VI*. Oxford: Oxbow, 74–89.

McNiven, T.J. (1995). "The Unheroic Penis: Otherness Exposed", *Source: Notes in the History of Art*, 15(1): 10–16.

Melykova, A.I. ed., (1970). *Poselenja I Mogilniki Kerchenskogo Polyostrova Nachala Nachej Eri/Settlements and Burials of Kerch Peninsula of First c. A.D.* Moscow: Nauka.

Meskell, L. (2004). *Object Worlds in Ancient Egypt: Material Biographies Past and Present*. New York: Berg.

Musche, B. (1988). *Vorderasiatischer Schmuck zur Zeit der Arsakiden und der Sasaniden*. Leiden: Brill.

Nicolay, J. (2007). *Armed Batavians: Use and Significance of Weaponry and Horse Gear from Non-Military Contexts in the Rhine Delta (50 BC to AD 450)*. Amsterdam: Amsterdam University Press.

Novák, M., Oettel, A. and Witzel, C. (2000). *Der Parthisch-Römische Friedhof von Tall Šēḫ Ḥamad/Magdala*. Berlin: BATSH.

Oberhelman, S.M. (2014). "Anatomical Votive Reliefs as Evidence for Specialization at Healing Sanctuaries in the Ancient Mediterranean World", *Athens Journal of Health*, 1(1): 47–62.

Ogden, D. (2002). *Magic, Witchcraft, and Ghosts in the Greek and Roman Worlds: A Sourcebook*. Oxford: Oxford University Press.

Pagano, M. (1999). "Ufficio Scavo di Ercolano", *Rivista di Studi Pompeiani*, 8: 180–83.

Pantano, D., Angelini, M. and Quaranta, P. (2006). "Necropoli della III Casa Circondariale di Rebibbia (Municipio V)", in Tomei (2006), 261–62.

Parker, A. (2015). "The Fist-and-Phallus Pendants from Roman Catterick", *Britannia*, 46: 135–49.

Parker, A. (2017). "Protecting the Troops? Phallic Carvings in the North of Roman Britain", in A. Parker (ed.), *Ad Vallum: Papers on the Roman Army and Frontiers in Celebration of Dr. Brian Dobson*. Oxford: Archaeopress, 117–30.

Parker, A. (2018). "'The bells! The bells!' Approaching *Tintinnabula* in Roman Britain and Beyond", in Parker and McKie (2018), 57–68.

Parker, A. and McKie, S. ed, (2018). *Material Approaches to Roman Magic: Occult Objects and Supernatural Substances*. Oxford: Oxbow.

Parker, A. and Ross, C. (2016). "A New Phallic Carving from Roman Catterick", *Britannia*, 47: 271–79.

Petersen, J.H. (2010). *Cultural Interactions and Social Strategies on the Pontic Shores: Burial Customs in the Northern Black Sea Area, c. 550–270 BC*. Aarhus: Aarhus University Press.

Petrie, W.M.F. (1972). *Amulets*. Warminster: Aris and Phillips Ltd.

Piotrovski, B.B. (1958). "Drevneegipetskie Predmeti, Naijdenii na Territorii Sovestkogo Sojuza/Ancient Egyptian Artefacts found on the Territory of Soviet Union", *Sovetska Archeologia/Soviet Archaeology*, 1: 20–27.

Piranomonte, M. (2006). "Un Antico Giardino Romano Sotto il Villino Fassi a Corso d'Italia (Scavi 2004–2005)", in Tomei (2006), 197–98.

Plouviez, J. (2005). "Whose Good Luck? Roman Phallic Ornaments from Suffolk", in N. Crummy (ed.), *Image, Craft and the Classical World*. Montagnac: Éditions Monique Mergoil, 157–64.

Pompianu, E. (2017). "Nuovi Scavi nella Necropoli Punica di Villamar (2013–2015)", *The Journal of Fasti Online*, http://www.fastionline.org/docs/FOLDER-it-2017-395.pdf [Accessed 05.01.2018].

Ramos Folques, A. (1973). "El Nivel Ibero-Punico de la Alcudia de Elche (Alicante)", *Rivista di Studi Liguri*, 34(1–2): 363–86.

Regev, D. (2013). "Egyptian Stone Objects from Miqne-Ekron. Canaanite-Phoenician Trade in Egyptian Cult-Objects and their Mediterranean Distribution", in L. Bombardieri, A. D'Agostino, G. Guarducci, V. Orsi and S. Valentini (eds), *SOMA 2012. Identity and Connectivity*. Oxford: Archaeopress, 103–10.

Richlin, A. (1992). *The Garden of Priapus: Sexuality and Aggression in Roman Humor.* Revised edition. New York: Oxford University Press.

Roberts, P. (2013). *Life and Death in Pompeii and Herculaneum*. New York: Oxford University Press.

Rtveladze, E.V. (1977). "Neskolko Drevneegypetskich Predmetov iz Severnoj Baktrii/ Some Ancient Egyptian Artefacts from Northern Baktria", *Sovetskaj Archeologia/Soviet Archaeology*, 2: 235–38.

Rudolph, W. and Rudolph, E. (1973). *Ancient Jewelry from the Collection of Burton Y. Berry*. Bloomington, IN: Indiana University Art Museum.

Sarkhosh Curtis, V., John Simpson, S.J., Kaboli, M.-A., Abdi, K., Ivanov, G., Katsumi, T., Akira, H., Kaim, B. and Kaimet, B. (2000). "Archaeological News from Iran and Central Asia: Third report", *Iran*, 38: 151–60.

Scatozza Höricht, L.A. (1989). *I Monili di Ercolano*. Rome: L'Erma di Bretschneider.

Scerrato, I.E. (2006). "Amuleti", in Tomei (2006), 205–06.

Schörner, G. (2015). "Anatomical Ex Votos", in R. Raja and J. Rüpke (eds), *A Companion to the Archaeology of Religion in the Ancient World*. Malden: Blackwell, 397–411.

Small, A., Small, C., Abdy, R., De Stefano, A., Giuliani, R., Henig, M., Johnson, K., Kenrick, P., Prowse, T., Small, A. and Vanderleest, H. (2007). "Excavation in the Roman cemetery at Vagnari, in the Territory of Gravina in Puglia, 2002", *Papers of the British School at Rome*, 75: 123–229.

Sono, T. and Fukai, S. (1968). *Dailaman III. The Excavations at Hassani Mahale and Ghalekuti, 1964*. Tokyo: Yamakawa Publishing Co.

Spasich-Churech, D. (2008). "Falichki Motivi iz Viminatsiuma/Phallic Motifs from Viminacium", *Glasnik Srpskogo Archeoloshkogo Drushtva/Newsletter of Serbian Archaeological Society*, 24: 121–74.

Stephens, J. (2008). "Ancient Roman Hairdressing: On (Hair)pins and Needles", *Journal of Roman Archaeology*, 21: 111–32.

Swift, E. (2003). "Late-Roman Bead Necklaces and Bracelets", *Journal of Roman Archaeology*, 16: 336–49.

Szilágyi, M. (2005). "Late Roman *Bullae* and Amulet Capsules in Pannonia", *Annual of Medieval Studies at CEU*, 13: 9–27.

Taylor, J.H. (2001). *Death and the Afterlife in Ancient Egypt*. Chicago, IL: University of Chicago Press.

Toll, N.P. (1946). *The Excavations at Dura-Europos. Preliminary Report of the Ninth Season of Work, 1935–1936. Part II: The Necropolis*. New Haven, CT: Yale University Press.

Tomei, M.A. ed., (2006). *Roma. Memorie dal Sotosuolo. Ritrovamenti Archeologici 1980/ 2006*. Rome: Electa.

Torino, M. and Fornaciari, G. (1996). "Analisi dei Resti Umani dei Fornici 7 e 8 sulla Marina di Ercolano", *Rivista di Studi Pompeiani*, 6: 187–95.

Turnbull, P. (1978). "The Phallus in the Art of Roman Britain", *Bulletin of the Institute of Archaeology, University of London*, 15: 199–206.

Tytgat, C. (1989). *Les Nécropoles Sud-Ouest et Sud-Est d'Amathonte. I. Les Tombes 110–385*. Nicosie: Imprimerie Nicolaou et fils.

van Loon, M.N. (2001a) "Beads and Pendants", in van Loon (2001b), 487–94.

van Loon, M.N. ed., (2001b). *Selenkahiye: Final Report on the University of Chicago and University of Amsterdam Excavations in the Tabqa Reservoir, Northern Syria, 1967–1975*. Istanbul: Nederlands Historisch-Archeologisch Instituut te Istanbul.

Vandiver, P. (1983). "The Manufacture of Faience", in Kaczmarczyk and Hedges (1983), 1–137.

Wehry, B. (2013). *Zwischen Orient und Okzident das Arsakidenzeitliche Gräberfeld von Tall Šēḫ Ḥamad/Magdala* l. Unpub. PhD Thesis, Freien Universität Berlin.

Whitmore, A. (2013). *Small Finds and the Social Environment of Roman Public Baths*. Unpubl. PhD Thesis, University of Iowa.

Whitmore, A. (2017). "Fascinating *Fascina*: Apotropaic Magic and How to Wear a Penis", in M. Cifarelli and L. Gawlinski (eds), *What Shall I Say of Clothes? Theoretical and Methodological Approaches to the Study of Dress in Antiquity*. Boston, MA: Archaeological Institute of America, 47–65.

Whitmore, A. (2018). "Phallic Magic: A Cross Cultural Approach to Roman Phallic Small Finds", in Parker and McKie (2018), 17–32.

Zaqzûq, A. (2001). "The Roman and Later Graves and their Contents", in van Loon (2001b), 515–68.

Zienkiewicz, J.D. (1986). *The Legionary Fortress Baths at Caerleon, I. The Buildings*. Cardiff: National Museum of Wales.

Ziviello, C. (1989). "I Cristalli", in *Le Collezioni del Museo Nazionale di Napoli*. Rome: De Luca Edizioni d'Arte S.p.A, 109, 228–9.

Zuravlev, D.V. (2006). *Ljubov i Eros v Anticnoj Kulture/Love and Erotica in Ancient Culture*. Moscow: Hudoznik i Kniga.

11 Roman and un-Roman sex

Sarah Levin-Richardson

The contributions in this volume have much to offer scholars of Roman material culture and social history. Not only have some of the chapters brought attention to sexual material in the heart of Roman Italy that is virtually unknown, even to those who study this material (e.g. flaccid phallic pendants from Herculaneum; see more below), the volume also raises important points about the influences of other Mediterranean civilisations (e.g. Pharaonic Egypt) on Roman culture, about similarities and differences in conceptualisations of gender and sexuality between Roman Italy and the Roman provinces, and about scholarly blind spots that have prevented us from seeing material that may not accord with our preconceived notions of antiquity. One of the most important impacts of this volume is that it invites us to reconsider what we think we know about Roman ideas of the body, encouraging us to re-evaluate long-held paradigms of male impenetrability and 'Priapic' sexuality. This volume thus forms part of a larger critical intervention in understanding Roman sexuality and serves as a welcome invitation to take new approaches to the body.

Priapic sexuality and the gendering of bodies

One of the major contributions of scholarship in the 1980s and 1990s was the explication of Roman sexuality as 'Priapic.' Formulated primarily by Amy Richlin in her 1983 book *The Garden of Priapus: Sexuality and Aggression in Roman Humor* to describe the phallic aggression present in Latin poetry, 'Priapic' sexuality is named after the ithyphallic woodland deity of Roman culture who was said to rape would-be garden thieves with his oversized phallus, and who was represented as the narrator of a set of obscene poems named the *Priapea* after their speaker. Scholars regularly note Richlin's role in advancing scholarly understandings of Roman sexuality (e.g. Skinner 2014: 4; Halperin 2015: 312): indeed, the 'Priapic paradigm' has become accepted as the major organising principle around which Roman sexuality was structured. As articulated in Holt Parker's influential 1997 *Roman Sexualities* essay ('The Teratogenic Grid'), this sexual paradigm holds that Roman men, in order to be considered normative, were expected to penetrate one or more of the three bodily orifices (vagina, anus, mouth) of a socially subordinate individual. To do otherwise—whether that meant a lack of interest in penetrating others or a desire to be sexually penetrated oneself—could result in social stigma as well as civic and legal disadvantages (Williams 2010[1999]; see also Walters 1997).

This understanding of Roman sexuality and its mapping onto the gender, status, and penetrability of bodies (note that in this paradigm, it is freeborn males who are normatively the penetrators, and women and slaves of both genders who are normatively the penetrated) explains so much of our literary and material evidence that it has taken on a hegemonic role in discussions of ancient sexuality. Yet in parallel with the popularity of this theory, some scholars have sought to supplement, nuance, or even challenge this model. James Davidson, in his 1998 book on Athenian sexuality (*Courtesans and Fishcakes: The Classical Passions of Classical Athens*), drew attention to the role of self-control in Greek conceptualisations of sexual roles, arguing that it, not penetration, was the major organising principle (though many scholars disagree with him (e.g. Fisher 2000); on Davidson, see also Skinner 2015). In his 2007 *The Greeks and Greek Love*—in some ways a continuation of his argument against the penetration model—he even called out (what he described as) scholars' fixation on sodomy (Davidson 2007: 4)!

Material culture has played a key, if sometimes under-appreciated, role in the critique of the penetration model. John Clarke (1998: 9–12, 17–18) has argued over the years that we can find alternative sets of norms and practices in Roman art since the producers and consumers of Roman art were much more diverse than the (usually) elite male authors and readers of Latin literature. In his work on Roman erotic art, Clarke (1998: 38–42, 2005: 293–6, 2014: 512–13) has highlighted sexual scenes that seem to defy the Priapic norms above, including a high-quality agate gemstone of the first century B.C. that shows one adult man penetrating another adult man, the latter of whom has a prominent erection. While scholars may reject Clarke's identification of the penetrated man as a *cinaedus*—it is debated whether the term *cinaedus* signifies primarily a male who enjoys being penetrated (Richlin 1993) or a gender-deviant male (Williams 2010[1999]: 177–8, 193–4, 232–43; Ormand 2018-[2009]: 23), let alone whether any Roman would identify as a *cinaedus* (Parker 1997: 60–3)—we certainly have a level of reciprocity (in age and mutual desire) that seems to push at the edges of the Priapic model. Clarke (1993: 292, 1998: 61–72, 2005: 291–3, 2014: 515) likewise notes that while side B of the first century A.D. Warren Cup (a masterpiece of silver drinking ware) is conventional for showing an idealised male penetrate a younger (surely servile) boy, side A, with the penetration of a fully developed (if unbearded) male, shows more equality between penetrator and penetrated. Clarke has argued that some sexual scenes show the agency of penetrated women, too. The clearest examples are on terracotta medallions from the Rhône Valley (dated to the late-first to mid-third centuries A.D.): one portrays the (penetrated) female figure as the conqueror of the male figure by means of the caption *tu sola nica*, 'you're the only victor', while another conveys a similar theme by showing the female figure with a soldier's shield (translation Clarke 2014: 527; see 1998: 260–1, 2003: 141–2, 147, 2014: 527–8). In another medallion, the visual echo between the woman astride her male companion and a painting on the wall with galloping horses draws attention to female sexual agency and movement (Clarke 1998: 257–8, 2003: 154–5, 2014: 528). Clarke (2014: 528) comments, 'Here the implication is that she is not just riding but galloping'.

Graffiti (mostly from Pompeii, where the largest number are preserved) have also been called upon for the same reasons. While many graffiti seem to uphold the phallocentrism and aggression of the Priapic paradigm (Williams 2014: 498), Kristina Milnor (2014: 191–232), Craig Williams (2014: 503–5), and I (2013) have teased out important glimpses of alternative sexualities. One poetic graffito (CIL IV 5296), written inside the entranceway of a house in Pompeii's Regio IX, shows a woman proclaiming her love for a girl in the manner of an elegiac lover. Milnor (2014: 196–206) has pointed out the lengths that scholars have gone to in order to erase the female homoeroticism of the inscribed poem, a wilful blindness that we see also in the study of other sexual material from Roman Italy and the provinces (see more below).

Other graffiti from Pompeii represent at least *some* penetrated women as sexual agents, either by using the female agent-ending *-trix*, as in *Murtis felatris* (= *fellatrix*), 'Murtis the sucktress' (CIL IV 2292), or by making such women the grammatical subjects of sexual verbs, as in *Rufilla felat*, 'Rufilla suks' (CIL IV 1651) (Levin-Richardson 2013). In one case, a woman is represented as an agent in the act of *futuere*, 'fucking': Μόλα · φουτοῦτρις, 'Mola the fucktress' (CIL IV 2204). These graffiti inspired Deborah Kamen and me (2015a, 2015b) to ask whether the conflation of penetration with sexual agency in scholarly discussions of Greek and Roman sexuality—that is, the convention of referring to the penetrating partner as 'active' and the penetrated partner as 'passive', a phenomenon marked as problematic also by Richlin (1993: 531), Williams (2010[1999]: 230), and Davidson (1998: 177)—accords with ancient evidence. Through careful reading of epigraphic and literary texts, we find that the Romans themselves could and did think of some penetrated individuals (both female and male) as sexual agents. Penetrated individuals could perform sexual acts (such as fellatio), could move their bodies during sex, and could desire sex. As penetrated individuals, however, they were still disparaged for taking part in acts characterised (by the Romans) as servile and effeminate (see the mapping of gender and status onto penetrative role, above) (Kamen and Levin-Richardson 2015a, 2015b; for how these works do, or do not, break with previous scholarship, see Halperin 2015: 319–20; Skinner 2015). While this analysis supports the claim that penetration is still the most important organising principle for Roman sexuality, it suggests that sexual agency could be an additional or subordinate axis upon which this sexuality was conceptualised. Moreover, it recovers the agency and subjectivity of penetrated individuals, who indeed are in the majority in antiquity.

Continuing in the sphere of literary analysis, Kamen (2012), J.H. Oliver (2015), and Maia Kotrosits (2018) each examine instances of non-penetrative eroticism in literary sources. In her analysis of Ovid's myth of Iphis (a biological female raised as a boy, who falls in love with a girl and is granted a sex change by Isis in order to consummate her love), Kamen (2012, see especially 31) suggests that Ovid acknowledges non-penetrative sex as a concept, even as he marks it as contrary to both law and nature, and thus 'inconceivable' in practice (leading, thus, to Iphis' sex change). Oliver (2015: 284) notes how the Priapic paradigm privileges genital sex, rendering other forms of desire invisible to modern scholars. Oliver points, too, to how the 'genital-sexual standard of proof' privileges literary genres that allow for graphic sexual descriptions over genres in which erotic desire and acts are represented in less direct ways (Oliver 2015: 284, n. 8). As a case in point, Oliver shows how Ovid's myth of Callisto (in short, Jupiter disguises himself as Callisto's patron goddess, Diana, in order to get close to, kiss, and then rape Callisto) alludes to other erotic possibilities. When Diana (or Jupiter-as-Diana) passionately kisses Callisto, the latter does not resist (as she does immediately upon Jupiter revealing himself); this, plus a profusion of amatory vocabulary, suggests an erotic relationship between Callisto and Diana (Oliver 2015: 288–92). We seem to have an awareness, then, of erotic behaviours (sexual kisses) that do not fit into the Priapic paradigm, as well as relationships that do not align with the penetrator–penetrated pairs the model calls for (Oliver 2015: 292–9). In a similar vein, Kotrosits (2018) argues that alternative (or additional) models of pleasure can be found in the *Acts of Paul and Thecla*. She draws out the importance of 'friction' as a way of describing sensual experience, noting the 'heightened sensual/sensory experiences, the moments of flush that pepper the story' (Kotrosits 2018: 356 and 364).

Finally, other scholars have called attention to the ways in which the erotic acts and emotions of individual Greeks and Romans may not have accorded with sexual norms. Mark Masterson (2014) has voiced just such a critique in his discussion of Roman masculinity. He argues that different experiences of masculinity—including 'indulgence in passivities of all kinds'—coexisted, in admittedly uneasy tension, with Priapic masculinity (Masterson 2014: 27). As he concludes, 'the model is one thing and reality another' (Masterson 2014: 26).

In a recent critical overview of the field, David Halperin (2015) has commented upon these and other shifts. He notes that 'it is the duty of scholarship to highlight pieces of evidence that seem not to fit [current models] or even to contradict them, to propose alternate models for theorizing continuity and change in the history of sexuality' (Halperin 2015: 316). He advocates care in assessing how new scholarship affects the validity of the 'Priapic paradigm' or 'penetration model' for sexuality described above. Like Masterson, Halperin (2015: 318–19) notes the difference between trying to understand the overarching structure of ancient sexuality—and its power dynamics—on the one hand, and how real individuals in antiquity might have thought of themselves, on the other. However, he reminds us neither to confuse the two, nor to say that because the latter (the reality) is not the former (the model), the former is wrong (Halperin 2015: 317–18). Summarising this view, he notes,

> Sexual relations for many people in the ancient world, as for many people in the modern world, were surely not *about* power, penetration, or hierarchy, but they were nevertheless organized and *structured*, then as now, by differences between the sexual partners in power, status, age, and sexual role.
>
> (Halperin 2015: 319)

Since the Priapic paradigm contributes to the gendering of bodies (in that to penetrate is masculine or masculinising, and to be penetrated is feminine or feminising), and since it gives pride of place to phallic penetration, it necessarily implicates bodies. Critiques of the paradigm, like Oliver's (2015) call to pay attention to physical incarnations of eroticism that do not involve genitals, do so as well. In that vein, I will briefly trace developments in the study of the body before turning to how the chapters in this volume contribute to and push forward scholarship in these areas.

At the same time as scholars sought to better understand the parameters of Roman sexuality and its lived variety, a wave of scholarship on the body flourished in the 1990s and early 2000s, inspired in large part by developments in feminist theory (Foxhall 2013: 12). Of the several edited volumes on this topic published during those decades, a special issue of the journal *Gender and History* (1997), edited by Maria Wyke, brought attention to the body both as a 'peculiarly privileged site for the production, display, and regimentation of gender identity and gender differentials' as well as something always in a state of flux and 'contradiction' (Wyke 1997: 427). Many of these same themes were continued in the following year's *Parchments of Gender: Reading the Bodies of Antiquity* (1998b), also edited by Wyke, which drew even more attention to the instability of bodies and gender, with the effect overall of 'destabiliz[ing] any simple binary division between masculinity and femininity and its association with hierarchical oppositions between domination and submission, penetration and receptivity, mind and body' (Wyke 1998a: 4). In the following years, *Constructions of the Classical Body* (1999b), edited by James Porter (1999a: 6) and appearing as part of the series 'The Body, in Theory: Histories of Cultural Materialism', showed how the body was a site of anxiety, while *Not the Classical Ideal: Athens and the Construction of the Other in Greek Art* (2000b), edited by Beth Cohen, investigated various forms of 'Others' and how that helped define Greekness.

In more recent work, scholars are quick to credit the strides forward made by this wave of scholarship, while also suggesting further avenues for exploration. Brooke Holmes, in *Gender: Antiquity and its Legacy* (2012), lauds 'the resistance, at least in principle, to totalizing accounts, matched by a collective enthusiasm for pluralism, diversity, and microhistories' in the study of ancient sex and gender, while also calling for more attention to 'genuine plurality of experiences in a range of societies over centuries, not just for different individuals (say, a citizen and a slave) but also at different points within individual lives' (Holmes 2012: 12 and 25). Marilyn Skinner, in a 2014 partially retrospective and partially prognosticating essay on 'Feminist Theory' for *A Companion to*

Greek and Roman Sexualities, suggests that individuals who blurred or flouted gender and sexual norms in antiquity such as the *cinaedus* and *tribas* may even approach something akin to 'third-gender forms' (Skinner 2014: 8). Foreshadowing some of the contributions of *Un-Roman Sex*, she suggests that boundary crossing in art 'may serve to undermine perceptions of a coherently gendered self' (Skinner 2014: 8), and that even the much-examined category of Roman men needs a fresh theoretical look (Skinner 2014: 8).

In all, scholars have noted that we are slowly moving away from rigid binaries in the study of ancient gender and sexuality—whether that means looking beyond male *or* female, active *or* passive, or self *or* other—though more work is needed in this area (Cohen 2000a: 11; Holmes 2012: 109; Skinner 2014: 8, 2015: 10–11). Porter's (1999a: 4) proclamation that 'the body continues to be one of the most elusive and most promising topics in the study of antiquity and its survivals' still holds validity today, two decades later.

It is in these contexts that this volume plays a key role in pushing forward new directions in research.

Challenging phallocentrism and Priapic sexuality

To start, the contributions of this volume challenge the phallocentrism of our conceptions of ancient masculinity and Priapic sexuality. Alissa Whitmore's careful study of flaccid phallic pendants not only illuminates their functions along the north-east border of the Roman Empire, but also draws attention to their appearance and functions in Roman Italy. For example, Whitmore notes that five flaccid phallic pendants have been found in diverse contexts at Herculaneum: in the drain of the forum bath; in the Palaestra (along with jewellery); and carried in a box by a refugee who was found in one of the vaults lining the shore (Whitmore, Appendix 10.1, nos 3–7). Another flaccid pendant, from Italy, was found in the grave of an infant (Whitmore, Appendix 10.1, no. 13). While this type of pendant was much more common along the coast of the Black Sea, the contexts there can help us understand their range of possible meanings in Roman Italy, too. Namely, their use in grave contexts—sometimes around the neck of the deceased, suggesting they were personal amulets; other times in connection with other magical items—suggests a protective function, even in their flaccid state. That the flaccid forms were almost, but not entirely, superseded by erect types—Whitmore also mentions (erect) phallic pendants found with an adolescent girl victim near Pompeii's Porta Nola and a three-to-ten-month-old in the Porta Nocera necropolis—suggests both a growing influence of Priapic ideas of phalluses, as well as the co-existence, even into the third century A.D. (at least in the East), of non-Priapic phallic protection. Indeed, one of the flaccid examples from Herculaneum was found together with an erect example (Whitmore, Appendix 10.1, no. 4).

In decentring the erect phallus, Whitmore's chapter contributes to a growing body of work challenging our fixation with penises and especially their perceived turgidity. Judy Hallett's recent analysis (2015) of Suetonius' *Life of*

Tiberius, for example, focuses on Tiberius' erectile dysfunction, and finds precedents in, and intertexts with, the poetry of Catullus and Horace. In doing so, Suetonius evoked pity in his readers for Tiberius' condition. Hallett (2015: 410) summarises that 'the cultural performance of Roman manhood in its fully realized state was indubitably hard, just like the optimal, if not everlasting, condition of the physical organ that served as its symbol'. Moreover, in a forthcoming essay on visual representations of Hermaphroditus (the intersex child of Hermes and Aphrodite in Greek and Roman myth), Linnea Åshede calls out our fixation on Hermaphroditus' penis—and its relative degrees of erectness—as the ultimate indicator of Hermaphroditus' 'true' gender identity. Rather, Åshede focuses on gender presentation as a whole, calling attention to the consistent depiction of Hermaphroditus' pale skin, long hair, and clinging clothing to argue that Hermaphroditus is portrayed as an ideal object of desire: an attractive, soft, androgynous (not 'female at first, and then surprisingly male') youth.

The Syston knife, in its turn, simultaneously seems to uphold and subvert the Priapic paradigm (according to John Pearce's cutting-edge analysis). The sexual scene on the knife handle focuses on a male about to penetrate either of two subordinate partners (the female figure reclining on the back of a subordinate male, or the kneeling subordinate male), and in that way seems to fit the Priapic paradigm described above perfectly (see Figure 2.1). One can interpret the knife handle from Liberchies with a phallically aggressive punched inscription (*qui fecit / memoro // pone au(t) / pedico*, 'Who did this I remember: put me down or I bugger you') in the same way. However, Pearce notes that as the user of the Syston knife folds up the blade for storage, the blade penetrates the buttocks of the male penetrator (or about-to-be-penetrator), destabilising the meaning of the handle and its relationship to the maintenance of the Priapic model of sexuality.

A similar combination of adherence to, and superseding of, Priapic norms can be seen among Roman soldiers in the provinces. As Tatiana Ivleva argues, a handful of funerary monuments and epitaphs show relationships between older, higher-status soldiers and younger, enslaved or freed males, corresponding to the Priapic expectations governing relationships between males. It would be hard to read Numerianus' commemoration of his former slave Victor, who died at age 20, in any other way, as Numerianus chose to add emotional language to the epitaph (he 'most devotedly conducted [Victor] to the tomb'; RIB 1064; see Figure 8.5), and commissioned for his former slave one of the fanciest tombs found in Roman Britain. As Ivleva adds, the acceptability of desiring younger males can also be seen in a graffito from Remagen in Germany (AE 1908, 0189=CLE 2153) that places loving *pueri* and *puellae* on an equal footing (in this case, as equally leading to destitution if carried out 'without end')! At the same time, Ivleva highlights potential evidence (especially in the form of funerary medallions with two men side by side; see Figures 8.6 and 8.8) for soldiers engaging in long-term relationships with other soldiers, an equality of age and status that would be at odds with the rules of Priapic sexuality.

Bodies and boundaries

Another contribution of the essays in this volume is the investigation of bodies. One of the most immediate lessons is the differential attention to, and representation of, female and male genitalia, both in antiquity and in modern scholarship. To start, Rob Collins, Stefanie Hoss, and Adam Parker demonstrate that the rules governing depictions of male and female genitalia differed greatly, from sheer numbers (more phalluses than vulvas by a landslide), to the amount of variation in the depictions and the types of materials used (more variety with phalluses than vulvas), to the detail of these representations (more detail in phalluses than in vulvas or vulva stand-ins). These differences point to long-standing negativity regarding the female body in antiquity, a derision found also in Latin graffiti (Williams 2014: 498). Moreover, the phallus was the *apotropaion par excellence* (though vulvic *apotropaia* do exist and are undercounted in the scholarship; see further below), protecting not only individuals, but also structures. Collins argues that fort headquarters and gates, barrack walls, the curtain wall, and bridges along Hadrian's Wall were protected with phalluses, a good number of which were carefully carved in relief, showing an investment of time and energy. The fact that some phalluses were inscribed in areas not readily visible (such as the drains at Vindolanda) suggests that the protective power of the phallus did not necessarily need to be 'activated' by viewers.

The lack of detail in Roman (and Greek) depictions of female genitalia also can be seen in one of the figures associated with the very origins of obscenity in Greek culture, Baubo, who was said (in some literary sources) to lessen the grief of Demeter by flashing her genitalia at the goddess (see, e.g. Olender 1991). And yet, as Hoss points out, even Baubo does not have a detailed vulva in the famous representations we think depict her from Priene. Similarly, in Roman art where we might expect graphic depictions of female genitals—when women are penetrated from behind and face frontal, or in scene IV of Pompeii's Suburban Baths (VII.16.a) showing a woman opening her legs wide while receiving cunnilingus—women's genitals are nevertheless 'sanitised' (to use Hoss's term). Hoss adds that the lack of detailed genitalia in the latter is even more surprising, since (as Clarke 2003: 123, 2005: 283 has argued) the sexually explicit frescoes (of which cunnilingus is only one scene) show increasing amounts of shocking and humorous obscenity, with the goal of producing apotropaic laughter to protect the vulnerable bodies of bathers as they removed their clothing in the changing room.

Male bodies, too, receive a critical intervention in this volume. Ivleva settles any lingering doubts that Roman soldiers could retain their masculinity while having sexual relationships with males, even pushing us to consider the co-existence of masculinity with relationships among equals. Pearce's careful attention to the likely contexts in which the Syston handle may have been used points to some of the processes by which males were turned into men. One such context is the barber shop, which is not only a potential place where males are given the physical appearance of men through proper grooming, but also a place where they are socialised into the norms and expectations of masculinity. In this case, the sexual handle can become a tool not just for shaving beards, but also for provoking discussion of what the parameters of acceptable masculinity are (or could be, or should be). This view of masculinity and bodies gives support to Maud Gleason's (1995: 59) assessment—based on how gender was deployed and constructed in oratory of the Second Sophistic—that masculinity, for the Greeks and Romans living and writing during the Roman empire, was an 'achieved state, radically underdetermined by anatomical sex'. Masterson (2014: 24) notes, too, that

> a constant refrain [in Roman rhetorical texts], implicit and explicit, is that gestures and voice are to be carefully cultivated so as to convey a natural masculinity. The irony of embracing artifice to reveal a natural manhood was productive of anxiety.

The process of shaving also brings to (ancient and scholarly) consciousness the vulnerabilities of the male body. Shaving was a particularly important and precarious activity, involving maintenance of norms, rites of passage, male bonding, and possible violation of bodily boundaries and harm if done incorrectly. Indeed, elite Roman men not infrequently voiced fear of being harmed while being shaved by slave barbers (Fitzgerald 2000: 47–50). It is in the context of possible harm that Pearce thinks the handle could also be apotropaic, combining the power of genital imagery with humorous sexual antics to provoke apotropaic laughter. Pearce's analysis can thus be added to other evidence from the Graeco-Roman world for the potential permeability of the male body (including soldiers; see further Walters 1997; Leitao 2014: 235–7; Masterson 2014: 25). For example, Sarah Currie (1998) argues that Roman anxiety about female poisoners is really about the vulnerability of the male body, which women could invade, control, change, and even feminise through poisons. Binding spells, too, demonstrate a fear that male bodies could be made impotent by 'an antaphrodisiac pharmakon or a spell' (Edmonds 2014: 284).

In general, though, vulnerability was not equally distributed among bodies, a point brought out by several of the contributors. Bodies of children were thought to be especially vulnerable, and various means were used to protect them in life and death. Both Whitmore and Parker mention flaccid and erect phallic pendants for children, for example, while Matthew Fittock points out that a six-year-old child with rickets was buried in London with three pipeclay Venus figurines (which were 200 years old by then!) carefully positioned around the body (along with other items). Women, in some areas, also received particular attention. Hoss suggests that jewellery and dress items with cowrie shells (a stand in for the vulva) were meant to protect women's bodies, while Whitmore notes that the bodies of adult women in the east were protected with phallic amulets, and that wear patterns on the objects indicate that they may have been worn in life as well.

The *apotropaia* used for protection also raise questions about the relationships between human, divine, and animal bodies. Parker wonders if the power of the phallus is as the disembodied member of Priapus, or if Priapus gains his divine power through the power of the (human) phallus. We also see the use of animal-based materials and symbolism in apotropaic imagery designed for human users and the use of human-based symbolism in apotropaic imagery meant to protect animals. Hoss and Parker mention the use of animal horn for *apotropaia* (in human graves, for example), while horses (and even mules) were protected by various *apotropaia* including those in the shape of vulva stand-ins like the 'coffee-bean' mount, the scallop shell, and the lunula, in addition to *apotropaia* that combine the mano fica with the phallus. This was not a phenomenon restricted to the north-west provinces, either; Hoss mentions three horse harnesses with a mano fica and phallus found in the Bay of Naples area, and a horse harness from Sicily that has a vulva in the centre! There were probably more in antiquity, Hoss comments, but they may have been overlooked by excavators.

As noted by Collins, Hoss, Parker, and Whitmore (and as can be seen in the famous examples of *tintinnabula* from the Bay of Naples area, e.g. MANN inv. nos 27837 and 27835), the disembodiment and multiplication of body parts are common features of *apotropaia* (and binding spells too, on which see, e.g. Edmonds 2014: 285). With this in mind, it is particularly interesting that so few *apotropaia* combine phallic and vulvic symbols, since one might think these would form a particularly potent apotropaic device. Some of the exceptions are well known: the threshold mosaic from the private bathing complex of Pompeii's House of the Menander (I.10.4; Plate 2; in this case, the ovoid shape created by a pair of strigils is vulvic, while a hanging lamp is phallic; see Clarke 1998: 212–40); the hanging pendants for personal use that combine a phallus on one end with a mano fica on the other (as in several examples from the Bay of Naples, e.g. MANN inv. nos 27808 and 27812; see also Figure 4.5); and the bowl from Catterick that depicts a scallop shell with phallus and mano fica combinations (Figure 4.6, middle). Others are less well known (at least to those who work on Roman Italy): for example, Collins notes three instances along Hadrian's Wall in which phalluses are combined with a pointed oval that may be vulvic (Figure 9.5, nos 12, 22, and 42) and Hoss notes an antler roundel from Cologne with both phallic and vulvic imagery (Figure 5.17). Others were just recently excavated, such as the sculpted stone found at Derbyshire representing a phallus, vulva, and the word *cuni* (Figure 4.6, right). In at least one case, multiple scholarly blind spots—the reluctance to identify certain symbols as stand-ins for female genitalia, and the ongoing focus on (ithy) phallocentrism—may have led us to overlook another example of this rare combination. Hoss points out that a 'coffee-bean' mount with a hanging pendant is conventionally described as 'heart-shaped'; she suggests, rather, that the latter is a stylised scrotum and testes.

Conclusions

The presence in Roman Italy of entire cityscapes—especially in the towns around the Bay of Naples and at Ostia—has led, on the one hand, to the ability to examine whole decorative ensembles in their architectural (and often urban) contexts. On the other hand, it has also led to relatively less scholarly attention on small objects, which are often overshadowed by larger or more eye-catching examples of art, or, in some cases, even ignored by previous archaeologists (as some of the chapters in this volume point out). The same can be said for the reliance on Latin literature for those who work on Roman Italy; with such abundant and evocative literary sources, there is less impetus to seek and apply theoretical approaches to material culture (which is not to say there is not theoretical work being conducted on material from Roman Italy). This volume can thus serve as a call to pay more careful attention to smaller objects, to be open to incorporating theoretical approaches, and to pay more attention to continuities and discontinuities across space and time. As one example, the chapters in this volume illuminate the extent to which Roman practices draw from other cultures. Egypt figures prominently here; Whitmore suggests that the power of flaccid phallic charms may have derived from their usage in that manner in Egyptian and Phoenician culture. Hoss likewise notes that the mano fica is attested in Pharaonic amulets and that cowrie shell symbols were used in Pharaonic jewellery. Other cultures were influential, too; Hoss mentions that scallop shells were used apotropaically in pre-Roman graves, where they were found in amulet strings and jewellery.

The methodologies exhibited in this volume also serve as reminders of how to create meaningful arguments from incomplete evidence (a scenario which pertains even to the well-preserved towns of Herculaneum and Pompeii), whether it is the lack of context because items were found via metal detecting (see, e.g. Chapter 2), or the lack of osteological data for burials (as at Emona and Poetovio; see Chapter 7). In some cases, this means careful study of artefact assemblages and their patterns (see, e.g. Chapter 7); in other cases, careful attention to the distribution of items or features (see, e.g. Chapters 3 and 9).

In addition, the chapters remind us that our desire to determine definitely the 'correct' interpretation of a work of art may in part miss the point. Ambiguity may have been the intent, or at least the effect, of certain objects and representations. For example, Hoss asks if the apotropaic symbols on one example of horse gear were symbolic vulvas or Celtic shields; ultimately, she suggests that the ambiguity may have been intentional as it combined or amplified the apotropaic elements (see the discussion of multiplication also in Chapter 4). Likewise, Chapter 2 points out that the ambiguity in the interpretation of the Syston knife's sexual scene may have provoked conversations among its users/viewers, and that the voice meant to be stating the threat against thieves on the inscribed handle from Liberchies is ambiguous (the voice could be perceived as that of the owner, the standing male figure, or the object itself). The fact that we are not sure of the user(s) of the Syston knife opens up, rather than restricts, interpretive possibilities, and in the process helps the field as a whole move away from looking for the solitary, omniscient viewer.

This is a trend we can trace in other scholarship, too. John Henderson (1999: 33 and 41) has argued for an 'open-ended' approach to reading and understanding Greek vase painting, while Williams (2014) has highlighted how the ambiguity of authorship and intent of Latin graffiti can lead to multiple interpretative possibilities. Kelly Olson (2015: 442) concludes that it is not always possible to tell the difference between the toga and *pallium* in visual representations, and she argues that ambiguity might even be the point (for nuanced takes on identity and clothing in this volume, see Chapters 6 and 7).

The alternative models of gender norms and sexuality present in the provinces are important in their own right, and also illuminate that the gender and sexual norms of Roman Italy were in fact a cultural choice and not a given. Fittock notes that rather than evoking love or sex, Venus figurines in the northwest provinces are found mostly in burials, and mostly for protecting children. Hoss reminds us that some depictions of female genitalia in eastern central Gaul are more realistic than their counterparts in Roman Italy, noting too that some scholars think that women enjoyed a more equal status in the former area (see Chapter 6; see also Clarke 1998: 254–65, 2003: 139–55, 2014: 526–30 on ceramic medallions from the Rhône valley). These findings illuminate the extent to which Roman norms were consciously created and maintained in the face of other options.

Moreover, these alternative models—and reactions to them in Roman Italy—point to a defining feature of gender and sexuality in Roman Italy: misogyny (for misogyny in antiquity, see, e.g. Chandezon et al. 2014: 301; Edmonds 2014: 293; Larson 2014: 215). While misogyny is not a new topic, it has received more critical attention lately (see, e.g. Holmes 2012: 7; Beard 2018 [2017]) and has become newly relevant in an era of increased awareness of *modern* misogyny.

For scholars, a focus exclusively on Roman Italy can result in an unconscious internalising and generalising of the gender and sexual norms present in the material culture (and literature) of the Italian peninsula. Studying the material culture of the provinces can thus decentre and defamiliarise Roman Italy, leading to more accurate and nuanced assessments of the Roman world as a whole (including Roman Italy).

Bibliography

Åshede, L. (Forthcoming). "Reappraising the Gender-Role(s) of Hermaphroditus in Ancient Art", in A. Surtees and J. Dyer (eds), *Exploring Gender Diversity in the Ancient World*. Edinburgh: Edinburgh University Press.

Beard, M. (2018[2017]). *Women and Power: A Manifesto*. Updated Edition. London: Profile Books.

Blondell, R. and Ormand, K. eds, (2015). *Ancient Sex: New Essays*. Columbus, OH: Ohio State University Press.

Chandezon, Ch., Dasen, V. and Wilgaux, J. (2014). "Dream Interpretation, Physiognomy, Body Divination", in Hubbard (2014), 297–313.

Clarke, J. (1993). "The Warren Cup and the Contexts for Representations of Male-to-Male Lovemaking in Augustan and Early Julio-Claudian Art", *The Art Bulletin*, 75: 275–94.

Clarke, J. (1998). *Looking at Lovemaking: Constructions of Sexuality in Roman Art 100 B.C.-A.D. 250*. Berkeley, CA: University of California Press.

Clarke, J. (2003). *Roman Sex: 100 BC-AD 250*. New York: Harry Abrams.

Clarke, J. (2005). "Representations of the *Cinaedus* in Roman Art", *Journal of Homosexuality*, 49: 271–98.

Clarke, J. (2014). "Sexuality and Visual Representation", in Hubbard (2014), 509–33.

Cohen, B. (2000a). "Introduction", in Cohen (2000b), 3–20.

Cohen, B. ed, (2000b). *Not the Classical Ideal: Athens and the Construction of the Other in Greek Art*. Leiden: Brill.

Currie, S. (1998). "Poisonous Women and Unnatural History in Roman Culture", in M. Wyke (ed.), *Parchments of Gender: Reading the Bodies of Antiquity*. Oxford: Clarendon Press, 147–67.

Davidson, J. (1998). *Courtesans and Fishcakes: The Classical Passions of Classical Athens*. London: HarperCollins.

Davidson, J. (2007). *The Greeks and Greek Love: A Radical Reappraisal of Homosexuality in Ancient Greece*. London: Weidenfeld and Nicolson.

Edmonds, R. (2014). "Bewitched, Bothered, and Bewildered: Erotic Magic in the Greco-Roman World", in Hubbard (2014), 282–96.

Fisher, N. (2000). "Review of *Courtesans and Fishcakes: The Consuming Passions of Classical Athens* by J.N. Davidson", *The Classical Review*, New Series, 50: 507–09.

Fitzgerald, W. (2000). *Slavery and the Roman Literary Imagination*. Cambridge: Cambridge University Press.

Foxhall, L. (2013). *Studying Gender in Classical Antiquity*. Cambridge: Cambridge University Press.

Gleason, M. (1995). *Making Men: Sophists and Self-Presentation in Ancient Rome*. Princeton, NJ: Princeton University Press.

Hallett, J. (2015). "Making Manhood Hard: Tiberius and Latin Literary Representations of Erectile Dysfunction", in Masterson et al. (2015), 408–21.

Hallett, J. and Skinner, M. eds, (1997). *Roman Sexualities*. Princeton, NJ: Princeton University Press.

Halperin, D. (2015). "Not Fade Away", in Blondell and Ormand (2015), 308–29.

Henderson, J. (1999). "Smashing Bodies: The Corinthian Tydeus and Ismene Amphora (Louvre E640)", in J. Porter (ed.), *Constructions of the Classical Body*. Ann Arbor, MI: University of Michigan Press, 19–49.

Holmes, B. (2012). *Gender: Antiquity and Its Legacy*. Oxford: Oxford University Press.

Hubbard, T.K. ed, (2014). *A Companion to Greek and Roman Sexualities*. London: Blackwell.

Kamen, D. (2012). "Naturalized Desires and the Metamorphosis of Iphis", *Helios*, 39: 21–36.

Kamen, D. and Levin-Richardson, S. (2015a). "Lusty Ladies in the Roman Imaginary", in Blondell and Ormand (2015), 231–52.

Kamen, D. and Levin-Richardson, S. (2015b). "Revisiting Roman Sexuality: Agency and the Conceptualization of Penetrated Males", in Masterson et al. (2015), 449–60.

Kotrosits, M. (2018). "Penetration and Its Discontents: Greco-Roman Sexuality, the *Acts of Paul and Thecla*, and Theorizing Eros without the Wound", *Journal of the History of Sexuality*, 27: 343–66.

Larson, J. (2014). "Sexuality in Greek and Roman Religion", in Hubbard (2014), 214–29.

Leitao, D. (2014). "Sexuality in Greek and Roman Military Contexts", in Hubbard (2014), 230–43.

Levin-Richardson, S. (2013). "*fututa sum hic*: Female Subjectivity and Agency in Pompeian Sexual Graffiti", *Classical Journal*, 108: 319–45.

Masterson, M. (2014). "Studies of Ancient Masculinity", in Hubbard (2014), 17–30.

Masterson, M., Sorkin Rabinowitz, N. and Robson, J. eds, (2015). *Sex in Antiquity: Exploring Gender and Sexuality in the Ancient World*. London: Routledge.

Milnor, K. (2014). *Graffiti and the Literary Landscape in Roman Pompeii*. New York: Oxford University Press.

Olender, M. (1991). "Aspects of Baubo: Ancient Texts and Contexts", in F. Zeitlin, J. Winkler and D. Halperin (eds), *Before Sexuality: The Construction of Erotic Experience in the Ancient Greek World*. Princeton, NJ: Princeton University Press, 83–113.

Oliver, J.H. (2015). "*Oscula iungit nec moderata satis nec sic a virgine danda*: Ovid's Callisto Episode, Female Homoeroticism, and the Study of Ancient Sexuality", *American Journal of Philology*, 136: 281–312.

Olson, K. (2015). "Toga and *Pallium*: Status, Sexuality, Identity", in Masterson et al. (2015), 422–48.

Ormand, K. (2018[2009]). *Controlling Desires: Sexuality in Ancient Greece and Rome*. Revised Edition. Austin, TX: University of Texas Press.

Parker, H. (1997). "The Teratogenic Grid", in Hallett and Skinner (1997), 47–65.

Porter, J. (1999a). "Introduction", in Porter (1999b), 1–18.

Porter, J. ed, (1999b). *Constructions of the Classical Body*. Ann Arbor, MI: University of Michigan Press.

Richlin, A. (1992[1983]). *The Garden of Priapus: Sexuality and Aggression in Roman Humor*. Revised edition. New York: Oxford University Press.

Richlin, A. (1993). "Not Before Homosexuality: The Materiality of the *Cinaedus* and the Roman Law against Love between Men", *Journal of the History of Sexuality*, 3: 523–73.

Skinner, M. (2014). "Feminist Theory", in Hubbard (2014), 1–16.

Skinner, M. (2015). "Ancient Sexuality at a New Crossroads: Beyond Binarism", Keynote lecture of "New Directions in Gender and Sexuality in Classical Antiquity" workshop at Amherst College, MA. Delivered March 27 2015.

Walters, J. (1997). "Invading the Roman Body: Manliness and Impenetrability in Roman Thought", in Hallett and Skinner (1997), 29–43.

Williams, C. (2010[1999]). *Roman Homosexuality*. Second Edition. New York: Oxford University Press.

Williams, C. (2014). "Sexual Themes in Greek and Latin Graffiti", in Hubbard (2014), 493–508.

Wyke, M. (1997). "Introduction", *Gender and History*, 9: 425–31.

Wyke, M. (1998a). "Introduction", in Wyke (1998b), 1–11.

Wyke, M. ed, (1998b). *Parchments of Gender: Reading the Bodies of Antiquity*. Oxford: Clarendon Press.

Plate 1 Bronze mirror cover, showing Eros and erotic scene. Museum of Fine Arts, Boston, inv. no. RES.08.32c.2.

Plate 2 Mosaic at the entrance to a caldarium in the bath complex of the House of Menander at Pompeii.

(Photograph: Sophie Hay)

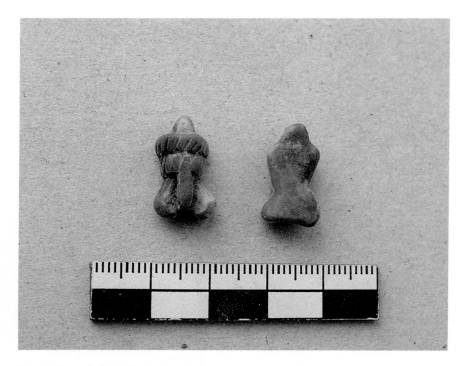

Plate 3 Front (left) and back (right) of glazed steatite phallic pendants, second–third century A.D., Gorny Altai (Russia).

(Reproduced with kind permission of E.S. Bogdanov from Bogdanov and Sljusarenko 2007)

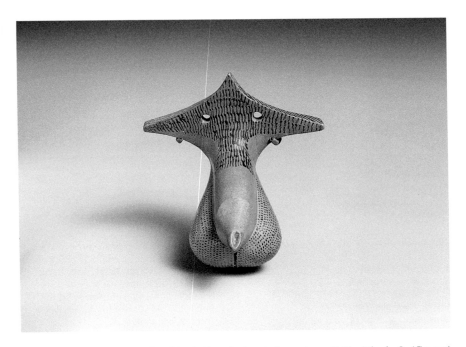

Plate 4 Greek terracotta flaccid phallus flask, sixth century B.C., Rhodes? (Greece). H 11.4 cm, W 10.2 cm, T 8.9 cm. Metropolitan Museum of Art, acc. no. 1999.78.

Index

Page numbers in italic refer to figures.
Page number in bold refer to tables.